RELIGION AND RESPECTABILITY
SUNDAY SCHOOLS
AND WORKING CLASS CULTURE 1780–1850

A

Perhaps those who commissioned this idealized representation of the Stockport Sunday School wanted to convey the impression that it was like a great country house set among open fields. They would, by analogy, assume the role of the benevolent squire-

RELIGION AND RESPECTABILITY
SUNDAY SCHOOLS
AND WORKING CLASS CULTURE
1780–1850

THOMAS WALTER LAQUEUR

YALE UNIVERSITY PRESS
NEW HAVEN AND LONDON
1976

For my Parents, Toni and Werner Laqueur

Copyright © 1976 by Yale University.
All rights reserved.
This book may not be reproduced, in whole or in part, in any form
(except by reviewers for the public press), without written
permission from the publishers.

Library of Congress catalog card number: 75–29728

International standard book number: 0–300–01859–2

Designed by John Nicoll and set in Monophoto Baskerville

Photoset by Thomson Press (India) Limited, New Delhi and
printed in Great Britain
by Robert Maclehose & Co. Limited, Glasgow

Published in Great Britain, Europe, Africa, the Middle East, India
and South East Asia by Yale University Press, Ltd., London.
Distributed in Latin America by Kaiman & Polon, Inc., New York
City; in Australasia by Book & Film Services, Artarmon, N.S.W.,
Australia; in Japan by John Weatherhill, Inc., Tokyo.

Contents

List of Illustrations, Maps, Graphs and Tables

TABLES

Preface

If there was a single experience common to the children of an agricultural laborer in Bedfordshire, of a stockinger or handloom weaver in the Midlands, or of a factory operative in south Lancashire, it was attendance at a Sunday school. Beginning in the early 1780s working-class children poured into these schools— 200,000 in 1800, 450,000 in 1818, 1,400,000 in 1833, 2,100,000 in 1851. So high was the proportion of the population enrolled in Sunday school by the late 1820s that, outside the Metropolis, nearly every working-class child must at some time have attended one. They were instructed, largely by teachers from their own class, in reading, writing, religion, and occasionally other subjects for periods of four to six hours each Sunday over a period of, on average, four years. Through the Sunday school children were inundated with the printed word. The Sunday School Union alone sold some 10,000,000 reading and spelling books in the first half of the century; its *Youth Magazine and Evangelical Miscellany* was a pioneer in children's periodical literature, and it was followed by some forty other magazines intended specifically for Sunday school scholars. Tracts, books, testaments and Bibles were distributed in tens of millions.

But the Sunday school provided more than literature and instruction; it was a central feature of working-class community life. The annual school outing was a highlight of the year; the school anniversary was, in some areas, an occasion for giving a new pair of shoes, a cap, shirt, or pinafore; the tea meeting was an important monthly social engagement for teachers. The Sunday school, through various clubs, provided clothes, money during illness, and a proper funeral upon death. Teachers and other students brought comfort and companionship to scholars who were absent through sickness. Attended entirely by the working classes, staffed largely by former students and their parents, often managed and financed by the community which it served, the Sunday school was a part of, and not an imposition on to, popular culture.

Although it nurtured radical, Chartist, trade union, and even secularist leaders, the Sunday school did not belong to the dramatic and much studied world of political struggle and agitation. It was a part of ordinary life, of a difficult and mundane week-to-week existence, of small-scale, personal struggles for education, decency, and self-improvement. It constituted a facet of working-class life different from, but no less important than, Peterloo, the Plug Riots, and all they represent.

Yet even its architectural vestiges are rapidly disappearing from view. The great Stockport Sunday School, which in its prime during the 1840s accommodated over five thousand children, was demolished in 1970, the victim of changing times, vandalism and urban renewal. Nothing remains on the hilltop site overlooking the famous railroad viaduct and the mills along the Goyt and Mersey to remind the visitor that here, during the early nineteenth century, fifty thousand children learned to read, write and cipher, listened to Handel, Mozart and Haydn, and participated in a thriving aspect of working-class culture. The Ancoats Sunday School in Manchester, which once held two thousand students, was used as an oildrum warehouse before being demolished to make room for a new building. Very little remains throughout England to remind us of the importance of Sunday schools to working-class children and their parents during the nineteenth century.

Furthermore, the powerfully argued and widely accepted central proposition of E. P. Thompson's *The Making of the English Working Class*—that 'in the years between 1780 and 1832 most English working people came to feel an identity of interests as between themselves, and as against their rulers and employers'—has focused the attention of historians on the process of conflict, of which Sunday schools were seldom a .part. It was the feeling of identity in opposition, Thompson holds, which constituted the formation of class; 'men as they lived their own history', a history of struggle, were its creators.[1] From the London Corresponding Society through the Luddites, radicals and early trade unionists of the Peterloo Period to the parliamentary reformers and Owenites of the 1820s and 1830s, to the birth of Chartism, the history of the working class is told as a story of combat against middle-class and aristocratic oppression. Religion generally, Methodism and Sunday schools in particular, are seen as agents of the middle class in this struggle to remould the innermost feelings and desires of working people.

[1] E. P. Thompson *The Making of the English Working Class* (New York, 1963) 9–11

This study began as an attempt to confirm Thompson's interpretation in one corner of nineteenth-century history. It ends by
concluding that the struggle against the bourgeoisie and its values
constitutes only a part of the story and that Sunday schools provide
a window through which another part of the truth may be glimpsed.
By adopting this perspective, however, important aspects of Sunday
school history have not been discussed. Their impact on Westminster
and Whitehall is almost totally ignored. They provided the infra-
structure for much Evangelical and Dissenting pressure group
politics. Their members were used in the fight against Brougham's
and later Graham's education bill; they were active in gathering
signatures for petitions in favor of the 1833 Factory Act and a
variety of sabbatarian projects. The history of Sunday school
organizations, particularly of the Sunday School Union, is only
briefly told. Even the relationship between the Sunday school and
the Church or chapel, though discussed at some length, is not
explored in full. Their role in recruitment, the development of
denominational Sunday school literature beginning around the
middle of the century, their views on various theological and
ecclesiological controversies of the day are only touched upon. This
is a study of the relationship between the Sunday school and the
working-class community it served and not a complete account of
the institution in all its aspects.

I have been extremely fortunate to receive help and guidance from
a large number of individuals and institutions during the preparation
of this study. Princeton University offered support for my first year
of research on this and related projects; the Warden and Fellows
of Nuffield College, Oxford, elected me to a Research Studentship
which allowed me to continue my research and writing under near
ideal conditions from 1971 to 1973. The Regents Faculty Fellowship
Program of the University of California allowed me to spend the
summer of 1974 doing research in England and the Committee on
Research of the University of California, Berkeley paid for a part-
time research assistant and other expenses incurred in the preparation of this book.

The staff at a number of libraries provided assistance during the
course of my research. In addition to the Bodleian and the British
Museum I worked for longer periods in the Manchester Central
Reference Library, the Stockport Reference Library, the Methodist
Archive Centre, the Institute for Historical Research, and the
Angus Library of Regents Park College, Oxford. I want to thank
Mr Christopher Makepeace in Manchester, Mr David Reid in
Stockport, and the Rev. Dr Bowmer and Miss Blessingham at the
Methodist Archive for their help and kindness. Dave Reid, to whom

I am particularly grateful, has supplied me with Xerox copies of documents, checked references, and been of assistance in a variety of other ways since I returned to the United States. Mr J. Bentley, Executive Secretary of the National Christian Education Council, gave me permission to use the uncatalogued archives of the Sunday School Union and provided lunch and tea when I was in the Council's Redhill headquarters. Miss Christine Kennedy and the staff of the Nuffield College Library secured more than a score of books for me via inter-library loans and were generally helpful and understanding far above the call of duty or usual library practice.

From a not altogether clear typescript Mrs Reba Lawless with great skill prepared a final copy of the thesis on which this book is based. Bojana Ristich and her staff at the Institute for International Relations, Ms Kathy Chapek and Ms Dorothy Shannon of the Department of History, Berkeley, were cheerful, prompt and accurate in typing various parts of my manuscript. I also want to thank Ms Ann Sullivan for her help in checking references and calculations, in doing tables and in other ways assisting in the preparation of this book. I am grateful to Ms Adrienne Morgan for preparing the maps.

I owe an especial intellectual debt to four of my teachers. Professor Lawrence Stone, Princeton University, provided invaluable encouragement, pointed and constructive criticism, and for want of a better word inspiration during the preparation of my thesis. His example, while I was a student and afterward, has been more important to me than can be adequately acknowledged here. While at Oxford I was fortunate to have Dr Brian Harrison of Corpus Christi College as my University Supervisor. He convinced me that Sunday schools were an important subject worthy of serious study; he also read several drafts of almost all of this book and helped me improve greatly its style and organization. My interest in the religious aspects of this project and in the social history of religion generally grew from when I first met Dr John Walsh of Jesus College, Oxford, at the Methodist Archive Centre. In addition to providing dozens of references he has shared with me his vast knowledge of eighteenth- and nineteenth-century religious history. His friendship and tutelage have infused this work and my historical thinking generally. Dr Max Hartwell of Nuffield College read much of my manuscript, but more importantly he was a critical and intellectually pugnacious presence during my two years at Nuffield whose dangerous influence might have made itself felt almost impreceptibly.

I want also to thank Dr Keith Hope of Nuffield for his help with my statistical analysis; he is, I hasten to add, in no way responsible

for its inadequacies. During my first year at Nuffield, Dr Chelly
Halsey offered me tutorials which helped provide the sociological
foundations for this book. I gained a great deal from debates on each
other's work with my friends Dr David Philips of Melbourne
University, Ms Mary Daly of University College Dublin, and
Dr William Irvine of Glendon College, York University, Canada.
My new colleagues at Berkeley—Natalie Zemon Davis, Ira Lapidus,
Sheldon Rothblatt, and Reginald Zelnik—helped me transform
my thesis into the present book. My editor, Mr John Nicoll, has been
a patient and understanding collaborator in the production of this
volume. I am grateful to Paul and Gretl Weyl, Gatley, Cheshire,
for providing a home during my three years in England and to my
parents for the years before. Finally, on the practical level, I want to
thank Dolores Heeb for reading and commenting on more versions
of each chapter than she might have liked and for assisting in
numerous other ways in the preparation of this manuscript. I hope
she knows how much else I owe her.

Thomas W. Laqueur
Berkeley
February 1975

1. Introduction:
Children, Philanthropy and the
Eighteenth-Century Origins of Sunday Schools

'The age was mad after innovation' declared Dr Johnson in a fit of pique over the abolition in 1783 of the procession to Tyburn and the introduction of the drop to hasten death by hanging.[1] And, while his diagnosis of madness might have been typically eccentric, his basic perception was correct; it was an age of innovation. Sunday schools were one product of the deep-rooted religious and philanthropic revival of the late eighteenth century; they were part of a movement to transform society, to change its sensibilities and moral perceptions, which had its roots in the middling classes but found expression in the classes both above and below.

Jonas Hanway (1712–86) might stand as the symbol of the new activist philanthropy. His concern for children was expressed in his work for the Foundling Hospital, his advocacy of acts in Parliament to provide complete records of children admitted to parish work-houses and to oblige masters to care for the material and educational needs of their apprentices, and of course in his support of Sunday schools. He was active in workhouse reform, founded the Marine Society, was president of the Magdalen Hospital for prostitutes and treasurer of the Misericordia Hospital for the control of venereal disease.[2] There were others like him. Joseph Massie began writing in the 1750s against the strictness of the poor laws and John Scott followed in 1783 with pamphlets on the wretched state of the impoverished; Thomas Gilbert, the most important of the eighteenth-century poor law reformers, sponsored the 1782 act

[1] Quoted in H. D. Trail *Social England* (1896) vol. V, 351
[2] See John H. Hutchins *Jonas Hanway* (1940) 185–6

for the reform of poor law administration.[3] The second half of the eighteenth century witnessed John Howard's campaign against the abominable conditions in prisons and on a smaller scale James Nield's society for the relief and discharge of persons imprisoned for small debts. Joseph Fielding's accession to the chief magistracy of Westminster in 1749 marks the beginning of an effective campaign against gin drinking and a reform in the administration of justice. Bear-, bull- and badger-baiting were under attack during the late eighteenth century. The anti-slavery movement began in 1765 when Granville Sharpe met an ex-slave whose life story spurred him to action.[4]

In London alone the number of medical, religious, educational and moral charities founded between 1780 and the turn of the century more than tripled the number founded during the previous twenty years; the number between 1800 and 1820 was almost twice that figure.[5] (Table 1).

Table 1 :   *Medical, religious, educational, and moral charities founded in London 1700–1850*

Year	Number founded
pre 1700	10
1701–1710	3
1711–1720	2
1721–1730	1
1731–1740	3
1741–1750	7
1751–1760	7
1761–1770	4
1771–1780	10
1781–1790	18
1791–1800	30
1801–1810	36
1811–1820	55
1821–1830	47
1831–1840	47
1841–1850	47

[3] For poor law reform see Dorothy Marshall *The English Poor in the Eighteenth Century* (1926) 51–5, and John Poynter *Society and Pauperism: English Ideas on Poor Relief* (London, 1969) 1–12, 26–7

[4] See B. K. Gray *A History of English Philanthropy* (1905), and David Owen *English Philanthropy, 1660–1960* (Cambridge, Mass, 1964), for prison reform, the anti-slavery movement, and the growth of associated philanthropy generally. For London, see M. Dorothy George *London Life: The Eighteenth Century* (1925) 6–14. For the suppression of popular blood-sports see Robert W. Malcolmson *Popular Recreations in English Society* (Cambridge, 1973)

[5] Calculated from list of charities in Ford K. Brown *Fathers of the Victorians* (Cambridge, 1961) 329–39

Even the number of new educational endowments, a relatively unpopular form of charity after the collapse of the charity school movement in the 1730s, increased in England from 255 between 1740 and 1760 to 298 during the next two decades, and to 334 between 1780 and 1800.[6]

Insofar as Sunday schools in the late eighteenth century were the fruits of efforts by middle-class Evangelicals they were in the mainstream of organized philanthropy and a successor to the charity schools founded earlier in the century.[7] But many, and perhaps most, early Sunday schools were only on the periphery of this tradition. They were the creation of poor and humble weavers, blacksmiths and shoemakers; Sunday schools indeed provide evidence that the currents of institutionalized benevolence ran far deeper in society than has been supposed.

The growth of Dissent and the advance of the Evangelical party within the Established Church had a more direct bearing on the advent of Sunday schools. After a half-century of stagnation or even decline Non-conformist membership began to increase rapidly around the middle of the century. The number of Congregationalists more than doubled between 1750 and 1800 and increased almost fourfold again by 1838; Baptists almost tripled their membership in the second half of the eighteenth century and more than trebled it again during the next thirty-eight years; the Methodists, numerically the most important, expanded from 22,642 members in 1767 to 93,003 in 1801 to over half a million by the middle of the nineteenth century.[8]

Dissent grew primarily by recruiting those usually untouched by organized religion. This new activist, lay dominated, largely poor, religious community provided a large proportion of early Sunday school workers. The growth of Anglican Evangelicalism is more difficult to quantify, but by 1800 there were probably 300 to 500 clergymen well placed throughout England to encourage the kind of religious activism which resulted in the founding of Sunday schools.[9] In short, by 1780 an increasing number of people, particularly in the lower strata of society, came to take religion

[6] See M. G. Jones *The Charity School Movement* (Cambridge, 1938) 351–2, Appendix I. Her tables are based on the Returns of the Commissioners of Inquiry into Charities, 1818–43

[7] This theme is developed in Jones, ibid. pp. 142–54

[8] See Alan Gilbert 'The Growth and Decline of Non-Conformity in England and Wales with special reference to the period before 1850: an historical interpretation of statistics of religious practice' (unpublished DPHIL thesis, Oxford University, 1973) 38–45

[9] See John Walsh 'The Anglican Evangelicals in the Eighteenth Century' *Aspects de l'Anglicanisme* (Paris, 1974) p. 102

seriously. The education of the young in the ways of godliness was a product of this revival.

The question remains, however, why the philanthropic and religious impulses of the late eighteenth century found such prominent expression in the founding of Sunday schools. There is of course no single answer as to what caused men and women from all classes to spend their leisure time teaching poor children to read the Bible, to write and to cipher. Motives varied from class to class and perhaps region to region. Furthermore, only the middle classes articulated their position, primarily through the sermons of select ministers and clergymen. Imagination will, therefore, be required to translate what they said into the language and thoughts of the thousands of working people who helped create the nineteenth-century Sunday school.

Three sets of ideas or feelings influenced to varying degrees the founding of Sunday schools. For some, the new institution was an instrument for the moral rescue of poor children from their corrupt parents, thereby at one stroke insuring the happiness of the little ones and the regeneration of society. Others saw in the schools primarily a means of spreading the Word of God, an end valuable for its own sake. Thirdly, a new, soft, kind, more optimistic and sentimental view of children and childhood induced benevolent men and women to direct their attentions to the young.

For some reason the decades after 1780 were seen by contemporaries as ones of national deterioration and depravity. Crime rates probably did not rise but more wealth to be stolen and more people to do the stealing, coupled with increased sensitivity to the sacredness of property might well have created the illusion of a crime wave. The increased availability of luxuries among the poor provided evidence to certain of the upper orders that, as Defoe put it, the Great Law of Subordination was breaking down. The long, bitter and losing war with the American colonies contributed further to the perception that the moral fibre of society was weakening. This deterioration was by no means thought to be confined to the poor; there was simply very little that could be directly done about the vices of the rich. 'The national depravity is great, and all ranks are infected. I will consider the lower orders of society,' said the Rev. Joseph Berington in 1788.[10] John Bowles, one of the high church Tories who founded the National School Society, was even more explicit. The education of those in Parliament afforded them no protection against vice; the 'irreligiosity' of middle-class and upper-class education was manifest. The House of

[10] Rev. Joseph Berington *An Essay on the Depravity of the Nation with a view to the Promotion of Sunday Schools and c.* (Birmingham, 1788) 17

Commons, he continued, had frustrated by a considerable majority a measure to curtail 'the prevailing, the increasing, and the unrestrained vice of adultery,' and yet very little could be done. Only the worst abuses of upper-class education could be corrected, while more positive steps could be taken with regard to the education of the poor.[11] Sunday schools represented such a step.

They were advocated by eighteenth-century Evangelicals and some of their successors as a means of removing children from the corrupt influence of their parents and providing them with a morally more salutary atmosphere. 'The children of the poor, by being drawn out of their obscurity into notice and protection, are humanized and civilized,' argued a friend of Hannah More.[12] Children were viewed as the most likely basis for the moral regeneration of society for two sets of reasons. First, adults and especially the adult poor were already far too set in the ways of corruption to be effectively reformed; children on the other hand were malleable and could be trained up in virtue or at least be more easily re-trained if they had already strayed. A second rationale grew out of a blend of neo-mercantilism and sentiment. Men like the Rev. Daniel Turner argued for increased provision of education because of the special and unique value of children and because the future of the commonwealth depended on them. Children are 'the heritage of the Lord and the fruit of the womb in His reward'; there is positive pleasure in bringing up a child who will react to kind attention by becoming a virtuous, reasoning being. Educate them now, he warns, for 'it is too late to correct them when they are spoilt.' Finally, 'Children belong less to their parents, than to the public; they are the children of the people, they are the hope and strength of the body politic.'[13] 'General instruction of the poor,' it was argued, 'will collect together all the ability which God hath distributed amongst mankind at large, and give it a direction for the public good.'[14]

Sunday schools as agencies of instruction represented an important step in the increased differentiation of educational activities during the late eighteenth century. For all those involved, whatever their immediate motives, these schools were the response to a feeling that the home, the small charity schools, and the patchwork of private,

[11] See John Bowles *Reflections on the Political and Moral State of Society at the Close of the Eighteenth Century* (1800) 103–8

[12] Rev. George Horne, DD *Sunday Schools Recommended—A Sermon* (Oxford, 1786) 12, or see the summary of this sermon in *Universal Magazine* vol. 79 (1786) 149

[13] Rev. Daniel Turner *Hints on religious education, Being Two Sermons in Favour of Sunday schools* (1794) 9–10

[14] Rev. John Liddon *The General Religious Instruction of the Poor, the Surest Means of Promoting Universal National Happiness* ... (1792) 24

pay-as-you-go day schools were proving inadequate by a number of criteria. For the middle classes and their clerical spokesmen Sunday schools were far from an ideal solution. A stable home with parents eager and competent to instruct their children in both secular and religious matters was preferable to an outside educational agency. 'Were every parent able and willing to do his duty', argued a defender of the schools against those who thought them detrimental to home religion, '[they] would be useless, and might even be harmful; and it is only because parents *do not* or cannot fulfill their proper duties that these helps become necessary.'[15] But parents were the weak link, either because of the exigencies of making a living or because of their low moral condition. As the Church schools in Manchester suggested during one of their fund-raising compaigns, 'In the present state of society, few [parents] have the leisure and capacity of forming and improving the minds of youth. The time of the labourer, the husbandman, the mechanic who constitute the majority of the people is fully occupied with the necessities of their families.'[16] Someone else, in this case the rich, therefore must be responsible for the education of the poor.

Sunday schools were necessary in short because 'though the Bible exhorts parents to teach their children, the poor are unable to give them instruction and it is feared some of them have no heart for it'.[17] Teachers must begin their work by 'unlearning the children much of what they have been taught', because 'being from the lowest order of people they have not been taught to associate happiness with virtue'.[18] Mrs Trimmer suggested to potential subscribers that the immoralities of the poor which 'keep their employers in a constant state of suspicion and uneasiness' would be a thing of the past now that, because of her school, the 'education of poor children is no longer entirely left to their ignorant and corrupt parents'. Only good could result from the fact that 'it [education] has in many places become a public business'.[19] The SPCK even went so far as to warn parents not to interfere with the socially beneficial transformation Sunday schools were working on their children. These schools, they were told, were being provided

[15] See the review of Daniel Dewar *The Nature and Obligation of Personal and Family Religion* in *The Christian Observer* vol. 22 (1822) 775

[16] *Report of the State of the Sunday Schools in Manchester and Salford belonging to the Church of England, July 1809-July 1810*

[17] Rev. J. W. Morris *A Discourse delivered at Clipstone ... in favour of Sunday schools and c. on Deut. xxi: 13.* (Market Harborough, 1792)

[18] Rev. Thomas Stevenson *The difficulties and encouragements attending the communication of religious instruction to the children of the poor: a sermon delivered ... April 11, 1814 ...* (Nottingham, 1814) 20

[19] Sarah Trimmer *The Oeconomy of Charity* (1787) 26–8

to limit the profligacy which grew out of parental ignorance on matters religious and moral; parents were to cooperate with their kind benefactors and refrain from setting bad examples for the sabbath school children.[20] In short, Sunday schools on this model were the agency through which 'gracious Providence dispensed relief' to those who 'through the miserable condition of their parents must be daily exposed to perishing'.[21] And, they offered the hope that the links of the 'great chain of society which has too long been broken and separated', the chain which once 'united rich and poor', could somehow be reforged.[22]

As the Sunday school became more of a working-class institution in the early nineteenth century views like these declined in popularity. But, the related motif of children, trained in the paths of righteousness, effecting the moral rehabilitation of their parents gained currency. It appeared with the first Sunday schools: 'If their [the children's] parents fortunately should be induced to cooperate, then they themselves will be in part reformed.'[23] By the early nineteenth century the theme of 'the child leading the man' to righteousness was everywhere. A typical story will serve as an example. It is in the form of a report from a country pastor on the reformation of a poacher whose change of heart was thought to constitute a 'very pleasing and striking instance of the great benefit derived by parents of children, as well as children themselves, from the institution [of Sunday Schools]'. The father, a man of 'the most depraved habits', was after much persuasion induced to send his daughter to the school. She was a star pupil, was given a Bible as a reward for her diligence and subsequently spent winter evenings at home reading to her parents who might otherwise have frequented the ale house. Everything having to do with the family became more decent as a result of the girl's education: she dressed better, the cottage was neater, the parents attended church punctually, etc. 'Time rolled on and the same consistency presented itself. Will—for such was the father's name—was now never seen to set a trap. He had not offered a hare or brace of birds for sale for more than five months. He was never caught, as used often to be the case, lurking among the copses.' And, after more evidence of his increasing

[20] *A Plain and Serious Address to the Parents of Poor Children on the Subject of Schools* (n.d. but *c.* 1800)

[21] Rev. William Peters *An exhortion to that greatest of Charities, Rescuing the Infant Poor from Sin, and educating them in the Principles of Virtue and Religion*, preached in the parish church of Towcester, Oct. 1787 and dedicated to John, Lord Bishop of Peterborough, on Prov. 22: 6, p. 5

[22] William B [rooke] *Plans of the Sunday-Schools and School of Industry established in the City of Bath* (Bath, 1786) viii

[23] Berington, *An Essay on the Depravity* ... p. 23

holiness is presented, the report ends with Will thanking the pastor for having established the Sunday school.[24]

Church and chapel authorities, of course, hoped that children would bring their parents to Christ and to the house of worship. The New Connexion Methodists[25], for example, suggested that teachers visit their students regularly because it would 'give [them] access to the hearts of irreligious parents by which they might become instrumental to their salvation'. 'The children are becoming the Spiritual instructors of their parents,' reported one Sunday school; 'O the joyful fact, as has been known,/That parents, by their children brought to see/the gain of Godliness ...,' exulted the author of a long and mediocre poem.[26] Over and over again children are considered by Sunday schools and religious organizations as the advance troops, leading an invasion of godliness into their parents' houses.

Purely economic reasons for taking education out of the hands of parents were seldom advanced. John Eden's view that the times required an educated working class or Earl Stanhope's point in the debate over Whitbread's education bill that an industrial and commercial nation would profit by having more educated mechanics and artisans were not often repeated. But early arguments for education as a form of social control—that it would lead people to see the beauty of England's constitution of laws and therefore compel loyalty to them—were put forward in a more economic context later on. The rational society postulated by classical economic theory demanded men able to reason; perturbations in the free market were, it was held, caused by ignorant men unable to see their real interests. As Edward Baines would put it 'Yet, there are too many proofs of want of information among the working classes in towns, and of their liability to delusion; and every one acquainted with these classes must acknowledge the necessity of a better system of education.'[27] The delusion in question consisted of believing in 'the ridiculous idea that by shortening hours of children's labour their labour would be cut and wages nevertheless maintained'.[28] The Royal Statistical Society pointed to some of the consequences of faulty education in 'the lamentable outbreaks and destruction of

[24] 'Recollections of a Country Pastor' no. 10, 'The Sunday School—The Poacher' in *The Church of England Magazine* vol. 3 (1837) 284–5. Another good example is the Sunday School Union Tract, no. 40 (*c.* 1806–11) 7–8—'The Reformed Parent'

[25] *Methodist New Connexion Magazine* vol. 53 (1850) 23

[26] 'Report of the Carpenter's Tower Sunday School, 1818' quoted in W. Walters *The History of the Newcastle-on-Tyne Sunday School Union* (1870) p. 190; George MacCarthy *The Rise and Progress of Sunday Schools: A Poem* (Sudbury, 1816) 55

[27] Edward Baines *History of Cotton Manufacture in Great Britain* ... (1835) 501–2

[28] Ibid. p. 501

property and life, which have occurred on almost every occasion in which temporary distress has pressed heavily upon the labouring classes, or imaginary grievances have aroused their discontent.'[29] Some of these ideas must have motivated those industrialists in the late eighteenth and early nineteenth centuries who supported Sunday schools.

But the passionate evangelical belief in the importance of the Bible probably moved more people than all the arguments based on the public utility of Sunday schools. Protestantism generally, and its evangelical strains in particular, held that the Word of God contained all that was necessary for the salvation of the soul. And, since evangelicalism was a highly individualistic form of religion, a religion of the spirit, it was thought essential that everyone have direct personal access to the truth of scripture. Literacy was the *sine qua non* of religious life. Men like Simon Lough heard the command, when he was fifty, to 'search the scriptures'; he learned to read, and in 1787 founded a Sunday school.[30] Learned divines preached of the importance of teaching the poor to read.

'The Bible is the gift of God to men in general, for general advantage,' said the Rev. James Dore. 'It must be admitted that the poor and un-learned are as much entitled to the Book, as the rich and the learned. Christ came to save all men.' 'As Protestants', he reminded his audience, 'you will countenance an institution that is animated by the very soul of protestantism and breathes its genuine spirit ... The work of truth, the fallibility of man, the perfection of Scripture, the liberty of conscience, and the right of private judgement and free enquiry ...'[31] all demand that the poor be taught to read. It was, another early supporter of Sunday schools argued, just as cruel and arbitrary to deprive the poor of the opportunity of learning to read the Scriptures as it was to prevent those who could read them from doing so.[32] Sunday schools deserve widespread support argued the Rev. John Liddon because they make the Bible accessible to the lower orders, because the Word of God 'is indeed a light shining in a dark place'.[33]

Finally, Sunday schools were the product of a new, more humane, more tolerant, indeed more optimistic view of childhood which grew up in the eighteenth century. In art and in life the suffering of

[29] *Journal of the Royal Statistical Society* vol. 3 (1840) 385

[30] W. Walters *History* ... p. 88

[31] Rev. James Dore *A Sermon Preached (on Isiah xxix: 12) at Maze Pond, Southwark, Sept. 27, 1789, for the Benefit of the Society for the Support and Encouragement of Sunday Schools* (1789) 12, 32

[32] W. B. [rooke] *Plans*, ... p. xi

[33] J. Liddon *The General Religious Instruction* ...

children became increasingly a source of concern; and the fact that so many early Sunday schools were founded by the working classes suggests that this new sensibility penetrated far down into society. It was expounded by two traditions of thought. First, there was a widespread belief in the power of reason to improve the condition of man and society; Lockean psychology, popularized by journals like Wesley's *Arminian Magazine*, taught that a child's mind was largely a *tabula rasa* at birth and therefore malleable by sound education and institutions. There was, secondly, what might be seen as the religious analogue to the Romantic vision of the child. Much of evangelical religion was highly ambivalent about the nature of childhood and one need not look far to find hymns and sermons which proclaim the aboriginal sinfulness of children and the necessity of harsh corrective discipline. But, just as Blake in the *Songs of Innocence*, or Wordsworth in *Intimations of Immortality*, proclaimed a unique vision of the world available only to children, so one strand of evangelical though regarded the child as especially capable of receiving God's grace and therefore able to teach and convert adults whose spiritual vision had become clouded. This vision penetrated, through sermons and pamphlets, to levels of society untouched directly by Wordsworth or Rousseau; it infused the thought of many of those who began Sunday schools. Furthermore, it laid the basis for a disciplinary regime based on regard for the specialness of childhood and the supremacy of love and kindness over force in bringing up children. If Victorian parents reverted to the cruel and brutal punishments of the seventeenth century—an unproven hypothesis—it is difficult to place the blame on that popular religious fervour which found expression in Sunday schools.

Those who supported Sunday schools accepted the educational theory, attributed by them to Locke or Rousseau, that 'everything not given at birth, we have from education'.[34] And very little was given at birth; in the words of one sermon 'the minds of children are like uncultivated land'.[35] All men are largely the product of their environment and become good or evil depending on how they were educated. Even a Methodist minister, committed in principle to the doctrine of original sin, remarked in a sermon to 'plain industrious people' that '... (notwithstanding the acknowledged depravity of human nature) a very large share of ignorance and

---

[34] *The Good Effects of Sunday Schools and other Charitable Institutions ... with a Plan for their Establishment* (Wrexham, 1789) opening page. See also the opening page of Turner *Hints on Religious Education*

[35] Morris *A Discourse ...* p. 9

wickedness of society is owing to the want of religious education'.[36]
Sunday school children on this model were not wicked little beings
who required a harsh disciplinary regime to control behaviour born
of sin, but rational, relatively innocent creatures who could be
'trained up in the ways of righteousness' through education.

Even for those who did not subscribe to a Lockean viewpoint,
the practical psychology of idealism, of a belief in innate ideas,
was similar in the context of Sunday schools. Children were
ultimately rational and educable. As the Bishop of Bristol put it
in 1795, 'the necessity for knowledge arises from both the nature
and the constitution of man. Born is he with the seeds and principles
of knowledge.'[37] Thomas Collins, Chaplain in Ordinary to the
Prince of Wales, cast Sunday schools still more clearly in an
Enlightenment mould. 'God has', he argued, 'given us reason, that
we should be influenced by rational motives.' Neglecting education,
therefore, is 'at once a contempt of the omniscient and all gracious
Providence, and of the powers and suggestions of nature and
the human soul.'[38] Over thirty years later in 1820 the writer
of a Sunday school manual reiterated this theme by arguing against
corporal punishment on the grounds that it pressed on man's
animal nature rather than appealing to the 'influence of higher
principles'.[39] This relatively optimistic view of a child's nature
pervades much of the early literature written to publicize Sunday
schools.

Isaac Watts' *Divine and Moral Songs for the Use of Children* represents
the beginning of a new more positive vision of childhood in religious
writings. The wide circulation of these poems makes them especially
interesting as both a source and a reflection of popular attitudes
towards children. Over 125 British editions of the work were
published between 1715 and 1800, another 189 before 1850 when
Watts' popularity finally began to decline. The opening stanza
of the song 'Against idleness and mischief' (How doth the little
busy Bee/Improve each Shining Hour ...) or of 'The Sluggard'
('Tis the voice of the Sluggard; I heard him complain) were still well
enough known in 1865 for Lewis Carroll to parody them.

[36] Robert Miller, M. G. (Minister of the Gospel), *The Duty of Parents considered
in a Sermon Preached in the Methodist Chapel, at Dewsbury, in Yorkshire, Sunday March 16,
1800* (Wakefield, 1800) 4

[37] Courtenay, Bishop of Bristol *Sermon on Prov. xix: 2 (Also, that the soul be without
knowledge, it is not good;)* (1795) 2

[38] Thomas Collins (Curate of Burnley, Rector of Compton Vallence, and
Chaplain in Ordinary to the Prince of Wales) *A Sermon Preached at Burnley
in Lancashire, Nov. 4, 1787, on the Institution of Sunday Schools There* (1788) 2

[39] Rev. R. M. Miller *The Religious Instruction of Children and Youth Recommended
to Christian Parents* (1820) 164

Watts, like many eighteenth-century religious figures, is profoundly ambivalent about the nature of man and especially about
the moral state of children. When the soul 'comes into the world',
he argues, 'it is unfurnished with knowledge'. But exactly what
would happen if an infant were left unattended, in a state of nature,
is problematic. 'If left entirely to ourselves', he concludes, '[we]
should *probably* grow up like the brutes of the earth.'[40] Not all, or
even the majority of the *Songs* emphasize the innocence of children;
some in fact exhibit the Calvinistic hard line with great ferocity.
For example, the song on 'On Obedience to Parents' warns the
child who breaks his father's word,

> What heavy guilt upon him lies!
> How cursed is his name
> The ravens shall pick out his eyes
> And Eagles eat the same.

'On Heaven and Hell' notes that 'There is a dreadfull hell,/ And
everlasting pains', awaiting those who do not follow his advice to
'read and pray'.

But Watts was also a great advocate of 'cheerful piety'. Religion
ought not to be overbearing and sad, he held, because that which
leads to 'everlasting pleasure' could not possibly be gloomy. There
is a quality of goodness and serenity about the *Divine Songs*, a playful
charm which symbolizes a new departure in religious sensibilities
and accounts also for their enormous popularity.[41]

Children for Watts were not by nature part of a savage Hobbesian
world:

> Let Dogs delight to bark and bite,
> For God has made them so;
> Let Bears and Lions growl and fight,
> For 'tis their Nature too.

But on the other hand,

> But Children, you should never let
> Such angry Quarrels rise;
> Your little hands were never made
> to tear each others Eyes.

[40] Isaac Watts *On the Improvement of the Mind* (London, 1841) 317–18; (my
emphasis)
[41] The best critical evaluation of Watts is in F. J. Darton's *Children's Books in
England: Five centuries of social life* (Cambridge. 1932) 106–111; see also A. P. Davis
Isaac Watts; his Life and Works (1948) 74–81. For a bibliographical history of the
Divine Songs see the introduction and bibliography by J.H.P. Pafford to Isaac
Watts *Divine Songs* (Oxford University Press Facsimile reproduction of first edition
of 1715 and an illustrated edition of circa 1840, 1971) especially pp. 60–96

> Let Love thro' all your Actions run,
>   And all yours Words be mild;
> Live like the blessed Virgin's Son;
>   That sweet and lovely Child.[42]

In the song 'Innocent Play' he first paints a picture of young lambs 'with fleeces so clean and so white' sporting about on a meadow and young doves nesting in an open cage. In contrast,

> If we had been Ducks, we might dabble in Mud:
> Or Dogs, we might play till it ended in Blood:
> So foul, or so fierce are their Natures.

Again, such is not a child's nature:

> But Thomas and William, and such pretty Names
> Should be cleanly and harmless as Doves or as Lambs,
> Those lovely sweet innocent Creatures.[43]

Of course much of Watts' poetry still lays emphasis on hell and damnation; some songs, those against scoffing and calling names, for example, are as gruesome as any of the seventeenth century.[44] But the content of many of the poems and the tone of the entire volume is indicative of a shift in religious attitudes.

The hymns of John and Charles Wesley are full of the same ambivalence but are also suggestive of a new metaphorical structure founded on the image of the innocent child.[45] For example, the first hymn on Mark 10:14, 'Suffer the little children to come unto me' proclaims of children that

> Born they are, like us, in sin
> Touch the unconscious lepers clean;
> Purchase of Thy blood they are,
> Save them by Thy dying prayer.[46]

But twenty-two lines later the hymn on 'For such is the kingdom of God' begins to develop the metaphor of the soul regaining childlike innocence in order to enter paradise:

> Thy church is here with saints supplied
>   Who childlike innocence regain;
> And every babe that ever died
>   Shall in thy heavenly kingdom reign.[47]

[42] Song 16, 'Against Quarrelling and Fighting' (1715 facsimile ed.) 171–2
[43] 'Innocent Play' (one of the unnumbered *Moral Songs*) (1715 facsimile ed.) 196
[44] Song 18 (1715 facsimile ed.) 174–5
[45] References are to the *Poetical Works of John and Charles Wesley*, collected and arranged in eleven volumes by G. Osborn DD (1871)
[46] 'Hymns on the Four Gospels' no. 982, vol. xi, 30
[47] Ibid. no. 984, p. 31

The image of childlike innocence is clearest in the 'Hymns for the Youngest' which begins with the famous couplet, 'Gentle Jesus, meek and mild/ Look upon a little child' and continues,

> I shall live the simple life
> Free from sin's uneasy strife:
> Sweetly ignorant of ill,
> Innocent and happy still.

> ***

> Keep me from the great offence,
> Guard my helpless innocence
> Hide me, from all evil hide,
> Self and stubbornness, and pride.[18]

In another of these hymns a child asks to remain in the state of innocence:

> Strong let us in Thy grace abide
> But ignorant of ill;
> In malice, subtlety and pride
> Let us be children still.[49]

Parents praying for a sick daughter ask God to 'Save her suffering innocence'.[50] Examples could be multiplied; but, the point is that there was an eighteenth-century religious mood wherein childhood and infancy were seen in the softer light of sentiment.

In part the Wesleyan attitude springs from its Arminian theology; the fate of each soul was not predestined from eternity. And, more importantly here, there was no scriptural foundation for the view that some infants, those whose souls were not destined for salvation, were reprobate from the womb. On the contrary, infants who died before they could choose redemption were destined for heaven because of their birthright of innocence. As Thomas Brocas, a Methodist lay preacher and early supporter of Shropshire Sunday Schools, argued against the ultra-Calvinist John Walker, the infants taken into the arms of Jesus could not be true believers, yet Jesus blessed them and therefore they could not be reprobates. 'For such is the kingdom of God', Christ said, and surely heaven could only be populated by the saved or the innocent young. Brocas continued to develop these themes by suggesting that the voice from the heavens referred to in Rev. 4:3–5 was the voice of the

---

[48] 'Hymns for Children' no. lxxii, vol. vi, 441–2
[49] Ibid. no. lxxix, p. 449
[50] 'Hymns for a Family', no. lxxi, vol. vii, 82

undefiled, of infants etc.[51] In short, through Watts, through the Wesleys, and through a mass of more obscure preachers, the religious culture out of which Sunday schools grew was suffused by the image of the innocent child.

But more is involved than a partial resolution of the tension between original sin and innocence in favour of the latter. The religious tradition being discussed here shared with the high culture of Romanticism a streak of anti-rationalism; children because of their relative ignorance, their innocence and their simplicity were more likely to perceive religious reality and to accept the Holy Spirit than were adults. The scriptural origins of this notion are in the Gospel of Mark: 'Verily I say unto you, Whosoever shall not receive the Kingdom of God as a little child, he shall not enter therein.'[52] It is a theme in the hymns of the Wesleys': 'My ruined innocence regive/My lost simplicity/And then with arms of love receive/The little child in me'; or, 'Lord, I would be brought to Thee/Passive as an infant be'; or 'A soul by sacred infancy' is freed from worldly sin so that it might lie innocent in the arms of Jesus; old age, because of the decline of reason is referred to as the 'infancy of grace', etc.[53]

A great body of Sunday school literature embodies in a more literal way Wordsworth's dictum that the child is the father of the man; the conversion of adults by children is one of its most ubiquitous themes. In a Wesleyan class meeting a man was reported to have stood up and announced, 'My son, who now sits beside me is my spiritual father. He heard me cursing, while in a state of drunkenness, and said to me, "Oh father, my teacher said today at Sunday school that neither drunkards nor swearers could enter heaven".' Needless to say the man subsequently mended his ways and joined the Methodist society.[54] In the same year an evangelist in Newcastle reported that he made 180 converts among the young who in turn were now bringing religion to their parents.[55]

The Romantic theme in religious literature is most perfectly expressed in Leigh Richmond's *The Dairyman's Daughter*. In this enormously popular story, whose sales before 1850 exceeded half a million, a clergyman narrator tells how successful a young girl had been in bringing the 'knowledge and experience of truth' to

[51] Thomas Brocas *God No Respecter of Persons, but Loving to Every Man: Being an Answer to the 'Friendly Address' of the Rev. Mr. John Walker* (Shrewsbury, 1808) 72–3

[52] Mark 10:15

[53] Wesley *Poetical Works* vol xi, no. 973, p. 27; no. 1483, p. 259; no. 985, p. 31; no. 986, p. 31

[54] *Sunday School Teachers' Magazine and Journal of Education* (1831) col. 478

[55] Ibid. (1832) col. 478

her parents. 'This is a lovely feature', he continues, 'in the character of a young Christian. If it have pleased God in the free dispensation of his mercy to call the child by his grace, while the parent remains still in ignorance and sin, how great is the duty incumbent on that child to do what is possible to promote the conversion of those to whom so much is owing . . .'[56]

'Her general conduct verified,' remarked an observer of the death of Sarah Sykes, aged nine, 'that out of the mouths of babes and sucklings God can perfect perfect praise.'[57]

There remains of course a great corpus of sermons and tracts full of horrific warnings to children as to the sinful nature of their souls. Indeed parts of the story just cited are in this tradition. But often actions belied words. The Rev. Joseph Milner for example advised parents to 'impress it on their [the children's] minds, that they are sinners by NATURE as well as by practice.' 'You must subdue by the rod, if it cannot be done by milder methods,' he suggested.[58] Yet his biographer points out that those who knew Milner by his preaching alone regarded him as 'severe and morose' and expressed surprise on meeting him that he was so 'easy, mild and affable'.[59] More to the point, however, he was the particular favourite of the young children in families he visited. They 'hung upon his lips, when he related to them the legendary tales which amused his infancy'.[60]

The contrasts between precept and practice is even more pronounced in the case of the Evangelical Richard Cecil. He was capable of preaching to children: 'I want to convince you that we are all, every one of us, perishing sinners.'[61] And yet the reports of his son and fragments of his diary paint quite a different picture. 'No parent could be more benevolent toward his family', his son points out and cites instances of parental indulgence. Once Cecil's daughter wanted the words to a song just as he was going into company; he wrote out the words while conversing, left the room, and presented them to his daughter. He hated punishment and

[56] Religious Tract Society edition (n.d. but *c.* 1830) p. 51; bibliographical information is from William Jones *The Jubilee Memorial of the Religious Tract Society, AD 1799 to AD 1849* (1850) appendix

[57] J. H. Walker *Memoirs of Sunday School Children who have lived and died in the Lord* (Northampton, 1823) 15

[58] Rev. Isaac Milner, ed. *Practical Sermons of the late Rev. Joseph Milner, MA . . . to which is prefixed an Account of the Life and Character of the Author* (Cambridge, 1801) Sermon xv. 'The Example of Abraham', pp. 213–14; see also Sermon vi, 'Lowliness Recommended from the example of Christ' p. 80

[59] Ibid. p. lxiv

[60] Ibid. p. lv

[61] Josiah Pratt, ed. *The Works of the Revd. Richard Cecil, MA with a Memoir of His Life by his son* (3rd ed. 1827) 2 vols. 'Sermon x on Prov. 4:1' p. 223

cringed in his study on those rare occasions when the mother disciplined the children; he wrote the tenderest of poems to console his son at the death of a one-month-old infant and was bathed in tears when his own child died. Family worship was short, useful, and tailored to the needs of his children.[62] Quite possibly, other Evangelicals who preached severity towards children often did not follow their own advice.

There was, however, no ambiguity in the Sunday school literature designed to guide teachers in their encounters with children. Instead of earlier views that children should adapt to adult forms of religious worship, early-nineteenth-century authorities argue that worship should be fitted to the needs of the child. A. H. Davis' recommendation that brevity is essential in dealing with children because of their limited attention span replaced John Cotton's warning that 'the devil rocks the cradle' of those children who fall asleep during long adult sermons.[63] Seldom in the literature are children treated as immature and, even more, wantonly sinful adults. The *Eclectic Review*, for example, advised the authors of children's books to suspend 'the superiority of their own maturity in knowledge and opinion' when writing for the young, because what might be lost in strict theology 'they would gain in *child-like simplicity*'.[64] Elsewhere, the same journal remarked that textbooks need not be entirely religious; what about pleasing tales and fables, it asked.[65] A sermon was praised because its style was 'lowered to the taste and comprehension of the smallest children'.[66] Those who advocated the strictest sabbath observance for children were countered by others who realized that special consideration had to be taken of the age of young family members.[67]

While one would not need to search very assiduously for eighteenth-century sermons and manuals which advocate a harsh disciplinary regime for children, it remains true that some of the most popular preachers advised precisely the opposite. The Nonconformist Rev. Phillip Doddridge (1702–41), for example, a man whose works and biography were widely circulated as Sunday school reward books, argued that the education of children should 'be done plainly,—seriously,—tenderly,—and patiently.' 'Do not', he suggests, 'desire to terrify or amaze them, to lead them into unnecessary severities, or to deprive them of innocent pleasures.'

[62] Ibid. p. 62, 63–7

[63] A. H. Davis *The Religious Instruction of the Young* (1826) 27–8; John Cotton *A Practical Commentary Upon the First Epistle of John* (1656) 102

[64] *Eclectic Review* vol. 1, pt. 2 (1805) 955

[65] Ibid. vol. 2, pt. 2, p. 840

[66] Ibid. vol. 7, pt. 1 (1811) 372

[67] For example see *Christian Observer* vol. 22 (1823) 769 ff

B

He took a very strong position against corporal punishment and ended his series of sermons on Prov. 22 with the caveat that humanity and patience should prevail in all of an adult's dealing with children.[68]

The ideal Sunday school teacher was not thought to be the stern and unyielding disciplinarian who followed Susannah Wesley's famous dictum to 'break the wills of children'.[69] 'Let yours be the government of love,' Thomas Raffles told Liverpool teachers in 1816. 'Let the law of kindness be ever on your lips. Imbue your spirit with the temper of him who said, "suffer the little children".'[70] The good teacher is 'affectionate in manner and mild in expression', said another guide book in 1826.[71] The future Bishop of Rochester noted in 1837 the ineffectiveness of corporal punishment and more importantly its opposition to 'that gracious spirit which should animate the managers of Sunday schools'.[72] Even so stern a periodical as the _Evangelical Review_ remarked in an article on 'Order in Sunday schools' that teachers 'must love little children, as Christ had loved them when he said "Suffer them to come unto me ..." He that makes a child happier for one half hour is a co-worker of God'.[73]

Indeed, the community spirit which pervaded Sunday schools made plausible the model of the teacher as an older, wiser and steadier friend : 'The Sunday school theory is that every scholar is sure of a friend who will visit him in sickness, procure help for him in want, and to whom he may apply for advice in an emergency.'[74] Teachers, according to a Wesleyan Sunday school organization, 'must not be haughty or distant, but condescending, and to a proper extent familiar—not irritable or impatient, but kind and forbearing—not gloomy or melancholy, but cheerful and pleasant—not partial or resentful, but administering favours with an equal hand, bearing with and forgiving the follies of youth.'[75] Kindness and a devotion to Christ were the two most important qualifications.

[68] Phillip Doddridge _Works_ (1804) 'Sermons on Proverbs xxii: 6' vol. III, 38, 41, 48; see also vol. II, 293–317; vol. V, 154, Hymn no. xcviii

[69] See Paul Sangster _Pity my Simplicity: The Evangelical Revival and the Religious Education of Children 1738–1800_ (1963) 29–30 for Susannah Wesley's views

[70] Thomas Raffles _The Sunday School Teachers' Monitor together with Hints for Self Examination ...being the substance of two addresses delivered to the teachers of Great George Street Sunday School, Liverpool_ (Liverpool, 1816) 17

[71] Davis _Religious Instruction ..._ p. 111

[72] J. C. Wigram, _Practical Hints on the Formation and Management of Sunday schools_ (London, 1833) p. 7

[73] Vol. 16, 2nd series (1833) 635

[74] _Sunday School Teachers' Handbook_ (1848) 9

[75] _The Sunday School Teachers' Re-Union_ (Leeds, 1848) 21

Conclusions

The men who wrote the tracts and sermons discussed above all thought that the education of children could no longer remain the sole responsibility of parents. They held this position in some cases for reasons having to do with the public good: a belief that, since the young constituted the hope of the commonwealth there was some public obligation to see that they were properly educated; a faith in education as an agency of moral regeneration; a hope that Sunday school educated children would serve as a moral advance force into the home of their parents; a conviction that the economy or in any case a rationally governed society required a reasoning population. More importantly, others became active in Sunday school work because of evangelical Protestantism which placed the Bible near the centre of Everyman's religious experience, thereby making literacy a prerequisite for godliness. Finally, Sunday schools were an expression of Romantic sensibilities regarding childhood transferred to the sphere of practical religion.

The question remains, of course, as to how many of the positions outlined above were shared by the working classes. Implicitly, if without literary justification, the Sunday schools of the poor as much as those of the rich, performed functions which parents could not, or would not, perform. Literate working people took the children of their less literate neighbors into their homes or into rented rooms each Sunday to teach them to read and write. Occasionally, as with the blacksmith cited in Chapter Two, an element of moral rescue seems to underlie a poor man's efforts at Sunday education. And, undoubtedly, the conversion to Methodism, which many early Sunday school workers experienced, brought with it a new aesthetic and moral sensibility which they sought to propagate. But the condescending statements of a Hannah More or a Sarah Trimmer are nowhere in evidence; most working-class people in fact made no comment at all on their efforts. If asked, they surely would have said that they simply wanted to help make their neighbor's children better. There probably was an economic demand for literacy which made both the giving and the reception of elementary education a more laudable and worthwhile exercise. But more importantly again, the Evangelical Revival, with the printed word so vital to its spirit, must have given impulse to literate working people to teach their less literate but eager neighbors to read the Bible. As for the softening of feeling toward children, recurrent expressions of affection and gratitude toward Sunday school teachers suggest that James Hillock, a Scottish schoolmaster of working-class origins, was not alone when he said 'The outcast or the careless may not hear the voice of Jesus, in his Word, saying 'Suffer the little children ...' but they may hear the invitation from the lips of a Sunday school teacher.[76]

In large part the Sunday schools originated as an expression of that faith in the efficacy of education and the malleability of human nature which is still dominant today. The desired results from a period of instruction varied between classes and over time, but the belief that something could and should be done systematically to influence the rising generation was common ground for all.

[76]James Hillocks *Life Story: A Prize Autobiography* (1860) 20

2. Sunday Schools : Their Origin & Growth

i. INTRODUCTION

The growth of Sunday schools, slow until 1780 and at a greatly
accelerated pace in the decades following, was but one product of
the religious and humanitarian movements outlined in Chapter One.
During the same period an evergrowing number of agencies
designed to ameliorate the condition of the poor generally and of
their children in particular were begun. Sunday schools, however,
were remarkable not only for the rapidity with which they spread,
for their wide geographical and religious distribution, and for the
degree of local support they enjoyed but most importantly for the
breadth of their social base. The impulse to found schools for the
religious and secular instruction of poor children was by no means
restricted to the middle and upper classes of the philanthropic
establishment. Working men and women in hundreds of
communities throughout England were at least as important in
building this educational patchwork as were the Hannah Mores,
Sarah Trimmers or Robert Raikes on whom exclusive credit is
usually bestowed. In fact, as these sorts of people dropped out of
Sunday school work, the schools became more and more agencies of
community self-help and self-improvement.

Robert Raikes, however, is most often named as the founder of
Sunday schools and he might indeed stand as a symbol for one
strand of their history. Within a decade of his founding four small
Sunday schools in Gloucester, he was hailed as a man whose
benevolence had earned him the right 'to be looked up to with
reverence and respect to the latest posterity'.[1] Raikes died in 1811
and very quickly assumed first place in the Sunday school pantheon.
He had left a monument, one clergyman declared, which would

[1] *European Magazine* vol. 14 (November 1788) 315–6

crown his head 'with a glory effulgent as the sun, and lasting as the throne of Omnipotence'.[2] If the seven cities of Greece contended for the birth of Homer, argued a sober denominational magazine, 'how much more may the city of Gloucester exult on account of this God-like and valuable man'.[3] In fact, however, Raikes was not so extraordinary. He was typical of the middle-class provincial philanthropist, the sort of person whose life 'seldom affords many particulars ... living constantly at his native place in the regular employment of his trade [and who] may be said to have passed his days in comparative retirement'.[4]

His father, Robert Raikes, Sr., was one of the earliest and most prominent provincial journalist-printers. As the partner of William Dicey, the famous publisher of chapbooks, Raikes founded the *Northampton Journal* in 1720 and eventually went off on his own to start the *Gloucester Journal*. The son, Robert, Jr., inherited the editorship of this paper in 1757 and immediately began to use his new position in the cause of humanitarian reform. He was a committed partisan of Howard's movement to improve the condition of prisons and the treatment of prisoners. He visited and corresponded with men condemned to death or deportation. His paper carried pleas for funds to pay the debts of men imprisoned for insolvency and to provide marriage portions for poor but virtuous young ladies; it was among the first to support the anti-slave trade movement. Sunday schools were but one of Raikes's efforts to do good, albeit the one that earned him national prominence.[5]

The story he tells of how the idea of a new educational charity came to him is revealing not only of his sensibilities but of the sensibilities of an increasingly important segment of society. One day in 1781

---

[2] Rev. Thomas Bailey *An Eulogium on the Character of Mr. Robert Raikes* (Nottingham 1815) 22

[3] *Methodist Magazine* vol. 41 (1818) 375

[4] Alexander Chalmer *The General Biographical Dictionary* vol. 25 (1812) 'Raikes' entry

[5] The primary biographical source for Robert Raikes, Jr. is J. Harris, ed. *Robert Raikes: The Man and his Work* (1899) compiled from the manuscript notes of the editor's father who had access to some sixty autographed letters of Raikes and had interviewed many of his co-workers in the early Sunday school movement. See also Alfred Gregory *Robert Raikes* (1877); Guy Kendall *Robert Raikes, A Critical Study* (1939); and P. M. Eastman *Robert Raikes and Northamptonshire Sunday Schools* (1880); Gray, *English Philanthropy* ... p. 194. For Raikes, Sr. see Roland Austin *Robert Raikes, the Elder, and the Gloucester Journal* (1915); Geoffrey Alan Cranfield *The Development of the Provincial Newspaper, 1700–1760* (Oxford 1962) pp. 48, 83, 198, 250; Victor Neuberg *The Penny Histories: A Study of Chapbooks for Young Readers over Two Centuries* (1968) pp. 26–27

I was walking into the suburbs of the city, where the lowest of
the people (who are principally employed in the pin-manufactury)
chiefly reside [where] I was struck with concern at seeing a
group of children wretchedly ragged, at play in the street.
I asked an inhabitant whether those children belonged to that
part of town, and lamented their misery and idleness.—Ah! Sir,
said the woman to whom I was speaking, could you take a view
of this part of town on Sunday, you should be shocked indeed;
for then the street is filled with multitudes of these wretches who,
released on that day from their employment, spend their time
in noise and riot and playing at chuck, and cursing and swearing
in a manner so horrid, as to convey to any serious mind an idea
of hell, rather than any other place ...

This conversation suggested to me, that it would be at least
a harmless attempt, if it were productive of no good, should some
little plan be formed to check this deplorable profanation of the
sabbath. I then inquired of the woman, if there were any decent,
well-disposed women in the neighbourhood, who kept schools
for teaching to read. I presently was directed to four: to these
I applied, and made an agreement with them, to receive as
many children as I should send upon the Sunday, whom they
were to instruct in reading and in the Church catechism.—For
this I engaged to pay them each a shilling for their day's employment. The women seemed pleased with the proposal. I then
waited on the clergyman before-mentioned, and imparted to
him my plan; he was so much satisfied with the idea, that he
engaged to lend his assistance, by going round to the schools on
a Sunday afternoon, to examine the progress that was made, and
to enforce order and decorum among such a set of little heathens.

This, Sir, was the commencement of the plan.[6]

It does not matter that Raikes's claim to having originated Sunday
schools was a source of much, often heated, controversy during
the nineteenth century. A plaque in the Reverend Thomas Stock's
old parish church of Ashbury, Berks., proclaims that this clergyman,
who appears in Raikes's story, conveyed the idea of Sunday
education to Raikes, and not the other way around. Long and
detailed articles in the national press argued Stock's case, and other
candidates for priority also emerged from time to time. Cardinal
Borromeo, the Bishop of Milan and a man especially concerned
with the education of children, is perhaps the earliest contender;

[6] *Gentleman's Magazine* vol. 54, pt. 1 (1784) 410–11; the letter had been written
to Colonel Townley of Bolton on 25 November, 1783; the earliest reference to
Sunday schools in this influential journal occurs on p. 377 ibid.

Jean Baptiste de la Salle who opened a Sunday school for the *gamins* of Paris in 1669 is close behind. During the late seventeenth century and increasingly during the eighteenth, other men and women went well beyond the requirements of ecclesiastical law to instruct the poor children on Sundays. The first Sunday school in England might have been started by the Ferrar sisters of Little Gidding in 1625. Fowler's Sunday School Charity was established in the Black Country in 1699, and the Rev. Joseph Alleine is alleged to have begun a school near Bristol about the same time.[7]

The pace quickened by the mid-eighteenth century. After 1750 philanthropically inclined clergymen like the Revs. Theophilus Lindsey, a Unitarian, John Valton, a Methodist, John Moffatt, an Independent, Thomas Kennedy, John Fletcher and David Simpson, Anglicans, followed suit. But more importantly, lay men and women, who were to become the mainstay of the Sunday school, also founded schools in the decades before Raikes. Catherine Cappe was considered something of an eccentric for teaching the poor to read on Sundays in Bedale during the 1760s. Hannah Ball of High Wycombe, Sophia Cooke of a village near Gloucester, one Mrs Dobinson of Derby, William King, James Hey, William Hallam, and John Brown, all began Sunday schools in the decades before 1781.[8]

[7] The most coherent case for Stock is made by Arthur B. Evans, headmaster of the Cathedral School, Gloucester, in *Gentleman's Magazine* vol. 101, pt. 2 (October 1831) 291–6. After a rebuttal signed by 'Cornelius' on pp. 392–3 of the same volume, Evans re-argues his position in vol. 102, pt. 2 (October 1832) 326–8. A good summary of the arguments over priority is in S. R. T. Mayer's *Who was the founder of Sunday Schools?* (1880). For Borromeo and biographical tidbits on many Sunday school pioneers see T. Timpson *Mirror of Sunday School Teachers* (1853); for de la Salle see David Miller *The Organization of Our Sabbath Schools* (Edinburgh 1880) 7; for the Ferrar sisters see Gray *English Philanthropy* p. 118; for Fowler's Charity see E. L. Glew *History of the Borough and Foreign of Walsall* (Walsall 1856) 182–3; for Alleine see Eastman *Robert Raikes* ... pp. 43–5

[8] For Lindsey and Cappe see *Memoirs of the Life of the late Mrs. Catherine Cappe written by herself* (1882) 118–22; for Kennedy see Eastman op. cit. 43–5; for Valton see W. B. Carter *History of the Nottingham Sunday School Union* (Nottingham 1869) 13; for Moffatt see A. McLellan 'Congregationalism and the Education of the People, 1760–1914,' (unpublished MA thesis, Birmingham University) 69; for Simpson, an Anglican Evangelical converted by Lindsey, see his *Memoir* by Rev. James Johnston (Macclesfield, 1800); for Hannah Ball see Nehemiah Curnock, ed. *Journal of the Rev. John Wesley* vol. 5 (1914) 104n., and also the article on early Sunday schools by Thomas Marriott, the son of one of the founders of the Sunday School Union, in *Wesleyan Methodist Magazine* vol. 71 (4th ser., vol. 2, pt. 1) (1848) 561–7; for Sophia Cooks see S. Mayer *Who Was* ... p. 33; for Mrs Dobinson and another anonymous woman see Henry Fish *Memoir of Joseph Pearson of Bath* pp. 6–7; for William King see H. I. Firth MA 'The Earliest English Sunday school' and Roland Austin 'The Dursley Sunday School Established 1784' in *Transactions of the Congregational Historical Society* (September 1928) 183–90, (April 1929) 228–33; for Hey see *Wesleyan Methodist Magazine* vol. 58 (3rd ser., vol. 14) (1836) 285–6; for John Brown, a Wesleyan from Bradford, see William Scruton *Pen and Pencil Sketches of Old Bradford* (Bradford, Bingley, 1889) 103; for Hallam see Carter, above, p. 14

However, Raikes's account of the founding of Sunday schools in Gloucester found its way, via Colonel Townley of Bolton, to the *Gentleman's Magazine*, thereby establishing his priority. From there it was disseminated throughout the country by that extensive network of magazines and newspapers available to the middle classes in the late eighteenth century.[9]

Sunday schools rapidly became the favorite charity of hundreds of provincial philanthropists; indeed, this educational humanitarian work became a form of cultural definition for some of the middle classes, an activity akin to participation in a literary and philosophical, anti-slave trade or prison reform society. One early guide pointed out that only 'a few serious neighbors need associate to form a school'; another reassured readers that two or three well-intentioned people, even one pious individual, could do the same.[10] The Sunday School Union went so far as to recommend to its supporters that they select a place in the country which had no Sunday school and spend their holidays there engaged in the good work.[11] Individually or in groups middle-class philanthropists answered these calls to action.

Joseph Strutt, the artist and antiquarian, moved into the Hertfordshire countryside in 1790 and immediately established two Sunday schools at his own expense.[12] The first Sunday school in Kendal was the result of efforts by James Arnslie, a doctor of physics, who three years earlier, in 1782, had founded the dispensary and who was involved in almost every philanthropic organization in the town.[13] William Hey FRS, chief surgeon of the general infirmary in Leeds and co-founder of the town's Sunday school, was at the same time a member of the Manchester Lit and Phil, an early supporter of the slave-trade abolition movement who owned £500 of Sierra Leone Stock, sometime President of the Leeds Bible Society, and a zealous worker for the Church Missionary Society.[14] Examples could be multiplied from the nationally famous, like

[9] Townley, who also sent a copy of Raikes's letter to the *Manchester Mercury*, was the son of a Rochdale mercer who was a small-time patron of the arts and local commentator on agricultural and other affairs. See A. P. Wadsworth 'The First Manchester Sunday Schools,' *Bulletin of the John Rylands Library* no. 33 (1951) 303. Via Townley, Raikes's letter also appeared in the Leeds paper (December 1783)

[10] 'Essay on the Formation of Sunday Schools' (3rd ed., 1813) 2; 'Hints on the Formation of Sunday Schools' in the *Evangelical Magazine* vol. 6. (January and February 1798) 15–18, 52–59 and also vol. 18 (1810) 224–5

[11] *Evangelical Magazine* vol. 23 (1815) 175

[12] John Nichols *Literary Anecdotes of the Eighteenth Century* vol. 5 (1812–15) 678–9

[13] Francis Nicholson and Ernest Axon *The Old Non-Conformity in Kendal* (Kendal, 1915) 515

[14] J. Pearson *The Life of William Hey, Esq. FRS* vol. 1 (1822) 163–93

Hannah More and her sisters in the Mendip Hills, Mrs Trimmer at Brentford, Sir Richard Stonehouse in Northamptonshire, or Lady Eleanor Venn, wife of the editor of the *Paston Letters* and herself a well-known writer of children's books, to hosts of more obscure people.[15]

A group of anonymous ladies founded a group of schools in Newington, Walworth and Cumberwell for 'members of their own sex'; a Mrs Loftus read about Raikes in a local paper and established a school in Sheffield; William Newsholme, a Reading snuff manufacturer, started the first Sunday school in the Worth Valley and kept it going with the help of his family, etc.[16]

The manner in which these and hundreds of others proceeded in their good works is illustrated by a contemporary poem:

> About this time, a pious man
> Pursued a well-adjusted plan,
> Took pity on the helpless poor
> And went around from door to door.
>
> Some called him Methodist and fool
> For he would have a SUNDAY SCHOOL;
> But some were willing to unite
> And said, they thought the man was right.[17]

Individual men and women of the middling classes, working at the local level, account for much of the early growth of Sunday schools. But there were also more organized and large-scale efforts by these sorts of people to further Sunday education.

In certain large or medium-sized towns and cities — Manchester, Liverpool, Birmingham, Stoke-on-Trent, Norwich, Shrewsbury, Colchester, Nottingham, Halifax, Stockport, Leeds — Sunday schools sprang from meetings of local notables called together by some variant of a notice like this one:

Sunday Schools. The utility of these Seminaries for the instruction of the lower class of people, and a due Observance of the Sabbath,

[15] For H. More see M. P. More *Mendip Annals, or a Narrative of the Charitable Labours of Hannah and Martha More in their Neighbourhood* ed. by Arthur Roberts (1858), below; Sarah Trimmer *The Oeconomy of Charity* (1787) *passim*; for Stonehouse see Eastman *Robert Raikes* p. 10 and the appropriate *DNB* entry. Stonehouse (1716–95) was a physician, founder of the county infirmary, writer of literature for the sick, and, after his ordination, an Anglican clergyman of Evangelical persuasion. For Venn see F. J. Darton *Children's Books* . . . p. 168

[16] *Protestant Dissenters Magazine* vol. 1 (1794) 415; John Salt 'Early Sheffield Sunday Schools and their Educational Importance,' *Transactions of the Hunter Archaeological Society* vol. 7, pt. 3 (1967) 180; J. W. Laycock *Methodist Heroes of the Great Haworth Round 1734–1784* (Keighley, 1909) 372

[17] 'The Sunday Scholar,' Religious Tract Society (n. d.)

being proved in different parts of England:—A Well wisher to such a laudable institution requests the Inhabitants of Birmingham to meet on that business at the hotel, on Wednesday morning, the 7th instant at ten o'clock precisely.

References to the 'ignorance, vice and misery', the 'idleness, play, lewdness, and every other species of wickedness' to which the lower orders were prone might also have been included. A nominally interdenominational committee was selected at the ensuing meeting to manage a Sunday school, which was created on the model of the infirmary, foundling hospital, or some such charity. (In Shrewsbury the dispensary and Sunday school annual reports were even bound together.)[18] Already existing small Sunday schools were incorporated, and a monopoly on Sunday education was declared.

By and large these interdenominational schools drew their support from a remarkably wide range of a town's lay and clerical elite. For example, the Manchester Sunday School Committee included the fervently evangelical Rev. John Bennett, Rev. Robert Hall, a mainstay of the 'Lit and Phil' who had been excluded from the Collegiate Church because his sermons were considered too 'popular', and the whole of the relatively indolent collegiate clergy as well. Laymen from the manufacturing and commercial upper crust included those who supported Pitt in his handling of the regency crisis and those who did not.[19] The Birmingham committee was led by the Revs Riland and Curtis, both active supporters of the anti-slavery cause and warm allies of the Wesleyans,

[18] For the two quotations see John A. Langford *A Century of Birmingham Life from 1741–1841* vol. 1 (Birmingham, 1868) 409–10 and *Manchester Mercury* (10 August, 1784); the very similar origins of Sunday schools in these cities may be seen for Liverpool in Sir James A. Picton *Memorials of Liverpool* vol. 1 (1873) 252; for Manchester in Wadsworth 'Early Manchester . . .'; for Birmingham see Langford, pp. 409–21; for Stoke, John Ward *The Borough of Stoke-on-Trent in the Commencement of the Reign of her Most Gracious Majesty . . .* (1843) lviii-lix; for Norwich and Shrewsbury, Lancaster Adkin *Proceedings for Sunday Schools and a Plan of that in St. Stephens, Norwich* (Norwich, 1785); for Colchester in the report in *The World* (June 1787); for Leeds in *Gentleman's Magazine* vol. 54, no. 5 (1789) 377 and Langford, pp. 411–12; for Stockport in W. I. Wild *The History of the Nottingham Union Stockport Sunday School* (1891—privately printed in London); for Nottingham in Carter, pp. 22–3 and R. C. Swift 'Methodist Sunday Schools in Nottingham,' *Proceedings of the Wesley Historical Society* vol. 23 (1961–2) 17–20, 36–40

[19] List of names from 'The Present State of the Sunday Schools in Manchester, April, 1, 1786' pasted in vol. 1 of *Minutes of the Manchester Sunday School for all denominations* Chetham's Library, MS. A 6-3; biographical information from Lewis's *Directory of the Towns of Manchester and Salford* for 1788 with MS. directory of 1,000 names and notes on *the directory* by Fred Leary, Manchester Central Reference Library 1942. 738.L4

but it included most of the town clergy as well.[20] The Revs George Wakefield and George Walker, Dissenting clergymen in trouble with the crown for the support of the French Revolution, started Nottingham Sunday schools, but their fellow workers included the rector of the parish, the master of the 'blue coat school' (who was later involved in fraudulent practices during the 1802 parliamentary election), the head of the local medical establishment, several silk manufacturers and merchants, and a naval officer who dabbled in reform.[21] In conclusion, a certain proportion, impossible to quantify, of early Sunday schools were the product of individual or group efforts by middle-class men and women working within the confines of their community.

The aristocracy was relatively immune to the educational and, indeed, most other philanthropic currents of the Evangelical Revival. According to Raikes, the 'ladies of fashion at Windsor' spent their Sunday afternoons teaching poor children to read, and Madam D'Arblay viewed the Gloucester printer 'almost with reverence'.[22] Here and there others at the very highest levels of society supported Sunday schools. The ennobled Evangelicals, Lords Barham and Teignmouth, were active in the Sunday School Society as in most other London charities; the Countess of Rothes established a school near Acton; Earl Spencer may have been responsible for one in Brington, Northants, and his mother, the dowager Lady Spencer, patronized a school at Bath. The very first Sunday school in Herefordshire was almost certainly the result of efforts by the Earl of Clarendon.[23] But beyond these few examples the aristocracy was little involved. The same, however, cannot be said of the working classes.

Historians, by concentrating their efforts on a few large schools, two London-based Sunday school societies, and a handful of

[20] Langford, *A Century* ... and W. C. Sheldon *Early Methodism in Birmingham* (Birmingham, 1903)

[21] See John F. Sutton *The Date Book of Remarkable and Memorial Events Connected with Nottingham and its Neighbourhood 1750–1850* (1852) 158 for names of founders. See Robert Mellors *Men of Nottingham and Nottinghamshire* (Nottingham, 1924), and Malcolm I. Thomis *Politics and Society in Nottingham 1785–1835* (Oxford, 1969) 131–2

[22] Raikes/Rev. Bowen Thickens, 27 June, 1788 in Harris *Robert Raikes* ... p. 128 and Kendall *Robert Raikes* ... p. 14; the Queen, too, wished she could spend her Sundays educating the poor to read. See *Gentleman's Magazine* vol. 58, pt. 2, no. 1 (1788) 654

[23] For Barham and Teignmouth see below, p. 34; for Countess of Rothes see *Gentleman's Magazine* vol. 58, pt. 1, no. 2 (1788) 109; for Spencer see Eastman *Robert Raikes* ... p. 26; for the Dowager Lady Spenser see *Diary and Letters of Fanny Burney* vol. 5 (1842) 250–53; for Clarendon see J. S. Hurt *Bringing Literacy to Rural England* (Chichester, 1972) 3

prominent Evangelicals, have obscured the part played by men
and women of the 'lower orders' in improving the lot of their
children. Local histories, however, turn up dozens of such cases
which are listed in Table 22, Appendix 1. There is no way of
knowing what proportion of the total number of schools was
founded by people such as these. But the fact that local sources
reveal so large a number of hitherto forgotten names suggests that
the Sunday school from its earliest days was to a large extent a
product of the working-class community. Education and improvement were not the monopoly of latter day puritans from the middling
orders of society.[24]

The schools listed in Table 22 (Appendix 1) were far less grand
in their origins than those discussed earlier. There was, for example,
no committee of town notables backing this notice, despite its
striking similarity to orthographically more orthodox Evangelical
rhetoric:

> This is to GIVE Notes to the Publick that Thomas Noble,
> Blacksmith, intends to open a Sunday Schoole on Sunday 4th April
> 1787, next, to any person mindfull to have their children tought
> in the Gospel of Christ Jesus and fear of God; and is in hopes
> that it will put a stop to so much vice that is committed every
> Sabbath Day; so all persons that is desireus of sending their
> children may apply to Thomas Noble in the meantime.[25]

Noble then proceeded to solicit funds, forms, teachers and other
necessities from his neighbors near Keighley and commenced the
school. In Stalybridge a laborer named Thomas Broadbent,
himself unable to write, began to teach his children to read on
Sundays because he could not afford to send them to weekday
school. His children brought others round, and the services of a
neighbor were required to teach the enlarged gathering; within
weeks the narrator of this account joined the school. Up to this
point the whole enterprise had been altogether makeshift. There
were no forms, tables, slates, etc., and children simply sat on the
cottage floor around their teachers. But the sheer numbers of
students that sought admission to the classes grew out of hand, and
the three founders began to call on neighbors who in turn solicited
funds to pay the rent for a larger room above a blacksmith's shop,
buy equipment, and generally establish the school more firmly.[26]
It was very much the same story in Blackburn, where working men

[24] As M. G. Jones *Charity Schools* ... has argued pp. 145ff
[25] Thomas Whitehead *History of the Dales Congregational Churches* (Keighley,
1930) 166
[26] *SS Teachers' Magazine* new ser., vol. 16 (1845) 365–7

begged the lumber from which to build desks and chairs and very soon found themselves with a school of over 400 children.[27] Furthermore, there are many cases in which the occupations or even the names of Sunday school founders have been lost but which nevertheless fall into the same pattern. Mr Richard Blinderfield and his wife, for example, kept a school in their cottage at Maesbury Marsh, Salop., for over twenty years. There were four sets of Sunday schools held in cottages of local Baptists near Salisbury from 1802 until 1824 when a collection was taken to rent a centrally located room. The missionaries from the Baptist Midland Association who walked out to nearby villages to set up Sunday schools were also probably not in the Hannah More mould.[28] The point is that, beginning in the 1780s, there was a remarkable growth of lay religious and educational philanthropy which was by no means limited to the upper strata of society.

It might have been expected that the parish clergy would have played a leading role in the movement to establish Sunday schools. The fifty-ninth canon enjoined that

> Every parson, vicar or curate upon every Sunday and holy day, before evening prayer, shall for half an hour or more examine and instruct the youth and ignorant persons of his parish.

Sunday schools would seem to be a logical extension of this activity. Furthermore, the seventy-seventh canon gave the clergy a monopoly over education in their parish, a right reinforced by 23 Eliz. c.i, 1 Jac. I.c.4, s.9, and 13 & 14 Car. II.c.4. In fact, however, after a period of initial enthusiasm on the part of certain members of the hierarchy, official support for Sunday schools subsided almost into nonexistence. Again, it is impossible to estimate how large a proportion of the Anglican Sunday schools owed their origins to the local clergyman, but efforts in the 1820s and later to involve the priest in his parish's schools suggest that, even in the Church, Sunday schools were essentially lay institutions. They were still more securely in the hands of the laity among Non-conformists, but occasionally Dissenting ministers did take the initiative in founding schools.

Evangelical churchmen called the town-wide meetings in Manchester, Birmingham and Norwich which resulted in lay

[27] John Ward *The Rise and Progress of Wesleyan Methodism in Blackburn* (Blackburn, 1871) 34

[28] Ernest Elliot *A History of Congregationalism in Shropshire* (Oswestry, 1898) 48; J. E. Watson 'The Educational Activities of the Baptists in England during the xviiith and xixth century with particular reference to the North West,' (unpublished MA thesis, University of Liverpool 1947) 236; J. Rippon *Baptist Annual Register* vol. 3 (1798) 120. These cases are not listed in Table 22, Appendix I

managed interdenominational schools. Many early London schools were begun by parish priests, and the reports of the Sunday School Society and other organizations contain accounts of local schools written by country clergymen.[29] The Rev. Mr Moore, Rector of Cuxton and Vicar of Boughton Blaen, Kent, for example, heard about the Sunday school founded by the Rev. George Hearne in Canterbury. He wrote to him for advice on how to start a school and upon being furnished with plans set out to collect subscriptions to visit every house in the parish to ask parents to send their children to hire two teachers, and to print up publicity broadsheets.[30] Moore, like others, even went to the trouble of printing up elaborate rule sheets for their tiny parish schools. Furthermore, until about 1800 when Sunday schools became suspect as strongholds of Jacobinism, the hierarchy actively supported the parish clergy in their philanthropic enterprise.

Bishops with Evangelical sympathies were, as might have been expected, particularly active. Beilby Porteus, after waiting a year or two for the new institution to prove itself, then preached a sermon on its behalf in Chester and supported Sunday schools throughout the diocese. Shute-Barrington was sufficiently enthusiastic to encourage his chaplain, Thomas Burgess, future bishop of St Davids, to write a set of textbooks for Sunday schools, and, once these were published, to promote their commercial success. In 1785 and again in his charge of 1797 he recommended the schools to his clergy. Even bishops who were not on the fringe of the Evangelical Revival propagated Sunday schools. Richard Watson, a pluralist of sixteen livings and the Bishop of Llandaff, gave them his blessings in his charge of 1788; Pretyman-Tomline did likewise in 1800. George Horne, President of Magdalen, Vice Chancellor of Oxford, and Bishop of Norwich 1790–2, gave one of the earliest and most publicized Sunday school sermons in 1785. The Archbishop of York, William Markham, is said to have been sympathetic; at least he contributed £20 to the York Sunday school.[32]

[29] See appendices of *Plan of a Society Established in London for the Support and Encouragement of Sunday Schools* 1787, 1788, 1789, 1797, 1812; Diana McClatchey *Oxfordshire Clergy 1777–1869* (Oxford, 1960) 146–7; see also S. Trimmer *Oeconomy . . .* appendix 129

[30] Account reprinted in S. Mayer *Who was the founder . . .* 60–62

[31] See, for example, the 'Rules of the Enford Sunday School' in *Orthodox Churchmans Magazine* vol. 5 (1803) 25–7

[32] The role of the hierarchy generally is discussed in William Turner *Sunday Schools Recommended . . . with an appendix concerning the formation and expense of these schools* (Newcastle, 1786) 56–7; for Porteus see Robert Hodgson *Life of the Rt. Rev. Beilby Porteus* (1811) 92 and also his *Letter to the Diocese of Chester Church of Concerning Sunday Schools* (1786) and *A Sermon Preached in the Cathedral Church of Chester, February 4, 1787, for the benefit of the Charity Schools in that City and with*

In the late eighteenth century Churchmen further down in the hierarchy also spoke up for Sunday schools. In a widely quoted series of sermons Richard Kaye, Dean of Lincoln and Archdeacon of Nottingham, recommended that his clergy start schools in their parishes. Andrew Burnaby, Archdeacon of Leicester, delivered at least two charges on a similar theme. William Paley, the theologian and protégé of the Bishop of Carlisle, wrote a textbook for the use of Sunday schools and encouraged their spread in at least one sermon.[33] But apart from these few men, there was little support for the new charity among those high in the Church, and after 1800 only the occasional hostile comment reached the public. Right wing attacks on Sunday schools as seditious institutions fomenting disorder among the lower ranks of society effectively silenced proponents of the schools, and it was not until the 1840s that they again came into official favor.[34]

Of course Dissenting ministers on occasion also started and supported Sunday schools during the late eighteenth and early nineteenth centuries. Rev. John Hawkes, for example, found the Dukinfield village chapel so deserted that instead of preaching to empty pews, he set about to establishing a school for the children who were 'run wild about the lanes and fields'. When he left in 1813 the school and revivified chapel were flourishing. Other cases could be cited: John Leppington, the Methodist circuit preacher, established a school in Luton in 1803; Rev. Alexander Redford

---

a view of recommending the establishment of a General Sunday school there (Chester, 1787); for Shute-Barrington see John S. Hatford *The Life of Thomas Burgess DD.* (1840) 104–6 and also Barrington's *Letter to the clergy of the diocese of Sarum* (1797) 22. He is quoted in Harris *Robert Raikes* ... p. 99 as having said in 1785 'I have established them [Sunday schools] in every parish where my property lies and warmly recommend them in my diocese'; for Watson see his *Charge* (1788); for Pretyman-Tomline see his *Charge* (1800) 21; for Horne see his *Sunday Schools Recommended* ... (Oxford, 1786) and also *Universal Magazine* vol. 79 (September 1786) 149 for a report of this sermon; for Markham see J. Howard *Historical Sketch of the Origin and Work of the York Incorporated (Church of England) Sunday School Committee established 1786* (York, 1887) 12–13

[33] For Kaye see excerpt from *Charge* ... (1786) in *Plan* ... 1787, or full text printed in London (1787) and also his *Charge* (1790); for Burnaby see *Two Charges delivered to the clergy of the Archdeaconry of Leicester in the years 1786 and 1787* (1787); for Paley see 'A Life of William Paley by Alexander Chalmer in the *Works of W. P.* vol. 1 (1821) xxv–xxxvi

[34] The Establishment was later sensitive to criticism of its early indifference to Sunday schools. In the first issue of the *Sunday School Teacher's Manual* vol. 1 (1843) a letter from the Rev. William Romaine is cited to show that the Sunday school system was indeed the work of Churchmen. See also the *Christian Remembrancer* vol. 1 (1819) 52–3, which argues rather lamely that while not directly a product of the Church controlled SPCK Sunday schools very soon came under Anglican influence.

began a school in Windsor during the same year, aided by his son and daughter. The Baptist George Osborn started one in Worcester in 1797.[35]

But, without writing off the part played by clergymen and ministers in the early history of Sunday schools, it is fair to conclude that laymen took the dominant role.

ii. THE NATIONAL SOCIETIES

National, London-based organizations were even less important in the development of Sunday schools than they had been in the charity school movement a century earlier.[36] The Sunday school was fundamentally a local, even neighbourhood, organization in which a distant authority could only play a minimal part. Nevertheless, there were two major and several minor national bodies which in different ways sought to coordinate and promote Sunday school work. (Table 2).

Table 2 : National Sunday School Organizations

Name	Date	Denomination
Sunday School Society	1785	Interdenominational
Sunday School Union	1803	Interdenominational but predominantly Dissenting
Sunday School Association	1833	Interdenominational but predominantly Unitarian
Methodist Sunday School Union	1837	Wesleyan
Sunday School Institute	1843	Church of England
Society of Friends First Day School Association	1847	Quaker

a.   The Society for the Support and Encouragement of Sunday Schools

The Society for the Support and Encouragement of Sunday Schools or, as it was usually called, the Sunday School Society, was formed in London on 21 September (or 7 September according to another account) 1785, primarily through the efforts of a Baptist merchant, William Fox. Its purposes, according to a circular prepared by Fox prior to the first general meeting, were

[35] Ann Parkinson *Beneficial Effects of a Sunday School at Duckenfield* (Hackney, 1816); Joseph Hawkes *The Rise and Progress of Wesleyan Sunday Schools* (Luton, 1885) 6; A. Elliot *Shropshire Congregationalism* ... p. 10; A. McLellan 'Congregationalism ... ,' p. 65

[36] Joan Simon 'Was there a Charity School Movement?' in Brian Simon, ed. *Education in Leicestershire* (Leicester 1968) 55–103

To prevent vice—to encourage industry and virtue—to dispel
the darkness of ignorance—to diffuse the light of knowledge—
to bring men cheerfully to submit to their stations—to obey the
laws of God and their country—to make that part of the community, the country poor, happy—to lead them in the pleasant
paths of religion here, and to endeavour to prepare them for a
glorious eternity.

The Society was expressly ecumenical; it had a governing body
composed of twelve lay Churchmen and twelve Dissenters 'united
to prevent the corruption of morals and advance the peace and
felicity of the country'. It was one of the earliest of several late
eighteenth-century organizations which sought to find a common
ground between the various religious communities of England, and,
indeed, for some of its members the Sunday School Society heralded
a new era of Christian unity.[37]

The Society shared directors with a number of interdenominational philanthropic agencies—the London Missionary Society,
the Anti-Slavery Society, the Society for the Suppression of Vice,
the Philanthropic Society, etc.[38] It was centralized in London and
had no local branches. Like the organizations just mentioned it
drew its directors and membership from the capital's Evangelical
haute bourgeoisie. Men like the eminent West India merchant
Benjamin Boddington and his son; Thomas Raikes, brother of
Robert and a director of the Bank of England; the bankers Robert
Barclay and Thomas Coutts; four members of the Thornton family
whose name appeared on almost every philanthropic subscription
list; William Wilberforce; and the Evangelical MP, William Morton
Pitt, a cousin of the prime minister, all played an active part in its
affairs. The Marquis of Salisbury's 100 guinea contribution, along
with his social position, earned him the honor of being the Society's
first president. Two MPs, James Martin and Brooke Watson, were
among the original vice-presidents. The social complexion of the
Society in 1812, when it issued its last full report, is evident from
its list of officers. Lord Barham was president, and of thirteen vice-
presidents, six—Sir Thomas Baring, the banker, John Maitland,
Sir Thomas Plummer, Samuel Thornton, Charles Grant and
William Wilberforce—were MPs.[39]

[37] See J. Ivemy *Memoir of William Fox, Esq.* (1831) 38 and 30 and *Plan* ... 1787
p. 6; see also p. 65 below

[38] List of subscribers in *Plan* ... 1787 ibid.; information of membership in other
societies from Brown *Fathers* ... and from a card file prepared by Dr Rusty Martin
in connection with his research which he was so kind as to let me use

[39] Biographical information from Brown *Fathers* ..., *Gentleman's Magazine*, the
DNB and Lewis Namier and John Brooke *The History of Parliament: The House of
Commons, 1754–1790* (1964)

The Sunday School Society did not, in fact, found or manage schools but confined itself to providing information to the general public and supplying free textbooks and occasionally cash to locally operated schools. In the first of these functions it helped make Sunday schools seem safe and respectable to those who doubted the wisdom of educating the lower orders. Within six months of its founding, the Society published William Morton Pitt's widely quoted *Plan for the Extension and Regulation of Sunday Schools*, a 'how-to-do-it' manual which served as a seal of approval from a socially prominent source. Endorsements of Sunday schools by highly placed clerics like those already cited and by prominent laymen like William Cowper or Adam Smith were solicited and circulated by the Society.[10]

Once the schools became an accepted part of the educational landscape the provision of books and funds became a more important activity. Within ten years of its founding the Society had given away 94,000 spelling books, 24,000 testaments, and over 5,000 Bibles to 1,002 schools with 65,000 students. By 1804 each of these figures had doubled, and it was reported that at least £4,100 in cash grants had been distributed since 1785.

Although the Sunday School Society issued its last full report in 1812, it appears to have limped along until at least mid-century.[11] The Methodist conference acknowledged its existence in 1827. In 1833 the *Baptist Magazine* drew readers' attention to the by now venerable body and reminded them that it was indeed distinct from the Sunday School Union. Finally, by 1850 the Sunday School Society's annual meeting was chaired by the secretary of the Sunday School Union from which it had become indistinguishable. At that meeting its record of 1,600,000 texts, 220,000 testaments, and 52,000 Bibles over sixty-five years of existence was made public. Nevertheless, by mid-century it was only the charitable branch of another organization's publishing business; its real importance had come to an end by 1812.[12]

The Sunday School Society was financed during its first fifteen years through subscriptions, charity sermons, and interest on

[40] For example, *The Good Effects of Sunday Schools ... conducted by good masters or mistresses, morally and politically considered, with a plan for their establishment* (Wrexham, 1789) contains long sections lifted from Pitt; Cowper's recommendation comes in a letter to the Rev. John Newton, 24 September, 1785, in *Letters of William Cowper*, ed. J. G. Frazer (1912) 367; Adam Smith's letter to the Sunday School Society is quoted in Timpson *Mirror ...* p. 277

[41] For 1795 see the *Evangelical Magazine* vol. 3, 374; for 1804 see the *Christian Observer* vol. 3 (February 1804) 110

[42] 'Miscellaneous Resolutions,' *Minutes of the Methodist Conference* (1828) 87; *Baptist Magazine* new ser., vol. 8 (1833) 376; for 1850 see *The Union Magazine for Sunday School Teachers*, vol. 7 (1850) 168

capital. In late 1785 it collected 1,636 guineas from 390 subscribers, 89 of whom contributed ten pounds or more; some of this was invested in 4 per cent bonds, and the remainder was used for current operating expenses. Sermons by such popular Evangelical preachers as the Revs Kaye, Romaine, Newton and Swaine raised over £400 during 1787 and 1788; this paid for between 20 per cent and 25 per cent of the operating expenses. A few legacies and donations completed the Society's annual income. By 1807 sermons were no longer profitable. Indeed, only 20 per cent of the Society's income of £940 came from any form of annual giving in 1812; only 16 per cent of £877 in 1829. Between 1834 and 1839 the Society spent £4,131 3s. of which only £1,315 came from current sources; the deficit was made up by selling property. By 1812 it was already dependent on the occasional legacy and interest on accumulated capital and was no longer a living charity. As for its expenditures, a sizable 15–20 per cent of the £6,850 budget between 1785 and 1795 was spent on offices and administration, 70–80 per cent on books, and up to 20 per cent on cash grants.[43]

Even in its role as a Sunday school charity, the Society's importance should not be overestimated. It gave assistance mostly to small country schools. While ten schools in Cullompton in Devon received aid, no schools in Sheffield, York, or Bradford, Manchester, Oldham, Bolton or Stockport were given any kind of grant, and only one each in Leeds or Huddersfield received help. At best, the Sunday School Society could have provided around 10 per cent of the total operating expenses of England's schools between 1785 and 1800, excluding capital expenditures.[44]

b. The Sunday School Union[45]

The Sunday School Union was socially far removed from the Society. It was formed by a group of young Sunday school activists,

[43] Plan ... 1787 for initial collection and first budget; names of those giving sermons in Plans ... 1787, 1788, 1789 ... 1797 ... 1812; for 1829 see Evangelical Magazine vol. 29 (new ser. 7) 255; for 1834–39 see SS Teachers' Magazine new ser. vol. 10 (1839) 380; budget to 1795 in Plan ... 1797

[44] Lists of schools aided are in each Plan. For estimates of Sunday school costs see Ch. 3, 94–9

[45] The two main sources for the history of the Union and its officers are W. H. Watson The History of the Sunday School Union (1853) and The First Fifty Years of the Sunday School Union (Southport, 1873). The minute books of the Sunday School Union Committee, under varying titles, are extant for the period 18 July, 1810 to 23 February, 1814 and from 1822 to the present. Until about 1850 this Committee managed all the affairs of the Union. Beginning in 1852 the publishing activities of the Union were taken over by a paid manager and supervised by a special sub-committee; various philanthropic and missionary activities also came under

aged eighteen to twenty-five, who met in Rowland Hill's Surrey
Chapel, and was to be a teachers' organization founded 'to stimulate
and encourage one another, to communicate and improve methods
of instruction, and to promote the opening of new schools'.[16]
W. B. Gurney, court reporter for the trial of Queen Caroline and
son of the inventor of a shorthand method, along with William
Marriott, Jr, a second generation Evangelical philanthropist, were
the most prominent of the group. Their first endeavor was to
publish a short pamphlet by Marriott on how to start a Sunday
school; next, in 1805, they began publication of the *Youth's Magazine*,
one of the first and certainly the longest lived of scores of magazines
for the young that were produced during the nineteenth century.
Except for these activities, the Union did very little other than
hold monthly meetings for London-based teachers to discuss their
work and to pray together for success. Their limited financial
needs were met primarily through annual sermons, the best known
of which was Bunting's 1805 pronouncement on 'The Great
Work'.

In 1812 the Union went public; its first open meeting was held
in the New London Tavern on 13 May. Under the new constitution
the Sunday School Union was to consist of all the teachers who
belonged to four auxiliary unions, one for each quarter of London
within five miles of the GPO. The governing body of thirty-four
men was drawn from these auxiliaries, while the day-to-day
operation of the organization—running the publishing business,
vetting books, acting as a pressure group for Sunday school
interests—was carried out by a small sub-committee of volunteers
who met at the Paternoster Street depot. Auxiliary local Sunday
School Unions—those of Nottingham and Hampshire were the
first—were entirely independent of the London organization.
Although the Union had distinguished presidents (first the wealthy
Methodist publisher and MP for Coventry, John Butterworth, and
then Lord Roden), held massive annual meetings at Exeter Hall, the
Evangelical Mecca, and provided information on Sunday schools
to several parliamentary committees, it remained both in London

---

the care of newly created sub-committees. As a result of these trends the minutes
of the parent Committee become increasingly less informative during the second
half of the nineteenth century; the minutes of the various sub-committees did
not survive the blitz. Newspaper clippings of annual meetings are pasted in the
'Minutes of the Committee'; a reasonably complete set of annual reports after
1838 are also available, along with the above material, at the National Christian
Education Council headquarters, Redhill, Surrey. A report from 1824 is available
in the British Museum

[46] Watson *History* ... (1853) 12

and in the provinces an organization of teachers who had banded together to secure books, discuss problems, and enjoy each other's company.

Religiously the Sunday School Union was non-denominational. Those forming the Bedfordshire and Huntingdon branch exulted that 'another hallowed spot had been discovered on which they might stand, and embrace each other with Christian affection, without even the slightest compromise of principle or dereliction of their private and relative duties.'[47] A speaker at the first meeting noted 'the growing disposition among Christians at various names and denominations to unite in great and glorious undertakings. I have happily experienced some of the most delightful moments of my life in the enjoyment of that brotherly communication with fellow Christians of other denominations.'[48] Until pressure from local unions in 1843 compelled the central committee to stop publishing the Church of England catechism, it sold catechisms from all parts of the religious spectrum and after it was forced to withdraw the Church's, it ceased selling any at all. But interdenominational harmony was only skin deep.[49]

Table 3:[50] *Schools, teachers, and students affiliated with the Sunday School Union,* 1819–35

Year	No. of Schools	No. of Teachers	No. of Students
1819	2,019	31,442	237,584
1820	2,568	32,337	274,845
1821	2,986	34,309	337,300
1822	3,063	48,254	442,456
1823	3,101	56,747	536,985
1824	4,367	59,036	566,676
1825	4,472	59,447	595,235
1826	4,713	55,485	608,018
1827	5,022	68,822	660,781
1828	5,280	77,897	655,391
1829	5,052	72,498	698,454
1830	5,735	79,753	739,340
1831	5,775	94,860	778,612
1832	6,272	97,670	838,161
1833	6,597	104,642	872,150
1834	6,826	110,702	926,412
1835	7,842	110,841	909,618

[47] *London Christian Instructor* vol. 1 (1818) 442; and Watson *History* ... (1853) 24.
[48] Watson *History* ... (1853) 23
[49] The case against keeping the Church catechism became particularly strong after the successful opposition to Graham's bill in 1843; see *Is the Union Right?* by 'One of Yourselves' (1843). As the minute books show, the committee resisted such sectarian arguments as vigorously as possible
[50] *SS Teachers' Magazine* new ser. vol. 11 (1840) col. 191–194

Church Sunday schools usually refused to join local unions, claiming that their nominal allegiance to the National School system precluded membership. Wesleyan Methodists were often reluctant to belong and after 1837 had an alternative organization which required their allegiance. Furthermore, the daily operations of the Union really involved very little of a religious nature. The Union was primarily a publishing house and bookseller, which, except when issues like that of the catechism arose, steered clear of sensitive areas. While they were theoretically ecumenical, most Unions contained only Dissenters and, with only rare exceptions, were more concerned with the operation of the schools than with theological niceties.

Beginning in 1819 annual reports make it possible to trace the growth of the Union and its branches. (Table 3).

Since country branches often conflated their membership figures and those of nonaffiliated schools, Union membership statistics are less than reliable. But as an upper limit, 39 per cent of the schools and 52 per cent of students in 1819 and 44 per cent of schools with 59 per cent of students in 1833 belonged to the Sunday School Union.

The work of the London branch and, to a lesser extent, of the provincial Unions fell into three areas. The most important of these was the publishing and distribution of textbooks, teaching aids, and magazines for students and teachers. The *Union Spelling Book* (in four parts) sold over five million copies between 1811 and 1850; a new graded religious reader sold as many between its introduction in 1830 and mid-century. The Paternoster Street depot stocked three hundred book titles in 1830 and over eight hundred in 1850, all of which had been carefully culled from titles submitted by publishers and authors.[51] These books and the Union's own publications, along with writing supplies, arithmetic tables, alphabet boxes, catechisms, and the like, were distributed by the London organization to local depots, which in turn sold them at cost to individual Sunday schools.

Both in the provinces and in London the Union provided a number of social and professional services for Sunday school teachers. The London teachers' library containing three thousand volumes was copied on a smaller scale in the provinces. Monthly tea meetings and great annual breakfasts or dinners that were attended by thousands provided a social life centered on Sunday school work. Area Unions organized Whitsun Walks, race week outings, celebrations of royal anniversaries, and all of the other social and recreational activities associated with the Sunday school.[52] The Union hired

[51] For publishing activities of the Union see below
[52] See pp. 175–9 and Ch. 6, below

a missionary in 1828 to travel up and down England and help local organizations expand or begin anew.[53] In London and the provinces it organized teachers' conferences to discuss new methods of teaching, new texts or equipment, discipline, and other matters having to do with the day-to-day operation of Sunday schools.

Finally, the Union nationally and locally acted as a pressure group for Evangelical and more often specifically Dissenting causes. It opposed Brougham's education bill of 1819 as inimical to Sunday school interests; it organized a petition drive against Graham's factory bill on the grounds that it gave the Church an unfair advantage in the provision of weekday education. The legions who supported the movement to close the GPO on Sundays, enforce Lord's day observance, keep the Notting Hill racecourse closed on the sabbath, and similar causes were often mobilized through the Sunday School Union network.

From 1811 the Union was financed almost entirely through the sales of books, magazines and materials. Its operations were in most respects exactly like those of any publisher or bookseller. The few hundred pounds that came in each year through donations or legacies, along with a share of publishing profits, went into a benevolent fund from which grants were made to Sunday schools in poor areas or overseas. In all, £29,000 was spent in this way, about half of it in England.[54] The miserable failure of the Union's attempts to raise funds nationally, in 1831 for the Sunday School Jubilee and in honor of its own fiftieth birthday in 1853, demonstrated the futility of such an exercise. Although hostile articles in the *Evangelical Magazine* may have had an adverse effect on the earlier solicitation, the real cause of failure was that each local Sunday school was far too deeply rooted in its community to contribute generously to a national fund.[55]

c. Other Sunday School Organizations

Other Sunday school organizations grew up from time to time during the late eighteenth and early nineteenth centuries, but they were of little importance, either for the development or the operation of local schools. Some, like the Midlands General Baptist

[53] The appointment of Mr Joseph Reed Wilson as full-time missionary and requests for contributions to finance his work were made public through the denominational press. See, for example, *Congregational Magazine* (March 1828) 194 and *Baptist Magazine* (March 1828) 222

[54] Watson *History* ... (1853) 189

[55] See *Evangelical Magazine* (1831) pp. 353–4, 394–7; *Wesleyan Methodist Magazine* 3rd ser., vol. 10, 636–7; and for 1853 see William Groser *A Hundred Years' Work for Children* (1903) 55

Sunday School Association or the Liverpool Methodist Sunday School Committee, were simply teachers' discussion groups.[56] Others, like the Wesleyan dominated Society for the Encouragement and Support of Sunday Schools in London or the Southwark Sunday School Society founded under the auspices of Rowland Hill, were smaller versions of the Sunday School Society and had the additional task of actually operating a half dozen neighborhood schools for a time.[57] Finally, a few national organizations tried to take over the functions of the Union within the confines of a single church or sect. The Unitarian dominated Sunday School Association broke away from the Union for 'conscientious theological reasons' but performed precisely the same functions as the old body, i.e., it 'suppl[ied] suitable books at low cost and establish[ed] and boost[ed] Sunday schools'.[58] By 1857, after twenty-four years of operation it had only 148 affiliated schools. The Wesleyan Sunday School Union was a similar such breakaway body, although many chapels apparently failed to join the new association or to buy their supplies from its book room.[59]

The case for the Anglican Sunday School Institute is rather different. For most of the century Church Sunday schools were at least nominally associated with the National School network. In fact, of the 10,965 Church schools queried in 1846, 6,470 were day *and* Sunday schools while 4,495 were Sunday schools only; of 996,760 students in 1837, 514,450 (52 per cent) were in day and Sunday schools and 438,280 (44 per cent) in Sunday school only. But a need was felt to have a separate organization, a separate magazine, teacher-training facilities, libraries and book depots for the Sunday school branch. The Church of England Sunday School Institute was supposed to fill this need. Its growth, however, was slow. In London its operations were similar to those of the Union but with two to three per cent of the annual turnover. Only in 1848 did it manage to get out its magazine, and by 1850 most Anglican schools were still buying their supplies through the National Schools or

[56] Adam Taylor *The History of the English General Baptists* vol. 2 (1818) 465–6; for Liverpool see *Philanthropic Magazine* no. 1 (1827) 35–7

[57] *Address of the Southwark Sunday School Society Instituted 1799* (1803); *Methodist Magazine* vol. 25 (1802) 430–5 and *Rules of the Society for the Encouragement and Support of Sunday Schools in London* (1802)

[58] Arnold Broadbent *The First 100 Years of the Sunday School Association 1833–1933* (1933)

[59] Wesleyan Sunday schools were under the direction of the Education Committee founded 1837. See W. J. Townsend et. al. *A New History of Methodism* vol. 1 (1909) 416–17. Parliamentary reports make clear that Wesleyan schools continued to use Union texts while the Sunday school periodical press reports Wesleyan participation in a variety of local Union activities well after the conference's 1837 declaration on Sunday schools

the SPCK. The Institute did manage to get a London library and teacher-training center into operation, run an essay contest for working men on the value of Sunday schools, and publish a few tracts before mid-century. But in the history of Sunday schools during this period its importance was slight.[60]

While the Sunday School Society was active in popularizing the idea of the Sunday school in the late eighteenth century and the Union was vital in providing textbooks, materials and magazines for their use, neither of these two organizations or the smaller Sunday school associations lay at the heart of the enterprise. Sunday schools were essentially individual local bodies that were proud of their traditions and of being financially and organizationally independent. They grew up through local efforts at all levels of society and were connected with national organizations only at the most superficial level.

iii. THE GROWTH OF SUNDAY SCHOOLS: ENROLMENTS, GEOGRAPHY, DENOMINATION

The explosive growth of Sunday schools in the late eighteenth century surprised even their most sanguine supporters. The Sunday school in Manchester opened with eighteen hundred students in 1784 and trebled that number by 1788; Birmingham Sunday schools grew to an enrolment of fourteen hundred within a few months and to over two thousand within a year. Leeds had a similar experience.[61] As John Wesley put it, 'I find these schools springing up wherever I go.'[62] There are no statistics for Sunday school enrolments in England as a whole until 1818, and even for that date the evidence is unreliable. The Rev. Dr Kaye's estimate of 200,000 children in 1785 and Raikes's of 250,000 in 1787 are purely speculative and wildly exaggerated.[63] There are, however, data on the number of

[60] 'General Inquiry made by the National School Society 1846–47,' summarized in *Special Reports on Educational Subjects* 1894 [c. 8943] xxiv. The Sunday School Institute's first report was published in 1845 when the organization had a budget of less than £200; the *Church of England Sunday School Quarterly Magazine* began publication in 1848 and vol. 1 of the *Church of England Sunday School Teachers' Magazine* was published in 1851; the *SS Teachers' Magazine* (1843) col. 887–90 claims there was a magazine of the same title published by the Institute in 1843, but it could not be located in the *Union Catalogue of Periodicals*, the Bodleian, or the British Museum catalogues.

[61] For Manchester see Wadsworth 'Early Manchester ...', pp. 325–6; for Birmingham and Leeds see Langford *A Century of ...* pp. 407–20

[62] Wesley's *Journals*, entry of 18 July, 1784, vol. 7, 3

[63] Kaye *Charge*; Raikes in *Gentleman's Magazine* vol. 57, pt. 2, no. 4, p. 948; there were even higher estimates of early Sunday school growth. See George C. T. Bartley *The Schools for the People ...* (1871) 370

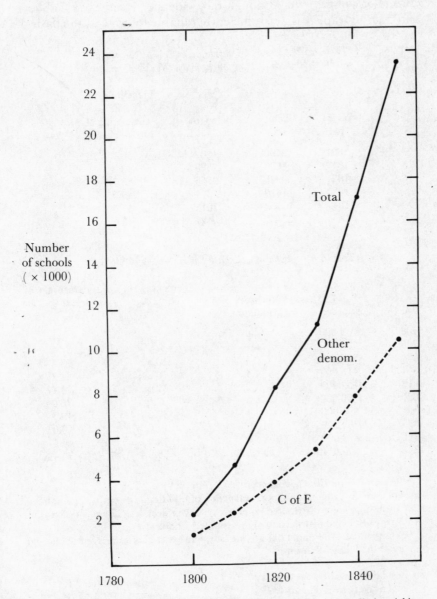

Graph 1: Growth of numbers of Sunday schools 1780–1850 distinguishing Anglican from other schools[64]

[64]Based on the data in Table 4

Sunday schools built or founded each decade beginning in 1801 which, when supplemented by other material, yield a rough chronology of growth. Although the evidence presented in Tables 4 and 5 and Graph 1 is not sufficiently reliable to serve as the basis of

Table 4:[65] *Numbers of Sunday schools built or founded* 1780–1850 *distinguishing Anglican and Non-Anglican*

Years to:	Total no.	No. Belonging to C. of E.	Percentage of Total no. Belonging to C. of E.
1801	2290	1282	56.4
1811	4687	2288	48.8
1821	8236	3766	45.7
1831	11910	5371	45.0
1841	17168	7815	45.0
1851	23135	10427	45.0

Table 5:[66] *Enrolment in English Sunday schools* 1788–1850

Year	Number	Percentage of Population	Percentage of Those Age 5–15	Percentage of Working Class Age 5–15
1788	59,980	—	—	—
1795	94,100	—	—	—
1801	206,100	2.5	10.3	13.8
1811	415,000	4.4	18.2	24.2
1818	452,325	4.2	17.6	23.4
1821	730,000	6.5	27.0	36.0
1831	1,096,000	8.4	37.2	49.6
1833	1,363,170	10.2	45.0	60.0
1841	1,679,000	11.4	49.8	66.4
1851	2,099,611	12.5	56.5	75.4

[65]Prepared from *Census: Education* 1852–53 [1692] xc, Table 25. Those schools for which no date of founding or construction of building is given, 1,071 Anglican, 420 Dissenting, were distributed equally over seven decades. There is no basis for a more sophisticated distribution of the undated schools

[66]Numbers of 1788 and 1795 are, at best, educated guesses arrived at through the use of the following formula:

$$\text{no. in schools aided by the Sunday School Society in 1788 and 1795} \times \frac{\text{no. of schools founded by 1801}}{\text{no. of schools aided by the Sunday School Society in 1801}}$$

The 1801 number is calculated by using the average size of schools aided by the Sunday School Society (90 pupils) × the number of schools in existence. For 1811

speculation about short-term rates of growth, two points can be made with confidence. After a slow start in the last two decades of the eighteenth century, Sunday school enrolment climbed steadily from 1800 to 1850, with perhaps some acceleration occurring in the late 1820s and 1830s. Furthermore, the magnitude of enrolment was such that very few working-class children after 1830 could have escaped at least a few years in Sunday school.[67]

Even if a reliable national series were available for Sunday school enrolments, it would be extremely difficult to explain its fluctuations. For example, the drop in enrolment 1842–3 might be explained by heightened political tensions, by economic distress, by a shortage of space, or, far more likely, by a combination of these and other factors. There is no way, even if an enrolment series were available, to isolate the mutually dependent variables. However, two local series, though susceptible to these limitations, do at least illustrate that by and large enrolment grew, with only minor perturbations, for most of the period 1800–50. Even in Stockport, a town at the center of working-class politics in the north of England, enrolment in the great interdenominational school, directed as it was by factory owners, was not seriously affected either by political strife in general or by Radical and Chartist Sunday schools in particular. (See Graphs 2 and 3, pp. 46–7)[68] The impact of Radical Sunday schools begun in Stockport around 1818 was short-lived; that of the small Chartist school in 1842 minimal or nonexistent.

---

and 1821 the same calculation was made using the average size of schools reported in *General Table showing the State of Education in England 1820* (151) xii, viz. 88. The 1818 figure is given in this report, but contemporary sources suggest that it is at least 25 per cent too low. For 1831 the average size of each school is taken from *Abstract of answers and returns relative to the state of Education in England and Wales* 1835 (62) xliii, pp. 1326–7; the 1833 figure is taken from this report. The average size of each school in 1841 is 8/18 of the difference between the average size in 1833 and that in 1851 from *Census : Education* 1852–53 [1692] xc., pp. 4–7, subtracting the schools and scholars in Wales. The enrollment for 1851 is taken from this report and is for England only. Ages of the population were not recorded in the 1801 and 1811 Census. In 1821 8/10 of the population enumerated gave their ages of which 241 were between 5 and 15. See 1821 *Census, Abstract of Answers and Returns*, 1822 (502) xv., p. 543. This fraction is used in the calculations for 1801, 1811, 1818, and 1821. The 1831 Census gave only the number of males over age 20. Ages of the entire population were demanded in 1841 and 1851, when .227 and .222, respectively, of the population were between 5 and 15. The 1841 proportion is used for 1831. See *Ages, Civil Conditions, etc.* [1851] *Census* 1852–53 [1691–I] lxxxviii, Table 3, p. clvi

[67] See further, pp. 101–2, below

[68] *Stockport Sunday School Enrollment Registers 1787–1850* 3 vols., MS. Stockport Reference Library. Admissions Register of the West Street Methodist School, Leek, Staffordshire Record Office, D 1114/2

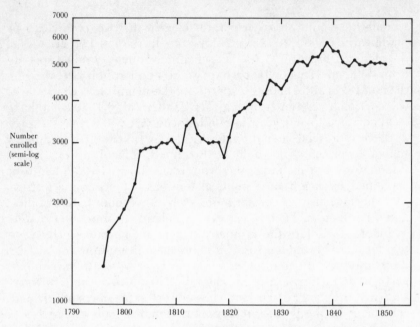

Graph 2: Total enrolment in the Stockport Sunday School, 1796–1850

The story in Leek, Staffordshire is much the same. If enrolment statistics are any indication, the preceding tables and graphs suggest that the popularity of Sunday schools among the working classes grew unabated during this period.[69] But it did not grow uniformly over the whole country, or in all religious bodies.

By 1851 the denominational pattern is clear. Anglicans controlled 54 per cent of all Church or chapel sittings but only 42 per cent of the total number of children in Sunday school (Table 6).

Among the Dissenting denominations, the Methodists did particularly well; of old Dissent the Congregationalists or Independents were far more successful and interested in Sunday school work than were Unitarians, Presbyterians and, to a lesser extent, Baptists. The Society of Friends and the isolationist Brethren played almost no part in the history of Sunday schools. The Roman Church, forced to compete with Protestant Sunday schools in the new industrial towns, did reasonably well in urban areas but overall failed to gain a share of Sunday scholars proportionate with its control of sittings.

Before 1851 the denominational picture is obscure. Tables 4 and 6 suggest that, after an early lead by the Church, Dissent came to

[69] On Chartist and Radical schools and working-class response to Sunday schools in general see pp. 78–86, below

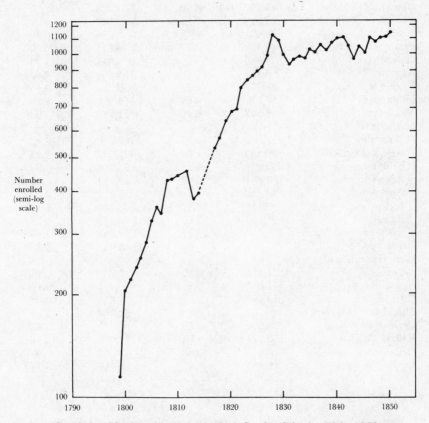

Graph 3: Total enrolment in the Leek Sunday School, 1798–1850

Table 6:[70] *Sunday school enrolment and number of sittings of Church of England and various Dissenting denominations showing percentage of total sittings and percentage of total Sunday school enrolment ascribable to each, 1851*

Denomination	No. of Sittings	Percentage of Total Sittings	Sunday school Enrolment	Percentage of Total SS Enrolment
Church of England	4,643,299	54.00	901,828	42.00
Church of Scotland	12,914	0.15	1,628	0.07
United Presbyterian	30,401	0.35	6,356	0.30
Presbyterian Ch. in Eng.	40,458	0.47	8,244	0.39
Independents	833,640	9.85	279,946	13.33
Baptists	568,464	7.72	155,398	7.40
Society of Friends	88,777	1.04	3,212	0.15
Unitarians	58,170	0.68	14,509	0.69
Moravians	8,523	0.10	1,788	0.08
Methodists				
Wesleyan	1,267,374	14.97	402,363	19.16
New Connexion	90,380	1.06	37,382	1.78
Primitive	357,056	4.21	96,706	4.60
Bible Christian	59,184	0.69	13,775	0.65
Association	90,720	1.07	43,217	2.05
Independent	2,144	0.02	3,902	0.18
Reformers	55,459	0.65	16,418	0.78
Total: Arminian Meth.	1,922,317	22.71	617,304	29.40
Calvinistic Methodists	7,866	0.09	6,461	0.30
Lady Huntingdon's Conn.	34,560	0.40	7,737	0.36
New Church	11,865	0.14	3,484	0.16
Brethren	15,599	0.18	638	0.03
Misc. Prot. (interden.)	—	—	60,888	2.89
German Protestant	200	0.00	20	0.00
Roman Catholic	159,271	1.88	32,973	1.57
Catholic and Apostolic	6,813	0.08	47	0.00
Latter Day Saints	19,985	0.23	741	0.03
Totals	8,463,122	100.00	2,099,661	100.00

dominate Sunday schools, a dominance particularly impressive in the early nineteenth century before the great membership gains of the 20s, 30s and 40s were registered. Since Anglican schools were usually smaller than those of Dissent, their share of the total number of scholars may be even less than their share of the number of schools. In 1829 the *Congregational Magazine* estimated that 700,000 children attended Dissenting Sunday schools, i.e. between 65 and 70 per cent of total enrolment.[71] On the other hand, the 1835

[70] *Census* [1851]: *Religious Worship* 1852–53 [1690] lxxxix; figures of Sunday school enrollment for Wales, p. clxix; numbers of sittings for Wales, p. cxciv, were subtracted from numbers in England and Wales, p. clxxxviii

[71] *Congregational Magazine* (1829) Supp., 393–4ff; see also Dearden's *Miscellany* vol. 2 (1839)

Table 7:[72] *Sunday school enrolment* per capita *on a county basis*, 1818, 1833, 1851

Counties	1818 Percentage of Population Enrolled in Sunday school	Rank by Enrolment *per capita*	1833 Percentage of Population Enrolled	Rank	1851 Percentage of Population Enrolled	Rank
Bedfordshire	6.1	8	15.7	3.5	19.7	1
Derbyshire	6.3	7	18.2	1	19.2	2
Yorks. W. Rid.	6.5	6	13.6	8	16.8	3
Cornwall	4.4	20	11.0	15	16.6	4.5
Huntingdonshire	3.2	30.5	12.3	12	16.6	4.5
Nottinghamshire	5.2	16	12.9	9	16.3	6
Buckinghamshire	7.3	3	15.7	3.5	16.0	7.5
Lancashire	5.2	16	13.9	6	16.0	7.5
Northampton	7.6	1	9.3	26	15.9	9
Leicestershire	7.1	5	15.3	5	15.4	10.5
Staffordshire	5.6	12	11.9	13	15.4	10.5
Dorset	7.2	4	12.8	10	15.1	12
Cheshire	6.0	9	17.4	2	14.9	13
Rutland	5.4	14	12.6	11	14.7	14
Wiltshire	7.4	2	13.7	7	14.6	15
Lincolnshire	2.2	38	9.9	21	13.9	16
Hertfordshire	3.9	24	8.7	29	13.1	17
Somerset	5.2	16	10.1	18	13.0	18
Westmorland	2.4	35.5	8.5	32	12.9	19
Gloucestershire	5.9	10	11.3	14	12.6	20.5
Yorks N. Rid.	1.3	41	9.6	24	12.6	20.5
Cambridge	3.3	28	9.2	27.5	12.5	22
Oxfordshire	4.3	21	10.8	16	12.2	23
Durham	4.1	22.5	9.2	27.5	12.1	24
Worcestershire	5.6	12	9.9	21	11.9	25
Berkshire	3.3	28	8.0	34	11.4	26
Hampshire	3.5	26	10.1	18	11.2	27
Norfolk	3.0	32,5	7.8	36	11.1	28
Suffolk	5.6	12	10.1	18	11.0	29
Essex	5.0	18	9.9	21	10.7	30
Cumberland	3.7	25	8.6	30.5	10.6	32
Yorks. E. Rid.	4.1	22.5	9.7	23	10.6	32
Warwickshire	4.5	19	9.5	25	10.6	32
Devon	2.4	35.5	8.6	30.5	10.0	34.5
Shropshire	3.3	28	8.0	34	10.0	34.5
Northumberland	2.0	39	7.0	39	9.8	36
Kent	2.4	35.5	7.6	37.5	9.4	37
Sussex	3.0	32.5	7.6	37.5	8.8	38
Herefordshire	3.2	30.5	8.0	34	7.7	39
Surrey	2.4	35.5	4.4	40	6.5	40
Middlesex	1.5	40	3.7	41	5.9	41

[72] The county *per capita* enrollments are calculated from the following parliamentary reports : 1820 (151), xii, 1835 (62), xliii, (1851) [1692], xc

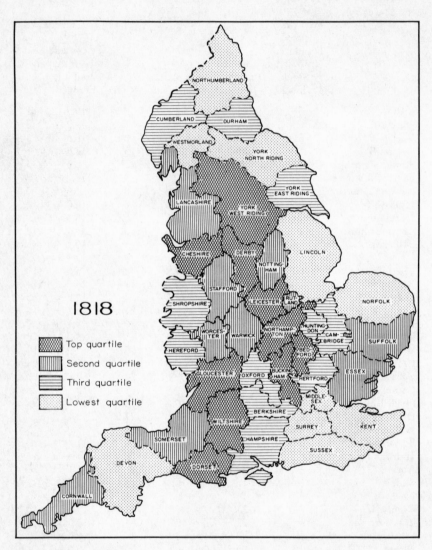

1. Density by quartiles of Sunday school enrolment per capita *on a county basis,
1818*

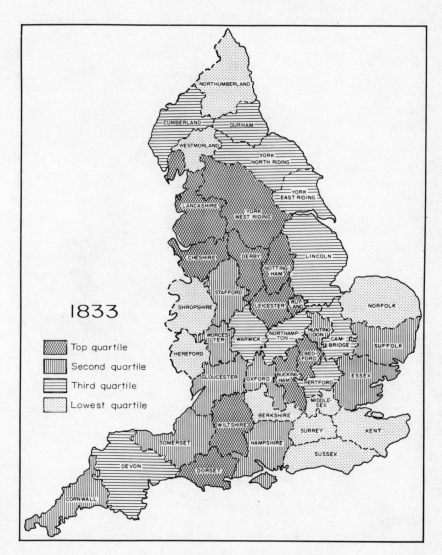

2. Density by quartiles of Sunday school enrolment per capita on a county basis, 1833

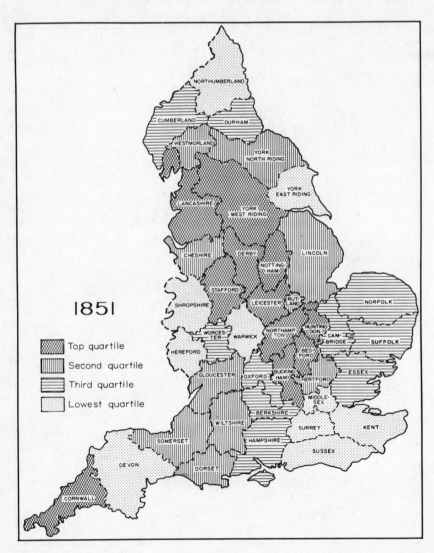

3. Density by quartiles of Sunday school enrolment per capita *on a county basis, 1851*

Education Returns list only 4,910 Dissenting Sunday schools with 618,770 students in attendance, i.e. 33 per cent of schools and 45 per cent of all students. All that can be said with certainty is that by mid-century the Sunday school was more closely associated with Non-conformity than with the Church; and furthermore, that quite probably the relative position of Dissent improved in the increasingly heated competition for new members after 1830.

Sunday school enrolments did not, however, grow uniformly throughout England. Working-class children in Buckinghamshire by the middle of the century were twice as likely to belong to a Sunday school as those in Herefordshire; one in five of the population was enrolled in a Sunday school in Bedforshire in 1851, but only one in seventeen of the population of Middlesex was enrolled. The following table and maps provide a basis for understanding the uneven popularity of Sunday schools in the various parts of the country.

The enrolment figures in Table 7 and the Maps 1, 2 and 3 belie the impression that Sunday schools were confined to the industrial north and Midlands of England. Bedfordshire consistently had higher *per capita* enrolments than Lancashire; Dorset, Wiltshire, Buckinghamshire, Bedfordshire were, at least after 1818, among the top one-third of counties in *per capita* enrolment as were Cornwall and Huntingdonshire after 1833.

Although both the culture and the popular mythology of the Sunday school were most highly developed in the industrial towns of Lancashire, Cheshire, the West Riding and Staffordshire, Sunday schools were not an essentially urban phenomenon. In primarily rural counties with a few urban concentrations Sunday school enrolments appear to have been distributed fairly uniformly between city and countryside. In 1851, for example, the cities and boroughs of Cornwall with a total population of 103,070 and a Sunday school enrolment of 13,576 accounted for 29 per cent of the county's population and 23 per cent of its total enrolment; the cities of Dorset with a total population of 40,341 and a Sunday school enrolment of 6,931 accounted for 22.7 per cent of the population and 26 per cent of the school membership. Bedford, the only city in the county, contained 9 per cent of its population but only 6 per cent of its school enrolment. The concentration of Sunday scholars was, in fact, slightly lower in urban areas than in the country considered as a whole. Boroughs and cities in 1851 had an enrolment ratio of 1:8.23 while 1 in 7.97 of the entire population were members of some Sunday school.[73] In short, factors other than

---

[73] Sunday school enrollments for cities and boroughs are taken from *Number of Day Schools and Sunday Schools, and Day Scholars and Sunday Scholars, in Each City*

settlement patterns must have been the primary determinant of Sunday school success or failure.

But why Sunday schools were popular in some areas and not in others is extremely difficult to answer if based primarily on the county as the unit of study. A county is too large a unit to be accurately classified as industrial, farming, or mixed, as having a high or low rate of population growth or a strong or weak Dissenting community. If, for example, a county is undergoing rapid population growth or if it has a high Dissenting membership *per capita*, it does not follow that these conditions pertain in those districts with high Sunday school enrolments. Even if certain economic, social and religious factors can be convincingly adduced as causes of human behavior, ecological correlations are always suspect. Nevertheless, while data on enrolment are available for individual parishes, commensurable material for other variables is not readily accessible at the local level. The county or the metropolis are, therefore, the only possible units of analysis with the data at hand.

London, as might be expected, had consistently low *per capita* Sunday school membership throughout the period. Its working class was notoriously irreligious. Attendance at worship in London on Census Sunday, 1851, was the lowest in the country; that only 2 per cent of the population of Bethnal Green were in church or chapel shocked the religious community. Both old Dissent and Methodism, which together provided the impetus for much Sunday school activity in the rest of England, were unable to make substantial gains in the Metropolis. London alone provided fertile ground for the secularist movement of the late nineteenth century. Furthermore, a long tradition of Sunday recreation—fairs, street markets, outings—particularly in working-class areas, might be pointed to as a compelling counter-attraction to the Sunday school. But, unfortunately, a more detailed analysis of London by divisions makes these kinds of explanations less plausible.

Clearly high Sunday school attendance was not confined to the working-class areas of east London; nor, conversely, was *per capita* enrolment invariably high in these districts. True, Bethnal Green ranked high in the proportion of its population age 5–15 belonging to a Sunday school; but so did suburban Wandsworth. *Per capita*

---

and Borough, In England and Wales 1852–53 (514) lxxix. 714. The concentration of Sunday scholars in urban areas given in the text is somewhat inflated since London, where Sunday school enrollment was particularly low, is not included in the table (except for the city) on which the calculation is based. The unreliability of the data for 1818 made it impossible to compare urban with rural areas for an earlier period

Table 8:[74] *Sunday school enrolment* per capita, *Church attendance and Dissenting strength in London with rankings* 1851 *(by districts)*

District	Percentage of Population Age 5–15 Enrolled in a Sunday school	Rank	Percentage Total Church Attendance/ Population	Rank	Attendance at Dissenting Places of Worship/ Total Attendance	Rank
Bethnal Green	33.5	1.5	14.9	36	12.8	34
St. Luke	33.5	1.5	35.4	18	71.7	1
St. Olave	33.3	3	51.1	6	30.9	24
Bermondsey	31.4	4	30.3	29	37.3	13.5
Wandsworth	27.6	5	65.2	2	23.5	28
Marylebone	27.3	6	38.4	14	31.8	22
Islington	25.8	7	44.8	9	32.8	21
London City	24.4	8	62.6	3	29.6	26
Hackney	23.7	9	58.3	4	51.2	8
St. Saviour	23.6	10	35.9	16	53.8	6
Greenwich	23.5	11	42.4	11	41.6	12
St. George Sk.	23.2	12	42.0	12	33.7	17.5
Whitechapel	22.7	13	30.7	26.5	33.7	17.5
St. George E.	22.2	14	23.6	34	37.3	13.5
Holborn	21.8	16	34.0	20.5	35.6	15
St. Martin	21.8	16	50.5	7	51.3	7
Poplar	21.8	16	28.0	31	54.3	5
East London	21.7	18	35.6	17	51.1	9
Lewisham	21.3	19	52.3	5	17.1	32
West London	21.1	20.5	30.5	28	3.7	36
Chelsea	21.1	20.5	39.2	13	27.6	27
Westminster	21.0	22	48.2	8	22.9	29
Stepney	20.8	23	33.2	22	54.8	4
Hampstead	20.0	24	69.2	1	12.1	35
Shoreditch	19.5	25	18.5	35	66.7	2
Clerkenwell	19.3	26	27.7	32.5	65.0	3
Rotherhithe	19.0	27	34.0	20.5	17.8	31
Newington	18.9	28	34.4	19	48.2	10
Camberwell	18.7	29	30.0	30	45.8	11
Pancras	17.4	30	43.1	10	31.0	23
Kensington	16.3	31	31.1	25	22.0	30
Lambeth	15.9	32	32.2	23	35.1	16
St. Giles	12.2	33	36.1	15	33.2	19
St. James	11.2	34	31.4	24	29.8	25
Strand	10.7	35	27.7	32.5	33.1	20
St. George H. Sq.	10.0	36	30.7	26.5	14.9	33

[74] Data are from the *Religious Census 1852–53* [1690] lxxxix, appendix, pp. 3–9 and from the *Education Census 1852–53* [1692] xc, appendix, detailed tables pp. 8–9, vol. lxxix, 309. Church attendance means the total number of persons attending morning, afternoon and evening services at Anglican, Roman Catholic and 'other' places of worship. 'Other' places of worship are almost exclusively those belonging to Dissent. The proportion of total church attendance enjoyed by these chapels is taken as an index of the strength of Dissent in a district

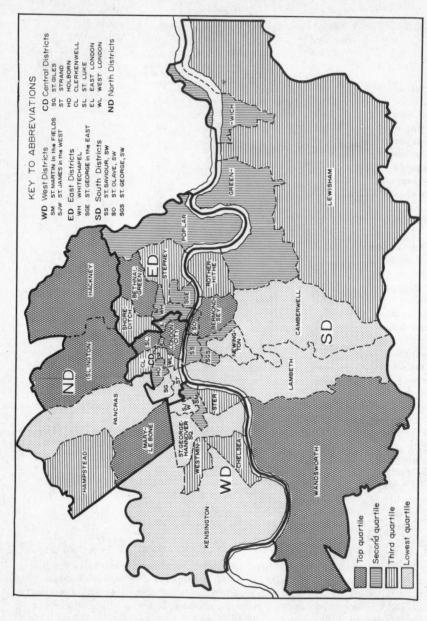

KEY TO ABBREVIATIONS

WD West Districts   **CD** Central Districts
SM ST. MARTIN in the FIELDS   SG ST. GILES
SJW ST. JAMES in the WEST   ST STRAND
   HO HOLBORN
ED East Districts   CL CLERKENWELL
WH WHITECHAPEL   SL ST. LUKE
SGE ST. GEORGE in the EAST   EL EAST LONDON
   WL WEST LONDON
SD South Districts
SS ST. SAVIOUR, SW   **ND** North Districts
SO ST. OLAVE, SW
SGS ST. GEORGE, SW

Top quartile
Second quartile
Third quartile
Lowest quartile

4. *Density by quartiles of Sunday school enrolment per capita by districts of London, 1851*

enrolment was lower in Stepney than in Chelsea, considerably lower in Whitechapel than in Marylebone. The popularity of Sunday schools had little to do with either church attendance or with the relative strength of Dissent. Bethnal Green, that national symbol of working-class irreligion, tied with St Luke's, which ranked only eighteenth in church attendance among London districts, for first place in *per capita* Sunday school enrolment. Bermondsey, which ranked twenty-ninth in church attendance, ranked fourth in Sunday school enrolment. Indeed, a rank order coefficient of .185 confirms what has already been suggested.[75] The relationship between church attendance and the popularity of Sunday schools in London is almost completely random. The same may be said with regard to relative strength of Dissent. St Luke's ranked first in both Sunday school enrolment *per capita* and total attendance at Dissenting place of worship as a proportion of the population; but St Olave, which ranked third in Sunday school enrolment, ranked only twenty-fourth in Dissenting strength. Shoreditch, on the other hand, ranked second in Dissenting strength but twenty-fifth in Sunday school enrolment. Spearman's coefficient for the ranking of the two variables is .090, suggesting that their relationship, at least on this level of analysis, is totally random. Without more research on the religious and social geography of nineteenth-century London the questions of why Sunday school enrolments were distributed as indicated in Table 8 and Map 4 remain unanswered.

While Sunday schools in London were relatively less popular than almost anywhere else in England, the institutional life of those schools which managed to thrive in the Metropolis, was indistinguishable from that of large and prosperous Sunday schools in Lancashire or the West Riding. The Silver Street Congregational school, for example, had a writing school; served tea, wine and biscuits at its great annual festivals; formed benevolent societies for teachers and students; taught singing in a special voice class for teachers; held 'old students' meetings every Easter Monday beginning in 1827; organized outings to Gravesend, Hampton Court, Highbury, Stratford or Ilford; and published the inevitable memoir book of pious scholars.[76] An old scholar from the Maze Pond Sunday School, when asked to discuss his Sunday school

[75] I have throughout this chapter used Spearman's rank correlation coefficient, sometimes called *rho*, in preference to Kendall's *tau* primarily because *rho* is more easily calculable and because for my purposes there was little to be gained by using *tau*. Both coefficients give a measure of the association between two variables whose values have been arranged in two ordered series. See Sidney Siegel *Nonparametric Statistics for the Behavioral Sciences* (New York, 1956) 202–23

[76] C. H. David *History of the Silver Street Sunday School Society* (1904) 12–26

experience, remembered the 'many happy hours we have spent amid the beautiful scenery of the Surrey hills ... how replete with pleasure [it was] for us to walk from the din of towns in the quiet of Norwood.'[77] Here and there in London the Sunday school with its constellation of activities did manage to gain a foothold; but the reasons why this hold was so precarious remain obscure.

Unfortunately, the reasons why Sunday schools were well attended in other parts of England is almost as mysterious. They have been seen as a response to the pressures of industrialization, especially to the increased requirements for child labor. The case of Wales immediately casts doubt on this hypothesis. Sunday schools there were far more popular and reached a far wider section of the population than in England, and yet the country was almost entirely non-industrial.[78] In England, too, there is no clear relationship between the degree of industrialization and the strength of Sunday schools. In 1818 the counties with high enrolments *per capita*, i.e. greater than 6 per cent, are more or less randomly distributed among agricultural, mixed, and commercial or industrial counties; the same might be said of those counties which had more than 11 per cent of their population enrolled in 1833. (Table 9).

Table 9:[79] *Distribution of countries with high Sunday school enrolment* per capita *with respect to their agricultural, mixed and commercial or industrial economy, 1815 and 1833*

	Agricultural		Mixed		Commercial & Industrial	
	1818	1833	1818	1833	1818	1833
No. of counties	5	5	7	8	4	3
Random distribution	6	6	6	6	4	4

Conversely, of the nine counties that had less than 3 per cent *per capita* enrolment in 1818, two can be classified as agrarian, three as mixed, and four as industrial or commerical. Of twelve counties with less than 8 per cent *per capita* enrolment in 1833, four are agrarian, four mixed, and three industrial. Among cities in 1851, Manchester, Oldham, Stockport and Ashton-under-Lyme had exceptionally high enrolments but so did Shaftesbury and Chippenham.[80] While the industrial revolution in some measure affected the entire country, and while Sunday schools viewed in a

[77] R. Reeve *History of Maze Pond Sunday School, 1801–1901* (London, 1901) 35; see also 'Reminiscences of an Octogenarian Teacher,' *Sunday School Teacher* (1890) 392–3

[78] For Wales see David Evans *The Sunday Schools of Wales* (1880)

[79] Classification of counties from P. Deane and W. A. Cole *British Economic Growth 1688–1959* (Cambridge, 1962) 103

[80] See *Number of Day Schools and Sunday Schools ... in Each City and Borough, in England and Wales ... 1854*

broad context were everywhere part of the educational response to industrialization, their pattern of distribution suggests that they were not merely an answer to the specific problems associated with the growth of large-scale machine-powered production.

It is tempting to associate the success of Sunday schools with the rapid population growth which accompanied the new industrialism. But there is no regular relationship between a county's rank in *per capita* enrolment and its rank in annual rate of population growth over the period 1800 to 1831. Nor is there a significant correlation between popularity of Sunday schools and either natural increase or rate of migration, the components of population growth.[81] In short, the distribution of Sunday schools over England, considered in county units, bears no clear relationship to any obvious social or economic determinants.

On the other hand, there is a connection between the strength of Sunday schools and certain religious variables, albeit one that is difficult to interpret. In 1851, for example, in cities and boroughs with populations over 10,000, there is a strong negative correlation between church attendance and *per capita* Sunday school enrolment. In a list of fifty-five cities for which data are available Stockport ranks highest in Sunday school enrolment but forty-first in index of church attendance, Halifax ranks fourth in strength of Sunday schools and forty-third in church attendance. Conversely, Exeter is second from the top in church attendance while sixth from the bottom in Sunday school membership; Ipswich's index of church attendance was the fourth highest of any English city, but its Sunday school enrolment *per capita* was next to lowest, etc. Spearman's rank order coefficient for the two series is a statistically significant $-.738$. That is, a strong inverse relationship holds between the two variables, suggesting that in certain urban areas, particularly in the north, Sunday schools replaced church or chapel as the focus of working-class religious life.[82]

But Spearman's coefficient between the counties ranked by Sunday school enrolment *per capita* and by an index of church attendance is a statistically significant $+.489$. Five of the top ten counties ranked by the popularity of Sunday schools were also among the top ten counties ranked by church attendance, viz. Bedfordshire, Huntingtonshire, Buckinghamshire, Northamptonshire, and Leicestershire. Bedfordshire had both the highest church attendance and the highest Sunday school enrolment *per capita* in England. It appears, therefore, that while in certain urban areas

[81] P. Deane and Cole *British* . . . pp. 108–09

[82] Indices of church attendance are from K. S. Inglis 'Patterns of Religious Worship in 1851,' *Journal of Ecclesiastical History* vol. 11, no. 1 (April 1960) 80–82

Sunday schools flourished as a substitute for traditional religious institutions and practices, in the country as a whole they tended to cluster in those counties where church attendance was high.

Since Sunday schools played so important a part in Wesleyan chapel life, it might be supposed that there would be a correlation between *per capita* enrolment and the Wesleyan Methodist membership expressed as a percentage of the population, the MPR. In 1818 no such relationship holds; the Spearman's coefficient of rank correlation is a non-significant .274. As the number of Sunday schools grew, however, there was some tendency for them to cluster in areas of Methodist strength. The rank correlation between Sunday schools in 1833 and Wesleyan MPR in 1841 is .337, significant at .05 level of confidence but not indicative of a very strong correlation.[83] Sunday school strength, however, correlates highly with a measure of overall Dissenting strength, i.e. the percentage of total sittings not held by the Establishment. A rank order coefficient of .537, significant at .01 level of confidence, may be calculated for the two series. The widely held opinion of nineteenth-century observers that Sunday schools and Dissent vary together is, therefore, partially vindicated.

Of course, the discovery of this and other relationships does not eliminate the problem of finding the social and economic determinants of Sunday school success or failure; it merely takes the argument one step further. It is true that the Sunday school was generally more a part of Non-conformist than Anglican religious culture, but the question still remains why the Church was strong or weak in a particular area. And here the historical sociology of religion, still in its infancy, fails to provide an answer. While the growth of Wesleyanism was most likely to occur in areas of Anglican weakness—in large parishes of pasture and upland farming areas, in rapidly growing cities, in parishes with absentee clergymen—the opposite relationship existed between old Dissent and the Establishment. Congregationalists, Baptists and Presbyterians tended to gain strength in those areas where the Church was strong.[84] The correlation of Sunday school enrolment with aggregate Dissenting strength, therefore, does not lend itself to a straightforward explanation. It is also true that Sunday schools flourished in cities where

[83] Wesleyan MPRs were kindly furnished to me by Mr Alan Gilbert and are now incorporated in his unpublished Oxford D PHIL thesis, 'The Growth and Decline of Nonconformity ...'

[84] The most complete discussion of the social basis of Dissenting strength is in Mr Gilbert's unpublished thesis. For earlier published expositions see Alan Everitt 'Non-conformity in Country Parishes' in Joan Thirsk, ed. *Land, Church and People*: *Essays presented to Prof. H. P. R. Finberg* (Reading, 1970) 178–99 and Robert Currie 'A microtheory of Wesleyan Methodist Growth,' *Proceedings of the Wesley Historical Society* vol. 26 (October 1967)

church and chapel attendance was particularly low, but again no
simple reasons can be given for why the working classes turned to
the new institution.[85]

Nevertheless, it is possible to offer an explanation of the popularity
of Sunday schools in certain areas in terms of the presence or
absence of alternative sources for the services they provided. In
the textile towns of Lancashire and the West Riding, among
certain elements in rapidly growing Midland cities like Nottingham
and Birmingham, in rural areas with mining or manufacturing like
the villages of Cornwall or Chipping Norton in the Cotswolds,
among increasingly poor framework knitters and handloom weavers
of the Midlands, Sunday schools provided educational, religious
and recreational services that were not available elsewhere. In rural
areas where Dissent was strong, the Sunday school became a center
of religious and cultural self-expression for the socially isolated
Non-conformist community. Conversely, Sunday schools were often
weak in areas where their services were already provided by other
institutions. In Durham and Cumberland a strong tradition of
weekday education produced one of the highest literacy rates in
England and made the purely secular part of Sunday schools less
relevant. Alternative educational and recreational facilities in the
Metropolis might have kept enrolments at the low level where they
remained for the entire period.

iv. CONCLUSIONS

The Sunday school grew up as part of the Evangelical Revival of
the 1780s and 1790s. This outburst of religious and philanthropic
fervor was by no means limited to the middling ranks of society,
and Sunday schools found early supporters among those classes
they were intended to serve. From the very beginning then Sunday
schools must be regarded, in part at least, as indigenous institutions
of the working-class community rather than an imposition on it
from the outside. The sheer numbers enrolled and their geographical
spread would suggest that few working-class children, except
perhaps in London, escaped at least some exposure to Sunday
school education. Though Non-conformity was generally more
active in this sphere, the Church was by no means quiescent.
Sunday schools were not the monopoly of any one region, religious
body, or class.

The next chapter will place the Sunday school more firmly

[85] Chapter 5 sets out a possible constellation of causes for this shift

in the context of the community it served. Its general independence from church or chapel, its source of funds, and its social composition all point the way to a consideration of the Sunday school as an institution of the working class.

3. The Sunday School : A Portrait in Context

i Introduction

The social background of those involved in Sunday schools—students, teachers, and managers—is such as to make the schools *ipso facto* a part of the community they served. The breakup of interdenominational schools forced their operations onto the neighborhood level; a burgeoning Sunday school subculture and long-lived tensions between clergy and laity reinforced the independence of the school from the congregation. This chapter argues that the Sunday school was a relatively autonomous, largely working-class institution. If this is true, its function as an agency of social control, discussed in Chapters Six and Seven, must be seen in a very different light indeed.

ii. The Sunday School as an Organization

The size of the late eighteenth- and early nineteenth-century Sunday school was sufficiently large to allow it to develop a communal identity and to require a formal organizational structure. Sunday schools initiated by the working class very soon outgrew the cottages of their founders and had to find larger quarters in lofts, barns, or warehouses. The practice of hiring ordinary day school teachers to receive children into their homes on Sunday was already in decline by the turn of the century. In short, Raikes's cottage schools were an anachronism almost as soon as they started.

While the average charity school of the eighteenth century contained no more than twenty to twenty-five children, the earliest Sunday schools of Northamptonshire had average enrolments of over eighty and those aided by the Sunday School Society of between ninety and a hundred. In 1818, when the ordinary day school held thirty children and the larger grammar schools of Lancashire about sixty, the mean Sunday school enrolment was eighty, varying from fifty-seven in Berkshire to 248 in Lancashire.[1] The Stockport Sunday school, largest in the world, had a peak enrolment of over six thousand, and many schools in large cities and even in smaller towns like Leek or Burslem gathered well over a thousand children under one roof and one management.

Increased complexity of organization accompanied the increased size of the Sunday school. Although on occasion some of its directors may have also served as churchwardens or chapel trustees, it was nevertheless a distinct, formally constituted institution. It had its own name, its own constitution and rules for management, and its own source of funds. The legal position of the schools varied. Two-thirds of the 10,159 Anglican Sunday schools met in buildings separate from the church; many of these were probably part of the National School system. But even without formal ties the Sunday school might well have been offered the use of the day school free of charge or for a nominal maintenance rent. Large Anglican schools like St Clement's or Bennett Street, Manchester owned their own buildings and were thus entirely independent of the Church. In 1851 only about 35 per cent of Dissenting Sunday schools met in separate buildings, but these would be entirely under the jurisdiction of the school trustees with perhaps a token chapel trustee on the board. In those cases where the school used chapel space, it was usually on a lease arrangement which could be, and was, liable to breakage by either side. Finally, about 10 per cent of both Anglican and Dissenting schools rented rooms outside the church or chapel and would therefore be entirely independent of their supervision.[2]

Almost all Sunday schools of similar size were similarly constituted. Large schools, especially those which owned property, had a governing body composed of major contributors, long-time teachers, important members of the congregation, and members of the clergy; this committee was responsible for all of the school's

[1] Size of charity schools is calculated from 'Account of Charity Schools for 1724' and 'A list of the Subscription Charity schools in and about London and Westminster for 1799' in M. G. Jones *Charity School* pp. 364–73; size of grammar schools calculated from N. Carlisle *Endowed Grammar Schools in England and Wales* (1818) Lancashire chapter; size of average private school in 1818 calculated from *State of Education in England* 1820 (151) xii

[2] 1851 *Education Census* 1852–53 [1692] xc, p. lxxix. Sunday school arrangements with chapel trustees become apparent in studying controversies between the two bodies. See below p. 82ff. If Manchester is at all representative a large proportion of National Schools were first built for Sunday school use alone. See MS. folders under town name and then school name in the National School Archive, 69 Great Peter Street, London

external affairs. It collected funds from the public, reported on their use, and managed the financial affairs of the school. The actual trustees of any buildings were usually drawn from amongst members of this committee. On the other hand, the internal affairs of larger schools and all of the activities of smaller ones were directed by a teachers' meeting that was chaired by a superintendent teacher and attended, where appropriate, by members of the governing committee. In addition to handling those matters left to the committee in larger schools, the teachers' meeting was invariably responsible for the day to day operations. It decided what subjects were to be taught, who was to be accepted or rejected as teachers and students, what textbooks to use, what procedures to follow in visiting absent scholars, and so on. Rich and locally prominent superintendents and committee members naturally exercised disproportionate weight in such meetings; but since the teachers were usually unpaid and could simply retire if displeased with the operations of the school, it was governed by consensus and not by naked authority and the cash nexus. High-handed tactics invariably led to trouble (see below p. 82).[3]

The Sunday school then was a comparatively large, highly structured, and generally democratic institution that was formally distinct from the church or chapel. In fact, its independence was more than a legal fiction; its life and customs grew up next to, and sometimes in conflict with, those of the traditional religious community.

iii. THE BREAKUP OF THE INTERDENOMINATIONAL SUNDAY SCHOOL

In her widely accepted account, M. G. Jones argues that Sunday schools began as non-denominational experiments in Christian collaboration which ultimately failed because the political tensions of the world at large impinged on the otherwise tranquil world of the Sunday school: 'Jacobinism split the Sunday school movement just as Jacobitism had split the early charity school movement. History repeated itself, but with a difference. As at the beginning of the century Dissent withdrew from association with the Church, so this time the Church withdrew from association with Dissent.'[4]

[3] This summary is based on a study of the rule books and guides to Sunday school practice cited in the bibliography

[4] Jones *Charity School* ... pp. 142–54, quote on pp. 153–4. W. H. Armytage *Four Hundred Years of English Education* (Cambridge, 1964) 75; R. A. Soloway *Prelates and People: Ecclesiastrical Social Thought in England, 1783–1852* (1969) 359–62; Richard D. Altick *The English Common Reader* (Chicago, 1957) 73, among others, base their accounts of Sunday schools during the French Revolution on Jones

The impact of the French Revolution and, more immediately, of warnings like those of the Bishop of Rochester against 'schools of Jacobinical dissent' was enough to make the Anglican clergy withdraw from interdenominational schools after fifteen years of quiet cooperation.[5]

A more recent interpretation retains the outlines of Jones' argument but places the breakup on non-denominational Sunday schools in the context of popular revulsion against the Establishment. On this account, the fundamentally non-denominational Sunday schools of the 1780s and 1790s were destroyed by clergymen who feared that these novel institutions had become the vanguard of Dissenting imperialism. When opinion among the lower orders moved against the Church after 1795, so the argument goes, the Church moved to combat this trend by breaking up non-denominational schools and thereby eliminating, it was hoped, that battle ground on which Dissent generally and Methodism in particular might prove most effective.[6]

These lines of argument can be faulted on four grounds: they underestimate the degree of friction from the start; they grossly exaggerate the effects of the French Revolution; they assign to the Anglicans the active role in breaking up Sunday schools whereas the Dissenters seem, in fact, to have been at least as responsible; and they draw attention away from those forces which worked long after the end of interdenominationalism to divide the Sunday school from the church or chapel. The short and unhappy history of these early schools is an important part not only of the history of religion in general but of the growth of the Sunday school community in particular.

There were, it must be admitted, both within and outside the Church a few men who believed in Sunday schools as a 'return to early Christianity when the true Gospel was preached by wandering itinerants', as a 'prelude to that happy day, when Christians will learn to unite together on the plain truths of their common Christianity'.[7] There were also those opposed, on principle, to interdenominationalism. They were satisfied with the religious

---

[5] See the most famous of anti-Sunday school sermons: *The Charge of Samuel [K. Horsley] Lord Bishop of Rochester to the Clergy of His Diocese* (1800) 25–6

[6] W. R. Ward *Religion and Society in England, 1790–1850* (1972) 12–16

[7] Rowland Hill *An Apology for Sunday Schools: The Substance of a Sermon preached at Surrey Chapel Feb.* 22, 1801 ... *with incidental Remarks on the Late Charge of the Rt. Rev. the Lord Bishop of Rochester* p. 19; Joshua Toulman, MA *The Rise, Progress and Effects of Sunday Schools considered in a Sermon Preached at Taunton, Mar. 28, 1789* p. 20; Hill goes so far as to recommend taking children to a different church or chapel as often as possible so that they could choose more intelligently which one to attend or more hopefully see the folly of religious differences and work for Christian unity

principles of a Sunday school only if it was completely under the control of the parish clergy, if masters and students attended church twice each Sunday, and if 'those who term themselves saints', i.e. Methodists, were completely excluded from playing any part.[8] By 1802 the ultra-conservative *Anti-Jacobin Review* declared quite simply that 'all sober thinking persons' could not but condemn the lay-dominated latitudinarian Sunday school.[9] And as late as 1821 a writer in the equally reactionary *Christian Remembrancer* inveighed against those few Sunday schools which still took children to church one Sunday and chapel the next, a practice through which 'they at last abandon in disgust a religion admitting, as they think, of so much doubt and uncertainty.'[10] But the virulent attacks of the right wing press or the Blagdon controversy pamphlets came well after the demise of Sunday school interdenominationalism, insofar as it ever existed. Breakups occurred for practical and not for ideological reasons.

Often there was not even a pretext of union between Anglicans and Dissenters. Sunday school supporters in Newcastle thought it a virtue worth commenting upon that each of their schools had from the beginning been associated with a single congregation.[11] The first Sunday school in Chester, 1782, was unashamedly denominated 'Methodist', that in Rushton, about 1780, 'Independent', in Stourbridge, 1785, 'Unitarian', etc.[12] In other towns, Rochdale, Leek, Keighley, and in sections of London, for example, schools that were *de facto* Methodist continued, sometimes for decades, to take their students to the parish church for worship. However, this was not because of their formal interdenominational character but due to the anomalous position, in the decades after 1790, of Wesleyanism, which hovered between Church and Dissent,

---

[8] See for example Rev. T. E. Owen *Methodism Unmasked or the progress of Puritanism* (1802)

[9] Vol. 11, p. 181; the sermon by Rev. Francis Wollaston, Rector of Chislehurst *A Country Parson's Address to his Flock, to caution them against being misled by the Wolf in Sheep's Clothing; or receiving Jacobin Teachers of Sedition who intrude themselves under the specious Pretense of Instructing Youth and Preaching Christianity* (1799) is another good example of similar views

[10] Vol. 3 (Jan. 1821) 13

[11] Rev. William Turner of Hanover Chapel, Newcastle-u-Tyne *Sunday Schools Recommended ... with an appendix concerning the formation and expense of these schools* (1786) 55

[12] *Rules of the Methodist Sunday School, St. John Street, Chester instituted in the year 1782* (Xerox supplied by Chester Record Office); A. G. Cumberland *Protestant Non-conformity in the Black Country, 1662–1851* (Unpublished MA thesis, Birmingham University, 1951) 163–4

unwilling to make the final break.[13] Finally, the whole issue of denominationalism did not arise for the hundreds of small neighborhood Sunday schools held in the cottages and lofts of humble people.

Even where a formally constituted interdenominational school did exist, its ecumenicalism was from the beginning only skin-deep. In the most widely publicized of the town-wide broadly based schools, that of Manchester, the governing committee was indeed made up of clergy and laity from both church and chapel. But the seeds of dissolution were planted in the original rules, just as they were in the rules of Birmingham, Stockport, Nottingham and a dozen other towns. All the children enrolled in Manchester were required to go to the school nearest their homes, except for the children of Dissenters who were allowed to travel some distance to find a master of their own persuasion; if possible, children were to be provided with such masters, and under no circumstances were Dissenting children subject to catechization by the Anglican clergy. Finally, and most important in the case of Manchester, the visitors of each school were permitted to decide the time and mode of attendance at divine worship. So, within an allegedly nondenominational organization, Dissenters were allowed to establish branches for their children under the supervision of persons appointed by them and with a provision that the children could attend their services.[14]

But even this loose organization could not contain its divergent elements. While the precise causes of the breakup in Manchester remain obscure, certain points are clear.[15] The question of church attendance and local autonomy undermined the stability of the school from the very beginning.[16] Its final dissolution was not precipitated by the secession of the High Church party but, on the contrary, by the refusal of two well-known Evangelicals to cooperate with the school.[17] One of these clergymen, the Rev. Cornelius

[13] Rev. John Ashworth *Strange Tales from Humble Life* 4th ser. (Manchester, 1870) 251; Thomas E. Brigden *The Old Leek Sunday School: A centenary Record* (Leek, 1897); J. W. Laycock *Methodist Heroes in the Great Haworth Round 1734–84* (Keighley, 1907) 376; John Telford *Two West End Chapels: or Sketches of London Methodism from Wesley's Day* (1886) 243

[14] *Rules and Orders for the Government of the Sunday Schools in Manchester, 1786* vol. 1 MS. A 6:3–6, Manchester Sunday School *Minute Books* Chethams Library

[15] The views of those who dissented from the committee are known only through the reports in the committee's minute books, i.e. through the committee's reaction to them

[16] Manchester Sunday School *Minute Books*, op. cit. 5 November, 1787, 7 February, 1791 (re extempore prayer); 5 March, 1798 (re tightening central control of the schools)

[17] The first hint of trouble is recorded, ibid. 3 December, 1798; see also 1 April, 1799, and 2 December, 1799

Bayley, had been brought up a Methodist, was at one time a teacher at the Kingswood School, and with Wesley's permission had preached at Oldham Road Chapel while he continued as minister at the proprietary Church of St James.[18] The other, C. P. Myddelton, was the author of a well-known defence of Sunday schools against the onslaughts of Horsley and other enemies on the right.[19]

Furthermore, far from accepting the secession by Bayley and Myddelton and then by three Methodist schools, the Anglican-dominated governing committee made every effort to keep the school united. On at least two occasions a delegation called on the clergymen to come back into the fold.[20] In July 1799, six months after rumors of Bayley's disaffection had arisen, a statement was issued reaffirming the desirability of a broadly based interdenominational school, and although the Wesleyans seceded at about this time, the committee continued to try to maintain the old order.[21] In December it was made clear that the question of attendance at worship rested with the local visitors so that, *de facto*, Dissenters could have control of this aspect of school life.[22] A revision of the rules reported in February 1800 reaffirmed the principle of freedom of choice in going either to church or chapel and pronounced that extempore prayer was not forbidden. By 3 March the committee had agreed that attendance at worship need be only one Sunday in four and that in any case this was a matter for local discretion; it also agreed to allow small classes and unpaid teachers, and it acceded to an escape clause, should future agreement be impossible.[23] Only after eighteen months of attempting to keep the schools united did the committee concede defeat; in May 1800 the rump of the old school organized a meeting of the Anglican clergy and their supporters to form a new Church Sunday school organization.[24] What really lay at the root of the unrest still remains in doubt. Two near-contemporary Methodist historians claim that an Anglican hostility to extempore prayer was the cause of it

[18] The main source for Bayley's life is a newspaper cutting on the centenary of St James Church, 1888, preserved in Fred Leary *Lewis' Directory with notes and MS. material on 1788* Manchester Central Reference Library 942.738 L4, vol. 1, signed EEP; for his relationship with Manchester Methodists see E. A. Rose 'Cornelius Bayley and the Manchester Methodists' *Proc. Wes. Hist. Soc.* vol. 34 (September 1964) 152–8

[19] *A Sermon in Defense of Sunday Schools* (Manchester, 1798); see also William E. Axon *The Annals of Manchester* (1886) 222

[20] Manchester *Minute Books* 3 December 1798, 17 June 1799

[21] Ibid. 12 July 1799

[22] December 1799, ibid.; a sub-committee waited on the gentlemen who had seceded—see 4 November 1799

[23] Manchester *Minute Books*, 3 February 1800, 3 March 1800

[24] Ibid. 5 May 1800; see also *Manchester Mercury* 1 July 1800

all. It is true, of course, that political tensions exacerbated Anglican anxiety about the danger of non-liturgical, free form worship. And, it is quite possible that Churchmen sought to prohibit this suspect mode of prayer. But it was an exuberant and self-confident Methodist community which made the break. Secession by the High Church party as a consequence of the political disturbances of the French Revolution cannot be assigned as a reason for the end of interdenominationalism in Manchester. Other disintegrative forces caused its demise.[25]

The story of the breakup of the town-wide schools in Birmingham and the Midlands at first glance appears to be more closely related to the politics of the day. In fact, the sordid details emerged only as part of Joseph Priestley's account of the High Church bigotry in which the King and Country riots were but the last episode.[26] Well before the fall of the Bastille and even before the emergence of the Test and Corporation Act repeal campaign, Dissent and Church had quarrelled in Birmingham over Sunday schools. It is not certain whether the original 1784 rules allowed children of Dissenters to attend their parents' place of worship; other children were automatically taken to Anglican services.[27] In any case, early in 1786, either for the first time or simply as a reconfirmation

[25] MS. *History of Sunday Schools in Manchester* signed at end by C. Rider, 10 December 1825. The author's father was one of the Wesleyan seceders who founded the new Sunday schools. He claims that the 'greatest liberality was maintained on both sides and the separation was amicably effected'; MS. *Sunday Schools in Manchester* by Rev. [James] Everett, n.d., both MSS. are in the Methodist Archive, London, Brotherton Collection

[26] In Priestley's *An Appeal to the Public on the subject of the Riots in Birmingham* ... (Birmingham, 1791) 5ff. he cited the breakup of the Sunday School and particularly the rescinding of the liberal rule as the kind of High Church bigotry which spawned the riots. The Rev. Edward Burn replied in *A Reply to the Rev. Dr. Priestley's Appeal to the Public ... in vindication of the clergy* ... (Birmingham, 1792) denying Priestley's charges. But apparently before the pamphlet was published someone pointed out to him the announcement in the *Birmingham Gazette* (2 October, 1786) where Priestley's charges were substantiated. He added an appendix claiming that the secretary had taken the minutes to the printer and had forgotten to pick them up so that they were never entered in the official minute books. In Rev. John Edward's *Letters to the British Nation ... A reply to Dr. Priestley's appeal ... on the riots in Birmingham being a joint production of the clergy of that place* (1791), pt. 2, no.6, p. 12 he prints extracts from the *Birmingham Gazette* which show that Burn was not only mistaken about the rescinding of the liberal law but also in holding that its passing was a minor affair

[27] The 1784 rules reprinted in Langford *A Century of Birmingham Life*, vol. 1, 410–11 allow church *or* chapel attendance; however Priestley and the other protagonists vary as to whether the schools began liberally, became restrictive, passed a liberal law and finally revoked the law or whether they began on the second step of this process

of accepted practice, Dissenters were given the right to take their children from Sunday school to chapel. By September, however,

> several gentlemen [had] threatened to withdraw their subscriptions to the Sunday school, in consequence of an alteration of the general rules made at the request of the Dissenters, on Friday, 10 Mar. 1786: Resolved that the resolution granting that request (which the Dissenters have not availed themselves of, and adhered to as they engaged) be rescinded; and, that in the future the rules, as they originally stood, be steadily attended to.[28]

According to Priestley the Dissenters continued to contribute to the old school in the hopes of its eventual liberalization, but they gave up after a year and formed their own schools. So, after a stormy two years interdenominationalism broke down in Birmingham.

The hatreds and lack of trust revealed in this pamphlet skirmish inspired a series of exposés on Sunday school breakups elsewhere in the region. The rector of Old Swinford claimed that ten schools, supported by communitywide subscription, were flourishing in his parish until 1789 or 1790.[29] Then the Presbyterians, in a spirit of proselytization, set up their own schools and bribed parents with money and clothing to withdraw their children from the religious and political safety of the old schools and to enroll them in the far less respectable Sunday schools of Dissent. Almost exactly the same charges were levelled in Warwick.[30] In both cases the Dissenters replied that, far from wishing to draw children away from the Church, they simply wanted to extend the field of service to those untouched by *any* religious or educational institution. The Unitarian Rev. J. Scott went so far as to reply that in many ways he preferred sending children to church rather than to chapel because the liturgy made Anglican services easier for the young to understand than the more free form worship of the chapel. As for teaching

---

[28] From the *Birmingham Gazette* (2 October 1786) reporting on a meeting 26 September 1786 reprinted in J. Priestley *A second appeal ... to which is added a letter from W. Russell ...* (Birmingham, 1792)

[29] Rev. Robert Foley *A Letter to Dr. Priestley, in answer to his late Publication, entitled 'An appeal ...'* (Stourbridge, 1793) answered by Rev. Benjamin Carpenter *A letter to Rev. R. Foley rector of Old Swinford in answer to the charges brought against the dissenters in Stourbridge ... To which is added an account of the proceedings at the Lyewaste by J. Scott* (1795)

[30] In Warwick the Anglican incumbent apparently preached a sermon against the Dissenters. This was answered in Rev. William Field *A Letter addressed to the inhabitants of Warwick in answer to ... charges against the dissenters ... by the Rev. Mr. Miller* (Birmingham, 1791); the reply came in Rev. Robert Miller and Rev. Hugh Langherne *Remarks upon a letter to the Printer of the Birmingham Gazette, dated Oct. 14, 1791 and also upon a letter ... by W. Field* (Warwick, 1791); Field rejoined in *A Second letter in reply to Remarks ...* (Birmingham, 1791)

a separate creed, he admitted that children in his school did not learn all the articles of the Anglican faith but that this was largely irrelevant since these were in any case too complicated for ten-year-olds to understand. Even the Anglicans could not and did not effectively teach the whole set. Finally, what money and clothes did change hands was only in compensation for those social services which parents allegedly lost as a result of leaving the Anglican schools.

Not all breakups produced such controversy; many were far less spectacular. In Stockport the interdenominational school split quietly in 1793 because one branch, dominated by the Methodists, found that it could raise more money and so could extend its services far more easily outside than inside the old organization.[31]

A Sunday school on the 'liberal Manchester Plan' was established in Coventry in 1785. But the clergy never attended committee meetings and refused in any way to cooperate with Dissenters who, they thought, had more than their share of students. After two years of sham 'liberality' all parties agreed that it was better to act separately.[32]

In Macclesfield teachers became exasperated with the lethargy of the interdenominational committee and set out on their own in 1797.[33] By 1812 they had two thousand children under their care and were willing to come to some arrangement with the Church. But the intransigence of the clergy prevented a rapprochement, and so the projected building which might have housed the interdenominational school, housed an Anglican institution instead. Meanwhile, the 'teachers' ' school solicited funds, mostly from the working classes, constructed their own buildings, and remained independent. Bingley Anglicans and Methodists held a common school until 1810 when they were split over the extempore prayer question; in Almondbury a joint Anglican-Methodist Sunday school formed in 1808 and met in the National School building until a quarrel over singing, prayers and opening addresses broke the partnership. And, despite decades of increasingly heated rivalry between Church and Dissent there were still in the 1830s a few schools like that in Portland which held its morning sessions in the Methodist Chapel and joined the Church school meeting in the afternoon.[34]

[31] W. I. Wild *The History of the Stockport Sunday School* (1891, privately printed)

[32] H. F. Burder *Memoir of the Rev. George Burder* (1833) 133

[33] *An Account of the Celebration of the Jubilee of the Macclesfield Sunday School, May 6, 1846* (Macclesfield, 1846) 19, 23–4

[34] John Ward *Historical Sketches of the Rise and Progress of Methodism in Bingley* (Bingley, 1863) 55; Richard Roberts *History of Methodism in Almondbury* (1864)

Finally, there were schools like those in Northampton or Nottingham which faded out of existence rather than ending crisply in a well-defined quarrel. In the former town the interdenominational school died quietly in 1820 as a result of denominational competition. In the latter a gradual takeover by the Methodists killed interdenominationalism. From the very beginning of this school in 1784, the problem of church and chapel attendance was prominent; in fact, the school was almost not started because of disagreement on this issue, and its opening was postponed for several months until it was cleared up.[45] Within four years there was also a separate Wesleyan school at Hockley Chapel, which may, in fact, have predated the interdenominational one on Exchange Street.[36] This school became increasingly the province of committed and energetic Methodist teachers, many of them recent converts, primarily from old Dissent.[37] The final breakup of the Exchange Street school was a consequence of the split within this dominant Methodist community. In 1797 the Kilhamite secession took over the institution, expelled the old Wesleyans, and established a New Connexion Sunday school. Other denominations followed suit in establishing their own schools—the Independents in 1798, the General and Particular Baptists the next year, the two parish churches of St Mary's and St Peter's in 1800 and 1801, and the old Wesleyans in 1803.[38]

In all these cases interdenominational Sunday schools broke up or faded away because of internal tensions: the increasing restiveness of Dissent with the confines of Anglican-dominated organizations, a clash of religious styles, and, perhaps most important, an increasing sense of identification of teachers and managers with the school. The French Revolution may well have intensified disintegrative forces; it certainly forced Evangelical Churchmen back into the traditional Anglican fold and made cooperation with Non-conformists in ventures like Sunday schools virtually impossible. But the very same practical issues which broke up the uneasy coalition of Anglicans and Dissenters in the

---

28–30; the latter provides an example of teachers opposing the split and setting up a school of their own based on broad principles; Robert Pearce *Methodism in Manchester and a Page of Church History* (1898) 131

[35] W. B. Carter *History of the Nottingham Sunday School Union* (Nottingham, 1860) 22–3

[36] See R. C. Swift 'Methodist Sunday Schools in Nottingham' *Proc. Wes. Hist. Soc.* vol. 33 (1961) 17–20, 36–40. John Blackner *History of Nottingham* (1815) claims the first Wesleyan Sunday school was founded in 1781, p. 128

[37] Swift ibid. and S. D. Chapman 'The Evangelical Revival and Education in Nottingham' *Trans. of the Thoroton Soc.* vol. 66 (1962)

[38] Swift *SS in Nottingham*, and Carter *Nottingham Union* . . . p. 59

late eighteenth century persisted into the nineteenth century causing conflicts and even schisms between Sunday schools and the churches or chapels with which they were nominally affi- liated. Interdenominationalism died because of the growth of the Sunday school community and not because of outside political forces.

This in turn points to the most important consequence of the failure of the early Sunday school experiment. So long as the schools were thought of as charities, taking as their models infirma- ries or almshouses, they remained agencies of the rich designed to do something to or for the poor. With the breakup of large town- wide schools into smaller units, they ceased being public charities and became the province of energetic and committed men and women of the local congregation or neighborhood. The death of interdenominationalism thus made possible the integration of the Sunday schools into the working-class community.

iv. SUNDAY SCHOOL, CHURCH AND CHAPEL

The degree of freedom that the Sunday school enjoyed varied bet- ween Church and Dissent and, within the Church, between Evan- gelical and other factions. But in general it was remarkably indepen- dent and so able to develop a life and spirit of its own.

For the non-Evangelical Churchman Sunday schools posed the problem of a lay agency with a vengeance. To meet the demand for education they would have to secure large numbers of lay teachers who would almost certainly demand some voice in the operation of the school and threaten to usurp some of the functions of the clergyman himself. On the other hand, as the Evangelical *Christian Observer* pointed out, if the Church of England did not use lay teachers, it might as well abandon popular education to the Methodists and other Dissenters who had no such scruples.[39] Churchmen yielded, if only through sheer necessity, but in so doing many became estranged from the Sunday school, which could thus achieve almost as much independence and self-govern- ment as the Dissenting school.

As early as 1790 the chaplain extra-ordinary to the King tried to reassure his colleagues that 'the comfort and ease and credit of the parochial clergy are connected with the prosperity of the Initiatory Seminaries [Sunday schools] for is not a considerable portion of that labour which properly belonged to us, hereby transferred to

[39] *Christian Observer* vol. 22 (1822) 105

others.'[40] They were not convinced and the political tensions of the French Revolution only made matters worse. Sunday schools, lay preaching, and itinerancy became equated in the minds of some clergy with anti-clericalism and sedition. That 'a vast number of those brought up at Sunday School were wandering from their proper callings, had become fanatical preachers, had deemed themselves qualified to hold disputations, had turned sceptic and infidel and anarchist'[41] was a common complaint. The hatred of the clergy for the Methodist preacher, a man without a parochial base, often with little education, wealth or standing, was transferred or extended to the Sunday school and other lay initiated projects. In condemning the Religious Tract Society, the *Anti-Jacobin Review* remarked that 'Sunday schools, then, (such at least as have been established by persons connected with this society) and lay preaching, it seems, are twin brothers.'[42] Their potential danger should not be overlooked for they were only too easily corrupted. 'A *school room* was erected—children were admitted—and a *mistress* was appointed; but alas! Short-lived was this delusive scene: The matron's armchair gradually grew into a pulpit—the children's benches were metamorphosed into *Pews*—and the School-Room became a Meeting house. Such practices merit exposure, and cannot fail to open the eyes of the world.'[43] Sunday schools were seen as the first step toward a lay religion with the consequent demise of the established church, good order, and stability.

Nowhere did these anti-lay feelings come out more strongly than in the so-called Blagdon controversy. The Evangelical Hannah More had established in the Mendip Hills at least seven Sunday schools, one of which was in Blagdon. Rev. Thomas Bere, curate of the parish, claimed that his wife heard the teacher in Miss More's school pray extemporaneously and asked that he be dismissed. Hannah More refused; this initiated a ferocious debate which was carried on in a half dozen periodicals and almost a score of pamphlets. Although the number of issues involved multiplied as the controversy wore on, the underlying question remained the degree to which laymen might participate in certain aspects of the Church's work. According to Bishop Lavington, it was 'one of the most glaring instances of lay interference, that [had] occurred since

[40] Samuel Glasse, DD, FRS *The Piety, Wisdom and Policy of promoting Sunday Schools . . . 24 Sept. 1786* (1786) 17

[41] *Anti-Jacobin Review* vol. 7 (October 1800) 216–17; the whole case is summarized in Rev. R. Polwhele, ed. *The Enthusiasm of Methodists and Papists considered by Bishop Lavington* (new ed. 1833) ccxxix-ccxxxi

[42] *Anti-Jacobin Review* vol. 13 (1802) 436

[43] *Orthodox Churchman's Magazine* vol. 1 (1801) 306

the institution of Sunday schools'.[44] The wisdom of teaching the poor to read was seldom questioned; William Cobbett, pioneer popular journalist, found himself on the side of the anti-Sunday school King and Country faction.[45] In fact, the debate revolved around Sunday schools almost by accident. They were simply the newest and potentially most important arena for lay activity within the Church and so were particularly suspect to the anti-Evangelical clergy. In the end, Hannah More's school survived, but one faction of the Church came away with the conviction that in Sunday schools, regardless of the potential good, 'no lay inter-ference can be allowed'; that the clergy must 'leave nothing to the discretion of a master or a mistress'; or at the very least that in all matters religious, 'the superintendence of a Sunday school should be entrusted, whenever their professional avocations render it practicable, to the clergy.'[46]

The reluctance of some Churchmen to give the lay-dominated Sunday school a free hand is reflected by the fact that in 1851 twelve per cent of the Church's teaching force still consisted of paid teachers who were far less independent than their voluntary counterparts and were only minimally identified with the school. Voluntary teachers were almost universal in Non-conformist schools.[47] The arguments of an 1822 pamphlet—that voluntary teachers were not trying to usurp the clergyman's place, that older students often left the Church school for one of Dissent because they preferred gratuitous teachers, that adherence to paid teachers gave competing schools an unearned edge were still being marshalled in the 1860s.[48]

Clerical hostility notwithstanding, the lay Sunday school flourished even within the establishment. Outright opposition gave way to indifference. Of course, some Church Sunday schools, like the one in Somerset taught by the rector, his cook, his servant, and the cook's wife, remained intimately tied to the clergy. The only known survey of Anglican Sunday school administration

[44] *Lavington* ..., Polwhele, ed., p. cxxxi; the most complete account of the Blagdon controversy is in F. K. Brown *Fathers* ... Ch. 6; fifteen tracts on the subject, which cover most of the ground, are bound together in the Bodleian under the heading. 'Hannah More, Blagdon Controversy'

[45] *Cobbett's Annual Register* vol. 2 (1802) col. 119–122

[46] *Anti-Jacobin Review* vol. 11 (1802) 181; Horsely *Charge* ... op. cit. p. 26; *British Critic* vol. 20 (1802) 437

[47] See p. 110 below

[48] *An Appeal to the Members of the Church of England on the Subject of Sunday Schools with especial reference to the effects of lay agency* (1823) especially pp. 18–22; Rev. J. Traviss Lockwood *Sunday Schools: How to Revive and Utilize them, with an intro-duction by the Lord Bishop of Oxford* (1868) 2–18

found that something less than half of all London schools were under the immediate direction of the clergy.[49] But qualitative evidence supports the view that Church schools were relatively independent.

A nationally publicized sermon for Sunday schools in 1832 complained of the 'little care that is taken to give efficiency to these establishments, by those who profess themselves to be their supporters and patrons', lay and clerical.[50] A leading Church magazine in 1842 tried to raise clerical enthusiasm by pointing out the practical value of Sunday schools in preparing children for confirmation, but apparently with little success.[51] The *Evangelical Magazine* pointed out that if something was not done to bring the schools nearer to the Church and the clergy, 'the great body of their children and youth will pass out of their hands into unregeneracy.'[52] The establishment's first venture into the Sunday school periodicals market in 1848 began with the admission that once 'it [the Sunday School] was in moral and mental isolation; it was a green oasis in a sandy dessert, the only means of secular education available', but added hopefully that, as it became more religious, it would draw nearer the Church.[53]

But twenty years later it was still hoped that Sunday schools would 'become for the future what they were intended to be in the past', viz. a part of the Church's catechumen system. Looking back, the same spokesman pointed out that 'In former days the relation of the Established Church to Sunday schools was merely theoretical. Beyond the administration of a religious rite, as little was attempted towards cultivation of the religious life in children as if the Church did not believe in the possession by them of religious susceptibilities.'[54] Like the Church Missionary Society, another lay organization ignored or rebuffed by the clergy, Sunday schools probably became increasingly close to the Church in the late nineteenth century. Earlier, their ties had been tenuous.[55] But all the forces which made for Sunday school independence within the establishment were more powerful and suffered fewer restraints within Dissent.

[49] *Journal of a Somerset Rector: John Skinner ... 1772–1839* ed. Howard Coombs (1930) 82; 'Church of England Committee of Enquiry: Report on the Metropolis' *Sunday School Teachers' Magazine* (1841) col. 126–132

[50] 'Sermon for Sunday Schools on Prov. xxii, 6' in the *Christian Remembrancer* vol. 14 (1832) 623–8, esp. p. 626

[51] *Church of England Magazine* vol. 13 (1842) p. 121

[52] *Evangelical Magazine* new ser. vol. 16 (1838) 628–9

[53] *The Church of England Sunday School Quarterly Magazine* vol. 1 (March 1848) 3

[54] *Sunday School Reform* (3rd edn. n.d. but *c.* 1870) 2–3

[55] The analogy is developed in Eugene Stock *The History of the Church Missionary Society* (1899) vol. 1, 243

First, Non-conformist theology allowed laymen a far greater
part in Christian work than did Anglican doctrine. By and large,
it placed the priesthood on a par with the flock, allowing the latter
more freedom to cultivate their own particular religious garden.
Second, from a purely practical point of view, Dissenting ministers
were severely circumscribed in controlling the religious activities
of the laity. In some congregations, they held their position at the
sufferance of the membership. In the various branches of Methodism, which claimed the allegiance of over twenty per cent of all
Sunday school scholars, ministers were only stationed a few years
in each community. Itinerants might come and go, but the Sunday
school community with its own management and traditions
remained unchanged. Furthermore, a shortage of manpower
made control of chapel life outside of the large urban centers
virtually impossible even for the highly organized Wesleyan
Connexion. In Yorkshire, for example, there were, in 1830, 658
chapels but only 118 preachers, most of whom might have to travel
ten, twenty, and in a few cases nearly thirty miles every sabbath so
as to give sermons in two or three scattered preaching places.[56]
The *Minutes of Conference* in 1851 reported 6,579 Wesleyan Congregations but only 1024 full-time preachers.

As a consequence of both theological and practical considerations,
the Sunday schools of Dissent were relatively free of congregational
or ministerial control. The *Methodist New Connexion Magazine*,
for example, noted that

> Another great evil which is gaining ground in these institutions
> is a progessive separation from the control and interference of
> the Church. In too many cases our Sunday schools are becoming
> distinct and separate communities, governed by laws which the
> leaders' meeting never made and executed by men whom the
> Church would never sanction or approve.[57]

This assessment gained support when a survey showed that six-
sevenths of all the Connexion's schools had management committees
chosen entirely by teachers and subscribers, with no say for the
leaders' meeting.[58] One Baptist source blamed the failure of Sunday
schools in recruitment on 'the dissension between the Churches
and the schools, for at present they scarcely seem to be parts of the
same system'.[59] Another noted that Sunday schools 'have hitherto

[56] William B. Haigh *Leeds Synopsis of Wesleyan Methodism in Yorkshire* (Leeds, 1830)
20–21

[57] New ser. vol. 4 (March 1826) 457

[58] *Report of the Committee on Sabbath Schools appointed by the Longton Conference as
per resolution 14 of Minutes 1840; Minutes 1841*

[59] *Baptist Magazine* vol. 25 (1833) 326

been too far removed, in most cases, from the efficient control, and too little aided by the experiences and counsel of Ministers and Churches'.[60] Rev. John Morrison, the famous Congregational preacher, berated the church for its neglect of the Sunday school, while the *Congregational Magazine* condemned Sunday school teachers for their ostentatious display of independence during the Jubilee celebrations in 1831.[61] And in Wesleyan Methodism, where antagonism between school and chapel surfaced most often, it was generally held by those in authority that the chief abuse of the Sunday school was that 'it should excite in any a spirit of insubordination, or infringement on the proper prerogatives of the pastoral office'. Teachers must not forget, though indeed they often did, that they acted legitimately only by permission and under authority of the pastor.[62]

Some ministers and some denominations did very little about this situation; they simply accepted the status quo and went about their business. As a well-informed writer of the late 1840s remarked, 'many of our larger churches lamentably disregard those [Sunday schools] they have instituted', while many Christian pastors, 'absorbed perhaps in their pastoral and more public duties, seem greatly to overlook, and even to forget these lowly subjects'.[63] Problems of membership and recruitment made such neglect dangerous. By the early 1840s the rapid growth of Dissent had come to an end, and earlier, during the 1830s, a revitalized establishment provided fierce competition. Outdoor preaching and great[7] revivals had lost their effectiveness in the more restricted market of the 1830s and 1840s.[64] 'We have trusted more for the increase of the church to remarkable interpositions of God's grace, in reference to individuals or multitudes, than to the use of the regular means which He has appointed for perpetuating the praise of His name . . .'[65] That is, the potential of Sunday schools for bringing in new members was not being exploited.

[60] *Liverpool Baptist Association Circular* (1832)

[61] Rev. John Morrison, 'The Obligation of Churches with Reference to Sunday Schools' *SS Teachers' Magazine* new ser. vol. 12 (1841) col. 449–59; *Congregational Magazine* new ser. vol. 7 (September 1831) 577–8. The editors were objecting to statements like 'Ministers of the gospel, 'tis true, are aware of the power possessed by Sunday School teachers but they too frequently appear as if they were jealous of it'; or 'Emancipate Sunday schools from the thraldom in which its half friends keep it', etc. made by Union and other school spokesmen. See also *Evangelical Magazine* new ser. vol. 9 (1831) p. 39; and W. F. Hook *Letter to the Bishop of St. David's* (1846) 47

[62] *Wesleyan Methodist Magazine* 3rd ser. vol. 14 (1835) 612–14

[63] Rev. Thomas Timpson *The Memoirs of Sunday School Teachers* (1849) 293

[64] See Allan Gilbert 'The Growth of Non-conformity . . .'

[65] Samuel D. Waddy *A Sermon on the Importance and Obligation of Early Religious Education* (Manchester, 1838) 20

'Statistics actually taken', another Wesleyan spokesman observed in 1854, 'have demonstrated beyond the possibility of doubt, that vast multitudes of children are incessantly passing through our Sunday schools and then becoming . . . utterly alienated from our religious fellowship.'[66] An Anglican school inspector lamented: 'It is a humiliating fact, yet nevertheless a true fact, that the Church of England appears to fail in retaining any but a minimal hold over young men of the artisan class. May it not be owing to the defect in our Sunday school teaching . . . ?'[67] Spiritual statistics from one county organization of Independent churches found that seventeen chapels and thirty-four village stations with 2,100 Sunday school students managed to recruit only ninety-one persons which, after sixty removals and deaths were subtracted, yielded a most unimpressive gain of thirty-one souls.[68]

Throughout this period statistics from Sunday school unions, from other organizations, and from individual chapels were equally grim. 87 out of 12,000 students in the Nottingham Union joined the church in 1822, a lower proportion than the 99 out of 11,000 who joined the year before.[69] 30 scholars joined the church out of some 14,000 belonging to the Halifax Union in 1843; 115 out of 13,000 joined in Hull three years later.[70] Even Sunday schools closely tied to a congregation did little better. In forty-seven years the famous Manchester school under the Rev. James Roby, with an average enrolment throughout the period of well over a thousand, induced only 260 students and teachers to join the church.[71] The first scholar to join Maze Pond Chapel in London came a full seven years after the school's founding; among the best records was that of Whitefield's Church, London, which held on to one in seven students.[72] Though evidence is scanty, only between 1.5 per cent and 4 per cent of total Sunday school enrolment would at any one time belong to a church or chapel.[73] In short, Sunday schools did very badly in recruitment, a fact which helps to explain

[66] Anon. (but attributed in Methodist Archive to Samuel Jackson) *Wesleyan Sunday Schools as They are and as They Ought to Be*; or, *the Isolated and Combined Methods of Evangelizing Children* (1854) 10

[67] Rev. B. W. Wilson, MA *Plain Hints for Sunday School Teachers* (n.d., c. 1870) 5

[68] *Congregational Magazine* 3rd ser. vol. 4 (1840) 540

[69] *London Christian Instructor* vol. 4 (1821) 391, and vol. 5 (1822) 614

[70] *SS Teachers' Magazine* new ser. vol. 14 (1843) 293–4, and vol. 18 (1846) 231

[71] *The Union Magazine for Sunday School Teachers* vol. 2 (1845) 279

[72] 'Historical Sketch of Whitfield's Churches' in John Campbell, DD *Letters on Wesleyan Methodism in England and the Colonies* (1847) 16–17; R. Reeve, *History of Maze Pond Sunday School: 1801–1901* (1901) 15

[73] For example see *SS Teachers' Magazine* new ser. vol. 18 (1847) 92 for Birmingham or *The Sunday School Teachers' Re-union* . . . (Leeds, 1848) 5 for Wesleyan schools in the four Leeds circuits

the eagerness with which denominational authorities sought to gain control of schools and set them on a more profitable path.

Their reactions to the situation varied in intensity. The Primitive Methodist Conference, for example, issued a directive in 1837 ordering due attention to Sunday schools and emphasizing the importance of harmonizing school hours with preaching; the New Connexion in 1841 took similarly timid steps.[74] Some Congregational boards insisted that Sunday schools be closely linked to the chapel as a condition for obtaining building grants.[75] Only the Bunting-dominated Wesleyan Conference pushed the issue of control to its limits, far enough to induce major schisms between school and chapel. Moreover, the fact that substantially the same resolution was passed by Conference in 1808, 1817, 1827, 1828 and 1841 indicates the difficulties it encountered in gaining control of Methodist Sunday schools. The first pronouncement ordered that '... all travelling preachers, where Sunday schools are established, be members of the Committees of those schools which belong to us; and let all the Superintendents preside at these meetings.[76] In 1817 Conference reasserted the principle that it is 'essentially necessary' for Sunday schools to be as closely connected with the Church of Christ as possible and to operate only such hours as do not interfere with divine worship.[77] The Revs Watson, Marsden, Newton, and Bunting produced a lengthy set of 'General Principles and Rules to be Observed in the Management of Methodist Sunday Schools' in 1827, the overriding principle of which was that Sunday schools were to be strictly concerned with religious education and therefore were to be directly under the management of religious authorities.[78] In practice this meant that all the officers of the school except the auditor had to be members of the Methodist society, that superintendent preachers were to be *ex officio* members of the governing body, and that the other members were to be chosen according to a strict formula which allowed teachers only one quarter of the places and even then only if the teachers were also Methodists. The rigid enforcement of these rules finally precipitated the crisis between chapel and school which had been latent in their relationship for decades.

In 1828 chapel building grants were made contingent on com-

[74] *Primitive Methodist Magazine* vol. 18 (1837) 22 and *Methodist New Connexion Magazine* new ser. vol. 9 (1841)

[75] *Congregational Magazine* new ser. vol. 4 (1828) 391; see also *Baptist Magazine* new ser. vol. 25 (1833) 325–6 and new ser. vol. 26 (1834) 14, 59–61

[76] *Minutes of the Wesleyan Methodist Conference* (1808) Q. 25

[77] Ibid. (1817) Q. 25

[78] Ibid vol. 5 (1827) 284–91

D

pliance with the 1827 regulations.[79] And finally in 1841 Conference's Education Committee once again laid down that Sunday schools 'shall avoid a latitudinarian character, by being avowedly and practically connected, as to their government and denomination, with Wesleyan Methodism'.[80] The necessity of repeating essentially the same rule over a period of thirty years and the tenacity with which the local community defended its schools against ministerial encroachment attests both to the continued independence of the Wesleyan Sunday school and to the support it commanded among the rank and file.

Three examples of school-chapel conflict, all arising out of a newly arrived Buntingite minister's attempts to assert his and the Conference's authority, illustrate this point. The Sunday school in Burslem was Wesleyan in origin, but somehow early in the century it dropped the denominational title in its name, although it continued to rent its building from the chapel trustees. A long dispute over conflicting times of worship and instruction finally came to a head when a school prayer meeting began to draw away large numbers of the congregation. This was exacerbated by the teachers' refusal to make preachers full committee members. Relations were strained still further and teachers displayed a marked hostility towards two leaders representing the Society, who were actually admitted. Finally, the preachers tried to evict the school from its building, and the committee, composed entirely of teachers, fought back by calling a town meeting, publishing a number of handbills, and taking the issue to the people. The school ultimately lost the battle but won the war. It seceded from the chapel and prospered on its own. Furthermore, it triumphed in maintaining what the Conference's defender derisively called 'the grand secret of all this maneuvering on the part of managers and teachers': '. . . a fixed determination to conduct the school upon the principle of *entire independence*'.[81]

Chapel authorities or superintendent preachers precipitated similar crises in Chester and Marple by trying to impose their authority on the Sunday school. The Rev. Robert Jackson in Chester first withdrew annual sermon rights from two schools which refused to allow their committees to be taken over by chapel appointees, then changed the locks on one so that the new superin-

---

[79] Ibid. (1828) Q. 18

[80] *Report of the Wesleyan Education Committee* (1841) section II. 1

[81] *A Vindication of the Measures Lately Adopted by the Trustees of the Wesleyan Methodist Chapel, Burslem, in Reference to the Sunday School Conducted on their Premises by* INVESTI-GATOR (Burslem, 1836), although written to oppose the popular cause, nevertheless quotes extensively from the relevant documents. See especially p. 18

tendents, but not the old, could gain admission, and finally when the new authorities were rejected by the children, ordered that the portals of the school be bricked up.[82] In Marple The Rev. H. Kellett tried much the same trick. On taking his appointment, he found the school which, governed by a gentleman who had once attended Methodist chapel, got its money from annual sermons but brought its scholars to chapel only every six weeks. After much struggle he got new rules passed, the most obnoxious of which, as far as the school party was concerned, gave a decisive voice to the leaders' meeting in the choice of school officials. The school refused to comply, and Kellett had a new door put on the building which was adjacent to the chapel. The school authorities broke the lock; Kellett put on a new one. After five weeks of new locks and breaking in, Kellett confiscated the school's library and records and won his victory.[83]

In the last two cases there is no record of what became of the dissident Sunday school or its members. Many other examples of controversy between school and chapel over attendance at worship, and more often over the acceptability of writing instruction on the sabbath, ended in a resounding victory for the school.[81] Although Methodist Sunday schools in the large towns were, by the 1840s, under the direction of the chapel authorities, they often faced the competition of rival establishments that were born out of the struggle for control. Sunday schools in small towns and villages without resident Conference preachers probably maintained their independence for the whole period of this investigation.

Many Anglican Sunday schools and the majority of those connected with Dissent were largely free of clerical interference up to 1850 and perhaps for decades more. Each school was in the hands of teachers or managers who were responsible only to themselves.

v. COSTS AND FINANCE

Before the voluntary replaced the paid teacher in about 1800, a Sunday school could be expensive. The customary fee for a day's instruction was 1d. per pupil. This expense, combined with the costs of heat, light, building rent and maintenance, books and supplies, resulted in a total expenditure of 3s. 6d. to 4s. per year

[82] Rev. T. Allin *Letters to the Rev. John Maclean Containing an Exposition of the Government of Wesleyan Methodism* (2nd ed. 1835) 41–5

[83] Rev. H. Kellett/Rev. Thomas Sayham, 24 February 1820, MS. letter, Methodist Archive

[84] See pp. 144 ff. below

for each student. When teachers ceased to be paid, the cost per pupil dropped to between 2s. and 2s. 6d. per pupil, a bit more in schools offering free copy books or arithmetic tables, perhaps a bit less at schools not offering free supplies or at those sufficiently large to reduce the overhead. On a *per diem* basis this compared favorably with the 10s. per year allowed for each student in day school by the 1863 Revised Code and, if gratuitous teachers are costed, comes to a good deal more. Using actual *per capita* costs and the enrolment figures from Table 5, it may be calculated that about £57,000 was expended annually on Sunday school operations in 1818 and between £200,000 and £300,000 in 1851.[85]

In addition to annual expenses there were the costs of the building. About half the Sunday schools in England occupied their own buildings, about forty per cent used church or chapel facilities, and the remainder rented rooms elsewhere. Of course, the church or chapel rooms might have been specially built for the use of Sunday schools and therefore ought logically to be included in the special purpose building category. Edward Baines estimated in 1847 that each of the 16,827 Sunday schools reported by Lord Kerry in 1835 had spent £250 on its building and that the voluntary principle could thus account for a total expenditure of £5,000,000 'to which the government contributed nothing—not so much as a smile'. His premises for carrying out the estimate are faulty, but the result is not far from the truth.[86]

An alternative estimate for 1851 might be calculated in the following way. Assume that half of the 2,100,000 children enrolled in Sunday school in 1851 were in that half of the schools which occupied their own buildings, yielding an average of just over a hundred pupils per school. Now schools of a size sufficient to accommodate such a number cost about £3.50 per pupil, using wage and materials estimates recommended by the Committee on Education of Privy Council. Multiplying this figure by the enrolment gives a building cost estimate of £3,700,000. If twenty per cent of the church and chapel space is presumed to have been built specially to accommodate a Sunday school and if its cost is also £3.50 per pupil, then a figure near Baines's £5,000,000 is

[85] Almost all sermons and guides on Sunday school practice give estimates of costs; annual reports give actual *per capita* expenditure. Newspaper and periodical reports of anniversary sermons often give the amount collected, the number of students in the school, along with the assurance that the sum given covers a year's operating expenses. Frederic Hill *National Education: Its Present State and Prospects* vol. 1 (1836) 113 gives 2s.–2s. 6d. as a reasonable estimate of annual *per capita* expenditure

[86] Edward Baines, Jr. *Letters to the Rt. Hon. John Russell on State Education* (7th ed. Leeds, 1847) 7th letter

obtained. However crude the estimates, at a five per cent discount rate, something on the order of £200,000 to £250,000, must be added to the current expenses of £200,000 to £300,000 in 1851.[87]

In the early days Sunday school finances followed old established patterns. Some schools were endowed, like the one in Twickenham which received a £100 legacy in 1789, or an Anglican school in Reading which collected an income of £127 each year from its invested funds; but by 1833 only 544 of 14,924 schools were even partially financed in this way.[88] Some schools, like those of Hannah More, or William Currie of Wellingborough, or the Strutts of Belper, were financed through the largesse of individual men and women. A few received money from the poor rates or from some other public sources.[89] Finally, the town-wide interdenominational Sunday schools and a few large schools throughout the nineteenth century got their funds through combining subscriptions solicited at large with contributions gathered at a charity sermon. But most Sunday schools throughout the nineteenth century received all their funds from annual sermons attended by a broad public, often of the same class as those for whom the schools were intended.

The commonly accepted model of the bourgeoisie buying social peace and political tranquillity through contributions to the Sunday school applies only in a few large cities or small company towns. Otherwise the annual sermon or anniversary was a major occasion for the working-class community, a time for celebration and generous giving. As one minister complained 'The Sunday school [in the mid-nineteenth century] was the most popular of social and religious institutions ... the anniversary the great religious festival of the year. Collections on this day were nothing

[87] Building costs are estimated from those given for schools of about 100 students in the *Minutes of the Committee of Council on Education* (1840) (254) xl. Estimates for the late 1810s are given in the *Annual Reports* of the National Society and are repeated with no change until the 1830s. It is not clear why these estimates are one-half to two-thirds of those given by the Privy Council for buildings which meet its standards. However the costs of individual buildings obtained for about 20 schools make it clear that regional variations and changes in cost over time make the estimates above only a rough guide to real expenditures

[88] R. S. Cobbett *Memorials of Twickenham* (1872) 149; *Abstract of Returns relative to the State of Education* op. cit. 1835 (62) xliii, pp. 1326–7

[89] M. More *Mendip Annals*; Eastman *Robert Raikes* ... p. 10; R. S. Fitton and A. P. Wadsworth *The Strutts and the Arkwrights, 1758–1830* (Manchester, 1958) 102–3; for finance out of the poor rates see Joshua Holden *A Short History of Todmorden* (Manchester, 1912) 197 which also provides an interesting example of cooperation between Methodists and Anglicans in the management of a Sunday school well after 1800; for other public sources see, for example, W. Scruton *Old Bradford* p. 336; and John Noake *Notes and Queries for Worcestershire* (1856) 38

like the ordinary collection.' The open plate and not, as usual, the closed box went around four or five times until enough had been collected to finance the school for the year. This, he adds, would never have been tolerated at other times.[90] Another minister objected to the secular frivolity of the annual sermon. When he arrived at one chapel to deliver his address, he 'found it crammed most inconveniently; the passages within its precincts were equally crammed.' He goes on to describe the large number of musical instruments, singers and other musicians, the children in new clothes, and the hundreds of proud parents who were there to enjoy the music and see the children rather than to listen to the sermon. And so that no doubts as to the profanity of the occasion could linger, he noted that 'The sums of money collected on these occasions were frequently very great; in many cases eight or ten times as much as could be obtained for any other object.[91] The *Northern Star* announced some forty-two separate anniversary occasions in its local intelligence section for 1838. Evidently Sunday school sermons were part of the lives and interests of those who read the Chartist newspaper: £83 were collected at Christ Church, Bradford, when Dr Hook preached to 'a church crowded to excess with both dissenters and others; a 'handsome collection' was taken at the Ashton New Connexion Sunday School, where pieces by Handel and Haydn were performed to enliven the occasion; readers were urged to attend an Easter oratorio and sermon at the Hunslet Chapel in benefit of the Baptist and New Connexion Sunday schools.[92] Clearly, the working classes were willing to pay for their Sunday schools.

vi. THE SOCIAL COMPOSITION OF THE SUNDAY SCHOOL

a. Students

Sunday schools in the late eighteenth century were intended to educate the children of those who could not, or would not, provide education themselves. Some explicitly excluded all except the lower orders:

No subscriber shall recommend any children whose parents may be supposed capable of sending them to any other school.

[90] F. W. MacDonald *Reminiscences of my Early Ministry* (1913) 20–2
[91] 'Sunday School Anniversaries' by 'S' in *Sunday School Union Magazine* vol. 7 (1850) 106–7
[92] *Northern Star* (5 May 1838) 5; (18 August 1838) 5; (10 March 1838) 5

No children admitted to this school but such as are by poverty
deprived of the means of learning on the weekday.

The objects of this charity shall be poor persons of either sex
over 6.[93]

Others, founded by working men and women, simply taught the
poor children of the neighborhood. And, although later rules were
not so explicit about the class of those suitable for Sunday school
education, it remained almost entirely the province of the working
classes.

'The children of the upper and middle classes do not generally
attend Sunday school,' said the usually well-informed educational
reformer Edward Baines. The *Baptist Magazine*, in one of a series
of articles, praised teachers for their work with the poor, ignorant
children who frequented Sunday schools. Horace Mann helped
readers of the 1851 education census interpret his statistics by
explaining that Sunday school enrolments were comprised mainly,
though not exclusively, of working-class children. The *New Connexion Magazine* in 1841 stated flatly that Sunday schools should be
for the poor only.[94]

Occasionally someone questioned the wisdom of admitting only
those who could not get an education elsewhere. Mrs Trimmer
went so far as to seek out 'a few children from parents who could
afford to send them to day school . . . [thus giving] the poor children
something to emulate'.[95] By the late 1830s some Sunday school
and denominational spokesmen began to view this policy as socially
undesirable in itself and as a barrier to the integration of the school
with the church or chapel community. Relations between church
and school, it was argued, were strained because the former identified the latter 'chiefly with teaching the children of the poor to
read'. They never saw the Sunday school as 'an institution to lay
the basis of a Christian society' and therefore middle-class children
never attended. 'The biggest defect with Sunday schools now',
suggested a writer to the *Teachers' Magazine* in 1843, 'is their identification with the very poor . . . they are disdainfully called charity

[93] 'Rules and Orders for the Government of the Sunday Schools of Manchester'
(1784); 'Rules of the Nottingham Methodist Sunday School' (179?) in R. C. Swift
Early SS in Notts. op. cit.; *Plan of a Society for the Support and Encouragement of Sunday
Schools in London and Vicinity founded in 1798* (1811)

[94] Edward Baines *The Social, Educational and Religious State of the Manufacturing
Districts* (1843) 25; *Baptist Magazine* vol. 24 (1832) 95–6; *Census: Education* [1851],
p. lxxii; *Methodist New Connexion Magazine* (1841) 383–4

[95] Sarah Trimmer *The Oeconomy of Charity* (1787) 139; see also *Evangelical Magazine*
vol. 6 (1798) 16

schools.'[96] The Revs Samuel Waddy and Samuel Jackson both argued that, as Sunday schools became less involved with teaching reading and writing and more exclusively involved with religious instruction, they should and would draw children from all classes of the congregation. 'Even those who had a respectable education, but on whose spiritual improvement no labour had been employed' should attend Sunday school, urged the *New Connexion Magazine* in 1848. The Rev. John Curwen in his 'Essentials of a Sunday School Reformation' gave a more positive reason for broadening the class base: 'it will bring the rich and poor together, and teach them from childhood, the salutary lesson that God is no respecter of persons.' Very little, however, had come of these movements by mid-century.[97]

Although it is clear that Sunday scholars came largely from the working classes, it is not possible to specify any more precisely from which strata of this broad group the students were drawn. Contemporary reports are ambiguous. In Yorkshire about 1812 there was apparently 'a prejudice amongst the better off of the labouring classes against sending their children because they thought [Sunday schools] suitable only for the lowest and most necessitous poor'.[98] On the other hand, by 1840 in the mining and manufacturing districts it was only the poorest and least provident of the working classes who failed to send their children.[99] James Hole, a leader of the Mechanics' Institute movement, saw in Sunday schools the potential for 'uniting class with class' because of the loyalty the schools commanded among 'the *superior* portion of the working classes'.[100]

Evidence from individual schools and from working-class biographies supports the conclusion that Sunday school pupils came from all strata of the working classes, skilled and unskilled alike. Of 101 children in the Spitalfields Sunday School, for example, half not surprisingly were from weavers' families. But children of four shoemakers, two tailors, two carpenters, two tripe dressers,

[96] *Sunday School Magazine and Journal of Christian Instruction* 40 (1838) 195; *SS Teachers' Magazine* (1843) 134, letter from 'Alfred' London

[97] Rev. Samuel A. Waddy *A Sermon on the Importance of Sunday Schools* (1838) and Rev. Samuel Jackson *Sunday Schools as they are and as they Ought to Be* (1852). Both are in the Methodist Archive pamphlet file; *Methodist New Connexion Magazine* (1849) 62–8; *Independent Magazine* (1842) 8 ff. reprints Curwen's pamphlet

[98] Society for Bettering the Condition of the Poor *Reports* vol. 6 (1812) 139–46

[99] This point emerges clearly from the accounts of Sunday school anniversaries in these areas and more generally from the sources from which these are taken. See Ch. 6, p. 177

[100] James Hole *'Light, More Light!' on the Present State of Education amongst the Working Classes of Leeds* (1860) 30 (my emphasis)

two basket makers, one lamplighter, a cooper, a bricklayer, shop-
keeper, turner, strap maker, dyer, and wirer were also represented.[101] The parents of most of the children in the great Stockport
Sunday School were employed in the town's dominant industry,
cotton manufacturing, but small tradesmen, artisans, and the
occasional victualler were also represented. Of the ninety per cent
of students in full employ, the great majority of both boys and
girls worked in factories, but a significant number were apprenticed
in more skilled trades—shoemaking, tailoring, and printing for
boys and bonnet-making, dressmaking, and hat-making for girls.
Reports for Birmingham in 1843 reveal similar occupational
patterns.[102]

Finally, the sheer numbers that attended Sunday school in some
regions imply that almost all children of the working class or the
'lower orders' must at one time or another have attended Sunday
school. As many as one-quarter of the population in parts of industrial Lancashire and Yorkshire attended Sunday school in 1843,
and almost one-fifth were enrolled in Bedfordshire, Derbyshire,
Huntingdonshire and parts of other counties in 1851.[103] More
than ninety per cent of those over fifteen employed by twelve
Manchester cotton mills in 1852 had at some time attended Sunday
school.[104] Almost eighty per cent of all children aged seven to
eighteen who were employed in the mines near Oldham actually
attended Sunday school and only among those between the ages
of eleven and twelve were less than seventy per cent enrolled.[105]
All the evidence thus suggests that, although different strata of
the working classes patronized different day schools that varied
in price and prestige, all sections sent their children to Sunday
school.

[101] *Annual Report of the London Mission* (1846) 6–7; I owe this reference to Anna
Davin who kindly sent me a Xerox copy of the pages cited

[102] Names and addresses of parents in Stockport were obtained from the MS. SSS
3 vols. *Enrollment Registers*, ... Using local directories it was possible to obtain
occupations of less than 15 per cent of these. Presumably the remainder were
employed in some occupation not worthy of listing, most probably that of a cotton
operative. For children's occupations in Stockport see *Supplementary Reports from
the Commissioners, appointed to collect information ... relative to the employment of Children
in factories ...* 1834 (167) xix, D1, p. 158; for Birmingham see *Appendix to the
Second Report of the Commissioners inquiring into the employment and condition of children
in mines and manufacturies 1843* [432] xv. f. 200–203, f. 98–99

[103] See E. Baines *State of the Manufacturing Districts* op. cit. p. 23; see also Table 7

[104] *Report from the Select Committee on Manchester and Salford Education, ... together
with minutes of evidence* 1852 (499) xi, p. 301. The figure is given as 8.2 per cent
who have *not* attended Sunday school

[105] Calculated from *Employment of Children: Appendix to the First Report of the
Commissioners (Mines) 1842* [382] xvii, p. 835

As for the Sunday scholars themselves, many were, in fact, not children at all. Their ages ranged from five to over thirty. On the one extreme there were Sunday schools exclusively for adults which by 1816 contained over four thousand students in twenty towns and cities. In Bristol alone between 1812 and 1832, 2,333 men and, more significantly given the discriminatory nature of elementary education for girls, 12,445 women attended Sunday schools which taught reading, writing, arithmetic, and, toward the end of the period, geography as well.[106] But even in schools not intended especially for adults, about ten per cent of the scholars were over fifteen during the 1830s; there was a considerably higher proportion of older students both in industrial areas where regular labor for children began at an early age and in Sunday schools with particularly diversified offerings. Thirty-two per cent of all students were over sixteen in one Halifax school; between fourteen and eighteen per cent were over fifteen in the schools of Bury, Salford, Manchester and Birmingham, twenty-one per cent of males and twenty-seven per cent of females were over that age in Stockport.[107] By way of comparison, the median age in one large Birmingham Sunday school was thirteen, while in five local charity schools it was only ten.[108] Various informants suggest that by 1850 the proportion of both older scholars and those under five might have increased, but Sunday schools were never the exclusive province of the very young.[109]

Some observers thought that women were more eager to attend than were men. 'I find mothers of the children and grownup women have begged to be admitted ... sorry I am to say that none of the other sex have shown the same desire,' reported Raikes. Hannah and Martha More too thought that girls were far more eager to be admitted and far quicker to learn than were boys.[110] Nevertheless, enrolment statistics for the country as a whole show an almost

[106] J. W. Hudson *The History of Adult Education* (1851) 6–13

[107] For estimates of ages in the country as a whole see J. G. Fleet *The Distinctive Features of Sunday Schools* (1850) and W. H. Watson *The Senior Class; and the Mode of Conducting it* (1845). For ages in Manchester, Salford, and Bury see *Report of the Manchester Statistical Society on the State of Education in Manchester in 1834* (1835), ... *in Salford in 1835* (1836), ... *in Bury in 1835* (1835); for Birmingham see Birmingham Statistical Society, 'Report on the State of Education in Birmingham', *Journal of the Royal Statistical Society* vol. 3 (1840) 25 ff.; for Stockport see *Factory Commission* ... 1834 (167) xix, D1, p. 158

[108] Second Report ... Employment of Children ... *Appendix*, 1843 [432] xv. f. 200–203

[109] See Watson *Senior Class* ...; Fleet *Distinctive Features* ..., and J. A. Cooper *The Senior Class: A prize Essay* (1847)

[110] Quoted in C. R. Newby *The Story of Sunday Schools* (1930) letter from Raikes to Fox, 1785, p. 17; M. More *Mendip Annals* p. 103 for example

even division of males and females.

The life situation of students is discussed in more detail below. In some areas the great majority of those in Sunday school worked during the week; in others as many as seventy-five per cent were enrolled in day school. The educational, economic and religious characteristics of a town or region determined the precise nature of the Sunday school population. Here the point is that Sunday schools were thought suitable for, and attended by, children from age five to over twenty who were drawn from all strata of the working classes.

b. Teachers

Charlotte Brontë's *Shirley* might lead its readers to believe that all Sunday school children were taught by the kindly vicar with the help of middle-class lady bountifuls. There were, of course, these sorts of teachers: 'Long may England's daughters hold the place which they now so often occupy, as the medium of charitable feelings between rich and poor.'[111] Mrs Trimmer, in soliciting teachers, thought that

> Perhaps it may be thought improper to take young ladies from whom genteel behaviour and elegance of expression is expected, among a set of vulgar, low bred children. [But], I do not apprehend any disagreeable consequences will arise from this circumstance ...[112]
>
> Can a woman, accustomed to the exercise of maternal affection towards her own beloved offspring be indifferent to the happiness of poor children, who have no means of learning their duty but what these schools afford?[113]

In most places, however, ladies and gentlemen of the more genteel classes were simply not forthcoming.

Between 1780 and 1800 the middle class dominated interdenominational Sunday schools, and some country schools run by the parish priest drew their instructors mostly from ordinary weekday school teachers who were supplemented by the services of 'decent labouring men, warehousemen and others of irreproachable character' hired for the occasion.[114] But as the numbers in Sunday school grew, this proved too expensive even for the most opulent

[111] *Church of England Magazine* vol. 8 (1840) 29–30
[112] Sarah Trimmer, *Oeconomy of Charity* (1787) 41
[113] Ibid. p. 19
[114] Mr. [James] Everett *Sunday Schools in Manchester* (n.d. but *c* 1835) MS. in the Manchester box, Methodist Archive.

Anglican Sunday schools; it was never a feasible system for the working-class and most Dissenting schools. Anglican schools reluctantly and other schools with great eagerness then turned to voluntary teachers. But much to the annoyance of clergymen and the managers of some schools, men and women of substance, prominent members of the congregation, were reluctant to step forward.

'Congregations do not even turn aside to see how the Sunday schools prosper,' complained the *Evangelical Magazine*. 'The too prevalent habit of more educated and genteel classes excusing themselves, on various pretexts, from the work', is decried by another authority. An Anglican writer cites anxiety over loss of dignity, fear of forming unsuitable friendships or being drawn into exessive familiarity with one's inferiors, and apprehension over finding few men of talent among colleagues as the reasons why 'persons of wealth in our congregations seem to abandon this field of labour ... to the more humble members of the community.'[115] As a result of these difficulties, most Sunday school teachers were drawn from the working classes.

'The bulk of our teachers, as well as our scholars, belong to the lower—some of the best of them to the lowest—classes of society,' reported the *Sunday School Magazine*. A working man told the Church of England Sunday School Institute that to his knowledge 'the greatest proportion of the instructors in Sunday school are individuals from our own ranks.' An agent for the Manchester Statistical Society remarked in 1833 that the Sunday school belonging to Christ Church, Manchester, was unusual in having educated men and women as teachers. The Children's Employment Commission ten years later thought it necessary to remark that most teachers could read and write, while the Secretary of the Sheffield Union told the same investigators that teachers were at least trying to make up for their lack of formal instruction through self-improvement classes.[116]

More important though for the development of a Sunday school community is the fact that a majority of teachers were themselves former students. In large Sunday schools there were special training classes for those intending to stay on. After a student had gone through all the reading, writing and arithmetic classes, he or she

[115] *Evangelical Magazine* (1838) 628; Rev. D. Morrison 'The Obligation of Churches in Reference to Sunday Schools' *SS Teachers Magazine* (1841) 444–59; A. H. Davis *Religious Instruction* ... pp. 87–91

[116] *Sunday School Magazine* 40 (1839) 195; *Church of England Sunday School Quarterly Magazine*, (1848–49) 274; *Children's Employment Commission (Mines and Manufacturies)* 1843 [432] xv, c91, e9

was, at age thirteen or fourteen, transferred to a 'first' class for boys' 'second' for girls, where intensive scriptural instruction was combined with further practice in secular subjects. In smaller schools older students simply moved on to become teachers. The proportion procured in this way varied from place to place but was seldom below fifty per cent: sixty per cent in 1832 out of 3,002 teachers in the Newcastle Union; in the 1840s eighty-six per cent of 389 in Stalybridge, fifty-seven per cent of 1,712 in the Manchester and Salford Union, seventy-three per cent of 178 in the Westbury Union, fifty per cent of 309 in the South Bucks. Union.[117]

Although of the 250,000 teachers in 1851 'a vast number were from the same position in life as the students', the drive to associate the school with the congregation had probably succeeded in bringing more middle-class men and women into the Sunday school by mid-century.[118] Still, the picture of a lady bountiful brought in from the outside continued to be unrealistic. The social and political message of the Sunday school, even in its most blatantly counter-revolutionary form, reached the children through teachers of their own class. As Andrew Ure was surprised to learn, Sunday schools were generally 'planted and upreared chiefly by the work-people themselves'. This similarity in the social background of students and teachers made it easier to develop a Sunday school subculture, an admixture of Smilesian self-help and self-improvement discussed in Chapters Six and Seven.[119]

Sunday school teaching became an important vehicle for the expression of working-class religion and of the desire, particularly among older students, to pass on the skills they had learned to their younger brothers and sisters. It also became a sign of mental culture. As the radical and Chartist James Watson said of his mother, '[she], although poor, was intelligent, as proof of which I may state that she was a teacher in one of the Sunday schools of the town.'[120]

c. Managers

Few generalizations can be made about those who managed Sunday schools. The early committees in large towns were usually drawn from the industrial and commercial élite and from the

[117] *SS Teachers' Magazine* (1835) col. 315; (1842) p. 763; (1845) p. 336; *Sunday School Union Magazine* (1847) 188; *SS Magazine* 40 (1839) 304

[118] See for example E. Baines *Manufacturing Districts, ...* p. 25

[119] Andrew Ure *Philosophy of Manufactures* (1835) 408

[120] William J. Linton *James Watson: A Memoir* (Manchester, 1880, Kelley Reprint 1971) 15

Anglican and Dissenting clergy. In some places governing bodies
retained this social complexion; in others quite a different sort
of person supervised school affairs. Two of the six directors of the
highly successful Knotts Lane School in Oldham could not sign
their names. A thirteen-year-old boy was accepted as a teacher in
one Midlands Sunday school when it was pointed out that he, in
contrast to most of the committee, could write. The superintendent
of a Methodist Association Sunday school in Nuneaton asked the
the commissioners inquiring into the condition of the handloom
weavers to excuse his 'wrighting', and the managers of a nearby
Wesleyan school replied to a question on discipline by saying

> Our Children are but Small and many friend Less so
> We Deel much in love with them.

Surely these were schools of the people.[121]

vii. Conclusions

Dissenting Sunday schools and, to a lesser extent, those of the
Church were lay-dominated institutions relatively free of ministerial
control. During the first half of the nineteenth century, predominantly working-class students were taught primarily by working-
class teachers in schools largely financed, and sometimes also run,
by working-class men and women. All schools, even those whose
managers were of a higher social standing than the teachers,
operated in a remarkably democratic fashion through the agency
of a teachers' meeting. The implications of these facts are developed
further in Chapter Seven; but before an analysis of the place of the
Sunday school in working-class life and politics can be undertaken,
it is necessary to examine its single most important contribution
to the community—the provision of elementary education.

[121] *Reports from the Asst. Commissioners on Hand-loom Weavers* op. cit 1840 [217]
xxiv, p. 129

4. Sunday Schools and Secular Education I : What was Taught and What was Learned

i. INTRODUCTION

Contemporaries differed about how important Sunday schools were in providing education for the working classes. The Secretary of the British and Foreign School Society told the 1834 Parliamentary Committee on Education that 'I never yet saw a Sunday school which [I] should consider worth taking into account as a place of literary instruction.'[1] But two and a half weeks later, the Secretary of the Sunday School Union told the same committee that in three years of Sunday school education a child could acquire 'a competent knowledge of the art of reading'.[2] Who was nearer the truth?

The opinions of contemporaries on the value of Sunday school secular education were far too closely tied to their stance on other emotionally charged religious and political issues to be of much use to the historian. Denominational authorities downgraded its importance because they felt Sunday would be better spent in exclusively spiritual pursuits. Advocates of more extensive government intervention in the provision of weekday education felt quite rightly that praise of the Sunday school system's educational value would minimize the urgency of their case. Commentators in the 1860s could look back on the patchwork of institutions that grew up during the nineteenth century to provide working-class education and condemn Sunday schools as the least professional and rational of them all.[3]

[1] *Report from the Select Committee on the State of Education, with Minutes of the Evidence 1834* (572) ix. 1; no. 310

[2] Ibid. no. 1228

[3] See for example the tract by the Rev. Samuel T. Waddy, 'Religious Education necessary for the National Well Being' (1838); see also the remarks by Joseph

On the other hand, a local historian faced in the early nineteenth century with the decision of including Sunday schools under the 'Religious Institutions' or the 'Literary Institutions' section of his work opted for the latter because 'they have in numerous instances been the means of opening the way to knowledge, and even to literary eminence.'[4] In general, those favoring voluntarism in education and radicals impressed with the progress of the working classes thought very highly of Sunday school secular instruction. It had produced in the thirty years before Peterloo 'many working men of sufficient talent to become readers, writers, and speakers in the village meetings for parliamentary reform', said Samuel Bamford. 'If there is any hero worship, let it be paid to those patient, unregarded, unrewarded, unknown, often much despised workers in the overcrowded garret or the dark underground school room,' who, according to Archibald Prentice, 'were creating THOUGHT amongst the hitherto unthinking masses'. 'If the poor in this country are generally well informed—able to converse freely and rationally on many literary subjects—we owe it to the Sunday schools in which they have learned to read,' wrote the editor of the Chartist *Northern Star*.[5]

Contemporary accounts are inconclusive about the value of Sunday schools in providing elementary education to the working classes. An assessment of their true significance will depend on answers to three sets of questions. First, how did Sunday schools fit into the larger pattern of working-class childhood? At what age did children attend, how long did they remain, what was the relationship between day schooling, Sunday schooling, and work or leisure?[6] Second, what were the institutional constraints of Sunday school education? What subjects were taught and how much time was devoted to them, what textbooks were used, how was instruction carried out, what size were the classes, etc.? Third, what was the role of Sunday schools in bringing the printed word to the great mass of working-class children? What part did they

---

Fletcher, some time H. M. School Inspector and advocate of increased government intervention in education, in *Reports from the Assistant Hand-Loom Weavers' Commissioners* Part IV 1840 [217] xxiv, p. 92; and W. L. Sargeant *Journal of the Royal Statistical Society* vol. 30 (March 1867) 112–13; Horace Mann's introduction to the 1851 education census which praises the moral efficacy of Sunday schools while dismissing their purely educational efforts. *Education* [1851] *Census* p. xx

[4] Edward Parsons *The Civil, Ecclesiastical, Literary, Commercial and Miscellaneous History of Leeds, Bradford ...* (Leeds, 1834) 106

[5] Samuel Bamford *Passages in the Life of a Radical* vol. 1 (1844) 7; Archibald Prentice *Historical Sketches and Personal Recollections of Manchester* (1851) 116; *Northern Star* (6 January 1838) 7

[6] See also Chapter 3, pp. 86–91, and Chapter 6, pp. 148–60

play in the informal educational network of the nineteenth century? This chapter will be concerned with these questions. Chapter Five will focus on the controversy over the propriety of teaching writing on the sabbath in order to explicate the intellectual, social and institutional forces which determined Sunday school curriculum. It also provides a case study of the intensely local concerns of many working men and women in contrast to those activities expressive of wider class consciousness.

ii. THE CONTEXT

Very little quantitative evidence is available on the place of weekday schooling in the life of a working-class child growing up during the early nineteenth century. The total amount of time spent in school, the pattern of attendance over the year, and the ages at which schooling was considered appropriate all varied between industrial and commercial cities, between rural and urban areas, between coal-mining and lead- or iron-mining regions, between artisans, small tradesmen, and factory workers, between periods of economic prosperity and periods of economic depression. No adequate study of the subject exists and what follows is no more than a sketch drawn to put Sunday school education in context.

In 1842, Edward Baines, a prominent advocate of working-class education and one of the leaders of the Dissenters' campaign to defeat the educational provisions of Graham's Factory Act, thought that five years of schooling for the working classes was the *best* any educational policy could aim for. It appears, however, that *c*. 1830 the actual amount of weekday schooling before beginning full-time work was more in the order of one or two years for the child in an industrial city and perhaps a bit longer in commercial towns. Two or three years might have been the norm by mid-century. Rural school life was probably longer than urban but more irregular; the same could be said of the schooling career of girls in comparison with boys. In both the city and the country, girls were often taken from school to help at home, nurse the sick, or do odd jobs. The ages usual for day schooling were obscure to contemporaries and impossible to reconstruct today. The Manchester Statistical Society in its first report on Manchester education attempted to gather empirical evidence on this subject but found the results so unreliable that they excluded the table (No. 4, 1st edition) presenting their findings from the second edition of their report. Most witnesses, however, agree that in the industrial north twelve was the absolute maximum age for leaving school although eleven was more usual. In mining areas, in cities and regions where lace or other sweated clothing industries provided opportunities for early employment, among match girls and chimney sweeps etc. schooling stopped earlier. In rural areas boys stopped going to school at about the age of ten but may have returned during the slack winter months. Girls may have remained until aged fifteen.[7]

But attendance at weekday school was not the norm for the working-class child at any age. As late as 1851 among those seven to eight years old, the age group with the highest percentage in day school, only sixty-four per cent of boys and fifty-one per cent of girls were classified as scholars. A negligible percentage were at work, and the remainder were returned as 'undescribed'.[8] So, a high proportion of working-class children ages five to fifteen were neither at school nor engaged in full-time work. In the best of circumstances their weekday education was an irregular affair with periods of attendance punctuated by periods of sickness, poverty, or other economic exigency which took the child out of school. Sunday schools were one of many agencies, albeit the most significant, which supplemented this short and precarious period of full-time elementary instruction.

The relationship of weekday to Sunday schooling in the lives of working-class children differed from place to place. (See Table 10.) Table 10 may be supplemented with somewhat less systematic or complete quantitative evidence for other localities. In Stockport,

[7] Baines, *The Sosicl, Educational and Religious State* ... p. 21. The length of schooling and the ages at which it was thought appropriate are discussed in Archibald Edward Dobbs *Education and Social Movements, 1700–1800* (1919) 158–9, which utilizes much of the available evidence. For Manchester and the cotton belt generally see David Winstanley *A Schoolmaster's Notebook* ed. E. and T. Kelly (1957) [*Remains Historical and Literary connected with the Palatine Counties of Lancaster and Chester* ser. 3, vol. 8] pp. 30–43. The author was employed as a schoolteacher in Miles Platting during the 1830s. For ages of schooling in agricultural areas see *Reports of the Special Assistant Poor Law Commissioners on the Employment of Women and Children in Agriculture 1843* [510] xii, pp. 28, 36–7, 217; *The Minutes of the Committee of Council for Education* are generally informative on this question; see for example Fletcher's report on 63 northern schools in *Minutes — 1844* (84) xxxviii, p. 219; John Glyde, Jun. *The Moral, Social, and Religious Condition of Ipswich* ... (Ipswich, 1850) 138–9 claimed that few children in Ipswich stayed in school for as many as three years and that twelve was the latest age for which schooling was thought appropriate. Richard Burgess in *Letter to the Rev. W. F. Hook, DD on his Proposal for a Plan for the Education of the People* (1842) 22 estimated that the duration of working-class schooling throughout England was 18–24 months and perhaps $2\frac{1}{2}$ –3 years in some seaports

[8] See *Census (Education)* 1852–53 [1692] xc. pp cx-cxiv. Equivalent statistics for 'an industrial city' suggest that a disproportionately large, but by no means all, of those not at school were working-class children. See ibid. pp cxv-cxvii

Table 10:[9] *The relationship of weekday to Sunday school education in selected places,* 1834–43

	1	2	3	4	5	6	7
	No. in day school only	No. in Sunday school only	No. attending day and Sunday school	Total in Sunday school (cols. 2 & 3)	Total in school —day and Sunday	Col. 2 as percentage of col. 4	Col. 2 as percentage of col. 5
Manchester and Salford	13,239	29,529	13,421	42,950	56,189	68.7	52.5
Birmingham	10,902	12,616	4,142	16,758	27,659	75.2	45.6
Bury	1,503	3,102	1,122	4,224	5,727	73.5	54.5
Coventry	4,229	4,295	1,199	5,494	9,723	78.2	44.2
Liverpool	17,815	3,719	11,649	15,368	33,183	24.1	11.2
York	2,228	842	2,521	3,363	5,591	25.0	15.0
Four Westminster parishes	3,215	666	889	1,555	4,770	42.8	13.9
Rutland	1,117	1,274	1,922	3,196	4,313	39.8	29.5
Bristol	3,483	7,171	4,513	11,684	21,865	61.4	32.8
Penzance and Madron	1,435	207	380	587	2,022	35.2	10.2
Ipswich	1,142	707	2,131	2,838	3,980	24.9	17.7

for example, only seven per cent of the boys and thirteen per cent of the girls out of approximately 4,600 students in the great interdenominational school were in day school; the great majority were employed in cotton factories. It was not possible to determine how many Sunday scholars in Leeds were also receiving weekday instruction but, since 11,429 attended Sunday school while only 6,759 attended day school, at least forty-one per cent, and probably many more, relied entirely on the Sunday school. In Newcastle on Tyne a 'considerable number' of all scholars were judged to be attending Sunday school only. Children of handloom weavers and framework knitters in the late 1830s and 1840s received their education almost exclusively in Sunday school. On the other hand,

[9] *Reports of the Manchester Statistical Society on the State of Education in Manchester in 1834* (1835) . . . *in Bury* (1835) . . . *in Salford in 1835* (1836) . . . *in York in 1836–37* (1837) . . . *in the Country of Rutland in the year 1838* (1839) . . . *in Liverpool in 1835–36*; 'Report on the State of Education in Birmingham' by the Birmingham Statistical Society in *Journal of the Royal Statistical Society* (*JRSS*) vol. 3 (1840) 25 ff.; C. B. Fripp 'Report on the Condition of the Working Classes in Bristol' *JRSS* vol. 2 (1839) 368 ff.; 'Second and Third Reports of the Statistical Society of London on the State of Education in Westminster' *JRSS* vol. 2, pp. 193 ff. and pp. 449 ff.; and also 'Fifth' report of same, *JRSS* vol. 6 (1843) 211 ff. For Coventry see *Reports* . . . *Hand-Loom Weavers*, op. cit., Part IV 1840 [217] xxiv, pp. 94–5; for Ipswich, see Glyde, op. cit., pp. 138–9; for Penzance and Madron see R. Edmonds 'A Statistical Account of the Parish of Madon containing the Borough of Penzance in Cornwall' *JRSS* vol. 2 (1839)

in 173 rural parishes only 2,680 out of a total of 12,510 scholars, that is twenty-one per cent, relied on Sunday schools exclusively.[10]

To summarize, on the basis of Table 10 and other information presented above, in the manufacturing centers of the North and the Midlands, the industrial and mining villages of the Forest of Dean, the West Riding, Staffordshire, Leicestershire or Lancashire the great majority of those in Sunday school received no other elementary education; half or nearly half of those receiving any education were receiving it on Sunday only. In places like Bristol, where a relatively high proportion of the relevant age group was receiving weekday instruction, Sunday schools could serve as a form of supplementary post-school education; hence, the majority of those in Sunday school were receiving no further instruction but only a third of those receiving *any* instruction were attending Sunday school only. Finally, in the Metropolis, in some commercial towns like York or Ipswich, and in rural districts, day schooling continued on and off for a longer period of time. A relatively small proportion of those in Sunday school were not also in enrolled weekday school; few of those under instruction attended school only on Sunday. Even here though the irregular nature of 'full-time' schooling must be borne in mind. In short, at least twenty-five per cent and up to seventy-five per cent of those who attended Sunday school in England were receiving no other formal education.

However, only a tiny proportion of those in Sunday school were below the age of five and thus too young to profit from elementary instruction. Increasingly the Sunday school became the province of adolescent boys and girls. As early as the 1830s more than ten per cent of those enrolled were over fifteen with a far higher proportion of older students in some areas; by 1850 the general opinion was that the proportion nationally had increased as well and indeed evidence from the second half of the century suggests that the proportion of older students increased steadily up to 1900. In fact the whole age structure probably shifted upwards. The average age of entrants in Stockport in 1800 was 9.75; in 1860 it was 13. In

---

[10] For Stockport see *Supplementary Reports from Commissioners appointed to collect information in the manufacturing districts, relative to the employment of children in factories ... with Minutes of Evidence and Reports of District Commissioners 1834* (167) xix, p. 156. For Leeds *JRSS* vol. 2 (1839) 41. For Newcastle *JRSS* vol. 1 (1838) 356. For rural counties, see survey by James Matheson, a prominent Congregationalist, in *The Patriot* (11, December 1843); *Children's Employment Commission: Appendix to the First Report of the Commissioners (Mines)* Part II ... 1842 [382] xvii, which inquired about the state of education in each locality studied suggests that many children in mining areas, even more than in the cotton textile belt, were solely dependent on Sunday schools for their education. See also below, Chapter 6, pp. 152–3

Leek the mean entrance age was 6.2 for the period 1803–12 and 11.2 for the period 1838–40.[11]

An officer of the Sunday School Union testified in 1816 that the average scholar spent a total of two years in Sunday school; in 1834 another official estimated that three years was the average duration in urban schools, five in rural areas. Frederic Hill gave four years as a national average in 1836. In 1842 the average length of stay in thirteen Leeds Sunday schools was between three and four years, ranging from two and a half to five.[12] The data for Stockport in Table 11 corroborates this evidence and suggests that the percentage of students remaining in Sunday school for relatively long periods of time increased between 1800 and 1860; conversely the proportion of short term drop-outs decreased.

Table 11:[13] Duration of stay at Stockport Sunday School for students in 1800, 1820, 1840 and 1860

Year	No. in sample	Percentage which stayed on in the SSS for the following no. of years or less										Average length of stay
		1	2	3	4	5	6	7	8	9	10	
1800	251	43	24	14	9	·	4		1			1¾ years
1820	255	71	46	30	21	14	10		4			2½ years
1840	368	58	38	28	20	17	14	11	10	8		2¾ years
1860	216	80	55	47	32	27	25	19	16	12	11	3¾ years

For most students the Sunday schools added three, four or five years of part-time education to a very limited and discontinuous period of weekday schooling, sometimes amounting to no more than a few months in a dame's school; for a minority it had to take the place of all full-time instruction. George Edwards, MP, of the Agricultural Labourers' Union, for example, claimed that Sunday schools provided the only education he ever had. Tom Mann of the dockworkers started work when he was nine after less than three years of day schooling; he went back to Sunday school when he was fifteen because 'it dawned on me that I had missed something in the educational line.' A chimney sweep who became a prosperous businessman and Methodist lay preacher left school at six and

[11] Calculated from MS. Enrollment Registers 3 vols., of the Stockport Sunday School in the Stockport Reference Library and from the MS. Admissions Register of the West Str. Methodist School, Leek, D1114/2, Staffordshire County Record Office. See also Chapter 3, pp. 90–1 ff. and the Epilogue, pp. 249

[12] Second Report from the Select Committee on the State of Education among the lower orders in the Metropolis 1816 (427) iv, p. 54; S.C.H.C. on the State of Education ... 1834 (572) ix, Q1227; Frederic Hill National Education: Its Present State and Future Prospects (1836) 102; Children's Employment Commission ... [Trades and Manufacturies 1843 [432] xv, E42

[13] Calculated from the MS. Enrollment Registers of the Stockport Sunday School

learned to write on Sundays; one Thomas Jones, an overlooker
in Salford, began work at eight and learned to read at a Sunday
school in the early 1790s. Another overlooker in Manchester
began work at ten and learned both reading and writing in a Sunday
school during the 1810s. Joseph Barker spoke for many: 'When
we had work we had not time for school; and when we had not work,
we had nothing with which to pay school wages; so Sunday school
was our only resource.'[14]

Secular instruction in Sunday schools must then be seen against
the background of a society in which the facilities for mass popular
education were still in their infancy. Cultural as well as economic
factors determined that the formal schooling available to a great
part of the population was only one-third of what is today considered sufficient to ensure functional literacy.[15] Sunday schools
with their accoutrement of reading clubs, libraries and improvement societies are probably the least known of a whole class of
institutions which filled the educational interstices of the early
nineteenth century. They offered one of the roads to those twin
Victorian virtues of 'self-help' and 'respectability'. But another
set of questions, those dealing with the institutional constraints
of Sunday school education, must be answered before the importance of these schools in providing elementary education can be
fully assessed.

iii. INSTITUTIONAL FACTORS

In a century during which surveys of almost every kind were
conducted, no national inquiry was made into the subjects offered
in Sunday schools. Local surveys dating from the 1830s and 1840s
and scattered evidence of a non-quantitative nature are all that
survive and probably all that ever existed. From this evidence it is
clear that variation between schools was enormous. There were
those rural Anglican schools which were reluctant to offer reading
instruction because the catechism and collects could be as effectively
taught verbally.[16] But there were also schools like that attached to
the Dukinfield Unitarian chapel in which the advanced classes

[14] George Edwards, *From Crow Scaring to Westminster. An Autobiography* (1922),
21; Tom Mann *Memoirs* (1923) 13, John Arthur Turner *The Life of a
Chimney Boy* (1901) 26. *First Report from the Commissioners appointed to collect information
in the manufacturing districts, relative to the employment of children in factories* ...; *with
Minutes of Evidence and Reports of District Commissioners, 1833* (450) xx, D2-124 and
D2-114; Joseph Barker quoted in J. F. C. Harrison, *Learning and Living 1790–1960*
p. 45

[15] Mark Blaug, *An Introduction to the Economics of Education* (1970) 260–7

[16] *British Magazine* vol. 2 (Nov. 1832) 270; (Dec. 1832) 395

used Carpenter's *Scriptural Geography*, Burder's *Oriental Customs*, and Murchason's *History of England* as texts; or the Unitarian Sunday School in Sheffield in which, according to a middle-class observer who was worried by the lack of religious instruction, 'girls who cannot read without spelling wade through one of Chamber's *Introductions to the Sciences*'. If evening classes attached to Sunday schools are included, the range becomes broader still. Benjamin Brierly met with his fellow students in Rochdale to read Shelley, Burns and Byron, and to produce Shakespeare plays for themselves and their neighbors; the improvement society of the Bennett Street Sunday School in Manchester began by studying English grammar and went on to Greek and Latin; the Leeds Ebenezer New Connexion school offered popular Sunday evening lectures on chemistry and electricity.[17]

Table 12:[18] *Proportion of Sunday schools in various cities teaching reading only, reading and writing only, and reading, writing and arithmetic, 1834–43*

Place	Total number of Sunday schools and scholars		No. of schools and no. of scholars in schools where READING is taught		No. of schools and no. of scholars in schools where WRITING is taught		No. of schools and no. of scholars in schools where ARITHMETIC is taught	
Manchester	86	33,196	84	32,811	10	2,560	3	684
Bury	12	4,224	12	4,224	4	1,696	1	330
York	22	3,201	22	3,201	1	116	1	40
Birmingham	56	16,757	56	16,757	25	7,329	7	2,067
Co. Rutland	69	2,529	69	2,529	3	101	0	0
Leek	5	1,527	5	1,527	3	975	no information	
Burslem	5	2,481	5	2,481	2	1,667	no information	
Kingston-upon-Hull	38	6,707	38	6,707	1	93	1	93
Longton	6	2,284	6	2,284	4	1,127	no information	
Salford	31	9,754	31	9,754	8	1,700	5	1,082
Liverpool	75	15,369	72	14,936	no information		no information	
	405	98,029	400	97,211	61	17,364	18	4,296
			98%	99%	18%	21%	5%	5%

[17] J. E. Hickey *History of the Dukinfield Sunday School* (Dukinfield, 1928) 25–6; *Children's Employment Commission* ... [*Trades and Manufactures*] ... 1843 [432] xv, E 28; Benjamin Brierley *Home Memories and Recollections of a Life* (Manchester, 1886) 38; *Bennett Street Memorials* (Manchester, 1868, 2nd ed.); *Methodist New Connexion Magazine* vol. 51 (1848) 382

[18] For the sources of this table see note 9, p. 99 and, for Leek, Burslem and Longton see *Children's Employment Commission* ... [*Trades and Manufactures*] 1843 [432] xv, C 94–96, C 60–67, C 91–93

Nevertheless, reading, writing and arithmetic generally defined the limits of a Sunday school and, for that matter, a day school education for the working classes. Almost all Sunday schools taught reading, perhaps 18–20 per cent of the schools, containing 20–22 per cent of the scholars, taught writing on the Lord's day, and between 5–6 per cent taught arithmetic and other subjects. Table 12 summarizes the available quantitative evidence.

The schools surveyed represent less than ten per cent of the total number of Sunday schools in England and, of course, do not constitute a random sample. Some of the gaps, however, can be filled with more impressionistic evidence while inter-regional variations can be partially explained by differences in the social role of Sunday schools (see above) and in the strength of denominations sympathetic or hostile to extensive secular instruction. Bury, Leek and Burslem seem to be representative of smaller industrial or mining communities in which, as the Curate of St James', Oldham, remarked, Sunday schools were thought of as '*the* schools for the working classes'. In 1830 the secular character of Sunday school instruction in Oldham was broken by the Church and Independents, but for competitive reasons the other denominations failed to follow suit.[19] In Clitheroe, another Lancashire cotton town, the Church attempted to suppress writing instruction on Sundays but was forced to reinstate the practice in order to compete successfully with Dissenting schools which offered more extensive elementary education.[20] The 1816 Parliamentary inquiry into education was told that no London Sunday school taught writing on the sabbath, but histories of at least two Wesleyan schools belie this claim. However a school to school survey suggests that by the early 1840s writing instruction had indeed ceased and only reading was taught on Sunday.[21] In Sheffield four schools, including the best attended in the city, taught at least reading and writing in 1841.[22]

The commissioners inquiring into the employment of women and children in agriculture were far less systematic than their counterparts in the mines and manufacturing investigations. Reports like 'with few exceptions [there is] a Sunday school in every parish in which reading is taught, and sometimes writing,' which refer to

[19] *Children's Employment Commission (Mines)* ... 1842 [382] xvii, op. cit. p. 860
[20] Nassau Senior *Letters on the Factory Acts* (1857, Kelly Reprint 1966) 44
[21] *Second Report S.C.H.C. on Education in the Metropolis* ... 1816 (427) iv, p. 54; Thomas Westerdale *Centenary History of the Radnor Street Day, Sunday, and Ragged Schools* (1898) and John Telford, *Two Chapels* ... pp. 255–66; and *JRSS* vol. 1 (Aug. 1838); vol. 3 (Jan. 1840) 50 ff.; vol. 6 (Feb. 1843) 44 ff.; (Aug. 1843) 211 ff.
[22] *Children's Employment Commission* ... 1843 [432] xv, E. 26–28

Wiltshire, Dorset, Devon and Somerset, represent the limits of detail.[23] However, accounts from rural areas sent to the Sunday School Union and the printed reports of the local unions themselves suggest that at least some non-urban schools offered more than cursory instruction in reading the scriptures. In the absence of statistical evidence it can only be surmised that the Sunday school in Tyd St Mary's, Lincolnshire, did not stand alone when it announced: 'We have the happiness to say, that the children are making advancement in their learning ... they are taught to read the scriptures, and instructed in the first principles of religion: and they are taught the art of writing, and instructed in their duties toward their parents and teachers.[24]

The pressures which forced a decrease in the amount of secular instruction, particularly writing, offered on Sundays during the first seventy years of Sunday schools worked differentially on the various denominations so that some abandoned writing and arithmetic instruction on Sundays earlier and more completely than others. The leadership of both Church and Dissent agreed that Sunday should be devoted, as much as possible, exclusively to religious instruction. But Anglicans generally were more successful than Dissent in limiting their Sunday schools in this way, although even they were of necessity forced to use elementary secular textbooks to teach reading. The Baptists were shocked to discover in 1833 that out of forty schools surveyed, eight admitted to teaching writing on Sunday, while in the others 'the greater portion of time seems to be occupied in elementary instruction'.[25] New Connexion Methodists, after more than a decade of official opposition to secular instruction on the Sabbath, found that of sixty-eight schools that returned a questionnaire on the subject, thirty-three taught writing on Sunday, twenty-eight taught it on weekday evenings only, and seven did not mention the subject.[26] Primitive Methodists and Unitarians almost universally taught writing, and Congregationalists seem not to have made much of a fuss about the issue. They gathered no statistics on the subject and apparently some of their schools did and others did not teach writing. Finally, Wesleyan Conference fought a prolonged battle against Sunday writing instruction and was, by the 1840s, largely successful in eliminating the practice. (See below, pp. 142–5.)

All of the foregoing refers only to what was taught on Sundays.

[23] *Employment of Women and Children in Agriculture 1843* [510] xii, p. 36

[24] Report of the Sunday School Tyd Saint Mary's in the *Second Half Yearly Report of the South Lincolnshire and Isle of Ely Sunday School Union* p. 21

[25] *Baptist Magazine* 3rd ser. vol. 7 (July 1833) 224–6

[26] *Methodist New Connexion Magazine* vol. 44 (1841) 383; see also vol. 48 (1845) 176

In some areas, the Potteries and the Black Country for example, weekday evening classes were attached to almost all Sunday schools. In industrial towns between one-third and two-thirds of all Sunday schools had such classes, which were usually attended by about ten per cent of the school's total enrolment. Thirty-three out of eighty-five Anglican schools in the Metropolis held weekday evening classes in 1848. In York, Liverpool and Co. Rutland, on the other hand, where relatively few students depended exclusively on Sunday schools for their education, few if any schools held evening classes although the schools might have been connected with week-day charity schools.[27]

In assessing the educational value of Sunday schools it must also be remembered that a student spent the greater part of the day under instruction (Table 13).

Table 13:[28] *Hours spent in Sunday school and the proportion thereof spent in direct instruction*, 1834–43

Hours spent in Sunday school	No. of schools and Percentage of total		No. of schools on which information is available	No. of schools using n% of their time on direct instruction				
				90–100%	80–90%	70–80%	50–70%	0–50%
1 to 2	3	1%	2	0	0	0	0	2
2 to 3	19	7%	16	13	1	0	0	2
3 to 4	104	39%	88	37	13	31	7	0
4 to 5	60	22%	27	12	5	2	7	1
5 and over	84	31%	53	26	0	26	1	0
Total	270		186	88	19	59	15	5
% of total	—		100%	47%	10%	32%	8%	3%

Over ninety per cent of the schools in the survey were in session for three or more hours and over fifty per cent for at least four hours. Almost ninety per cent of the schools spent at least half their day in direct instruction, almost sixty per cent spent four-fifths of their time in this way. This means that not only was most of each Sunday spent in a class situation but that only a few minutes were available for opening exercises, exhortations by the managers, or other large group activities. Even when those who directed a

[27] For Anglican schools in the Metropolis see *Church of England Sunday School Quarterly Magazine* vol. 1 (1848) 165; there are almost two columns of references to Sunday schools in the Index 1845 [608] xlii. 195 to the *Second Report and Evidence of the Children's Employment Commission* ... 1843 [430] [431] [432] xiii-xv which support the view presented here of the educational role of Sunday schools in the Midlands and North; each of the reports cited in note 9, p. 000 also provides evidence on this subject

[28] Again, the sources of the data in this table are the reports cited in note 9, p. 99

Sunday school wanted to 'indoctrinate' the children, the time at their disposal was less than a half hour divided between morning and afternoon sessions.

Attendance at Sunday school was invariably in the neighborhood of seventy-five per cent; that is, three-quarters of the registered students were likely to turn up for one or both of the sessions on any given Sunday. There is no evidence on how attendance varied from morning to afternoon; in Stockport, however, between fifty-five per cent and sixty per cent of all students were present at both sessions and the proportions were probably comparable in other schools.[29] For the majority of scholars, Sunday schools thus provided a period of instruction more or less equivalent to one day at an ordinary weekday school.

The importance attached by Sunday schools to secular education is reflected by the fact that children were grouped according to ability, not age, and assigned to the appropriate class and textbook. Benjamin Brierley, the Lancashire poet, tells of being put in a Bible class because of his facility at spelling; he so provoked the older boys by his smugness after spelling 'gimlet' correctly that only a liquorice peace offering prevented a fight.[30] The simplest grading scheme involved a three-way division, which was used, for example, by the Southwark Sunday School Society: group one read in the New and Old Testaments and spelled in the Spelling Book; group two read and spelled in the Spelling Book; and group three read in the Alphabet Book, that is, they learned the alphabet. The Primitive Methodist manual on Sunday schools recommended four classes and further noted that it took only half an hour to find the correct ability level for a whole school with only a one-in-twenty chance of error. J. C. Wigram, the secretary of the National Society, suggested that Anglican schools adopt six divisions: a first class for learning monosyllables, a second for 'Reading Made Easy' lessons, a third for reading about miracles, parables, and simple Bible history, a fourth for studying Mrs Trimmer's *Scripture History*, and finally two advanced classes for reading the New Testament and full Bible. He also recommended textbooks from the SPCK catalogue which he felt would be suitable for the three more elementary classes. The Methodist Sunday School Society in London used seven gradings and one authority even recommen-

---

[29] [1851] *Census: Education* p. clxix; for Stockport see *Teacher's Register 1799*, MS. S 3/1 and uncatalogued *Registers* for 1800 and 1809 [Stockport Reference Library]. These give results of 43 per cent and 54 per cent respectively but the managing committee's minutes suggest that attendance improved after the turn of the century

[30] Brierley, op. cit. p. 12

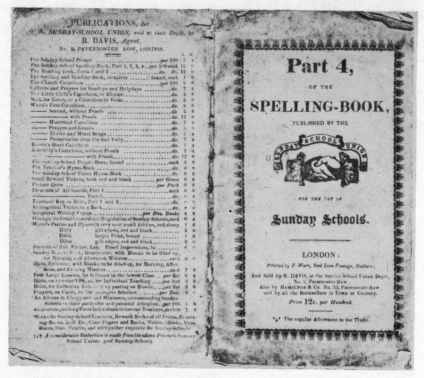

1. *The cover of the final part of the Sunday School Union's Spelling Book. It was in fact a small dictionary catering to those about to embark on serious Bible reading. The list of books printed on the back of this little volume is suggestive of the range of material the Union had for sale, from Arithmetic tables, to a wide range of catechisms, to supplies for collective teaching.*

ded ten.[31] In addition to reading classes, those schools in which writing and arithmetic were taught had separate sections for these subjects; and, in highly articulated institutions, like the Stockport or Bennett Street, Manchester, Sunday schools, some students spent part of the day in teacher-training sessions.

Classes tended to be small, personalized and, in theory at least, conducted according to well-developed teaching methods. Although most early experts recommended a ratio of twenty to thirty students per teacher, this was prohibitively expensive as

[31] *Rules of the Southwark Sunday School Society* (1797); *Primitive Methodist Magazine*, vol. 5 (1824) 'Treatise on Sunday Schools' (in four parts) part 2, 148; J. C. Wigram *Practical Hints on the Formation of Sunday Schools* (1833); *The Plan of a Society Instituted AD 1798 . . . for the Establishment and Support of Sunday Schools in London and its Vicinity* (1811). This Wesleyan organization at one time operated six schools; [Mary A. Maurice] *Glenrock Sunday School; or Lessons Illustrative of a Simple Method of Conveying Religious Instruction to Children of the Poor* (1840, 2nd ed.) 'Introduction'

28

church or at school, go not with them.

Walk not thou in the way with them; for their feet run to evil.

Trust in the Lord: be not wise in thine own eyes: fear the Lord and depart from evil.

Trust in the Lord, and he shall be thy help, and shall keep thy foot from being taken.

V.

Do no hurt to any thing that is less than thyself. Sport not with the pain of others.

Pierce not the smallest insect for thy sport: for they are all the work of the Lord: and he hath blessed them in their season.

Rob not the poor bird of the nest, which is to keep her warm from the cold and rain; nor take her eggs, nor her young ones, which she loves as much as a child is loved by his mother.

The Lord perceives thy cruel pastime; and will turn his ear from thee in thy distress.

29

VI.

Happy is the man that findeth wisdom, and the man that getteth knowledge.

Go to the ant, thou sluggard; think of her ways, and be wise.

My son, make much of time: life is short. Our life shall pass away as the trace of the cloud, and come to nought as the mist.

VII.

Christ commands us in the Gospel to pray to God, and hath taught us how we ought to pray.

He hath told us, if we pray to God in his name, God will grant us what is proper for us, if we deserve it.

We must pray to God to forgive us our sins, and that he would help us with his holy spirit to lead a good life.

But God will not forgive us our sins if we do not forgive each other.

B 3

2. These pages from the Salisbury Reader *give a fair impression of the religious and ethical precepts found in it and other Sunday school textbooks. There is perhaps more of an emphasis on trusting solely in the Lord than is usual*

long as teachers still collected 1*d*. or so for each child whom they taught.[32] Manchester school, as well financed as any, had thirty-eight and forty-three students to a teacher in 1785 and 1787 respectively.[33] Those schools which utilized voluntary teachers maintained, before 1800, the low pupil-teacher ratios more common later on. Bolton, for example, had eighty teachers for its approximately 800 students in 1787; the Wesleyan school in London maintained a similar ratio.[34]

For reasons of ecclesiastical polity as well as finance, the Dissen-

[32] See for example, Beilby T. Porteus, Bishop of Chester *A Letter to the Clergy of the Diocese of Chester Concerning Sunday Schools* (1786) 8 or *Evangelical Magazine* vol. 6 (1798) 15–21. Almost all of the early plans and manuals on Sunday school practice carried the same advice. See bibliography section IIc.

[33] *The Present State of the Sunday Schools in Manchester, April* 1, 1786 in *Proceedings* of the Manchester Sunday School Chetham's Library MS. A6–3 and the annual report for 1788 in the *Manchester Mercury* (19 August 1788)

[34] John Wesley *Journals* (27 July 1787); *Plan* ... 1798 (1811) op. cit.

ters relinquished paid teachers with far greater alacrity than the
Church.[35] The pattern in Manchester is illustrative of the national
case. In 1816 with half of their Sunday school budget going to pay
teachers, the Anglicans could afford to maintain a pupil-teacher
ratio of only 1:22 compared with 1:10.5 for the Dissenters and
Methodists who used gratuitous teachers exclusively. By 1833
the student-teacher ratio in Church schools had dropped to 1:16,
while that of the Methodists remained 1:10, and that of 'other
sects' stood at 1:9. Still, in 1851, both nationally and in Manchester,
the Church of England and the Roman Catholics, the two groups
who had the highest proportions of paid teachers, also had the
highest pupil-teacher ratio. 12.3 per cent and 6.39 per cent respectively, of their teachers were paid compared to less than 1 per cent
in all Dissenting denominations; their pupil-teacher ratio was
12.4:1 and 14.5:1 compared to 5:1 or 6:1 in all other schools.[36]

Generally each class in the Sunday school was autonomous and
not part of a monitorial scheme. The only complete survey on
Sunday school organization found in 1818 that only eleven per cent
of 452,817 scholars were in the eight per cent of the total number of
schools using the 'new' system, that is the schemes devised by Bell
and Lancaster.[37] Occasionally their methods found an advocate
in the periodical press; one writer argued that 'discipline must be
exercised to correct the irregularities of human behaviour' and
that, since the system of monitors and the establishment and preser-
vation of order were really the same thing, all Sunday schools
should adopt it forthwith. Twenty years later, the organ of the Sunday School Union suggested that the monitorial scheme was the
most perfect known, 'like the British Constitution, *sui generis*'.[38]
But the Union's secretary told the 1834 Parliamentary inquiry
into education that the monitorial system was avoided wherever
possible. J. R. Wood, who conducted the educational inquiries for
the Manchester Statistical Society, thought that it was invariably
a stop-gap measure adopted whenever there was a lack of gratuitous
teachers, that it encouraged rote learning, and that it led to gross

[35] See pp. 75-6, Chapter 3, above
[36] For 1816 see *Select Committee on the State of the Children in Manufactures of the
United Kingdom 1816* (397) iii, p. 97; Anglican Sunday school budget is taken
from the *Annual Report of the Sunday Schools belonging to the Established Church* (1818),
treasurer's account; for 1833 see *Report of the Manchester Statistical Society on ...
Education in Manchester* op. cit. p. 38; for 1851 see *Census: Education*, p. clxix, Table Q
[37] *General Table Showing the State of Education in England* 1820 (151) xii, pp. 151-2
[38] *Sunday School Repository* vol. 2, no. 13 (1815) 195; *Sunday School Teachers' Magazine
and Journal of Education (SS Teachers' Magazine)* new ser. vol. 3 (1832) col. 513-524

inefficiency in the operations of the school.[39] And even Joseph Lancaster, one of the inventors of the monitorial method, eschewed its use in Sunday schools; he recommended instead a method of teaching reading in which children gathered in small groups of eight around a teacher who used a graduated series of lessons pasted on boards visible to everyone in the circle.[40]

While small classes did not guarantee superior instruction, if other things were equal they became an important determinant of how much a child could learn. More importantly, because of the emphasis on personal, non-mechanical instruction Sunday schools overcame the resentment of many parents against the British and Foreign or National schools in which the older children of their neighbors could exercise an arbitrary tyranny over their own children.[41]

Working-class autobiographies are rich in material appreciative of the secular and spiritual value of Sunday schools but almost silent on classroom methods. To judge from the frequent reports of amazing memory feats, some Sunday school classes probably followed their weekday counterparts in requiring students to learn by heart long passages which were then recited in the school or before patrons on special occasions. For example, a nine-year-old boy from Sunderland repeated from memory 797 verses of the Bible, Lonridge's five parts of the Cathechism, and the whole of the church catechism before a large gathering in 1834. In one small Sunday School Union children managed to learn 1,015 complete chapters plus 22,190 separate verses, 9,906 catechisms, 6,076 spelling lessons, and 3,502 hymns in a single year.[42]

Indeed, More's method—'To make them read the same parts so often, that the most important texts shall adhere to their memories'— or the *Baptist Magazine*'s advice that 'simplify and repeat, simplify and repeat are the maxims for a school' were probably followed in all too many classes.[43] But in order to memorize long texts the ability to read was generally required, and Sunday schools took the teaching of this and other elementary skills seriously.

[39] *S.C.H.C. . . . on the State of Education 1834* (572) ix, Q 1187; for Wood's testimony see *Report from Select Committee on the Education of the Poorer Classes in England and Wales, together with Minutes of Evidence 1837–38* (589) vii, Q 1183

[40] Joseph Lancaster *An Address to the Friends and Superintendants of 'Sunday Schools'* (1809) 20–32

[41] See [Thomas Wright] *Some Habits and Customs of the Working Class by a Journeyman Engineer* (1867) 15–16

[42] *Annual Report of the Sunderland Sunday School Union* reprinted in the October issue of *SS Teachers' Magazine* (1834) 625; *SS Teachers' Magazine* (1835) 328

[43] William Roberts, ed., *Life and Correspondence of Hannah More* vol. 3 (1834) 150; *Baptist Magazine* vol. 12 (1820) 246

The Sunday School Union, the Anglican Sunday School Institute and numerous, independently published handbooks decried rote learning and advocated in its place more sensitive and productive methods of instruction. Warnings against the assumption that a pupil was stupid solely on the grounds of his inability to memorize were common. The Union, for example, was a strong advocate of David Stow's 'training system', first published in 1826, which demonstrated the weakness of learning by rote, the fallacy of 'compounding instruction with education' and the importance of the 'interrogative, illustrative and elliptical methods of teaching'. It also re-published for Sunday school use Henry Dunn's *Popular Education; or the Normal School Manual*, a standard pedagogical text-book in British School Society training colleges.[44] Furthermore, the concern in Sunday schools for effective secular education was manifested by a plethora of short articles that suggested one or another improved methods of instruction.

The Sunday School Repository advocated a mode of teaching writing by using certain elementary strokes suitable for use on slates; in another issue it suggested teaching spelling by means of writing. A Methodist New Connexion authority thought that instead of using 'the old, dry method', spelling instruction should be inter-spersed with explanations about meaning and with affectionate addresses, nevertheless making sure that 'pronunciation is clear with no singing tones'. The Sunday School Union recommended using letter boards and lessons written on a large wall panel, the so-called collective method, in place of books; they argued that large letters made learning to read easier. The Institute developed a letter box which made alphabet instruction as painless as possible.[45] In short, there was widespread concern that Sunday schools use the most modern teaching techniques available.

Undoubtedly the teachers, themselves without much formal education, were less systematic than some observers might have hoped. But the three, four or five hours that were spent each week in small classes devoted to instruction in reading and sometimes writing or arithmetic must have made an impact on working-class

---

[44] See Groser *One Hundred Years* . . . pp. 32 and 103

[45] *Sunday School Repository* vol. 1 (1814) 462 and vol. 2, pp. 55 and 415; *Methodist New Connexion Magazine* vol. 35 (new ser. vol. 1) (1833) 384 ff.; there is scarcely an issue of the *SS Teachers' Magazine* which does not give some tips on how to use the collective method, letter boxes, wall panels, etc. W. H. Watson, a longtime activist in the Union, thought that their ABC system was one of the nine great claims to success the Union could put forward. See his *History of the Sunday School Union* (1853) 182–3; as the opening essay of the *Church of England Sunday School Quarterly Magazine* vol. 1 (March 1848) makes clear, technical innovations in teaching were undertaken so as to leave as much time as possible for purely religious instruction

children deprived of a prolonged period of weekday elementary
education.

iv. BRINGING THE PRINTED WORD TO THE PEOPLE

A working-class child in the mid-eighteenth century seldom saw
the printed word. By 1850 children were inundated with textbooks,
periodicals and pamphlets produced expressly for them. The growth
of Sunday schools was almost exactly contemporaneous with the
growth of publications for children,[46] and no other institution was
more instrumental in bringing the printed word to the working-
class child.

Specialized reading textbooks were produced and used on an
unprecedented scale. In the very beginning Sunday schools used
teaching material taken over from the ordinary day schools for the
'middle classes'. One guide recommends James Talbott's *The
Christian Schoolmaster* (1707); another suggests either George Fisher's
The Young Man's Best Companion, in its twenty-eighth edition by
1798, or Henry Dixon's *The English Instructor,* first published in
1728 and in its sixty-ninth edition by 1823.[47] All three of these
books are lengthy, relatively advanced, and, except for the last,
completely unsuited for beginning students. For some reason
charity-school textbooks were never adopted by Sunday schools,
and new works, specifically for their use, were written.

Thomas Burgess, the future bishop of St David's and later
Salisbury published his so-called *Salisbury Reader* in 1786; William
Paley followed with *Reading Made Completely Easy* in 1790. The
Sunday School Union began a series of spelling books in 1811 and
a second collateral series in 1830; the SPCK which supplied many
Anglican schools published at least a dozen pedagogical booklets
suitable for students at various reading levels from monosyllables
to the New Testament. Furthermore, commercial publishers like
Westley in London or Richardson & Son in Derby produced
readers or spelling books for the Sunday school market; and individual schools on occasion also commissioned works for their own
use and for sale to neighboring institutions.

Some of the above texts were enormously popular. Paley was

---

[46] See F. J. H. Darton *Children's Books in England; Five Centuries of Social Life*
(Cambridge, 1958)

[47] See [Lancaster Adkin] *Proceedings for Sundays [sic] schools, and a plan of that
in St. Stephen's Norwich, established 1785* (Norwich, 1785?); George Horne, DD *Sunday
Schools Recommended—A Sermon* (Oxford, 1786) Appendix 1; the bibliographical
information is from the title pages of the copies used

E

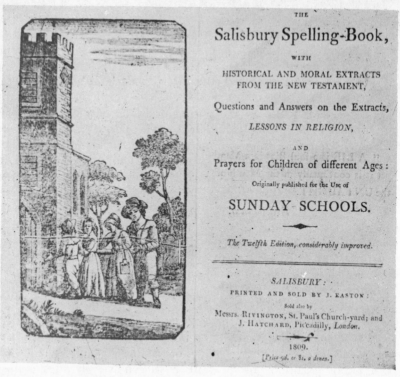

THE

Salisbury Spelling-Book,

WITH

HISTORICAL AND MORAL EXTRACTS
FROM THE NEW TESTAMENT,

Questions and Answers on the Extracts,

LESSONS IN RELIGION,

AND

Prayers for Children of different Ages :

Originally published for the Use of

SUNDAY SCHOOLS.

The Twelfth Edition, considerably improved.

SALISBURY :
PRINTED AND SOLD BY J. EASTON;
Sold also by
Messrs. RIVINGTON, St. Paul's Church-yard; and
J. HATCHARD, Piccadilly, London.

1809.
[*Price 9d. or 8s. a dozen.*]

3. Frontpiece illustration from one of the most popular early Sunday school texts. Note the 'ABC tables' which one girl is carrying in. The children are quite clearly wearing their best clothes.

still being reprinted in 1855; the *Salisbury Reader* was in its twelfth edition in 1809; the Union continuously reprinted and revised its texts.[48] Moreover, the numbers involved are staggering. About ten million copies of the two Union texts were sold between 1824 and 1830 and perhaps another 1,500,000 between 1811 and 1824. Depot sales during the period 1821–50 totalled almost £150,000; in 1841 the turnover of £9,000 wholesale was four times the text-book outlay of the British and Foreign Schools and almost £3,000

[48] Bibliographical information for Burgess and Paley from C. W. J. Higson, ed. *Sources for the History of Education* (1967), B 917, D 1011; I used the 1809 12th ed. of the *Salisbury Reader* and the 1855 edition of Paley; for the Union's 1811 *Spelling Book* see *Christian Observer* vol. 11 (1812) 847, appendix. The publication history of the Union's 1830 *Scriptural Reading Book* may be followed in the *Minutes of the Committee . . . at the Depot*. See Appendix 1, Table 23; publication dates for the remaining texts are taken from the copies actually consulted. See Chapter 7, pp. 000–00 for an analysis of content

more than the Anglican National Society.[49] (See Appendix I, Table 24.) Between March 1790 and March 1799 the Manchester Interdenominational Sunday School alone bought 11,700 spelling books from various distributors, twice the total number of Bibles, testaments and Books of Common Prayer purchased for the use of children. Many Anglican schools after 1811 bought their textbooks through the National Society, while large schools like Stockport printed their own *Reading Made Easy*, excess copies of which were sold to neighboring schools.[50] In short the size of the Sunday school textbook market was prodigious.

In both form and content these books were like those used in ordinary weekday schools, except that by the 1830s, when ordinary textbooks were becoming more secular, those used in Sunday school

4. *Most Sunday school spelling books opened with illustrated alphabets like that from* Reading Made Completely Easy *below.*

[49] By 1812, one year after entering the book trade, the Union had published 150,000 copies of *Introduction to Reading, part 1*, and 85,000 copies of *part 2*, precursors of the four part spelling book, see *Christian Observer* ibid.; for textbook sales of the British and Foreign School Society and the National Society see J. M. Goldstrom 'The Changing Social Context of Elementary Education as reflected in school books in use in England, 1800–70' (unpublished Birmingham Univ. PHD thesis, 1968) 220–1

[50] *Manchester Sunday School Minute Books* MS. A 6–4, Chetham's Library—summary at end of volume for 4 May 1789–5 May 1800; Stockport Sunday School *Annual Reports* 1805 ff.

were becoming less so.[51] All of them began with an alphabet section in which a word and picture were used to teach the value of each letter. They then proceeded to words of one syllable, or in some cases lists of nonsense syllables, then words of two syllables accented on the first, words of two syllables accented on the second, and so on. Throughout the texts, graded reading copy made use of the words being taught. In addition to the Bible and New Testament, which were used as reading copy by the more advanced quarter to a third of students, Sunday schools used vast numbers of specialized textbooks designed according to the principles of then current psychology of education.[52]

But the 'march of the intellect' also reached young people through at least forty-two youth magazines published or distributed by various Sunday schools or school organizations and through the juvenile sections of adult periodicals. Children, it was realized, constituted a distinct group of readers which had to be catered for in a special way. With the possible exception of one ephemeral magazine published by John Newberry in the mid-eighteenth century and half a dozen extremely short-lived periodicals *c.* 1800, the *Youth's Magazine* begun by the eighteen-year-old William Lloyd of the Sunday School Union was the first sustained effort at publishing periodicals for children.[53] A specialized press for Sunday school teachers grew along with the burgeoning children's press. (See Appendix I, Table 23.) Between 1805 and 1850, almost forty magazines aimed directly at Sunday school children began publication. These ranged from magazines of a general religious and 'improving' nature like the interdenominational *Youth's Magazine and Evangelical Miscellany* published by the Union, or the Baptist, Primitive Methodist, Wesleyan, and Church of England children's magazines to the youth publication of tract or temperance societies like the *Gospel Tract Magazine* or the *Juvenile Rechabite Magazine*. In addition over a dozen periodicals for teachers were published during these years. They range from the Union's unofficial house organ, the *Teacher's Magazine*, to the Anglican Institute's *Sunday*

---

[51] See Chapter 7, p. 213–14

[52] For percentage in scripture classes see Edward Baines *The Social, Educational, and Religious State of the Manufacturing Districts* (1843) Table III; the associationist psychology upon which most early nineteenth-century textbooks were based is discussed in Howard C. Warren *A History of Association Psychology* (New York, 1921) 8 ff. *passim*, 87 ff. *passim*. For the most complete exposition of the 'look and say method based on the principle of association' in the Sunday school literature see John Curwen *Sunday School Papers* (1849) and *Look and Say Method of Teaching to Read* (1842)

[53] Sheila Egoff *Children's Periodicals of the nineteenth century* Library Association

School Quarterly Magazine, or *Church of England Sunday School Union Magazine*, to unattached journals like the *Sunday School Magazine*.

The circulation of these magazines was relatively large by nineteenth-century standards. The Primitive Methodists, then a small and young denomination, announced in 1823 that they needed two thousand firm orders to begin publication of their children's magazine, and within six months they had over six thousand. Carus-Wilson's three gory and, to modern readers, unsavory magazines (*The Friendly Visitor, The Visitor's Friend*, and the *Children's Friend*) may have sold up to 50,000 copies per month. By comparison the *Edinburgh Review* sold 13,500 copies at its peak in 1818 but only 7,000 by 1860 and the *Westminster Review* sold 4,000 in the same year. No religious monthly had a circulation over 2,000 in 1860.[54]

Finally, in addition to providing specialized textbooks and distributing a growing periodical literature for children, Sunday schools disseminated the printed word through libraries and books or pamphlets given as rewards to scholars. The Sunday School Union, greatly dissatisfied with the finding that in 1834 only 2,000 of 10,000 schools had libraries attached to them, began in 1835 a program to distribute collections of 100 to 200 books. During the next fifteen years, it contributed 2,100 of these libraries, i.e. 210,000 to 420,000 volumes, to schools attended by over 300,000 students.[55] Although no figures are available for the Religious Tract Society before 1850, that organization gave away some 53,700 libraries of comparable size, with a total value by 1898 of £214,000.[56] Parochial libraries, distributed by the SPCK, received support from even the most hidebound and conservative rural vicar if only for reasons of social control.[57] As a result of all this and supplementary local activity, between a half and three-quarters of urban Sunday schools had libraries by 1840 and perhaps a quarter

[54] *Primitive Methodist Magazine* vol. 5 (1824) 94–5; Alvar Ellegard 'The Readership of the Periodical Press in Mid-Victorian Britain—II. Directory' *Victorian Periodicals Newsletter* No. 13 (Sept. 1971) 12–13, 16. For circulation statistics of Carus-Wilson's magazines see Edwin W. Rice *The Sunday School Movement 1780–1917 and the American Sunday-School Union* (Philadelphia, 1917) 482

[55] Calculated from the Union's 'Annual Reports' pasted into the *MS Minute Books*, op. cit.

[56] [Anon] *The Story of the Religious Tract Society* (1898) 13

[57] Sunday school and parochial or parish libraries tended to be the same thing. See W. O. B. Allen and Edmund McClure *The History of the Society for Promoting Christian Knowledge, 1689–1898* (1898) 153–5; see also E. W. Grinfield 'The Bulwarks of the English Church ... To which are added some observations on the origin and progress of Parochial Libraries for the use of the common people' (Bath, 1820 (?)) and the discussion thereof in the High Church *Christian Remembrancer* vol. 2 (1820) 429

of the rural schools, if Rutland is at all representative.[58] Large
collections like the 4,000 volumes at Stockport or Bennett Street,
Manchester and the 1,700 volume library in Hanley, near Stoke-
on-Trent, rivalled similar facilities at the largest Mechanics
Institutes or reading clubs.

The number of tracts printed and distributed was in the tens of
millions. The Union began publishing one tract a month beginning
in 1806—*The Spanish Armada*, *The Gunpowder Plot*, *The History
of the Reformation*, *Honesty the Best Policy*, etc. These twelve-page
booklets were issued in editions of twelve to fourteen thousand, and
many were reprinted two or three times within five years of publication.[59] Private publishing houses like Richardson & Son of
Derby produced scores of reward books about twenty pages long,
many handsomely illustrated with woodcuts. The RTS distributed
much of its prodigious output through Sunday schools. In addition
to its ordinary tracts in the so-called 'first series' the society published
little books like *The Fortune Teller's Conjuring Cap or Tom Topper's
Tale over his Jug of Ale* designed to compete with popular chapbooks;
an English history series for the young with such serious titles as
The Reigns of the House of Stuart and *The Britons and the Saxons*; and
popular editions of classical works. The sheer volume of these
publications is staggering. Twenty-five to thirty million of the
'Hawkers' Tracts were distributed by 1839; 9,710,666 tracts and
4,040,793 children's books left the depository in 1849 alone. A
Union committee for vetting publications approved on average
300 book titles per year in the 1820s and over 800 by 1850.[60]

Children could also choose from hundreds of titles in the Union
and SPCK catalogues. In an Anglican Sunday school in Liskeard,
for example, forty-one Bibles, forty prayer books, fifteen *Pilgrim's
Progress*, thirteen Richmond's *Annals of the Poor*, and four Baxter's
Saint's Book were selected for the annual reward day. Fox's *Book of
Martyrs*, books on secular and ecclesiastical history, collected
sermons, and treatises on 'useful knowledge' were popular choices in
other places.[61]

Sunday schools, through the publication and distribution of all

[58]Same sources as given in note 18, p. 103

[59]Tracts No. 1–62, 1806–1811 are collected in one volume in the Hull University
Library; the edition size is from the printing history of a selected few of these
tracts in the Angus Library, Regents Park College, Oxford

[60]For RTS see William Jones *Jubilee Memorial of the Religious Tract Society* (1850)
103–133; for Union, 1820s figures calculated from *MS Minute Books*; 1840s figure
from Watson *History* ... pp. 182–3

[61]*Church of England Sunday School Quarterly Magazine* (1849) 287. See also *Catalogue of the Book Repository of the Sunday School Union, Paternoster Street* (1824) and
History of the RTS ... p. 13

the texts, magazines and books discussed above, produced a flood of literature aimed at the working-class child. In contrast to the eighteenth century, skills in elementary reading, once learned, were probably retained because of constant exposure to the printed word.

v. SUNDAY SCHOOLS AND SECULAR EDUCATION: AN ASSESSMENT

It would be startling if all of the efforts described above had not had a marked effect on the level of literacy among the working classes and therefore upon the economy and society as a whole. But both personal testimony and more quantitative data attest to the fact that they did. Thomas Whittaker, the temperance reformer, for example, was given a Bible by his mother and told to read it. 'I did so, for I could read; I had learned to do that in the sabbath school, and I say, God bless the sabbath school!' he relates in his autobiography.[62] A mother in Pendleton told an investigator that her daughter had learned to read and write in a Sunday school but believed that she 'ne'er got much good at a day school'. The wife of a handloom weaver in the same place lamented her inability to send her children to day school but said that 'they go to Sunday school and larn a deal o'good there.'[63] A sixteen-year-old chimney sweep reported that when his mother first suggested he go to Sunday school to 'keep his hand into writing', he was reluctant to do as she suggested, but, having overcome his reticence, he found that 'in the space of a few weeks I improved my reading and writing also.'[64] In fact, Sunday schools appeared to many religious authorities to be far more successful as 'instruments of instruction' than of conversion.[65]

Four sets of data support this literary evidence. The New Meeting Sunday School in Birmingham provided the 1843 Commission on Children in Manufactures with a list of all boys and girls on their register: the age, occupation, and an estimate of ability with reading and writing of all students was included.[66] By dividing all those scholars who are employed full-time, and thus getting no day school education into an older and a younger age group, and then

[62] Thomas Whittaker *Life's Battles in Temperance Armour* (1884) 26

[63] *Report of the Manchester Statistical Society on the state of education in Pendleton* (1838) 4–5

[64] *Sunday School Repository* vol. 2, 265–6—letter

[65] For example Rev. Miles Atkinson *Practical Sermons ... To which is prefixed a short memoir of the life and character of the author* vol. 1 (1812) xxiv. Atkinson was one of the leaders of the Leeds Sunday school movement in its early days and became bitterly disappointed with its failure as a means for religious reformation

[66] *Children's Employment Commission ...* 1843 [432] xv, F 200–204

comparing the educational attainments of the two groups, one can get some idea of the contribution made by this Sunday school in improving the reading and writing ability of students (Table 14).

Table 14: *Level of reading and writing competence in the Birmingham New Meeting Sunday School, 1843*

Ability level	Boys				Girls				Boys and girls			
	12 or less		over 12		12 or less		over 12		12 or less		over 12	
Reads: well	24	45%	61	67%	28	58%	32	76%	52	52%	93	70%
Reads: little	28	53%	29	32%	18	38%	10	24%	46	46%	39	29%
Reads: none	1	2%	2	1%	2	4%	0	0%	3	3%	2	1%
Writes: well	17	32%	46	50%	9	19%	29	67%	26	26%	75	56%
Writes: little	21	40%	39	42%	22	46%	3	7%	43	43%	42	31%
Writes: none	15	28%	7	8%	17	35%	10	24%	32	32%	17	13%
Total	53	100%	92	100%	48	100%	42	100%	101	100%	134	100%

While the differences between the reading abilities of the two age groups are marked, the differences in writing are much more so, particularly among girls. For both boys and girls, however, the greatest difference between the two groups is in their ability to read and write well. This suggests that while Sunday schools may be solely responsible for teaching skills to only a small proportion of the students, they help to improve the standard of literacy among many more.

Evidence from the Stockport Sunday School points in the same direction. Using the enrolment registers, which give the ability of a student upon entry into, and exit from, the school, one can estimate the degree to which it contributed to the elementary education of its students. Although it is not possible to isolate those students who went to day school from those who did not, only 7.7 per cent of the boys and 13.3 per cent of the girls fall in the former category.[67] The extra education factor would therefore not be large enough to explain the improvement which occurred. (See Table 15.)

It is clear that attendance at the Stockport Sunday School, at least for some, was indeed beneficial. A lower percentage left the Sunday school in the lower three divisions than entered in them for

[67] Calculated from MS. returns for each class made in compliance with a request from the 1833 Factory Commissioners. Stockport Reference Library

Table 15:[68] *Level of competence of students upon entering and leaving the Stockport Sunday School for those first enrolled in 1800, 1820, 1840, 1860*

Level of Instruction		Number and percentage of total in each category							
		1800		1820		1840		1860	
a. Letters and spelling	entry	262	29%	20	2%	49	8%	16	3%
	exit	26	6%	5	1%	0	0	0	0
b. "Reading made easy"	entry	286	30%	436	41%	167	28%	159	34%
	exit	116	27%	136	23%	38	11%	17	8%
c. Testament	entry	156	16%	185	17%	142	24%	103	22%
	exit	59	14%	84	14%	71	22%	36	17%
a, b, and c	entry	704	75%	641	61%	358	61%	278	60%
	exit	201	46%	225	39%	109	33%	53	26%
d. Bible	entry	159	17%	382	35%	224	38%	161	35%
	exit	36	8%	103	18%	103	31%	67	32%
e. Writing	entry	82	9%	42	4%	10	2%	24	5%
	exit	139	32%	230	40%	117	36%	85	41%
f. Accounts	entry	0	0	0	0	0	0	0	0
	exit	47	11%	26	4%	0	0	0	0
d, e, and f	entry	241	26%	424	39%	234	39%	185	40%
	exit	222	53%	359	61%	220	67%	152	74%
Total	entry	945		1,065		592		463	
	exit	423		584		329		205	

each of the years considered. There is also a slight decrease in the percentage of those who entered in the lower divisions, reflecting the increased age of entrance and perhaps some minimal improvement in the quality of day education. More important than the decrease in the lower division over time is the gain in those leaving in the higher divisions each year and the upward trend for leaving in these higher divisions from 1800–60. In other words, for each year more people left in the higher divisions than entered in them, and the percentage leaving in one of these divisions increases from 53 per cent in 1800 to 74 per cent in 1860.

The proportion leaving, and the proportion of the school enrolled in, the writing division remained constant at about one-third throughout the first half of the century. It is this one-third which corresponds to the proportion of students who remained in the school about three years or longer and gained the most from its services. A smaller percentage, between five and ten per cent made the Sunday school a major part of their lives. They remained eight, nine or in some cases up to seventeen years; they joined the various improvement societies, night classes, etc.; and it is for them that the Sunday school had the greatest educational value. Factory children, it should be noted, were less likely to reach

[68] Calculated from *MS Enrollment Registers* op. cit.

the highest levels of the school than those in other employ.
(Table 16.)

Table 16:[69] *Representation of factory and non-factory children over age* 13 *in the higher and lower divisions of the Stockport Sunday School,* 1833

Level of Education		Total number	Number in factory	Percentage in factory	Percentage employed
Low.	Reading classes—M	626	480	76	100
High.	Writing classes —M	349	230	66	100
Low.	Reading classes—F	592	544	92	100
High.	Second class —F	162	95	59	100

They were under-represented in the boys' writing classes and were
proportionately even less well represented in the most advanced
girls' class. Nevertheless, the movement from the lower to the higher
divisions suggests that, except for the decreasing proportion who
left within a year of entering, the Sunday school had some educational value for the great bulk of its students.

Finally, there is evidence from the Manchester Statistical
Society's investigation into education in Pendleton and Kingston-
upon-Hull, which sought to ascertain the educational attainments
of 21,165 minors and to correlate this data with the length of time
the children had been in school.[70] Of these minors, 4,949, most of
whom were under five years old, had never attended school. Of
the remainder, 12,642 had attended or were still attending day or
evening school; 200 were still or had been under private instruction; for 2,688 no information could be obtained; and, finally,
663 had attended or were still attending Sunday school only. It
is this last group which provides the relevant evidence. (Table 17.)

Table 17: *Educational acquirements of minors attending only Sunday school in Pendleton and Kingston-on-Hull,* 1838, 40

Attending only Sunday school	Level of attainment								
	READING			WRITING			CIPHERING		
	Well	Barely able	None	Well	Barely able	None	Well	Barely able	None
No. 663	226	147	290	105	35	523	22	6	635
% 100	34	22	44	16	5	79	3	1	96

[69] Calculated from MS. returns for each class made in compliance with a request
from the 1833 Factory Commissioners. Stockport Reference Library
[70] *Report of the Manchester Statistical Society on the State of Education in Pendleton* ...
Kingston-U-Hull op. cit. Table IX

Despite the fact that the number who only attended Sunday school included those too young for day school—which means that these data underestimate the value of Sunday school education—the levels of attainment in reading are roughly comparable to those of one to two years of day school. The writing attainments of the 'Sunday school only' group are equivalent to about four years' day schooling.[71] Insofar as schooling determined the level of basic literacy, the quantitative material presented here confirms the overwhelming impression gained from literary sources that, not surprisingly, those who attended Sunday school benefited from the secular instruction offered there.

vi. CONCLUSIONS

This section has not argued that Sunday schools provided an adequate substitute for extended day education; nor has it sought to deny by exclusion the religious and purely social aspects of Sunday school life. It suggested that within the context of a working-class childhood, three to five hours of instruction each week for an average of four years, using specialized textbooks in small classes graded according to scholastic ability, had a significant impact on the creation of mass literacy in nineteenth-century England.

Perhaps the *Morning Chronicle* exaggerated when it claimed that many of the richest men in Manchester owed their ability to read and write to the Sunday schools. But it was right when it said that

> Long before educational committees of the Privy Council and British and Foreign Societies were heard of, long previous to the era of Institutes, and Athenaeums, the Sunday-schools were sedulously at work, impregnating the people with the rudiments of an education which, though always rude and often narrow and fanatical in its teachings, was yet preserving a glow of moral and religious sentiment, and keeping alive a degree of popular intelligence which otherwise would assuredly have perished in the rush and clatter with which a vast manufacturing population came surging up upon the land.[72]

From the Sunday schools came the managers and foremen of industry and the political and trade union leaders of the working class. The place of these schools in their lives and in the lives of more ordinary men and women will be considered in Chapter Six.

[71] The reports give attainment levels for students who have left school after N years. I used as equivalent the year wherein the distribution of achievement was nearest to that of the Sunday school

[72] *Morning Chronicle* (15 November 1849) Letter IX, col. 1

5. Sunday Schools and Secular Education II : The Determinants of Curriculum

On Sunday, 5 July 1834, over a thousand Sunday school students streamed down one of Bolton's main streets. Teachers and other supporters of writing instruction on Sunday lined one side of the road, opponents of secular instruction on the sabbath waited on the other. As the students walked between the two factions over nine hundred veered to the pro-writing side and marched in triumphal procession to Moor Lane where ordinary classes gave way to a victory celebration marked by speeches and hymn singing. By the time things finally settled down, the Hanover Street Chapel had lost two hundred adult members and 1,100 Sunday school scholars to the congregation which grew up around the rebellious pro-writing party.[1]

This was only one among scores of similar, albeit less dramatic, skirmishes in the long battle by denominational authorities, particularly the Wesleyan Methodist Conference, against writing instruction on the sabbath. The controversy over writing instruction in fact touched on the most sensitive issues regarding the nature and place of the Sunday school in the working-class community. An understanding of what this apparently trivial dispute meant in its nineteenth-century context will, therefore, provide additional insight into the role of these schools in the lives of those who used them.

According to one view, the limitation of the Sunday school curriculum was a special case of a more generalized opposition among the ruling classes in the late eighteenth and early nineteenth century to the 'education of the people'. In this view, 'the dominant attitude of the Evangelicals, that the function of education began

[1] Stephen Rothwell *Memorials of the Independent Chapel, Folds Road, Bolton* (Bolton, 1887) 133–7; and John Musgrave *The Origins of Methodism in Bolton* (1865) 34

and ended with the moral rescue of the poor' combined with
pervasive counter-revolutionary sentiments to keep writing out
of Sunday schools from the start or to curtail, if not to eliminate,
it as soon as possible.[2] Or conversely, it is argued that Sunday school
authorities opposed writing instruction because they regarded use
of the pen as an upper-class accomplishment; and historians might
therefore, conclude that the schools were not for education but
rather for indoctrination.[3]

Indeed, the time-honored arguments of the early eighteenth
century against mass popular education still found currency in the
1780s and 1790s. Bernard de Mandeville considered charity schools,
and presumably all schools for the laboring classes, 'very pernicious
to those whose livelihood has no dependence on these arts and who
are forced to get their daily bread by daily labour'. Richardson
thought that 'The low and illiterate are the most useful people in
the commonwealth', for whom schooling is, by and large, undesirable since 'a lettered education but too generally sets people above
those servile offices by which the business of the world is carried on.[4]

In the late eighteenth century, a few still used the argument
that any education for the poor beyond teaching them to read their
Bibles would 'produce in them a disrelish for laborious occupations'.[5] George Hadley, for example used the section on Sunday
schools in his history of Kingston-upon-Hull to launch a near
hysterical attack on the very notion of teaching the poor to read and
write. Education led to obscenity he argued; 'learning extirpates
industry' and 'a husband-man who can read and write is an incum-
berance to a parish.' Educational philanthropy was but a ploy
'ardently promoted, from motives of vanity in individuals, impelled
by a desire of becoming conspicuous in a popular measure'. Finally,
the worst of all, education encouraged itinerant preaching with its
panoply of levelling tendencies. It not only caused men and women
to abandon 'the more irksome labour of their hands' for the 'indolent labour of their heads', it caused them to place themselves on a
level with the clergy of the established church. The number of
itinerant preachers, 'of these pernicious vagrants [will] be increased
when ALL CAN READ, and when all claim the right of putting

[2] E. P. Thompson *The Making of the English Working Class* (1963) 377–8; for this
view see also Brain Simon *Studies in the History of Education, 1780–1870* (1960)
132–3; Raymond Williams *The Long Revolution* (New York, 1961) 135–7

[3] Charles Foster *Errand of Mercy*; *The Evangelical United Front, 1790–1837* (Chapel
Hill, 1960) 80

[4] Bernard de Mandeville *Essay on Charity and Charity Schools* (1727) 62; Samuel
Richardson *Works* (1811) 160–1, quoted in Christopher Hill, *Puritanism and
Revolution* (1968) 362–3

[5] Quoted in Williams *Long Revolution* p. 135

their own construction on what they read'. Duties of the present
life will be ignored and fanaticism and strife will pervade the land.[6]

The French Revolution exacerbated these fears and consequently arguments over education took on the more overtly political
and repressive tone evident in Davies Giddy's remarks on
Whitbread's proposal to provide two years of free instruction in
reading, writing and arithmetic for poor children:

> ... instead of teaching them subordination ... it would render
> them factious and refractory; it would enable them to read
> seditious pamphlets, vicious books and publications against
> Christianity; it would render them insolent to their superiors;
> and in a few years, the results would be that the legislature would
> find it necessary to direct the strong arm of power towards
> them.[7]

Indeed the *Anti-Jacobin Review* argued again and again that such
dangers were a thing of the present and not of the distant future.
Sunday schools, according to another periodical, had helped to
create a literate audience for the thousands of seditious tracts and
pamphlets that were distributed throughout England and sometimes even scattered indiscriminately along the King's highways.[8]

Jonas Hanway, one of the founders of the Sunday School Society,
though not in principle opposed to teaching *some* of the poor to
write and do arithmetic—a master might find it necessary to teach
his servants the three Rs so that they could perform their duties
more satisfactorily—nevertheless thought that 'if one in twenty
acquires this skill, it may answer for the other nineteen.'[9] He
elaborated this position in his influential and widely cited book
on Sunday schools: 'It certainly cannot be meant to exceed the
proper bounds of instruction. As to the connection between *reading*
and *writing*, as vulgarly understood, I discover none that concerns
those who depend for their bread on their manual labour and not
on their *pen*.'[10] The laboring classes should learn to read so that
they might read the Bible, fill up their leisure time more construc-
tively, and thereby keep out of mischief.

Others who supported Sunday schools in the late eighteenth
century, although not actively opposed to teaching the lower

[6] George Hadley *A New History of Kingston-upon-Hull* (Kingston-upon-Hull,
1788) 379–381

[7] *Parl. Debates* (Hansard) vol. IX, 789, 13 July 1807.

[8] *British Critic* (March 1798)

[9] Jonas Hanway *Letters on the Importance to the Rising Generation of the Labouring
Part of our Fellow Subjects* (1767) 38

[10] Jonas Hanway *A Comprehensive View of Sunday Schools and a Copious Schoolbook*
(1786) xii–xiii.

orders writing or arithmetic, nevertheless thought these subjects irrelevant to the real aims of their undertakings. 'Rescuing them [the poor] from low habits of vice and indolence', 'inur [ing] children to early habits of going to church and spending the leisure hours of Sunday decently and virtuously', 'training up the minds of children to love of VIRTUE' did not require intensive secular instruction.[11] (A small minority took this position a step further and supported Sunday schools, while opposing more widespread elementary education, precisely because of the former's more limited objectives.)

The controversy over teaching writing on Sundays, which festered in some Dissenting denominations and became most virulent in Wesleyan Methodism, might be seen as an outgrowth of the obscurantist position outlined above. E. P. Thompson, for example, highlights the confrontation between the high Tory Jabez Bunting, who opposed writing in Sunday schools as a 'secular art' from which 'temporal advantage' might accrue, and the 'former Jacobin' James Montgomery, who defended 'the children's cause' in the pages of the Sheffield *Iris*.[12] James Angel James, one of the most famous Dissenting preachers of the early nineteenth century and an oft quoted authority for the anti-writing faction, argued like Hanway or Sarah Trimmer, that 'it [writing] was not absolutely necessary for their temporal interests, because the poor may acquire nearly all the advantages and comforts of their station without being able to write.'[13] Finally, those who opposed teaching writing on Sunday seem tainted by the undisputed political conservatism of the Wesleyan Conference leadership, which for thirty years was in the vanguard of the struggle to suppress secular education in Sunday schools.

Conversely, the proponents of writing appear more liberal by association with men and groups of radical political persuasions. Joseph Barker, for example, replied to J. A. James that 'In this happy land the poor have every station of life open to them, and no one can tell, when he looks at a ragged child, what situation he

---

[11] *Plan of a Society ... for the support and encouragement of Sunday schools* (1787) 5–6; quoted in William C. Northcott *For Britain's Children, The Story of the Sunday School Union 1803–1952* (1952) 15; Anon. *An address to parents earnestly recommending them to promote the happiness of their children by a due regard to their virtuous education* (Uxbridge, 1787)

[12] Thompson *The Making of the English Working Class* p. 389

[13] Rev. J. A. James *The Sunday School Teacher's Guide* (Boston, 1819) 163. An earlier English edition was widely used by the anti-Sunday writing instruction faction of Wesleyan Methodism

may fill a few years hence.'[14] A letter from William Hill, the editor of the *Northern Star*, argued in 1838 that the elimination of Sunday writing instruction would be a national calamity, and the Owenite Sunday school in Keighley carried a flag bearing the inscription 'NO SIN TO WRITE' in the town's Whit Monday walk.[15] Furthermore, those Methodist sects—the Primitive, Band Room, and to a lesser extent, New Connexion Methodists—with a more predominantly working-class membership, a more democratic organization on the national level, and perhaps a greater propensity on the local level to become associated with radical causes, were also the denominations least concerned about eliminating writing instruction from their Sunday schools.[16] At least part of the 'writing controversy' then, appears to have been between those who thought poverty was a station ordained by Providence and those who favored education as a means by which the poor might find their place in a hierarchy open to talent.

But the case is not so simple. By the time of the debate on Whitbread's bill in 1807, the central issue at the parliamentary level was no longer whether the poor should be given an elementary education but who should provide the necessary schooling and to what religious or political ends. Whitbread's bill, and indeed every attempt between 1807 and 1870 to institute a national system of mass instruction, failed because of the struggle between competing interests for control of projected facilities, not because of principled opposition to working-class education.

As for Sunday schools, the obscurantist tradition played almost no part in the debate over curriculum. On this subject Hanway and More were not representative of Evangelicals, and in any case a great many Sunday schools between 1785 and the late 1820s did in fact teach writing on the sabbath. By the time the controversy over eliminating such instruction reached its peak in the late 1820s and the 1830s, the principle of popular education had become almost universally established. Furthermore those who were strongest in their opposition to Sunday instruction were generally active in promoting more extensive weekday education, and, in a majority of schools, provision was made for weekday evening instruction in those subjects not considered suitable for the sabbath. The propriety of such subjects for the working classes was beyond question. Finally, the sabbatarian arguments advanced against secular

[14]Joseph Barker, 'Minister of the Gospel' *Mercy Triumphant, or Teaching the Children of the Poor to write on the Sabbath Day; Proved to be in Perfect Agreement with the Oracles of God; with plain and full answers to* . . . (1843, 3rd edn.) 27

[15]*Northern Star* (6 Jan., 1838) 7 and (9 June 1838) 5

[16]Robert Currie *Methodism Divided* (1968) 54–8

instruction on Sunday, which will be examined later in this section, cannot be interpreted as having a distinct anti-working-class bias.

The debate in Parliament over the educational provisions of Samuel Whitbread's poor law reform bill was the first time that popular education was discussed at the highest level. Unfortunately, the significance of this debate has been distorted by historians who have selected Davies Giddy, by far the most rabidly hostile speaker against the principle of the bill, as representative of the other twenty-six members of the Lords and Commons who spoke with reference to it.[17] His oft quoted (see p. 126 above) warning that political dangers arise from mass popular education is as unrepresentative of the debate as the Earl Stanhope's condemnation of those who adhered to 'the abominable principle, that no part of the country ought to receive education unless in the tenets of the established church' or his assertion that in a manufacturing country like England, continued prosperity 'depended on a clear understanding and some degree of mathematical and mechanical knowledge' among the workforce.[18] A few opposed the bill because it was too expensive but most speakers were hostile to it because of its provisions for the control of education. They argued either that Whitbread's proposals left the adoption of schools in each parish to the discretion of parishioners 'without any reasonable discrimination of rank and property' which ought 'to have their proportionate weight'; or that, if there was to be public provision of elementary education, it would have to be strictly under the direction of the Established Church which under the proposed measure would not have been the case.[19]

Further evidence for the absence of generalized opposition to limited popular education is the fact that within five years of the defeat of Whitbread's bill the two main school societies were founded. The Anglican National Society, started by three high Tories in 1811, was committed to instruction in the elementary subjects despite some earlier statements to the contrary by Andrew Bell, its pedagogic mentor. The Society's central school in Baldwin's Gardens, Holborn, for twenty years the most visible center of its operations, taught reading, ciphering up through multiplication and division, and writing, first on sand tables, then slates, and occasionally in copy books.[20] British and Foreign Society schools

[17] For the debate see *Parl. Debates* (Hansard) vol. IX, 798–804, 13 July 1807; 853–860, 21 July 1807; and in the Lords, 1174–78, 11 August 1807

[18] Ibid. 1178

[19] Ibid. 1174–75, 1176, 11 Aug. 1807

[20] H. J. Burgess and P. A. Welsby *A Short History of the National Society 1811–1961* (1961) 7–8

taught the three Rs and some history and geography as well.[21]

The support for these societies within the governing élite was almost universal. Lords Eldon, Grenville and Redesdale, all of whom had spoken against Whitbread's bill, were among the vice-presidents of the Anglican body, whose contributors included the Queen and the Prince Regent, the Dukes of York, Cumberland and Cambridge, and the Stock Exchange Committee. Spencer Perceval, Lords Hawkesbury and Redesdale, the Archbishop of Canterbury, and Hawkes Bourne contributed some £683 10s. between 1811 and 1816; all had opposed the 1807 education measure.[22] The Prince Regent was patron of the interdenominational British and Foreign Society, the Dukes of Kent and Sussex were vice-patrons, and the Duke of Bedford served as president with a board of vice-presidents almost as impressive, if rather more whiggish and heavy with Dissent, then that of the National Society.[23]

Only a handful of men saw the diffusion of education as valuable in itself, elevating or enlightening the lower orders for their own benefit. Most men had a more external, instrumental motive in supporting education; they hoped that it would make the lower orders more virtuous, more loyal, more firmly attached to the Church, more moral, easier to control, and perhaps healthier and more productive as well. But opposition in principle to teaching the poor how to read, write and cipher was minimal.

The reactionary farmers encountered by Hannah More in Somerset undoubtedly had their counterparts elsewhere, but their views were unfashionable and were seldom found in print. Sir Thomas Eden writing in 1797 was perhaps more representative when he observed that

> ... with respect to education in general ... it is now admitted on all hands, that intellectual acquisitions are beneficial to every class of the community, and that children of our labourers are not the less likely to become useful members of the State in that sphere of life for which they are destined, from having been instructed in reading, writing, and arithmetic.[21]

By 1808 belief in the value of education was so widespread that, as Playfair remarked, 'the man who should dispute the wisdom of Sunday schools would be considered as unworthy of attention.' The Mr Dombeys of the world, who approved of schools so long as

[21] H. B. Binns *A Century of Education, Being a Centenary History of the British and Foreign School Society* (1908) 73

[22] *5th Annual Report of the National School Society* (1816)

[23] Binns *A Century* ... pp. 72–3

[24] Sir Thomas Eden *The State of the Poor* (1798) vol. 1, 427

they taught the inferior classes how 'to conduct themselves properly', ⤶
had come to be more common among the respectable classes than
the Major Bagstocks, who held unequivocal views: 'Never educate
that sort of people, Sir. Damme, Sir, it never does. It always fails.'[25]
To see simple obscurantism as a major element in the debate over
writing on the sabbath, or in any other nineteenth-century educational debate, is to miss their true significance. It was control of
schooling that was at stake.

Moreover, during the period when the obscurantist case might
have been at its strongest in Sunday schools, the late eighteenth
and early nineteenth century, writing was regularly taught on the
sabbath. As a letter in the *Bolton Express* noted:

> It is well known that writing has been taught the children in
> most, if not all, the Methodist Sunday Schools from the commence-
> ment of the Godlike Institution, and that the teachers were
> encouraged therein by the best men that ever advanced the
> Methodist Connection not excepting the venerable Mr. Wesley
> himself.[26]

The Nottingham Sunday School in the late eighteenth century,
dominated by Methodists though in theory interdenominational,
taught reading and writing on Sundays and arithmetic on weekday
evenings; Stourbridge Unitarian Sunday School spent a large
proportion of its budget on slates, copy books, pencils and writing
desks during the same period.[27] A private Sunday school in Yorkshire, begun about 1805 by a lady in correspondence with the
Society for Bettering the Condition of the Poor, used Bell's system
to teach boys and girls to read, write, and cast accounts.[28] The
curate of Ayleston suggested to readers of the *Gentleman's Magazine*
in 1786 that the best six readers in a class of thirty-five be admitted
to a writing class and that, until students became sufficiently
competent, adults be admitted to the advanced class.[29] Raikes
himself advised a young tinplate worker who was setting up a
Sunday school in Rochdale to teach reading and writing.[30]

Hanway and More were, therefore, not speaking for the country

[25] Quoted in M. Dorothy George *London Life in the Eighteenth Century* (1925;
1966) 26; Charles Dickens *Dombey and Son* (Fireside ed.) 87, 334
[26] 31 Jan. 1824, quoted in Rothwell *Memorials* ... p. 133
[27] J. W. Wakerly *Centenary History of Wesley Sunday School, Nottingham* (1885);
A. G. Cumberland 'Protestant non-conformity in the Black Country, 1662–1851'
(unpublished MA thesis, Birmingham University, 1951) 163–4
[28] *Reports of the Society for Bettering the Condition of the Poor* vol. 6, 139–46
[29] *Gentleman's Magazine* vol. 59, no. 3 (1789) 204
[30] William Jessop *An Account of Methodism in Rossendale and the Vicinity* ... (Manchester, London, 1880) 170

as a whole, or even for the Evangelical party. James Montgomery, the champion of the successful pro-writing faction in Sheffield, was an Evangelical Moravian song-writer and poet.[31] The Rev. William Romaine, a prominent Evangelical and one time chaplain to Lady Huntingdon, wrote to a friend in 1784 that 'the Lord God has marvellously favoured the plan' to get children together on Sundays and 'teach them to read, *write*, and learn the catechism'.[32] The Rev. William Turner proposed to the Annual Conference of the Associated Dissenting Ministers in 1786 that children be 'united each Sunday and carefully taught to read and *write*' and, of course, be given religious instruction. Teachers who could only give reading instruction, he suggested, should get 1s. 6d. per Sunday; those who could teach writing as well ought to get 2s.[33]

Furthermore, those who did oppose writing instruction on Sundays made every effort to provide it on other days of the week. Their scruples forbade teaching writing on the sabbath, not teaching the poor to write. The Church of England Sunday schools in Manchester, for example, specifically prohibited writing instruction on Sunday. 'But', the relevant rule goes on to say,

> the school rooms may be open two evenings per week for the purpose of gratuitously teaching the children to write and cast accounts and the Visitors and teachers are earnestly recommended to encourage and promote this plan amongst the children of their varied schools as a reward for regular attendance and good conduct.[34]

The *Evangelical Magazine* suggested a similar arrangement and expressed the hope that parents would be sufficiently aware of the benefits of writing instruction to allow their children to attend weekday evening classes.[35] 'Where the scholars of a Sunday school have not the advantage of attending a daily school', argued the Secretary of the National Society, in 1833, 'very great benefit may arise from assembling them one or two evenings a week ... for the boys to learn writing and arithmetic; and the girls the same ,or needlework and knitting.'[36]

[31] George Padgin 'James Montgomery—Christian Poet, Hymn writer, Philanthropist, and Pioneer of Sunday Schools' Robert Raikes Historical Society Bulletin no. 15, mimeographed (March 1965)

[32] *Letters of The Rev. William Romaine* in *Works* vol. 7 (1809) 130–1 (my emphasis)

[33] Rev. William Turner *Sunday Schools Recommended ... with an appendix concerning the formation and expense of these schools* (Newcastle, 1786) 45

[34] 'Rules of the Sunday School belonging to the Established Church' in *Minute Books of the Committee* ... after entry for 27 Dec. 1815, MS. Chetham's Library A 6–5

[35] *Evangelical Magazine* 2nd ser. vol. 2 (1824) 196

[36] Wigram *Practical Hints* p. 80

Although the interdenominational Sunday School Union did not take an official stand on so controversial an issue—some of its affiliated schools did, and others did not, teach writing on the sabbath—it published advice on how to teach writing and sold copy books for that purpose. In the Union's annual sermon for 1819, Robert Watson noted that some schools taught writing but that 'in all well-regulated Sunday Schools of this description, it [writing] is not taught on the Sabbath. There are teachers, who much to their honour, are willing to sacrifice one or two evenings a week for this purpose, to making the sanctity of that day unimpaired . . .'[37]

Wesleyan Sunday schools generally adopted the weekday evening plan once Sunday instruction had been eliminated. James's guidebook noted that in many schools which obeyed the Conference's prohibition on writing 'two or three evenings of the week are devoted to the subject'.[38] At the local level, the Congleton Methodist Sunday School arranged for evening classes before voting against writing in 1837; the Bacup Sunday School in Yorkshire hired a young man at £4 per year to teach writing and arithmetic on Saturday evenings; the Burnley Methodist Sunday School, which in 1821 had successfully withstood a boycott on charity sermons imposed by the Rev. Robert Newton in order to suppress writing instruction on Sunday, freely abandoned the practice in 1826 and introduced alternative classes on Saturday evenings for boys and Monday evenings for girls; free paper and pens were provided out of general funds.[39] In fact, weekday evening classes, which were attended by about ten per cent of students, were common in most parts of the country.[40] Even those who in the late eighteenth century thought that reading instruction on Sunday constituted a violation of the sabbath made provision for Saturday evening classes.[41]

There was undoubtedly a streak of anti-intellectualism among some Evangelicals and particularly among the successors of Wesley. Perhaps their belief in the immediacy of religious experience and the knowledge of one's salvation made literary attainments beyond the ability to read the Bible seem less important. But even Jabez

[37] Rev. R. Watson *Sermon* (*Mark ix*: 36) *to the Sunday School Union* (1819)
[38] James *Guide* . . . p. 164
[39] J. B. Dyson *History of Wesleyan Methodism in the Congleton Circuit* . . . (1856) 159; Jessop *An Account* . . . p. 311; B. Moore, JP *History of Wesleyan Methodism in Burnley and East Lancashire* (Burnley, 1899) 115
[40] See Chapter Four, p. 103
[41] See for example the *Protestant Dissenters Magazine* vol. 1 (May 1794) 242 and (Sept.) 372–3; this was a journal of Old Dissent, e.g. Congregationalists, Baptists, and Presbyterians

Bunting, the leading proponent of the Wesleyan campaign to stop Sunday writing instruction, was quite clearly not motivated by a desire to keep the working classes ignorant. 'If', he wrote, 'by Lancaster's plan children can be taught to write, while learning to read the scripture, and if that plan were feasible in Sunday schools, my scruples would be greatly relieved.' But such was not the case, and Bunting suggested that 'therefore it [writing] ought to be taught in the six days allotted to us for secular purposes, not on seventh reserved for spiritual exercises.' He went on to propose Saturday evening as an appropriate time throughout the year or, at the very least, during the summer months when presumably long hours of daylight made evening instruction more practicable.[12]

Finally, the drive to suppress writing and other forms of secular instruction in Sunday schools coexisted with efforts by those involved to make weekday instruction more readily available. Popular ignorance, therefore, was not the aim of the anti-writing faction. Far from being opposed to further instruction for the working classes, the Wesleyan Methodists and Congregationalists established denominational schools during the late 1830s and 1840s just as the writing controversy reached its peak and was beginning to subside.[43] Those responsible for the integration of the Sunday school with church or chapel welcomed the spread of literacy. 'But the general means of education for all', wrote a commentator in the 1870s, Sunday schools have 'risen to a higher plane, and may now be confined to spiritual instruction'.[44] In the 1860s the Bishop of Oxford expressed the hope that 'the use of Church Sunday schools as instruments for conveying mere secular instruction [had] probably and happily gone by.' 'The existence of such schools', he continued, 'was an evil necessity engendered by widespread weekday neglect.'[45] A society was even formed in 1844 to 'assist Sunday school teachers and committees throughout the country, and of every denomination, to obtain general education for their children during the week, and to secure them from those encroachments so frequently made upon their classes'.[46]

Chapter Four and the evidence presented above make it clear that

[42]T. P. Bunting *Life of Jabez Bunting* vol. 1, 320 and 322–3 quoted from the private memorandum Bunting drew up to clarify the issues for himself

[43]The Methodist Education Committee was founded in 1837, the Congregationalist Society in 1843. Members of both denominations had of course supported the British and Foreign School Society before these dates

[44]Jabez Burns *A Retrospect of Forty Five Years of Christian Ministry* (1875) 369

[45]Introduction to J. Traviss Lockwood *Sunday Schools: How to Revive and Utilize Them* (1868) iii

[46]*Circular of the Sunday School Society for the promotion of General Education on the Principles of the British and Foreign School System* (1844)

Sunday schools for the whole period under discussion were engaged in the provision of secular education. Hostility to writing instruction on Sunday was grounded in sabbatarianism not obscurantism. But sabbatarianism in the late eighteenth and nineteenth century is a complicated and little understood phenomenon; as an explanatory device it raises as many questions as it answers.

For the Evangelicals of the 1780s, as for the supporters of the Lord's Day Observance Society in the 1830s and after, violation of the Sabbath was the most corrupting of sins. 'Does not a strict observance of the Sabbath promote the Discharge of ALL obligations? All the important duties of morality?' asked an early sermon on Sunday schools. Indeed, 'the PROFANATION of the Sabbath is the root of every evil.'[47] 'Harm in reading, writing, travelling, visiting, etc. on the Sabbath?' Bunting mused in a personal memorandum: 'Religious observances of the Lord's day must be upheld by some public and visible distinctions. Every liberty, every trespass is as proceeding as from a secret contempt of the Christian religion.'[48]

Insofar as the working classes were more dependent on Sunday schools for secular education and on public facilities generally for their everyday needs, efforts to suppress writing instruction on the sabbath or to restrict Sunday markets, transport, drinking etc. affected them more than other classes.[49] But of course there were also numerous and well-recognized advantages of sabbatarian legislation. In addition to assuring the working man and woman time for relaxation, recreation, learning, or for simply doing nothing, it also formed a barrier against the encroachments of a capitalist economy. 'Oh! precious day!' proclaimed a working man's essay on the sabbath

the workman's jubilee—the slave's release—the shield of servitude—the antidote of weariness—the suspension of the curse . . . It does homage to the glorious attributes of THE MAN, even when it finds him in the condition of the SERF. In most cases, it proclaims to the servant equal liberty with the master. It is a perpetual rebuke to the reigning rapacity of the world.

[47] Lancaster Adkin, Rector of Belaugh *The Sabbath—A Sermon Preached at the Parish Church of St. Stephen's, Norwich, to Promote the Establishment of Sunday Schools* (Norwich, 1785) 16, 31

[48] Bunting, op. cit. pp. 322–3

[49] See Brian Harrison 'The Sunday Trading Riots of 1855' *The Historical Journal* vol. 8 (1965) 219 ff. for a statement of this view. Perhaps the classic statement of the thesis that the polarization of sabbatarianism and the reaction against it followed the cleavage between the working and middle classes is in Marx's article 'Anti-Church Movement—Demonstration in Hyde Park' reprinted in *Marx and Engels on Britain* (2nd ed., 1962) 434–40

It deals out, with even-handed justice, the essential rights of mankind to all classes alike; and it is designed to protect the poor from the bribes of wealth, and the weak from the encroachments of power.[50]

Practical as well as psychological motives, therefore, induced some of the working classes to support strict Sunday observance.

Furthermore, sabbatarian strictures in both the private and public sphere were intended by their proponents to apply to all segments of society. The Wesleyan Methodists were particularly active in the campaign against Sunday writing, but they also discountenanced doing Latin or French exercises and taking public school children out for drives on the sabbath, both of which applied exclusively to the upper and middle classes.[51] Josiah Pratt advised his son in Cambridge to spend Sunday as follows: before college chapel—read privately; breakfast to church time—read scripture; attend morning and afternoon sermons, and outline each; go to evening prayers, and afterward retire alone for tea.[52] A widely circulated pamphlet on the sabbath warns its readers not to read public journals or other non-religious works, read or write business letters, entertain idle friends, or take public walks on the sabbath; and William Lovett, the Chartist, wrote that on Sundays his mother 'strictly prohibited all books but the Bible and a Prayer book' and did not allow him 'to enjoy a walk unless to chapel'.[53] Saintliness was expected from all classes.

The psychological and theological roots of sabbatarianism during this period are obscure. The desire to create a more regular rhythm of work and rest, so prominent in sixteenth and seventeenth-century puritanism, played little, if any, part in the nineteenth century.[54] The Protestant belief that godliness was the obligation of all Christians, and not just the priesthood, surely motivated some of those who strove for that purification of society in which observance of the sabbath played so large a part. Real and imagined evidence of secularization may have led others to erect quite arbitrary 'visible

[50] *The Workmen's Testimony to the Sabbath* (1851) 25; see also *Prize Essays on the temporal advantages of the Sabbath* (1849) esp. pp. 12–15, 18–21, 26–27, 84–89, 152–3, and 184–5

[51] *Methodist Magazine* vol. 24 (1801) 266

[52] Josiah Pratt *Memoirs* (New York, 1855), quoted in George Ellis 'The Evangelicals and the Sunday Question,' (unpublished PHD thesis, Harvard University 1951) 8

[53] Rev. Baptist Noel *The Sanctifications of the Sabbath* ... (1835) 13; William Lovett *My Life and Struggles* (1876) 7

[54] For a discussion of sabbatarianism in early modern England see Christopher Hill 'The Uses of Sabbatarianism' *Society and Puritanism in Pre-Revolutionary England* (1964)

distinctions', as Bunting put it, to demarcate the religious from the secular.

Although the roots of sabbatarianism are complex, the arguments about writing instruction on Sunday are not. The sanctity of the Christian sabbath entailed certain restrictions on Sunday activities; Sunday schools were justified insofar as they served to sanctify the day through moral and religious instruction; and to teach writing on the sabbath constituted an appropriation of that day 'to a purpose for which it was never intended, without a sufficient reason to justify such a misapplication'.[55]

This argument, like most sabbatarian discussions, was elaborated in one of two directions.[56] First, since it was by no means clear to the entire religious community, much less to everyone associated with Sunday schools, that the strict Mosaic law regarding the seventh day applied with equal force to the first day of the week, there was considerable debate on the precise relationship of the Christian Sunday to the Hebraic sabbath. If one held that the Jewish code was no longer in full force, one *might*, though one need not, countenance extensive secular instruction on Sunday simply because there was no reason to do otherwise. It was argued along similar lines that writing instruction in Sunday schools was justified because it was nowhere explicitly prohibited in scripture, a point not overwhelmingly convincing to those who retorted that going to fairs, horse races, and such activities were also nowhere singled out in the Bible but were, nevertheless, clearly not permissible.

Most of the debate over what could be taught on Sundays did not, however, revolve around the 'nature of the sabbath' question or the strict constructionalist argument but instead held as common ground a belief in the sanctity of the Christian sabbath and the sinfulness of using it for worldly pursuits. It was the nature of the

[55] James *Guide*, pp. 162–3
[56] The following discussion of the writing controversy is based on James, *Guide*; Barker *Mercy Triumphant* ... Rev. Valentine Ward *Observations on Sunday schools; Principally to their connection with the divine institution and public worship on the Lord's day, Instruction in the art of writing and the pastoral duties of Christian ministers* (2nd ed., Leeds, 1827); J. A. Mayer *A Defence of Sunday Schools: attempted in a series of letters addressed to the Rev. M. A. Olerenshaw* (1798) and *Candid Animadversions on the Rev. Thomas Whitaker's four Letters* (1798); Rev. M. A. Olerenshaw *A sermon (on Gen. ii: 3) on the Sanctification of the Sabbath and the right use and abuse of Sunday Schools* (1797); Rev. Thomas Whitaker *Four Letters to Mr. J. Mayer of Stockport on his Defence of Sunday Schools* (1798); Rev. Abraham Watmough *Observations on Teaching the Art of Writing in Sunday Schools* (1832); Rev. Robert Martin *An address to the Superintendents, Committee and Teachers of the Methodists Sunday School in Bury— on the Impropriety and Sinfulness of Teaching Children to write on the Lord's Day* (Bury, 1819); Anon. ['A Minister of the Gospel'] *An Important Question Discussed* (Sheffield, 1834); Ward provides the clearest summary of the debate

exceptions to the general prohibition on such activities which constituted the nub of the dispute.

Writing instruction was, of course, not alone in being proscribed on the sabbath. Any activity had to meet certain conditions before it could escape the strictures of the fourth commandment. Absolute necessity was one cause for exclusion; it was as necessary to eat and drink on the seventh day as on the other six; one might also call a doctor, prepare medicines or take other steps to preserve one's own or someone else's life.[57] Furthermore, an activity was permissible if it was associated with religious observance, i.e. if it was an act of worship or instrumental in an act of devotion, or if it was an act of mercy or a form of charity which could not wait for a weekday. Most of the debate over what was to be taught in Sunday schools was focused by the opponents of secular instruction on whether the three Rs were acceptable by any of these criteria.

Reading was a relatively easy and uncontroversial subject. A few, like the Rev. Richard Cecil, felt that Sunday schools should offer exclusively religious instruction to children who could already read with some degree of fluency.[58] But it was generally acknowledged that since the Bible was the font of all religious truth and since each Christian had a right, indeed an obligation, to read and study the Bible for himself, the ability to do so could be legitimately transmitted in Sunday school. Writing and arithmetic, however, were more problematic. Not only were their religious merits less apparent, but opponents associated these subjects with still more secular and prohibited activities—the distribution of books, slates, paper and pens, the lending of library books, the sale of Bibles, and the collection of dues for sick and burial societies.[59] In short, writing was for many a symbol for all of those things which served to transform what ought to be a religious institution into a veritable bazaar.

Nevertheless, defenders of writing instruction argued that it could be made into an act of devotion and that it was already an act of charity. The same arguments were made for arithmetic. While, admittedly, neither 'the making of letters nor the learning of them' could be made into a religious exercise, both might be seen as necessary antecedents to genuine acts of devotion. Children could learn their letters using scripturally based writing copy and

[57] At one time, not calling a doctor on Sundays even when seriously ill was viewed as particularly virtuous; though by the late eighteenth century and early nineteenth century, this seems no longer to have been the case. See Keith Thomas *Religion and the Decline of Magic* (1971) 621

[58] *Works of the Rev. Richard Cecil* ed. by Josiah Pratt (1811) 529–34

[59] *Wesleyan Methodist Magazine* vol. 45 (1822) 109–11

then practice what they had learned by writing from memory certain Bible passages. Beginners, for example, could start on sentences like 'Amen—Allelujah—Aaron held his peace' and then move on to 'Abstain from all appearances of Evil'. The Sunday School Union made similar suggestions but added that students might be asked to write out scriptural proofs for certain doctrinal points rather than reciting them from memory. Others pointed out that writing enabled hearers to note down sermons which would cause them to make a more permanent impression.[60]

The case for arithmetic, or ciphering as it was called, was more tenuous. Joseph Mayer, for example, argued that Genesis 7:11–12, 20, 24; Exodus 16:35–36, 26:1–30, 38:9–31; Leviticus 25:8–13; Numbers 1:17–46, 2:1–34; the whole of Ezra, Nehemiah and Esther, large parts of the prophetic books, much of the New Testament, and particularly Revelations are 'totally incomprehensible' to the innumerate. While such claims were perhaps exaggerated, it is clear that those who defended writing and arithmetic instruction on Sunday did so convinced that it had significant religious value. Though perhaps not the prime motivation, these arguments of religious utility provided a convincing rationale.

If, however, writing instruction could not be defended as an act of devotion or as a necessary antecedent to one, it could be justified as a form of charity. Knowledge was either a great good in itself, expanding and invigorating the mind, or it was a means by which the poor man could improve his life and that of his family. As Barker put it

> All ranks, all callings, and all arts require its [writing's] assistance, and without its help [all] would sink into a savage state. Even digging, spinning, etc. cannot be done so well without being able to write, and those who cannot cast accounts are ever at the mercy of unscrupulous men who would otherwise have to keep their records of what they owed or what was owed them.[61]

In either case, to impart knowledge is to do good and hence constitutes an act of charity. To those who tried to disqualify writing instruction precisely because of its worldly value, Mayer quoted the scriptures: 'Godliness is profitable unto all things; having promise of the life that now is, and that which is to come.'

The Rev. Valentine Ward offered the most extensive rebuttal to the arguments that writing instruction constituted either an act of

---

[60] *An Essay on the Formation and Management of Sunday schools* (1813); Sunday School Union *Annual Report* for 1811, reprinted in Watson (1853) op. cit.; *Evangelical Magazine* 2nd ser. vol. 2 (1824) 102, and vol. 24 (1816) 502–4, esp. p. 502

[61] Barker *Mercy Triumphant* ... pt. I, 1

devotion or an act of charity. His response to the first was simply
to deny the religious significance which proponents of writing
instruction claimed for it. Alternatively he argued that the pro-
writing faction's line of reasoning was very much like that which the
Papists used to justify icons and was therefore suspect. Furthermore,
since writing instruction often required that children spend the
hours of worship in school instead of in church or chapel, it was
religiously counter-productive even if it did have some devotional
value. His response to the second argument, that writing instruction
was an act of charity, was that it was not *necessary* to undertake it
on Sunday; other days would do as well, and so the act of charity,
if indeed it was one, could be postponed. Secondly, Ward argued,
'There are no obligations binding upon that charity [Sunday
schools] equal to that which binds us to obey the law of God. It is
a work which came not under the Lord's exceptions; it was a
benevolent thing that had no character of mercy, either to the
bodies or to the souls of men.'[62] And finally, he suggested that
perhaps there were not even conflicting obligations—to do good
and to honor the sabbath. The ultimate effects of teaching writing
on Sundays was to do harm to the working man:

> It is pleaded that, to teach their children to write is to do good
> to the poor ... they [who make this case] are not *practically*
> the friends of the poor, but their dangerous enemies. For, the
> strict observance of the sabbath is the grand bulwark of Poverty
> against the encroachments of Capital ... The abolition of the
> sabbath would, in truth, be equivalent to a sentence, adjudging
> to the rich the services of the poor for life. The sabbath is the
> poor man's fence against excessive toil; to apply any part of it
> *systematically* to the *teaching* of a *secular art*, for the *sake* of *secular
> benefit* is to break this fence.[63]

It does not matter that Ward's newly found friendship for the
poor might be less than sincere. The feeling behind this remark—
that some quite arbitrary set of social conventions must be enforced
in order to set apart the day traditionally allocated to public worship
in an age when fewer and fewer of the working classes were bothering
to attend church—lies near the heart of sabbatarianism and goes
far to explain why rational debate did so little to settle the writing
controversy. As the *Wesleyan Methodist Magazine* noted, those not
convinced by *An Important Question Discussed* ... and James's *Guide*
had, quite simply, 'in their minds some radical and fundamental

[62] Ward *Observations* ... pp. 26–7; see also *Wesleyan Methodist Magazine* vol. 49
(1826) 173
[63] Ward *Observations* ... p. 18

difference of opinion on the subject of the sabbath and perhaps on other doctrines ... '. [64] There was little possibility of communication between the factions. For the proponents of writing there could be no response but disavowal to Bunting's categorical assertion that it was 'in all its direct and immediate uses a secular art. The religious use of it [was] at best remote, contingent and indirect.' [65]

But while sabbatarianism certainly supplies a necessary part of the explanation for the writing controversy, it is not in itself sufficient. Organizations which in all other spheres were zealous in the cause of Sunday observance nevertheless countenanced and indeed encouraged writing and other kinds of secular instruction on the sabbath. The Stockport Sunday School is a case in point. In 1797, the governing committee felt it necessary to print the laws relating to sabbath-breaking; these were distributed about town, and a hundred copies were reserved for distribution in the school. In 1802, John Carrington, one of the trustees, proposed that someone should ride around Stockport's streets and the surrounding fields in order to scoop up children engaged in frivolous games. Though not adopted then, in 1807 a similar plan was suggested and this time apparently put into practice. In 1809 the committee petitioned the magistrates to close a fruit shop which was tempting students; soon thereafter the problem of scholars' buying sweetmeats on the way to and from school was discussed. Again in 1814 and 1817, petitions were sent to the magistrates, the first asking that the school's sabbath patrol be put under the direction of the constables and the second demanding action against 'boys playing football etc. on the outskirts of town'. If sabbatarian zeal determined what subjects were taught, the Stockport Sunday School would have offered only the most minimal reading instruction, but, in fact, its program was probably amongst the most varied in England. [66]

The same case can be made for the Sunday School Union. It was extremely active in organizing support for the parliamentary battles against Sunday opening of the post office and Sunday trading, and yet it publicly advertised methods of teaching secular subjects more effectively and, through its depots, sold material to futher this end. [67] The Primitive Methodists were one of the denominations strictest about sabbath observance, and yet nearly all its

[64] *Wesleyan Methodist Magazine* vol. 47 (1824) p. 763
[65] Bunting *Life* ... p. 322
[66] Stockport Sunday School Committee *Minute Books*—MS. in Stockport Reference Library—entries for 30 June 1797; 28 March 1802; 29 March 1807; 19 March 1809; 3 April 1814; 10 February 1817
[67] Sales of writing materials are recorded along with other sales. See note 48, p. 114

Sunday schools taught writing throughout this period. The Rev. John Ashworth, active in the Sunday closing movement, advertised an adult reading and writing class for Sunday afternoons in his Rochdale chapel.[68]

Since both sides of the writing controversy included strict sabbatarians, belief in the sanctity of the sabbath alone will not provide the explanation of why so long and furious a battle raged over so apparently trivial an issue. Clearly something more profound was at stake.

Writing instruction on the sabbath came to be considered the identifying mark of the independent, lay-dominated, and locally controlled Sunday school. Particularly in Wesleyan Methodism, but to a lesser extent in other denominations, the elimination of such instruction became the *cause célèbre* of those determined to assert ministerial domination over Sunday schools and turn them into agencies of proselytization. Controversy, indeed almost pitched battles, arose when local interests, particularly teachers, sought to defend their schools against ministerial encroachment.

On the one hand, there was the 'general rule of the modern Sunday school', which was adhered to by the supporters of extended elementary instruction: 'Anything which will expand the minds of the children, and lead them to love and adore their Creator, or make them more capable of promoting His cause in the world is directly within the purpose of this institution.'[69]

But those who opposed writing instruction on the sabbath took a much narrower view. William Hey, for example, whose letter to the Methodist Conference in 1807 first brought the writing issue into the open, argued that 'even reading itself is but preparatory to the great business of religious instruction' and that Sunday schools existed solely to make students 'but true Christians, that they may glorify God here and be prepared for the society of saints and angels in glory.'[70] The Methodist Conference and, by the 1850s, ministers of most other denominations as well held similarly circumscribed views on the proper function of Sunday schools. 'They should be strictly and entirely religious institutions; and ought, therefore, to be schools for the *Christian* instruction and education of the children of the poor.'[71] Everything, the *Wesleyan Magazine* argued, pertaining to sabbath instruction should be

[68] Rev. John Ashworth *Life and Labours* ed. by A. C. Calman (Manchester, 1875) 99–102 and advertisement following text

[69] Mayer *A Defence* letter 5—'promoting His cause in the world' is given a loose interpretation which includes the doctrine of self-help and all that it implies

[70] Pearson *Life of William Hey* ... p. 310

[71] Wesleyan Conference *Minutes* (1827) 284

connected with the spiritual welfare of the children of the poor.[72]
New Connexion Methodist authorities wrote in 1805 that 'Religious
instruction ought doubtless to be considered as the leading feature
of these seminaries [Sunday schools]: but is it not a matter of
thankfulness, that so many thousands are now learning to read and
write in this nation, who were it not for these means, might have
lived and died in heathenish ignorance.'[73] By 1826, they condemned
writing instruction as a waste of the 'precious moments of God's
holy day more profitably spent in teaching the immortal beings
entrusted to their care, the principles and duties of the Christian
religion.'[74] Local resistance to the elimination of such instruction
was seen as resistance to the authority of the church and its ministers.

Indeed, the whole conflict over secular education must be seen,
from the denominational authorities' point of view, in the context
of Sunday schools' failure to recruit for the church, their laxness
in bringing children to worship, and occasionally their outright
hostility to any ministerial meddling in their affairs.[75] While all
denominations encountered these difficulties, the highly centralized,
hierarchic and authoritarian nature of the Wesleyan polity under
Jabez Bunting caused them to become the focus of overt political
conflict. The controversy over writing, as Bunting's son confirms,
was in reality a conflict over control. When certain ministers,
including his father, objected to writing in Sunday schools, 'grave
questions arose between the active managers of the schools and the
authorities of the circuit, as to the nature and extent of the control
which the latter might rightfully claim over the former. This [the
writing controversy] was the second great struggle of my father's
life.'[76]

The issue of writing also involved questions of power and control
when viewed from the perspective of the local Sunday school.
Teachers and managers, who had generally run the affairs of the
school and determined its educational as well as its religious policy,
were suddenly faced with a new set of rules imposed from the outside. These rules sought to set strict limits on what the school could
teach, on what hours it should keep, and on who should be on its
governing body. Rather than submit to the dictates of the Wesleyan
Conference or some other distant authority, local interests often
preferred to secede from the chapel to which they had been nominally attached. And although writing was the most important issue

[72] *Wesleyan Methodist Magazine* vol. 47 (1824) 763
[73] *Methodist New Connexion Magazine* vol. 8 (1805) 519
[74] Ibid. new ser. vol. 4 (1826) 457
[75] See Chapter 3
[76] Bunting *Life* ... vol. 1,320 ff.

which divided Sunday school personnel from religious authorities, it was only one of many areas of conflict between local interests and national authorities within Wesleyanism.[77]

In 1808 and 1817 the Methodist Conference passed resolutions that were designed to bring denominational Sunday schools under ministerial, i.e. Conference, control and to eliminate secular interference with their primary, religious purpose. Conference, 'discountenancing the plan of teaching the *art of writing* on the Lord's day', argued, among other things, that it took up time 'that might be more profitably employed in catechetical and other religious instruction'. Most importantly, the 1827 'General Principles and Rules to be Observed in the Management of Methodist Sunday Schools', which made the travelling preacher a member of the governing board and restricted the teachers to a quarter of all places on the board, also declared that 'neither the art of writing, not any other merely secular branch of knowledge shall be taught on the Lord's day.' Although the controversy over writing had arisen as early as 1800, it became far more widespread after 1827 in the context of the new regulations.[78]

Bunting's experience in Sheffield early in the century set the pattern for future battles. He arrived in the town as the newly appointed circuit preacher and immediately set out to ban writing in the local Sunday school despite local opposition. The pro-writing faction withdrew and started the Sunday school in Red Hill, which was to become, because of the excellence of its educational program, the largest school in Sheffield. But even this pyrrhic victory was soon undone. Mr Myles, 'that easy superintendent conceded the matter in dispute and altered his own views'. Those who had been expelled were readmitted by the consent of the leaders' meeting, while Bunting's allies—the Revs. Hare, Valentine Ward and Davis McNicoll—sat by 'in an indignant silence'.[79]

Rev. Thomas Kaye arrived in Newchurch in 1820 determined to suppress writing in the Sunday school. He appointed his son superintendent, unilaterally issued a new set of rules, and when teachers refused to comply proclaimed a sermon boycott of the school. Justifiably angry, the teachers attempted to compromise; and, when Kaye refused to negotiate they, along with the majority of

[77] See Currie *Methodism* ... pp. 17–84

[78] Wesleyan Methodist Conference *Minutes* (1808) Q 25, (1817) Q 25. Maldwyn Edwards in *After Wesley: A Study of the Social and Political Influence of Methodism in the Middle Period* (1935) 107 claims that the conference forbade the teaching of writing in 1814. I could not find reference to this in the *Minutes* of 1814. *Minutes* vol. 4 (1823) 426; *Minutes* (1827) 284 ff.

[79] Bunting *Life*, vol. 1, 320 ff.

trustees and students, withdrew from the chapel, leaving the minister with a sadly depleted school and congregation.[80] Teachers in Macclesfield issued the following declaration to the Rev. Bretnell when he sought to 'bring the Sunday school people under control': 'we are perfectly satisfied ourselves that the liberal foundation upon which [the school] is established is by far the most catholic and honourable, as well as the best adapted to the circumstances of the town.'[81] In Bury there was great resentment among teachers when the minister attempted to impose the 1827 Rules. On the Sunday following the beginning of his efforts, 176 teachers and 863 students did not proceed as usual to the chapel school but instead made their way to a woollen warehouse where they held worship and organized a new school. In appealing to the public for funds, they declared that: 'We have then, *to preserve our own freedom* and to render our labours energetic and efficient as heretofore, been compelled to take over premises, and supply them ...'[82] Many other local conflicts followed much the same pattern—in Bolton, Congleton, York, Burslem, Tunstall, Leeds, Bollington, Burnley. The Stockport School, founded by a close associate of Wesley, Mathew Mayer, suffered a boycott of Wesleyan preachers at least until 1850 because of its insistence on maintaining a full curriculum.[83]

Eventually, of course, Bunting and his supporters won. By the 1840s most Wesleyan schools had abandoned writing instruction, and by the 1850s Sunday schools probably were more closely tied to the chapel than had hitherto been the case. Nevertheless, the writing controversy stands as another instance of local resistance to national control within Wesleyan Methodism.

Conclusions

Four points emerge from this chapter. First, that unequivocal

[80] Jessop *Methodism in Rossendale* ... pp. 248–50

[81] *An Account of the Celebration of the Jubilee of the Macclesfield Sunday School, May 6, 1846* (Macclesfield, 1846) 23 and 107; see also Rev. Benjamin Smith *History of Methodism in Macclesfield* (1875)

[82] T. P. Dale *The History of Brunswick Chapel, Bury* (Bury, 1896) 19 (my emphasis)

[83] S. Rothwell *Memorials ... Folds Rd., Bolton* pp. 133–7; Smith *Methodism in Congleton* ... J. Lyth *Glimpses of Early Methodism in York* ... pp. 216–17, 236; *A Vindication ... by INVESTIGATOR* ... *Children's Employment Commission* op. cit. 1843 [432] xv. E 26; Bunting *Life* ... W. H. Oliver Lake *A Centenary History of the Wesleyan Methodist Church in Bollington* (Bollington, 1908) B. Moore *Methodism in Burnley* ... pp. 115–17; 'Memorial to the Methodist Conference' in Stockport SS *Minute Books* 28 August 1808); see also No. 12 (1810) and the letter from Beaumont to Mayer S2–5 (1844)

F

opposition to the education of the poor was rare in the late eighteenth and early nineteenth century; obscurantism played no part in the controversy over writing which raged in Sunday schools.

Second, the evidence suggests that while the sabbatarianism of those who opposed writing instruction was indeed strongly felt, it cannot serve as a complete explanation of the controversy. Two rival conceptions of Sunday schools had specific implications both for whether writing was taught or not and for who was to exercise control over the school. The writing controversy was in this way tied into the struggle of the Wesleyan ministry to gain control of the affairs of their denomination. Both the debate over Whitbread's bill and the controversy within Methodism over writing in Sunday schools suggest that as schooling developed a public function it also became a political prize worth fighting for. The issue of school curriculum involved only incidentally educational philosophy, concern for students' needs, or the desires of parents and students; the salient consideration was the requirements of the group which controlled educational facilities.

Third, the continuous local resistance to the Wesleyan Conference's wishes on secular instruction in Sunday school is clear evidence that the views of the hierarchy cannot be conflated with those of local Methodists. Even in urban centers where the ministry might have exercised some control, the congregation, and specifically the Sunday school, had a life of its own. The political doctrines of a Bunting or a Stephens are largely irrelevant to a study of the social consequences of Methodism at the grass roots.

Finally, the writing controversy points to the importance of local political issues in the lives of working men and women in the early nineteenth century. During the period 1780–1850 the question of who controlled the Sunday school was perhaps of more importance than the great questions which later on were to divide class from class.

6. Sunday Schools and the Working Classes

i. INTRODUCTION

Institutions for providing education or religion or social services cannot be adequately considered in isolation from the lives of those they seek to serve. And yet this has been precisely the fate of Sunday schools in the historical literature. Their political and economic role in society at large has often been touched upon, and the overwhelming verdict of scholars is that they existed as more or less overt agencies of social control and class manipulation. Their educational services, it is argued, were minimal and severely curtailed by the obscurantist mentality of those who managed them. Their textbooks committed a real 'psychological atrocity' upon the children; their burial clubs constituted one of 'the more gruesome stories' in the history of the period, according to E. P. Thompson.[1] Genuine religious motivation for Sunday school attendance is ruled out by the prevailing interpretation which pictures the working classes as wantonly and hopelessly irreligious. The clergyman who at the turn of the century remarked that 'it is not that the Church of God has lost the great towns; it never had them,' is echoed with only few qualifications by modern historians.[2]

But the fact remains that, by 1850, two million working-class children were enrolled in Sunday school; and 250,000 men and women, most of whom were from the same class as the students, taught there. The question is Why? What part did Sunday schools play in their lives? Surely the answer is more complex than that attributed to Charles Booth: in a house with little privacy they

[1] Thompson *Making* ... p. 377 and 290

[2] A. F. Winnington-Ingram *Work in Great Cities* (1896) 22 quoted in K. S. Inglis *Churches and the Working Classes in Victorian England* (1963) 3; see also Henry Pelling 'Religion and the Nineteenth Century British Working Class' *Past and Present* no. 27 (1964)

offered a free Sunday afternoon when the parents could have intercourse without fear of being disturbed by children.[3]

ii. The Demand for Secular Education

In order to prove conclusively that there was a strong working-class demand for the secular education offered by Sunday schools, two quantitative indicators would be needed. First, it might be shown that schools of denominations which taught writing and arithmetic on Sundays, or which taught reading in a more proficient way, were proportionately better attended than the churches or chapels to which they belonged. So, for example, assuming that other factors are equal, if say three denominations which offered the most extensive elementary education attracted twenty per cent of the total number of worshippers but fifty per cent of all Sunday school children, then it might be concluded that parents discriminated in favor of these denominations' schools because of the one feature which distinguished them from all other schools, viz. the amount of instruction offered. Second, and less satisfactorily, the demand for education might be gauged by studying the substitution of Sunday school for weekday instruction; in other words, if, as weekday education became curtailed or in some way unavailable, Sunday school instruction could be shown to have taken its place, then it could be argued that the latter grew in response to a demand no longer satisfied by the former. Unfortunately, for reasons which are discussed at length in Appendix 2, neither approach is feasible. In the absence of such statistical proofs a more traditional approach based on literary and qualitative sources is all that remains.

There is considerable evidence that the demand for secular education among the working classes kept Sunday schools from becoming purely religious institutions until well after mid-century. Parents quite clearly sent their children to Sunday school, in part at least, to gain an elementary education; older scholars attended of their own free will in order to participate in the institutions for self-help which grew up around these schools. An examination of the generally unrestricted educational market-place of the late eighteenth and early nineteenth century bears this out. Schools which offered extensive instruction tended to do better than those with more limited curricula; conversely, restriction, relatively or absolutely, in the amount of elementary education provided often

[3] Interview with the Rev R. S. Reaney, vicar of Christ Church, East Greenwich in the Booth Collection in the LSE Library, B 287, pp. 49–51. I owe this reference to Dr Hugh McLeod

led to a diminution of enrolment. The rector of Almondbury, Yorkshire, 'regretted that a great number of children are tempted to go to Sunday schools of the dissenters owing to the inducement being held out by teaching writing on Sundays', and Mr Coales, a paid teacher in an Anglican Sunday school in York, complained that his children were being enticed away by a new school which taught more subjects than he offered.[4] One reactionary clergyman writing in the *Christian Remembrancer* argued that Sunday schools should exist *solely* for religious instruction and that even in weekday schools the lower classes should under no circumstances be educated beyond the ability to read the Bible. Nevertheless, fear that the Non-conformists would meet the working-class demand for secular education, and thereby reap the harvest of souls, was too much even for a man of such strong scruples. In their Sunday schools the Dissenters

> doubtless from the best intention, have carried the education of the poor much further than this, and with a very natural zeal for making proselytes, have endeavoured, as it were to entice children by larger supplies of intellectual food ... and though this prevails to a much less extent in the schools of the Established Church, yet *they are compelled, however reluctantly to make some advances in order to prevent absolute desertion.*[5]

A good example of the process at work is to be found in the Lancashire cotton town of Clitheroe. There a print-work owner named Thomson tried to have the children in his factory educated on the part-time system but found that they could not easily make the transition from being 'like pins in a machine', using only their 'animal labour', to being thinking persons capable of doing mental work. He tried, therefore, to put the onus of providing an education on the parents by making the ability to read and write prerequisites for the best paid and most prestigious apprenticeships in calico printing. As a result, Anglican Sunday schools which did not teach writing were abandoned for those of the Methodists and Catholics which did, although the introduction of twice weekly evening classes by the Established Church redressed the balance.[6] Similarly, the Church Sunday school in Nuneaton enjoyed a great accession of students as soon as it began to offer more elementary instruction in evening classes.[7] 'The greatest attraction which secured atten-

[4] *Digest of Parochial Returns* 1819 (224) ix, p. 862; John Lyth, DD *Glimpses of Early Methodism in York and the Surrounding District* (York, 1885) 172

[5] *Christian Remembrancer* vol. 3, no. 1 (1821) 12–14. My emphasis

[6] Nassau Senior *Letters on the Factory Acts* (1837) 44

[7] *Reports from the Assistant Hand-loom Weavers' Commissioners Part IV*, 1840 [217] xxiv, Midlands District, p. 83

dance on the part of young people was that, in addition to reading instruction, we taught them to write', reported the working-class temperance reformer Joseph Livesey.[8] Edwin Rose, an engineer millwright from Manchester, testified that he had abandoned the Methodist Sunday school in Lever Street because it taught only hymns and prayers, and went instead to the Unitarian school on Lower Mosley Street, 'where they taught reading and writing, which he found useful'.[9] Indeed, that school claimed that children flocked to it from three or four miles around because of the secular education offered.

Conversely, schools which curtailed secular instruction found themselves in dire straits. Union Chapel in Bury lost 863 pupils when it imposed a ban on writing instruction; seventy-five per cent of its 1,900 students left Hanover Street Sunday School in Bolton for the same reason.[10] In fact, when in 1810 Jabez Bunting had wanted to abolish Sunday writing instruction there, he was warned 'that an attempt to lay [it] aside would be ruinous—I think it necessary to be cautious.'[11] A boycott of one small school in Oldham occurred when it followed Bunting's advice, and parishioners took a similar course in Ripponden when the vicar refused to support the Anglican Sunday school because it would not give up sabbath writing instruction.[12] Occasionally the children took direct action. One Methodist preacher was taunted with the call

> Here comes the Rev. Mister Grundy
> Who'll ha' no writing upon a Sunday.[13]

The fact that elementary instruction beyond reading was used as a reward in many Sunday schools provides further evidence of the considerable working-class demand for education since rewards are only effective if they are highly prized. Those who could recite the ten commandments, were over eleven, and had attended Bible class for six months without breaches of discipline were rewarded

[8] *The Life and Teaching of Joseph Livesey, Comprising his Autobiography* with an introductory essay by John Pearce (1885) 42

[9] *Report from Commissioners on Employment of Children in Factories* op. cit. 1833 (450) xx. D1–122

[10] Thomas P. Dale *History of Brunswick Chapel* . . p. 19; Stephen Rothwell *Memorials . . . Bolton . . .* p. 137

[11] Entwisle/Bunting, 20 May 1809, quoted in E. P. Stigant 'Methodism and the Working Class, 1760–1821: A Study in Social and Political Conflict' (unpublished Keele MA thesis, 1968) 218–19

[12] J. F. [John Fletcher] *Greenhill Methodist Sunday School, Block Lane, Oldham 1849–1949* (Oldham?, 1949) 8; *Northern Star* (12 June 1841) 8

[13] C. W. Bardsley *Memorials of St. Anne's Church, Manchester* (Manchester, 1877) 120–21

by being admitted to the writing class of the Burslem Sunday School. No more than forty students, admitted because of good behaviour and regular attendance and then only with a recommendation from a teacher, were allowed in the writing classes of the Spitalfield Sunday School; withdrawal from the class was used as punishment. 'Writing is to be taught as a reward and as a further means of religious instruction,' read the rules of an Exeter Sunday school. It was taught and 'valued as a great privilege' in Haslingden. An 1841 Anglican Committee of Enquiry in the Metropolis found that 'in a considerable number of cases' writing was taught because 'it [was] an incitement to good behaviour, and tended to prevent desertions.'[14]

Extensive elementary instruction was apparently so attractive that it could be held out as bait for capturing and retaining older students. The secretary of the National School Society, which maintained both weekday and Sunday schools, told a parliamentary committee that the institutions under his supervision 'carry the writing out to a greater extent than we might otherwise think necessary, considering the station which the children will occupy in life, for the sake of retaining the scholars under our discipline for a greater length of time.'[15] Joseph Mayer in 1798 argued that writing and arithmetic instruction would draw older students into the Stockport Sunday School at a time in their lives when they were most in need of careful supervision; thirty years later, the same argument was still popular among those who advocated writing, arithmetic, grammar or geography instruction on Sundays.[16]

An impressionistic analysis of the market in education suggests, in short, that part of the Sunday school's appeal lay in the elementary instruction it provided. Parents discriminated between schools on the basis of the educational services offered, and children remained in attendance longer when more subjects were offered or were better taught. The importance of this instruction is most evident in the lives of those who, because of poverty, were completely deprived of weekday instruction; and at the other end of the scale, those who thrived on the culture of self-improvement, shading over into popular radicalism, which developed around the Sunday school.

[14] *Rules for the Management and Internal Government of the Burslem Sunday School* inst. 1787 (1821); 'Spitalfield Wesleyan Sunday School: Rules for Writing' (1824); Allan Brockett *Non-Conformity in Exeter 1650–1875* (Manchester, 1962) 173; John Stott *Notices of Methodism in Haslingden* (privately printed in London, 1898) 108; *SS Teachers' Magazine* (1841) col. 130

[15] *Report from the Select Committee on the Education of the Poorer Classes* 1837–38 (589) vii, Q 749

[16] Mayer *Defense . . . to Ollerenshaw*

For framework knitters and handloom weavers, for unemployed factory hands, for women, and for those whose parents were illiterate and thus unable to provide education at home, the Sunday school and the Sunday school teacher provided an alternative or supplementary source of instruction. One knitter told a parliamentary commissioner that he was far too poor to afford to send his children to day school but that he sent them to Sunday school to compensate for their misfortune:

A.   They have a good education there. I have to return thanks to Mr Pratt, of Narborough for that. He has been very kind to us.

Q.   Is he the minister?

A.   No, he is an old hosier, who was laid by business, [sic] and he takes the trouble to give the poor children a little education in writing and summing.[17]

'Sunday school education is all the education my children have had,' reported John Benson, another knitter. 'It is not in a poor man's power to give them any [weekday] education.' 'I have one son who has come on well at the Sunday school,' said a third, who went on to bemoan the impossibility of providing more extensive education for his children.[18]

There were 2,834 handloom weavers' children in the twenty Gloucestershire parishes investigated by the 1839 Commissioners; 272, a mere 9.7 per cent, of these were in day school but 1,882, 66.7 per cent, were in Sunday school.[19] Of 494 weavers' families scattered over various regions, 64.5 per cent sent at least one of their young to Sunday school; only 18 per cent could afford to have a child in weekday school. Of the 1,820 children surveyed 40 per cent were in Sunday school, only 8 per cent in weekday school.[20] Clearly those in the dyeing trades often had to rely on Sunday schools as their only source of education.

Women were more likely than men to suffer from a lack of elementary instruction. In the 1780s 68 per cent of men but only 39 per cent of women could sign the marriage register; by the 1840s the gap had narrowed from 22 per cent to 16 per cent; 68 per cent of

---

[17] *Appendix to the Report of the Commissioners Appointed to Inquire into the Condition of the Framework Knitters* 1845 [618] xv, Part 1, Leicestershire, 3304–3305

[18] Ibid. nos. 447 and 1799

[19] *Reports of the Asst. Hand-loom Weavers' Commissioners* Part V 1840 [220] xxiv, pp. 489–90

[20] Ibid., Part II 1840 (43–I) xxiii, pp. 415–16, 418–20, 423–6, 429–32 and Part V, 1840 [220] xxiv, pp. 439–47

grooms and 52 per cent of brides were able to sign but the continued existence of the gap bore witness to the inferiority of women's education.[21] Furthermore, while the numbers of boys and girls in *all* day schools was the same throughout the period, both nationally and in most localities, girls occupied a far higher proportion of the places in the most inferior schools. In Finsbury 18 per cent of female enrolment but only 11 per cent of male enrolment was in dame school, and in this borough total male even exceeded total female enrolment by 10 per cent. During the 1830s 19 per cent of the girls and only 12 per cent of the boys occupied dame school places in York; 22 per cent of girls but only 14 per cent of boys in Liverpool; 31 per cent of girls and 16 per cent of boys in Salford, etc.[22] Finally, of course, there was a cultural bias against extensive education for girls which is reflected in these statistics but which becomes more real in the context of an individual life. For young women the Sunday school or even a single teacher could be the way out of ignorance and depression.

Marianne Farningham provides a good example. She was born of strict Particular Baptist parents near Eynsford, Kent and went on to become editor of several Dissenting journals. It is clear that her father, who dominated the family, thought that all secular knowledge was more or less useless and that it was particularly so for girls. She was consequently forced to withdraw from school, very much against her wishes, in order to help with housework. Reading, she claims, was her only consolation, and her father gave her two Sunday School Union periodicals, *Teacher's Offering* and the *Child's Companion*, which each month contained success stories of poor ignorant boys who, though beginning life with great handicaps, 'became useful if not great'. The absence of women in these stories precipitated what appears to have been a severe adolescent crisis. 'I was bitter and naughty. I did not pray, and was not anxious to be good.' And it was her Sunday school teacher, who read with her, loved her and brought her through this bad spell, and who apparently gave her confidence both as a Christian and as a woman.[23]

Finally, the Sunday school flourished in a period when rapid economic and social change must have exacerbated the isolation

[21] R. S. Schofield 'Dimensions of Illiteracy' unpublished paper given to the Cambridge New Economic History Conference, Sept. 1972 or see my paper 'Literacy and the Industrial Revolution', *Past and Present* August, 1974

[22] 'Report of the Education Committee on the Borough of Finsbury' *Journal of the Royal Statistical Society* (*JRSS*) (Feb. 1843) Table 1, 35; 'General summary of schools and scholars' *Report of the Manchester Statistical Society ... on York, on Liverpool, ... on Salford*

[23] Marianne Farningham *A Working Woman's Life* (1907) 44

of children from parents. The growth in literacy noted earlier meant that a far greater proportion of children than parents could read and write, a situation reflected in the common motif of children reading scripture or newspapers to their parents. While fathers were able to teach their sons a trade or mothers able to pass on skills in sewing, needlework or other household crafts, it was less likely that they could pass on the non-traditional skills of the printed word. A literary education beyond the bare rudiments was not available within the home, and other institutions, among them the Sunday school, grew up to fill the gap.

Consequently, for a man like Adam Ruston, whose father was an eight shilling a week farm laborer, instruction at the Sunday school was almost like the initiation into a secret rite:

> I worked hard and strove eagerly to get into one of these [writing] classes, and very soon did so. And then came the glorious lines and straight strokes, pothooks and ladles. How fascinating these elementary strokes seemed. How in admiration, I fixed my gaze upon them, and how easily, to my surprise I made them. Then, more exhilarating still, came forth words, and sentences, and even my own name, written in large strong strokes of my quill pen. No engineer, architect, inventor, discoverer, or commander could have felt more exquisite pleasure in their moments of conquest and triumph, than was experienced by me.[24]

For many others the Sunday school or an individual teacher provided instruction that could not be obtained at home. Joseph Barker, whose father had learned to write as an adult so as to communicate his religious experiences to his wife while he was away from home as a soldier, was taught Latin and Greek by a Methodist preacher he met through Sunday school; George Holyoake, the Chartist and socialist, made his first contacts with logic and mathematics as well as with Owenite socialism through the teachers at a Unitarian Sunday school; Francis Soutter, a leader in the fight against church rates and a champion of women's rights, came under the influence of G. M. Murphy, the Lambeth radical parson, through the Saturday evening newspaper readings that were organized by the Surrey Chapel Sunday School. Countless factory children in Manchester came under the influence of Travers Madge, who taught them geography, history and grammar, visited their homes, and took them on walks and rambles.[25]

[24] Adam Rushton *My Life as a Farmer's Boy, Factory Lad, Teacher and Preacher 1821–1909* (Manchester, 1909)

[25] Joseph Barker *Life of . . ., Written by Himself* ed. by J. T. Barker (1880) 77; Joseph McCabe *Life and Letters of George Jacob Holyoake* (1908) 12; Francis W. Soutter

A highly developed culture of self-help, self-improvement and respectability, which nurtured many of the political and trade-union leaders of the working class, emerged from the late eighteenth- and the nineteenth-century Sunday school. The school joined together the world of respectability and roughness, political activism and resigned quietism.

The liberating quality of knowledge and the potential power of a working class freed from the shackles of ignorance is nowhere clearer than in the poetry of Robert Milhouse. He was born in 1788, the second of ten children and began work when aged six; at ten, he was employed full time on a stocking loom. He learned to read, write and do arithmetic at Sunday school. Education was for him both a shield and a weapon against tyranny and degradation. In a song on 'Black Injustice' he says:

> I feel, black injustice, thy hand;
> Yet ne'er shall thou conquer my soul;
> And though bitterly falls thy command,
> My mind shall outwing thy control;
> And long as Remembrance shall hold
> Her power to reflect in my brain,
> Though tyrants are shield in gold,
> This tyrant I shall disdain.

His ode to Robert Raikes, the legendary founder of Sunday schools also plays on the theme of knowledge as liberation.

> Raikes! thou hast laid the axe into the root
> Of ancient tyrannies grown grey in crimes,
> And shall receive the thanks of future times,
> Tho' not from despots sickening at thy fruit.[26]

'Let our Sunday schools become the UNIVERSITIES OF THE POOR, in which the infant mind shall be taught to look through nature up to nature's source ... ,' declared Rowland Detrosier, the working-class radical who was superintendent of the Swedenborgian Sunday School in Hulme. Indeed, he taught himself the rudiments of natural history, astronomy, electricity, 'galvanism',

---

Fights for Freedom: The Story of a Life (1925) 18, Murphy identified in G.D.H. Cole's MS. *Directory of Labour* two copies of which are in the Nuffield College Library; H. Brookes, ed. *Travers Madge: Memoirs* (1867) 3

[26] John Potter Briscoe, ed. *The Sonnets and Songs of Robert Milhouse, with a biographical sketch of the author* (Nottingham, 1881) 68, 53

mechanics, and 'all the subjects connected with them' in order to meet the educational demands of his students.[27]

John Wilson of the Durham Miners' Association provides another example of a man for whom the Sunday school was the gateway to education and to the political culture he later espoused. He had attended Sunday school as a boy but had apparently strayed from the paths of righteousness. After one particularly heavy drinking bout, he promised a friend that he would become a Sunday school teacher. 'From that day, drink has had no attraction for me ... I felt there was more required; I had only made a start, and must go further. I felt that to be a teacher in the Sunday school in the proper sense, I must be fitted for it ... I took to reading avidly; still the want was there.' In fact, he underwent a conversion experience in a Primitive Methodist class meeting and subsequently began a new life consisting of politics, preaching and daily self-education sessions.[28]

But Wilson was far from unique. The Lancashire Chartist shoemaker, John Latchford, taught in a Wigan Sunday school and became the superintendent of another school in Hindley; John French, Black Country socialist, managed a school in Dudsley; Joseph Linney, another Black Country Chartist was also a Sunday school superintendent; John Fielden, the Halifax Chartist, began teaching in Sunday school when he was seventeen.[29] W. J. Davis was induced to attend Sunday school when he was fourteen by the promise of further instruction in writing and arithmetic; he became a teacher, joined the training classes and Barr Street Improvement Society, learned grammar, won Queen's Prize of the Science and Art Department, and, of course, eventually became secretary of the brassworkers' union.[30] Thomas Cooper, William Lovett, George Holyoake, Issac Ironside among the Chartists, Mann and Tillett of the dock workers, William Ancott of the Ironworkers, Thomas Burt and John Normansell of the mineworkers, George Edwards of the second Agricultural Labourers' Union, William Bates, the Chartist and co-operator, John Mitchell,

[27] Rowland Detrosier *An Address ... on The Necessity of an Extension of Moral and Political Instruction Among the Working Classes* (1831) 8–9; see also the 'Memoir' of Detrosier by James Shuttleworth which forms the preface of the London, 1834, version of the speech cited; and Gwyn Williams *Rowland Detrosier—A Working Class Infidel* (York, Borthwick Papers no. 28, 1965) 8

[28] John Wilson *Memories of a Labour Leader* (1910) 204–8

[29] C. Deane Little *Our Old Sunday School: 150 Years of Wigan Methodism* (1933) 23; G. Barnsby *The Dudley Working Class Movement 1832–1860* (Dudley, 1970) 10; J. Freeman *Black Country Stories and Sketches* (Bilston, 1930) 204; J. L. and B. Hammond *The Town Labourer 1760–1832* (1917) 287

[30] William A. Dalley *The Life Story of W. J. Davis J. P.* (Birmingham 1914) 14

the co-operator and temperance reformer, and Owenite socialists, like John Finch and Edward Craig, participated in the culture of self-improvement which centered on the Sunday school.[31]

In fact, the educational program of Sunday schools grew in response to the demand for more advanced instruction from men such as these. 'Aspiring to know more than could be taught at the Sunday school', wrote the Lancashire poet Benjamin Brierley 'Hollinhead and I joined the one known as the "Old School". We banded together with other young men and formed a mutual improvement society. My uncle Richard Taylor, bought books for us from Manchester book stalls.' As a mark of their success Brierley points out that from among his group came 'the Crossley brothers who were merchants and manufacturers, a successful farmer in America, a partner in a south eastern firm of auctioneers, and a man with a good position in a manufacturing firm in Pendleton'.[32] Adam Rushton reports that he and twenty-five friends from his Sunday school near Macclesfield formed a group to study grammar and other subjects in the evening.[33] The improvement society that was attached to the Anglican Bennett Street Sunday School was begun by three young men who were passionate in their commitment to self-education: George Milner, a man of humble origins who began attending the school at eleven, Ralph Nicholson, who had been abandoned early by his father and began work in a mill at age six, and George Lawton, whose origins are not given but who began his career as a machinist's apprentice. Milner became a schoolteacher at the Wilmslow National School, having resigned his position in the manufactury at the age of twenty-four because of bleeding in his lungs. Nicholson, who was most influential in setting up the evening class to study grammar, was finally forced to quit the factory because of a severe trade depression and accepted the mastership of the Bowden National School; he started studying Greek while in the Sunday school but was sidetracked when told he would have to learn Latin first. George Lawton left the engineering trade when his employer went bankrupt and became librarian to the Mechanics Institute and

[31]Thomas Cooper *Life of, by Himself* (1876) 36 ff.; William Lovett *Life and Struggles in Pursuit of Bread, Knowledge and Freedom* (1876) 7; Holyoake *Life* 33; Tom Mann *Memoirs* (London, 1923) 4; Ben Tillett *Memories and Reflections* (London, 1931) 26–8; Thomas Burt *An Autobiography* (London, 1924) 44; *Life and Labours of John Normansell* reprinted from the *Barnsley Chronicle* (1 January 1876); George Edwards *From Crow Scaring to Westminster* (London, 1922) 21; for Bates, Mitchell, Finch and Craig see John Saville, ed. *Dictionary of Labour Biography* vol. 1 (1972); for Ironside and Ancott see *Dictionary* . . . vol. 2 (1974)

[32]Benjamin Brierley *Home Memories* (Manchester, 1886) 36

[33]Rushton *My Life* . . . p. 43

collector for the Royal Infirmary.[34] Thousands of men, though apparently few women, initiated and benefited from the Sunday school improvement societies which grew up in most parts of England.

To return then to the initial question—why did the working classes attend Sunday school—at least part of the answer is clearly that they attended because of the education they could acquire there. Schools with the widest offerings of elementary instruction were better patronized than others, secular instruction was seen to be sufficiently attractive to be used as a reward in many Sunday schools, and a whole subculture of self-help and self-improvement developed out of the more mundane educational program of Sunday schools. Finally, as Frederic Hill put it, the value that the working class placed on education '. . . is shown by their readiness in educating others, even at the sacrifice of a portion of the only day of relaxation which they can command'.[35] Indeed, by 1850 over 200,000 men and women, mostly from the working class, spent every Sunday teaching the children of their neighbors to read. But why, if there was this widespread demand for education, could contemporaries, followed by modern authorities, hold to the judgment that 'while some parents appreciate education, most do not'?

Parents had to decide how much education to purchase for their children on the basis of two economic considerations, viz. the cost of schooling and the potential benefits, both in terms of wages and less tangible returns, that might accrue from their investment. It appears likely that the ability to read, write and do arithmetic would be of considerable value in an increasingly industrial and commercial economy and that it was perceived to be so by a large segment of the working classes. On the other hand, the costs of even an elementary education were high when set in the context of the average family income. First, direct expenditures were far from negligible. Dame schools cost from twopence to fivepence, and ordinary day schools around eightpence to tenpence per week, in addition to the costs of the extra shoes and clothing that were required for regular school attendance.[36] The opportunity costs were, however, far greater; children could be put to work in casual employment in urban and rural areas at a very early age; full-time work could begin at ten or by mid-century perhaps at eleven or

[34] *Memorials of the Founders . . . of Bennett Street Sunday School* with additions by Benjamin Milner (2nd ed. 1882)

[35] F. Hill *National Education . . .* p. 117

[36] Each of the reports cited in note 9, p. 99 give estimates of direct costs of education in various grades of schools

twelve. A family with three children between the ages of six and thirteen would thus incur over two shillings in direct costs and would lose about ten shillings in potential earnings if all three were enrolled in full-time study.

However, direct expenditures on the order of two shillings per week were completely unrealistic. In Northumberland, where the high demand for education among farm laborers was often commented upon, a family of four earning sixteen shillings per week might be expected to spend only sixpence of this on education, while a family with six children could budget only fivepence per week for the same purpose.[37] It was estimated that in industrial Lancashire a prudent factory worker earning a handsome twenty-six shillings and sixpence per week could be expected to spend sixpence of his wages for the schooling of his children.[38] The two great advantages of Sunday schools were that they were free and that they did not interfere with weekday labor and therefore did not reduce family earnings. The large amount of Sunday school education consumed suggests that working-class demand for instruction was considerable, if only the costs could be reduced to tolerable proportions. But costs were not the only factor which differentiated Sunday schools from many of the day schools available to the working classes in the early nineteenth century.

Sunday schools were part of the local community; the schools of the National and the British and Foreign Society were not, and were therefore less likely to meet the needs, and win the approval, of working-class parents. Sunday school teachers were largely from the same class and quite probably from the same neighborhood as those they taught. Teachers in the schools of the two educational societies, i.e. in publicly provided schools, were brought in from the outside and were potentially objectionable on a variety of personal or political grounds. The rector of Warrington, for example, told the National Society that the schools in his parish had declined precipitously because a Miss Saunders and a Miss Churchill at the girls' school were not only inefficient but also enforced church attendance, short hair, and other noxious forms of discipline. Under the new mistress the numbers had increased again. The boys' school had gone into decline because the teacher was secretary to a Tory politician and made speeches on political

---

[37] 'Expenditures on Education in Bellingham, Northumberland' *JRSS* vol. 1 (1839) 420

[38] Henry Ashworth 'Statistics on the present Depression of Trade at Bolton; showing the mode in which it affects the different Classes of a Manufacturing Population' *JRSS* vol. 5 (1842) 74–81, esp. p. 78

occasions.[39] Sunday school classes were small and instruction adjusted to the individual; in publicly provided schools the monitorial system reduced the child to a small cog in a great and impersonal educational machine. Discipline in Sunday schools with regard to cleanliness and dress, although apparently strict, was flexible enough to allow for the exigencies of working-class life. In the National and British schools this was not always the case. The attractiveness of Sunday schools was thus enhanced for the same reasons that dame and ordinary day schools were more popular among the working classes than the relatively cheaper National and British schools. In both cases the education offered filled the perceived needs of the community and was provided at a low enough economic and psychic cost to attract millions of working-class children.[40]

iii. SUNDAY SCHOOLS AND THE RELIGION OF CHILDREN

Although Sunday schools in general were a failure as recruitment agencies for church and chapel, they nevertheless sustained a Christian culture among working-class children. As a source of the biblical rhetoric which influenced popular writing and speech during the nineteenth century, as a place of comfort at times of sickness and death, and as an instrument of conversion, the Sunday school played a central part in the spiritual lives of its students.

The Bible and *Pilgrim's Progress* were to be found in almost every working-class home.[41] Their aesthetic power must have had a special attraction for children growing up in a hard, often cheerless and always precarious world; their language remained long after attendance at Sunday school had ceased. As John Wilson said of Bunyan's characters, 'I am thankful their reality still lives and I hope it will never fade until I too, with Pilgrim, pass over the River.'[42] The grand themes and the stately beautiful language in which they were told fed my very life,' said Marianne Farningham of the Bible passages she learned as a girl in Sunday school.[43] 'Stir up, oh Lord, we beseech thee, the wills of thy faithful people', the opening words of one of the Church collects, stuck in the mind of

[39] Rev. Horace Powys/J. C. Wigram 4 June 1836 in the MS. Warrington National School File, National School Society Library, Great Peter Street, London

[40] For further discussion see T. W. Laqueur 'Working Class Demand ... '

[41] The extraordinary penetration of the printed word into the working class home is suggested in 'Social Condition of the Working Classes in Eight Kent Parishes' Central Society for Education *Reports* vol. 1 (1837) 344

[42] Wilson *Memories* ... p. 54

[43] Farningham *Life* ... p. 20

Tom Mann, the dockers' leader, to his death.[44] The first miners' MP, Thomas Burt, told of an argument between his father and the Sunday school superintendent over what Thomas was to recite at the annual sermon. The latter had chosen 'an uninteresting goody-goody sort of piece, poor and empty', while his father chose the thirty-fifth chaper of Isaiah and coached him in it. It is indeed 'strong lofty melodious prose'.

> The wilderness and the solitary place shall be glad for them; and the desert shall rejoice, and blossom as a rose'... Say to them that are fearful of heart, Be Strong, fear not: behold your God will come with vengeance ... And the ransomed of the Lord shall return, and come to Zion with songs and everlasting joy upon their heads: they shall obtain joy and gladness, and sorrow and sighing shall flee away.[45]

Powerful stuff for a boy in his teens and a rich source for the man who later addressed mass meetings of the Durham Miners' Association.

But the religion of the Sunday school went deeper than the beautiful language of the Bible, Bunyan or the prayer book. The assurance of salvation and the community of their fellows provided students with the psychological strength to face the all too familiar spectre of death and disease. A religion which places great emphasis on the promise of an afterlife is not just 'the chiliasm of the defeated and the hopeless', the solace of failed revolution.[46] It is also the religion of those for whom death from consumption, smallpox, cholera, fever or accident is an ever-present oppressive reality. In England as a whole the age specific death rate was nine per thousand for those aged five to nine, and five per thousand for those aged ten to fourteen; in the overcrowded, damp and cold cities of south Lancashire, northern Cheshire and the West Riding, the chances of dying young were much greater. In 1850, when the life expectancy for males in the country as a whole was forty, it was only twenty-four in Manchester. Infant mortality was well over three hundred per thousand, and between ten and twenty per thousand could be expected to die each year between the ages of eight and twenty.[47] So, almost all children in the early nineteenth century would have watched one of their infant brothers and

[44] Dona Torr *Tom Mann and his Times* vol. 1 (1956) 30

[45] Burt *Autobiography* p. 44

[46] Thompson *Making* ... p. 382

[47] See E. A. Wrigley *Population and History* (1969) fig. 5.3 'Age specific death rates—England and Wales, 1840–1960'; for Manchester see W. Farr *Vital Statistics* (1885) 478, 181 and fig. 1.1 in Wrigley; see also parts iv, v of Farr *passim*

sisters, or those of neighbors, succumb to some common disease. In a Sunday school with an enrolment of two hundred, one or two students would die each year; and, if the school was in an industrial city, this number would be doubled. Against such a background, the eschatological bent of so much Sunday school religious literature appears less perverse and its potential psychic satisfactions more manifest.

The Watts hymn which proclaimed:

> There is an hour when I must die,
>   nor do I know how soon 'twill come;
> A thousand children young as I
>   are called by death to hear their doom.[48]

was not conjuring up some gruesome fantasy. It reflected the uncertainty and precariousness of existence which were the subject of hundreds of poems like:

> The mother left her work awhile
>   To watch her smiling babe at play
> When evening came it would not smile
>   For stiff upon her knees it lay
> Its lip was white, its cheek was cold
>   Why did it die it was not old?

***

> Too well I read the awful truth
>   That all mankind must thus expire
> In pale decay or blooming youth . . . [49]

A whole literature grew up in the late eighteenth and nineteenth centuries which related, with varying degrees of truthfulness, the way in which children faced this danger.

One form of this vast literature was the deathbed fable. These either portrayed the horrible death of a famous infidel like Voltaire or Tom Paine; the accidental and inglorious deaths of wicked Sunday school students who played truant, lied, stole, broke the sabbath by swimming or skating, or acted immorally in some other way; or the glorious deaths of semi-mythical regenerate sinners. While interesting in its own right, there is little to be learned from this literature regarding the way real children faced death.[50]

---

[48] Isaac Watts, Song 10 'Solemn Thoughts on God and Death' *Divine and Moral Songs for Children* (London, 1971 Facs. ed. of 1848 ed.) 224

[49] *The Christian Child's Faithful Friend* vol. 1 (1833) 143

[50] See *The Death Bed of Tom Paine* reprinted in F. K. Brown *Fathers* . . . pp. 458–9 and Brown's discussion on the preceding page; or for example *The Death of an*

Secondly, there grew up an extensive body of accounts describing the last moments of historically identifiable adults whose lives had displayed signs of extraordinary piety. The authenticity of these accounts is less important here than the fact that they undoubtedly came to serve as a model for dying, as a prescription for meeting death. As such they have much in common with the memoirs of children.

These are in some respects similar to the two forms just discussed; they are didactic in the sense of the fable and exemplary or prescriptive in the sense of illustrating a way of dying acceptable to some social group, in this case Sunday school teachers. But both internal and external evidence suggests that memoirs of children to a large extent also constitute reports of what actually happened and as such provide an insight into the religious lives of Sunday scholars. Although difficult to convey without citing large numbers of stories, there is a ring of truthfulness about a certain set of memoirs. A small child nearing death might well have said to her mother, 'Will Jesus take me? Mother do you think he will?'; or another, when asked whether she wanted to live, could well have said 'Oh no!; I am going to be with Jesus Christ in heaven. They are singing for me there. I do not wish to stay any longer.' As the introduction to the *Stockport Sunday School Memoir Book* put it,

> ... they [the deathbed accounts] state simple facts in the simple language made use of by the children themselves. And though their expressions may not have been exactly such as the scholar or the divine would have used, yet they will be perfectly intelligible to all, and the genuine simplicity manifested in them will not fail to make a deep impression on pious minds.[51]

Modern investigations of terminally ill children contain very similar language and thereby lend credence to nineteenth-century accounts.

Furthermore, the social context described in the stories was, as other sources prove, true to life. Sunday school teachers routinely visited sick students, classmates were organized to pay calls on their indisposed colleagues, and the last moments were thought of as a

---

Infidel: or the last Hours of the Hon. Francis Newport RTS, no. 16 (B. M. 863 K 1); conversely there is RTS no 6 *The Repentance and Happy Death of the Celebrated Earl of Rochester to which is added a Letter from a nobleman, on his deathbed, to a profligate companion.* For the death of bad Sunday school scholars see for example William Richardson, *Dialogues for Sunday Schools on Interesting Topics* (1822)

[51] *Sunday School Gleanings* (2nd ed. 1823) 122; *The Children's Friend* vol. 2 (1825) 161. The relatively restrained story from which this quote comes is typical of deathbed literature as a whole but not of Carus-Wilson's work in general; *Memoir Book of the Stockport Sunday School* (compilation from the 1790s to the 1870s) 1–2

public rather than a private occasion. The descriptions of moist walls, cracking plaster, dirt, filth and such, which appear over-dramatic to the modern reader, might not have been unrealistic when written about the rural cottage or urban slum dwelling. Even in sound housing there could have been little privacy in a two-up, two-down house containing a family of eight, and this overcrowding might well have appeared squalid to Sunday school observers.

Finally, many stories are so detailed as to make wild exaggera-tions a risky business for the compiler; too many people would have been able to identify the case and catch out gross inaccuracies. Jane Thrupp died in Abingdon on 17 May 1821 after a prolonged illness; James Brown of High Felling Sunday School near New-castle suffered a fatal accident in the coal pits during the winter of 1823–4.[52] Medical details of the illnesses in question are often provided. In Stockport personal or biographical details emerge clearly: Samuel Gordon flirted briefly with deism while away from Stockport; Ann Milward's abilities as a teacher were not splendid or calculated to draw attention to her; John Lodge had a great taste for music and performed both vocally and on his instru-ment, etc.[53] Visiting scholars in Stockport was a highly organized activity; accuracy in reporting death scenes was urged upon teachers; and the superintendent even kept an account in his private diary of the number of children who died happy, the number who died unattended, and the total.[54]

If finally the authenticity of deathbed accounts is accepted, they in many ways speak for themselves. Three important points emerge: first the religion of the Sunday school in its eschatological form provided a way of dealing with the fear of death; second, evangelical forms of dying provided a dignified and socially sanctioned form of deathbed behaviour, which to a great extent was actually carried out; and third, the Sunday school bands visited the sick scholar on his deathbed, and such visitations were not the product of morbid fascination with death but an expression of communal support in times of crisis.

In addition to the aesthetic and eschatological aspects of religion, the Sunday school encompassed the process of conversion and dedication to Christ. Moreover, it represented an acknowledge-ment by adults of the special spiritual needs of children and adoles-

[52] *Sunday School Gleanings* ibid; *The Child's Magazine and Sunday Scholar's Compa-nion* vol. 1 (1824) 54

[53] *Stockport Memoir Book* memoirs of Milward and Lodge

[54] *Diaries of Joseph Mayer* vol. 1–7, MS. Stockport Reference Library, and *Committee Minute Books passim* (1798–1830)

cents. Religious styles, of course, varied considerably between Evangelicals and non-Evangelicals, between rural and urban schools, and between middle-class and working-class managed schools. The spectrum ranged from the relatively meaningless memorization of collects and catechism in a high Anglican Sunday school to 'some delightful specimens of meek and unostentatious piety' in a rural Church school to well disciplined revivals in some urban Dissenting schools to three and four day long, emotionally charged camp meetings among rural Primitive Methodists.[55]

Furthermore, some aspects of religion in Sunday schools, and of popular religion generally, shaded over into superstition or idolatry. The *Baptist Magazine* condemned the 'overfanciful descriptions of heaven and hell' with which Carus-Wilson tried to scare children.[56] Marianne Farningham tells of being terribly afraid of approaching a certain spot outside her village because a Sunday school teacher had told her that it was the opening to hell.[57] The dockers' leader, Ben Tillett, remembers asking one of his teachers what the animals on top of the church meant. 'The beasts were to watch the four quarters of the earth against the devils and enemies of Christianity,' she replied. 'Would they eat them up?' he asked; 'Yes, and eat them up,' was the answer. Tillett and his friends, of course, could not resist the temptation of testing these gargoyles and played truant from school for precisely this purpose. After watching the ugliest of the statues for a while a shadow seemed to cut across it. 'Then the figure seemed to squirm like a cat as though about to jump. We saw the twist of the body, the mouth snapped, the eyes blinked, and thereupon two screaming, howling boys ran madly away, gasping, white with the fear of nightmare devils, and finally falling down helpless and scared to death.[58] Most Sunday school religion, however, was not so unorthodox, although it was often highly emotional, free flowing, and near to primal feelings of guilt, damnation and salvation.

Guides to Sunday school practice recommended special kindness and consideration in the treatment of children; advocates of religious education argued the importance of 'training up children in the way they should go' so that they would not *become* corrupted by a wicked world; the uniqueness of the young, in fact, was implicitly or explicitly acknowledged in a variety of ways. Yet, Sunday scholars were not spared the rigors of guilt and conversion. 'The

[55] See for example *British Magazine* vol. 3 (1823) 300–1; W. Pilkington *The Makers of Wesleyan Methodism in Preston* (1890) 70; *Primitive Methodist Magazine* (1839) 318; (1840) 25; (1841) 61; *SS Teachers' Magazine* (1839) col. 133
[56] *Baptist Magazine* vol. 18 (1827) 343
[57] Farningham, *Life* ... pp. 28 ff.
[58] Tillett *Memories* ... pp. 27–8

main purpose of Sunday school instruction is to lead children to a knowledge of themselves as sinners and to show them the need of a Saviour.[59] 'We shall at once admit that these institutions are intended to convert and save the souls of children.'[60] 'You must be born again,' warns one tract given to Sunday school children, while another asked them to learn the hymn:

> A sinful creature I was born
> And from the birth I strayed:
> I must be wretched and forlorn
> Without Thy mercies aid.[61]

It seems that significant numbers of Sunday school children were 'born again' and at more or less the same age as twentieth-century adolescents who go through a conversion experience (Graphs 4 and 5, p. 167). The middle to late teens were defined as a period of intense inner turmoil, which among evangelical families was supposed to lead to a new life in Christ. In less religious families, on the other hand, adolescent conversion might result in often bitter generational conflict. Thomas Swann, son of a London bricklayer was evicted from his home because his father was annoyed by his new found righteousness; the *Primitive Methodist Magazine* reported the story of a young girl who angered her mother by insisting that the family engage in prayer and other religious exercises; finally, there were numerous almost archetypal stories of parents who after a period of intense hostility to religion were brought around by the piety of their children. These tales usually begin with some variant of the scene in which a parent ripped the Bible from the little hands of a child intent on going to Sunday school and thereby prevented his or her attendance. As the Bible was hurled across the room, there was usually some modest protest from the little boy or girl like, 'O mother, that precious book, to use it so!' The child would then fetch the Bible and read various passages to the parent who would in turn have a change of heart and end up going to chapel with the young scholar. But while the dynamics of religion in the working-class family remain obscure, outward manifestations of religious experience are more accessible.[62]

---

[59] *Baptist Magazine* vol. 24 (1832) 387

[60] *Methodist New Connexion Magazine* (1845) 176

[61] Religious Tract Society, no. 33 (1830?) and RTS, no. 52 (series 1810–20)

[62] Guida Swann, ed. *Journals of Two Poor Dissenters 1786–1880* (1970) conversion of Thomas Swan, c. 1803, p. 5; *Primitive Methodist Magazine* (1823) 64; the reverse could, of course, also be a source of conflict—'Mrs. Collier' reports her anxieties with regard to her son who after eight years in Sunday school was still not converted, lied, etc.—*A Bible-Woman's Life Story* ed. by Elizabeth Nightingdale (1885) 28–9. See for example Davis, *Religious Education* . . . pp. 62–63

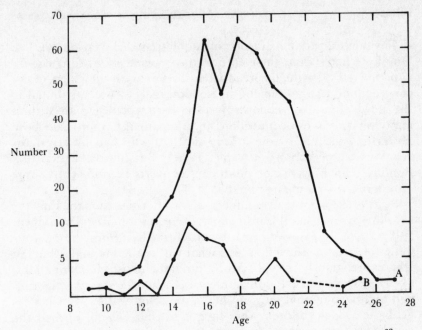

Graph 4 : Distribution of ages of conversion for two groups, 1770–1835[63]

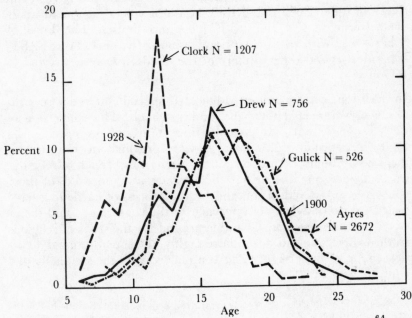

Graph 5 : Distribution of ages of conversion, for four groups, 1900–32[64]

[63] Graph 1, line A is calculated from ages of conversion of 507 ministers or candidates for the ministry in *Congregational Magazine* (1835) 647; line B is calculated from Timpson *Mirror* ... which gives the age of conversion for 48 Sunday school workers born between 1770 and 1820

[64] Michael Argyle *Religious Behaviour* (1958) 61

The organizational forms of adolescent conversion varied. Sunday schools from their earliest days were centers for denominational revivals which spread from the young to the elders of the congregation. An awakening in London in 1795 was attributed to the newly founded schools; 'I have been privileged to witness many revivals in our connection, and in many the young have been powerfully visited,' wrote a lady in 1829 who had observed the religious life of Bolton since the 1790s.[65] But the realization that Sunday schools were not producing converts in sufficiently large numbers led to a change in style.

By the 1830s most denominational authorities thought that the revival was an unsuitable instrument of conversion. Regular, diligent and religiously inspired work by teachers, free from the onerous duties of secular instruction, was what was needed to make Sunday schools religiously useful. More fundamentalist denominations, like the Primitive Methodists, integrated children into the vigorous and highly emotional religious life of the congregation. In Chesterfield the school children were taught to sing, which 'opened the way for extensive usefulness' especially in the processing services:

> The children were all in attendance, or we could not have begun at the time. They raised their youthful voices high, and made Chesterfield-street ring with Jehovah's praises. The Lord of hosts was with us in a glorious fashion. In the LOVEFEAST, besides several others, many of the children were converted to God.[66]

In addition, certain writers advocated special children's revivals that were organized through Sunday schools. The conversion of the young was not only possible, important and promised in the Bible, but specific examples of it were provided in scripture, so there could be no excuse for not beginning this branch of religious work, argued one authority.[67] Schools are *not* composed 'of those who have grown old in sin, and by the process of hardening have sealed up every avenue of approach to the conscience', and therefore constitute the most favorable ground for the seeds of religious truth. Conversion did not require highly developed rational faculties; in fact, Christ ought to be approached with the simplicity of a child, it argued.[68]

[65] James Everett *Adam Clarke Portrayed* vol. 2 (1843) 23; Elizabeth Rhodes *Memoir* (1829) 139

[66] *Primitive Methodist Magazine* (1839) 178–9

[67] Rev. Edward Miller 'On the Conversion of Sunday School Children' (1842) reprinted in *SS Teachers' Magazine* (1842) 776 ff.

[68] *The Revivalist* conducted by Rev. Joseph Belcher, vol. 7 (1838) 17–18

But whatever the form of efforts to convert the young, the experience itself was always emotional, often ecstatic, occasionally hysterical and obviously sexual. Girls seem to have been more susceptible than boys, but weeping and other emotional displays were apparently common to both sexes and to students as well as teachers. One boy who first saw himself as a sinner aged ten or eleven remembered his teachers 'especially Mr George Gardiner, who used to weep over me and others of the scholars'.[69] A superintendent of a Methodist Sunday school in Manchester dated the beginning of his success in that role to the time when he was first able to address children with sufficient fervor to elicit tears. After that, '[he] was often cheered by the sight of weeping countenances', and was particularly encouraged when a laborer came up to him and reported looking through a keyhole in one of the classrooms to see a group of girls kneeling in a circle, praying and weeping.[70] One twelve-year-old girl approached her Sunday school teacher 'with streaming eyes' to tell him that 'God had pardoned her sins and that she loved God because he had loved her first.'[71] Elsewhere, after four nights of preaching at a Sunday school revival, all the young were bathed in tears. One girl sobbed, 'I have tonight been invited to come to Christ, I see that he is inviting me to come. I can not lie down another night without him.'[72] In a small Cambridgeshire revival, children were said to have shouted, 'Oh save me now! Save me or I perish!' as the spirit moved them.[73]   Exhibitionist.

It remains an open question whether Sunday schools induced a sense of guilt and a state of emotional turmoil so that they could then offer the means of assuaging them. But the appeal of highly charged fundamentalist religion to those whose ordinary lives were disorderly, unpredictable and hard is not difficult to understand.

iv. SUNDAY SCHOOLS IN THE LIFE OF THE INDIVIDUAL AND THE COMMUNITY

Sunday schools helped to bring order into the daily lives of their students, to provide social services not readily available elsewhere,

[69] Quoted in Hawkes *The Rise of Wesleyan Sunday Schools, Luton* (1885) 13
[70] *History of Sunday Schools in Manchester* MS. Methodist Archive, signed at the end by C. Rider (10 December 1825)
[71] *Report of the Wesleyan Sunday Schools* in *Plan of a Society . . . founded* 1798 (1811) 56
[72] *The Teachers' Offering; or Sunday School Monthly Visitor* (1844) 212
[73] Histon, Camb. *SS Teachers' Magazine* (1842) 124; regarding the special susceptibility of girls to conversion see also *Primitive Methodist Magazine* (1838) 258

and to offer recreational and cultural activities where few were available.

In inculcating values relating to personal behavior, Sunday schools appear to have been a remarkably successful agency of bourgeois moral imperialism.[74] To some extent they were, of course, just that; but on closer examination what appears to have been an imposition from above was, in fact, a way in which those who spent their lives in disorder, uncertainty, dirt and disease brought some order into this environment. Cleanliness in body, punctuality, neatness in dress and in one's home, and orderliness in one's life style were very much part of the fabric of 'respectable' working-class society and by no means inhibited those engaged in their pursuit from attacking the repressive aspects of the contemporary political and economic system; rather the reverse.

Cleanliness especially appears to have been a symbolic expression of the love and concern felt by parents for their children: 'Her cleanliness in her house was remarkable! her care for her children was apparent.'[75] Lovett says of his mother, 'she took great pains in keeping me scrupulously clean and respectable in my person'; Alexander Somerville writes of this, 'her motherly affection for me, and indirect pride in the good appearance of her family, had led her to suggest to my father that I should not be sent to school again until we had got the silken we were waiting for to get new clothes.'[76] When Benjamin Brierley's mother was very ill, he commented later that his first thought had been of 'other boys who had been left motherless [and so] gone to rags both in clothing and in morals'.[77] An anonymous working man describes his mother in terms that suggest an almost pathological dislike of dirt: 'My mother was a very industrious woman and quite remarkable for her love of cleanliness. She carried her dislike of dirtiness so far as to request every person coming into her house to be careful not to soil, or otherwise put out of order the well scrubbed and neatly sanded floor.'[78]

Cleanliness of person and clothing came to be associated by children and parents with the Sunday school, which in turn represented all that the weekday was not—order, neatness, self-respect. It is striking how many men and women writing their autobiographies in the late nineteenth century remember just

[74] See Chap. 7

[75] [Anon.] A Brief Memoir of the Late Mrs. John Richards (Wednesbury, 1854) 11

[76] Lovett Life ... op. cit. p. 8; Alexander Somerville The Autobiography of a Working Man vol. 1 (1848) 32

[77] Brierley, Home Memories op. cit. p. 25

[78] [Thomas Carter] Memoirs of a Working Man (1845) 22

this aspect of their school experience. George Edwards, for example, recalls that:

> My sister and I went to bed early on Saturday nights so that my mother might be able to wash and mend our clothes and we have them tidy for Sunday. This work kept my mother up nearly all Saturday night, but she would be up early on Sunday morning to get our scanty breakfasts ready in time for us to go to Sunday school.[79]

The specialness of Sunday school, its transcendence of the mundane and the ugly, comes across even more strongly in the biography of a one-time pottery worker and Primitive Methodist preacher:

> I got a washing that morning such as I had not time to get on other mornings. I had poor enough clothing to put on, but my eldest sister always helped me in my toilet on Sunday mornings, and my hair got brushed and combed and oiled (with scented oil) ... Amidst these unfriendly and perilous circumstances, the influences of the Sunday school stood me in good stead. It was not so much that I understood the evil about me and saw into its baleful depths, as that I had an inward influence which gave me an opposite bias and always made me think of the Sunday school.[80]

It must be emphasized, however, that this euphoria about the Sunday school did not produce a rejection of political radicalism. Indeed, the author loudly condemned the Wesleyan leadership for its conservatism and included in his autobiography an appreciation of the Chartist Joseph Capper.

> I knew [of] two different worlds—one belonging to the God and Father I read about in Sunday school every Sunday; and the other belonging to the rich men, to manufacturers, to squires and nobles, and all kinds of men of authority. These I supposed made the world of men what it was, through sheer badness in treatment of all who had work.[81]

Sunday school anniversaries too were occasions to display respectability and self-esteem. In fact, on Clog Sunday in Manchester parents bought their children new shoes, and the Sunday school

---

[79] Edwards *From Crow Scaring* ... op. cit. p. 21

[80] *When I was a Child* by an Old Potter, introduction by Robert Spence Watson (1903) 7–8

[81] Ibid. p. 35; for his views on the Wesleyan leadership and on the Chartists see pp. 143–5

provided for those unable to make the purchase.[82] The anniversary, not Christmas, was the day for making gifts of clothing in the Potteries, and the same was true in parts of Kent, Cornwall and Northamptonshire.[83] 'I had no new clogs for prize giving day,' reads one autobiography, 'but I washed my feet for a long time. I was determined that if I could not get anything to cover my ten toes, I could make them look clean.'[84] In fact, much to the annoyance of some religious authorities, who considered it a form of worldly vanity, parents were far more concerned to present their children to the world neat and in new clothes than to strive for their religious edification.[85]

Sunday schools developed a wide range of social services because older forms of charity, poor relief, and even to some extent informal community or family networks could no longer meet the needs of a rapidly growing population that was prey to the trade cycles of an industrial economy. These services varied from *ad hoc* informal acts of kindness on the part of students and teachers to highly organized and well-financed sickness, burial or clothing clubs. When an old teacher in Petersfield, Hants. broke his leg, five children from his class spontaneously visited him and put fourpence into his hand.[86] Children in the Portsea Lake Lane Sunday School collected a halfpenny from each student and gave the resulting £1.11s. 8½d. to a classmate suffering from a gangrenous leg.[87] In Armitage, Staffs. scholars were asked to contribute a halfpenny whenever one of their colleagues died to help pay for his funeral.[88]

On another scale, Bolton Parish Sunday School Sick Society paid 2s. 4d. per week, up to £7. 5s., for a weekly contribution of 1d., had 580 members, and assets of £597. 8s. 0d.[89] German Street Sick and Burial Society, Manchester, paid between 2s. 6d. and 5s. per week for sickness based on contributions of 1d.-2d. per week and £3. 8s. for a funeral.[90] Bennett Street Society had 975 mem-

[82] *The Manchester Guardian* (10 November 1879)

[83] For example see *When I was a Child* p. 205; Farningham *Life . . .* p. 30; W. J. Bain *A Study of Rock; but not Geological—A Paper on the early history of Sunday Schools especially in Northamptonshire* (2nd ed., Northampton, 1875)

[84] Rev. John Ashworth *Life and Labours* ed. by A. L. Calman (Manchester, 1875) 17

[85] See for examples pp. 85–6 above. Working-class accounts of anniversaries always note children's clothing or prowess at recitation and seldom if ever mention the sermon or other more religious aspects of the festival

[86] *SS Teachers' Magazine* (1839) 454

[87] *SS Gleanings . . .* p. 67

[88] A. G. Mathews *The Congregational Church in Staffordshire* (1924) 196

[89] *First Report of the Factory Commissioners . . .* 1833 (450) xx. D 2, p. 137

[90] J. Kirkham *Centenary History of the German Street Sunday School* (1903) 11

bers in its 'sick department', 955 in its funeral section, and took in
£3,742. 7s. 11d. between 1812 and 1830, while paying out over
£2,700.[91] The Birmingham New Meeting Sick Society, founded in
1798, offered benefits of 2s. or 4s. for sickness based on ½d. or 1d.
payments each week, and by 1834 had a capital of £1,467.[92]
Depending upon age of entry, the Anglican society in Leek paid up
to 7s. per week for six months, 6s. per week for the next six months
and 4s. for life to its members on the basis of a 2s. entry fee and a 1s.
per month contribution.[93] Cockermouth, Cumberland, Sunday
School offered 3s. sick pay for a 1d. per week contribution, 2 gn. and
a coffin for a ½d. a week payment to the funeral society, and 50
per cent premium on all funds paid into the clothing society.[94] By the
1830s benefit societies at this level of organization had become so
acceptable that the *Baptist Magazine* recommended that each of
the denomination's schools should have one. Contributions of
1d. per week, the article suggested, could yield benefits of 1s.–1s. 6d.
per week in case of sickness, 15s. for a funeral, and still allow full
repayment of unused funds at the end of the year.[95]

If the benefit societies of Manchester and Stockport were at all
typical, women and factory children, the groups most vulnerable
to economic exigencies, were more likely to become members than
men and children employed outside the factory. (Table 18.)
Almost twice as great a proportion of factory as against non-factory
workers belonged to benefit societies; a significantly higher propor-

Table 18:[96] *Membership in the Bennett Street and Stockport Sunday School Sick Societies
among factory and non-factory employed scholars and teachers*, 1833

Males	1 No. examined	2 No. in Sick Society	Col. 2 as a percentage of Col. 1
In factory	426	130	33
Not in factory	252	47	19
Females			
In factory	625	279	45
Not in factory	332	80	24

[91] *Bennett Street Memorials* ... p. 131
[92] Frederic Hill *National Education* ... pp. 119–20
[93] New Leek Sunday School [Anglican] 'Humane Society for Sick and Aged
Members' Staffordshire Record Office D 1114/1
[94] *SS Teachers' Magazine* (1842) 623
[95] *Baptist Magazine* (1834) 145
[96] *First Report of the Factory Commissioners* ... op. cit. 1833 (450) xx. D 1, p. 87

tion of women than men were subscribers. But for all of those involved, sick and benefit societies provided social services no longer
readily available from traditional sources and not yet provided by
the welfare state.

After sick societies, clothing clubs were probably the most
common form of Sunday school social services. In schools with rich
patrons, these were simply a more organized form of traditional
charity. An unknown donor, for example, provided over thirty
separate gifts of shoes and clothing to parish Sunday school children
in Monks' Eleigh.[97] Rev. Joseph Pearson wrote of his experiences
in Nottingham around the turn of the century that: 'Boys entitled
to shoes and stockings, etc. called on me ... I led them through
the town and got their wants supplied, which gave me great pleasure. Sixty-nine boys, in the course of a few weeks, were relieved
by these means, and £14. 8s. 4d. expended.'[98] In other schools
children paid a halfpenny each week and received, dependent on
good behavior, a fifty to a hundred per cent bonus on their contribution at the end of the year. Poorer schools used the same system
but without the bonus. And, of course, clothing was also supplied
on an *ad hoc* basis. Working-class teachers in Blackburn, for example,
organized relief efforts to collect clothing, food, and money for
children suffering in the 1841 depression.[99]

Sunday schools also formed part of a network which could be
used by scholars to obtain employment in cities where they could
have few other contacts with potential employers. The hero in
Philip the Reprobate by Jane Strickland finds a patron and
enters business 'for which the neat handwriting and good arithmetic acquired in the Sunday school qualified him sufficiently'.[100]
In real life, the Liverpool Methodist Sunday School Committee
announced in 1827 that it had given characters for trade and service
to 220 boys and 180 girls.[101] The obituary of Richard Evans, Esq.
of Worcester remarked that 'he took especial delight in forwarding
young men in business, especially such as had been Sunday
scholars'; and the Rev. James Griffin of Rusholm Road Sunday
School was told by a Manchester manufacturer that: '... Whenever
steady men are wanted for confidential positions, the masters or
overlookers apply to the superintendents of the Sunday school to

[97] Rev. the Hon. A. F. Northcote *Notes on the History of Monks' Eleigh* (Ipswich,
1930) 43
[98] Quoted in R. C. Swift 'Methodist Sunday Schools in Nottingham' *Proc.
Wesley Hist Soc.* vol. 23 (1961–62) 28
[99] *Sunday School Magazine* (1841) 265
[100] Part 3, reprinted in *SS Teachers' Magazine* (1839) 135
[101] *Philanthropic Magazine* vol. 1 (1827) 36

recommend them young men of ability and good character.'[102] J. C. Wigram told a parliamentary committee that a tradesman who superintended a Sunday school circulated a small notice in which he offered to act as a negotiator between shopmen who required help and boys who wanted positions and that he was instantly flooded with notices of positions being offered.[103] Lloyd, an officer of the Union, told the 1816 inquiry into education that Sunday school managers generally recommended senior scholars for positions in the warehouses or offices of their friends.[104] Teaching in a Sunday school also apparently helped provide access to certain relatively secure and prestigious jobs. Three hundred and fifty of the four hundred men and women selected for British and Foreign School Society training colleges were Sunday school teachers according to the Society's secretary.[105]

The range of informal and formally constituted services provided by Sunday schools was wider still. They offered assistance where lack of access to political authority rendered the individual helpless, like securing the release of a student from a press gang in London.[106] They provided small-scale savings banks for children which, it was optimistically argued, 'often save whole families from destitution'.[107] They organized the benefit societies, clothing clubs, and employment exchanges discussed above. In short, they provided for the working-class community a wide range of services not readily available elsewhere during the first half of the nineteenth century.

Finally, the Sunday school was a social and recreational center for a significant part of the working-class community, especially, but not exclusively, in the new industrial towns. For teachers of whatever class it could absorb a major part of their free time. Benjamin Braidley, owner of a commission warehouse and guiding light of the Anglican Bennett Street Sunday School in Manchester, spent his free time as follows: Monday—writing class at the Sunday school; Tuesday—prayer meeting with scholars; Wednesday—Church Missionary Society meeting and writing and accounts classes at the Sunday school; Thursday—writing and accounts classes; Sunday—all day at the school.[108] Many working-class

[102] SS Teachers' Magazine (1848) 528; Rev. James Griffin Memories of the Past: Recollections of a Ministerial Life (1883) 231

[103] S. C. H. C. . . . Education op. cit. 1835 (465) vii, Q 31

[104] S. C. H. C., Second Report . . . Education in the Metropolis op. cit. 1816 (427) iv. p. 79; on this topic see also C. of E. SS Quarterly Magazine, (1848–49) 272

[105] Education Magazine (June 1835) 423

[106] Thomas E. Westerdale Centenary History of the Radnor Street Day, Sunday, and Ragged Schools (1898) 18

[107] SS Teachers' Magazine (1846) 219

[108] Benjamin Braidley Memoir (1845) diary entry for 1 December 1816

lay preachers developed their avocation through the Sunday school. James Haigh of Mossley, for example, learned to read and write at the Sunday school, began attending class meetings with his companions from the school, remained there after his conversion, became an exhorter who went around from class to class giving short religious lessons, and ended up a New Connexion lay preacher.[109]

From teas to funerals, the role of the Sunday school was central to the lives of many teachers. Local histories and the specialized school press reported a never-ending series of special and regular gatherings. There were Christmas, Whitsun and harvest teas; there were meetings held in honor of a colleague or a superintendent who was leaving or who had achieved thirty, forty, even fifty years of service. Secondhand bookshops today are still packed with presentation copies of the Bible, the *Wesleyan Hymn Book*, a *Book of Common Prayer*, or a *Pilgrim's Progress* given to some deserving teacher during the nineteenth century.

Teachers accompanied students in the funeral processions of Sunday school members: they followed the coffin of Stephen Strains, a 'humble schoolmaster' in Stratford; the superintendent and older teachers carried 'little Mary' to her grave in Petersfield. They organized special events like that in Burgh, Lincs. at which Church Sunday school students, headed by a band and followed by the inhabitants, marched out to meet the vicar and his new wife.[110] And, of course, they went to improvement societies and lectures organized by the school or by some other organization. Anglican teachers in London, for example, could attend monthly lectures at the Sunday School Institute and hear, in addition to topics of religious interest, talks on subjects like 'Ancient and Modern Egypt Contrasted' by the Headmaster of the City of London School.[111]

But the recreational, cultural and social activities of the Sunday school were far more important to students than to teachers. For adults in the early nineteenth century public recreation was largely confined to the pub; drinking, cock-fighting, gambling, and prize fights were the primary diversions.[112] In the countryside traditional annual wakes and fairs were by 1800 rapidly declining;

---

[109] Joseph Barker *Memoirs of Several Eminent Christians Lately Members of the Methodist New Connexion* (1839) 4–6

[110] *SS Teachers' Magazine* (1839) 141 and (1842) 312–14; *Sunday School Magazine* (1846) 142

[111] *C. of E. SS Quarterly Magazine* (1848) 85–8

[112] See Brian Harrison *Drink and the Victorians* (1971) 32–49

in towns, race week, though open to children, was not designed for
their particular pleasure. Before the growth in the late nineteenth
century of organized youth movements and public sporting events,
Sunday schools provided the only institution designed, even i .
part, for the pleasure of the young.   +

The anniversary celebration has already been discussed in the
context of fund raising and will be discussed again as a counter-
recreation designed to combat the evils of traditional festivals.
Here it is important as the major event of the Sunday school year
which provided, for months in advance, a focus for the students'
energies.[113] They were an occasion to dress in new clothes, to parade
through the town, to recite specially memorized passages in front of
parents and subscribers, to hear music, and often to go to the
country for a picnic.

In larger schools special hymns were written for the occasion.
Music was always central. A Bagsdale minister's son, in training to
be a shoemaker, taught children to sing oratorios.[114] Frederic
Macdonald, in describing the anniversary at which even 'the
poorest houses turned out little girls in white frocks, sometime
white shoes, with hair generously combed and oiled', remarked
also on the long rehearsed and carefully prepared performances
of the *Messiah* and *Judas Maccabeus* which were presented.[115]
Another school in the Midlands performed medieval miracle
plays at its annual fete.[116] The *Northern Star* reported that a little
boy at Hanley in the Potteries recited 'Factory Bell' from the works
of Mr Hicks, the Chartist, at his school's anniversary; Joseph
Barker preached the sermon at Ashton New Connexion Sunday
School where music by Handel, Haydn and Taylor was per-
mormed.[117] Fiddles, flutes, cellos and trumpets provided the
music in Wigan, where people from all around came together
for the anniversary.[118]

Sometimes associated with the anniversary, sometimes an event
in its own right, the Sunday school outing was the second great
occasion of the year. These varied considerably from school to
school and grew enormously in the 1840s with the coming of cheap
mass transportation. In Alberthorpe the Sunday school celebrated
its twentieth annual festival with a march through the village by 250

[113] For a more modern account of these preparations see Arthur Cossons 'The
Villagers Remember' in *Transactions of the Thoroton Society* vol. 66 (1962) 67–82

[114] Ashworth *Life* ... p. 15

[115] Macdonald *Reminiscences* ... p. 21

[116] *Children's Employment* ... [*Trade and Manufacturies*] op. cit. 1843 [431]
xiv, Q. 85.

[117] *Northern Star* (6 March 1841) 1; (18 August 1838) 5

[118] Little *Wigan SS* ... p. 14

G

students, sixty teachers, and a band, which was followed by ale and buns for all and dinner for the teachers.[119] The procession in Rockland St Peters, Norfolk, was headed by the Primitive Methodist Sunday School banner which was followed by eight other banners, by two men playing instruments of music, by two travelling preachers, by the superintendent and then by the children themselves, 'all neat and clean, every one carrying a little flag'.

> It was the greatest procession ever seen in Rockland St. Peters ...
> We proceed to the field where a table was set out for the children to take tea. Mr. James Fielding, sen. who raised this Sunday school, provided a sufficient number of custards, which were placed on a table so as to form the words, 'Sunday schools'. Ninety-six children sat down to tea, and every one of them had a custard. They were all highly delighted.[120]

In fact, feasts were among the earliest Sunday school innovations. Raikes provided one for the children in Painswick in 1787; Hannah More gave dinner to over a thousand children and parents every year; over a thousand children in Bath drank toasts in beer to the king, to the corporation, and to Sunday schools at their annual banquet in 1815.[121] The new parish Sunday school in Medmenham, Bucks. was inaugurated with a feast of beer and buns for the children.[122] And, though usually without alcohol, most Sunday schools provided some kind of annual treat for its scholars.

Even before the existence of the railways the annual outing could proceed beyond walking distance of the school. London children from the East End were taken by wagon to Richmond Park via Kew Gardens and other parts of the city that they seldom if ever saw.[123] Manchester children were taken by canal boats on their Whitsun outings.[124] But trains made far more elaborate excursions possible. 3,000 children and 500 teachers from the Birmingham Sunday School Union were taken by train to Cheltenham on 8 and 9 July 1846, to visit the pump room, various gardens, and a nursery; on 15 July 600 children and 400 teachers from Cheltenham visited Birmingham.[125] 3,000 children and teachers from Maccles-

[119] *Northern Star* (8 September 1838) 4 'And a very bad custom it is', remarked the editor

[120] *Primitive Methodist Magazine* (1841) 61

[121] *Sunday School Repository* vol. 2 (1815) 31

[122] Arthur H. Plaisted *The Manor and Parish Records of Medmenham, Bucks.* (1925) 312

[123] 'A friend of Sunday schools' *The Sunday School Treat to Richmond Park* (1860)

[124] MS. account 'Sunday Schools 100 years ago', labelled also 'Manchester London Road Sunday School' in Methodist Archive Centre, letter from Sarah to Ann, June 3rd, 1836

[125] *SS Teachers' Magazine* (1846) 399

field visited Stockport by train in July of the same year; 'railways and Sunday schools seem related and both will work wonders in their departments', it was very aptly remarked.[126] 2,300 passengers went from Derby to Matlock in two trains with sixty gaily decorated carriages in 1849; 6,125 parents, teachers, and students, along with 500 ladies and gentlemen, at first-class rates, went on the Norwich Sunday school outing to the sea at Yarmouth in 1846 at a cost of 3d. per child and 1s. per adult.[127]

v. POLITICAL SUNDAY SCHOOLS

The most striking fact about radical, Owenite, Chartist, and other 'alternative' or 'counter' Sunday schools is their small number. By 1851, the only date for which quantitative data exists, a mere 60,000 children, less than three per cent of total enrolment, were in non-denominational or 'other Protestant' schools, i.e. schools not even nominally attached to a church or chapel.[128] Since most of the towns in the north of England had at least one 'ordinary' school of this nature, often with an enrolment well into the thousands, there is little room in the statistics for 'alternative' school places. But a more careful analysis of the peak periods of political activity—the late 1810s, the early 1830s, the Chartist decade from 1838 to 1848— provides only scanty additional information.

There were reports in the spring of 1817 that 'schools of politics' were being opened up 'in almost every manufacturing village in the kingdom'. The most careful student of Lancashire radicalism, however, was unable to turn up any facts which support these alarmist government reports. There was almost no public mention of the subject in 1818, although by the end of the year a new or even a first beginning was being made in the field of radical education.[129] A spy report from Stockport, filed 12 February 1818, notes that reformers had rented a room for debate, but whether it served as a Sunday school as well is not known. In any case, by November 1818 the existence of a radical Sunday school there is beyond doubt.[130] The *Manchester Chronicle*, which considered schools like that in Stockport 'one of the worst features of the present day', set out to

[126] *Sunday School Magazine* (1846) 205

[127] Ibid. (1849) 287; reprint from *Norfolk News* in *SS Teachers' Magazine* (1846) 483–4

[128] See Table 6, Chap. 2, p. 48

[129] W. W. Kinsey 'Some Aspects of Lancashire Radicalism, 1816–1821' (unpublished MA thesis, Manchester Univ., 1927) pp. 24–6

[130] Lloyd/Hobhouse (12 February 1818) HO 42/174; ibid. (7 December 1818) HO 42/182

investigate the problem when it received news of a school being founded in Liverpool.

> Stockport led the way. The teachers who were expelled from the great school there for their principles of insubordination, went and joined Harrison and Co. The next school established of the kind was in Oldham; where, not long ago, some person happening to look in, saw one of the teachers run out for a Bible to save appearances. The Manchester school was next in order and one has recently been established at Bury.[131]

Another Manchester newspaper claims there was a school founded in Leeds sometime in 1819.[132] Radical journals give little additional information on Sunday schools. The usually well-informed *Black Dwarf* mentions a thriving school in Manchester and another with about two hundred students in Oldham. Nothing more.[133] Intensive local inquiry may bring other schools to light, but a search through Home Office spy reports and the Manchester papers for the period, both of which would have, if anything, exaggerated the danger of revolutionary Sunday schools, was unsuccessful.

Owenite Sunday schools are similarly hard to discover. 'It has often been the subject of regret to me that Socialists have done so little practically in educating the rising generation', lamented a correspondent to the *New Moral World*. 'With one or two exceptions,' according to a response to this observation by one 'W',

> I believe, no attempt has been made to establish either day or Sunday schools, in connection with branches of the association. We have been lecturing and dancing, while our children have been left to receive all the vitiating influences which the old society has thrown around them, without any means of counteracting them beyond those which are offered by the parents' example and instruction.

These assessments were probably not overly pessimistic. The *Proceedings* of the third Co-operative Congress reported a mere six schools, of which only one was definitely listed as a Sunday school. The fourth Congress later in 1832 heard reports from thirty-eight societies, only one of which stated that it had a Sunday school; two others answered the question 'Any schools, lectures, or dis-

---

[131] *Manchester Chronicle* (27 November 1819) 3

[132] *Manchester Exchange Herald* (12 October 1819) 325

[133] *Black Dwarf* vol. 3 (1819) 217–18, 345; a meeting to celebrate the release of Hunt was held in a Union schoolroom in Rochdale, but it isn't clear whether this was used by a radical Sunday school or was merely rented from some schoolmaster. See vol. 9 (1822) 705 ff.

cussions?' affirmatively but did not specify which of these activities they maintained.[134]

By the early 1840s there were a few more Owenite schools. One of the most thorough students of the subject found references to some twelve Sunday schools—those of the Honley, Oldham, Rochdale, Bradford, Hyde, Failsworth, Congleton, Ashton, Padiham, London, Sheffield, and Leicester branches—in the *New Moral World* between 1840 and 1842. A few other branches probably also supported Sunday schools during this period. There was an Owenite Sunday school in Stockport early in 1839 which ended its report with an exhortation to other localities to open similar institutions as soon as possible; perhaps the Bury Sunday School for All Denominations which met in the Peoples' Hall beginning in June 1839, or the 'infidel' Sunday school in Keighley were linked with Socialist groups. The Bethnal Green branch proposed a school of some sort in 1840 but it is not clear whether it was ever actually instituted; Birmingham held literary and scientific classes but there is no evidence that these were for youth or that they were held on Sundays. Of course, the great Salford Interdenominational Sunday School had strong socialist connections and might therefore be counted. All told, there were something of the order of sixteen to eighteen Owenite Sunday schools in existence.[135]

But, while some of these schools were firmly established and enjoyed a long life, others were more ephemeral. The Failsworth school was built by subscriptions in 1785; the Church party withdrew in 1837, after which the school came to be identified with the Owenites and later with the Secularists. New rooms were added in 1880 and there were still some 180 scholars in 1902. On the other hand, the Oldham school which subsisted between 1840 and 1842 cannot have been in existence continuously because in 1845 the Socialist branch reported with well deserved pride that its recently opened Sunday school was a great success due to the excellence of its educational program.[136]

[134] Letter from John Firmin in *New Moral World* (11 July 1840) 23 and the reply by 'W' in *NMW* (24 October 1840) 262; William Carpenter, *Proceedings of the 3rd Co-operative Congress 23 April 1832* (1832) 'Statistical Table' bound into front of volume; for the fourth Congress see the report bound in the *Lancashire and Yorkshire Co-operator*, no. 10, new ser. 135. See Brian Simon, *Studies in the History of Education* ... p. 242; *NMW* (9 February 1839); *Northern Star* (22 June 1839) 5 and (8 June 1839) 5; *NMW* (new series I, 1840) 5 and ibid. 141; H. Silver. *Concept* ... pp. 177–8 and the *Lancashire and Yorkshire Co-operator* no. 8, new series, pp. 10–13

[136] See the report of G. W. Foote in *Freethinker*, (24 August 1902); *NMW* (1 March 1845) 288; I owe this and the following reference to Dr Edward Royle who has in addition been extremely generous in sharing his ideas and materials on Owenite education

In general the Owenites did not lay great stress on Sunday schools and concentrated their efforts on Socialist alternatives to mechanics' institutes. It might indeed be questioned whether in practice the education of the young was a very high priority among the Owenites:

Regarding schools, the Board would be sorry to damp the energy of any of our Members but the most we can accomplish at present will be to keep the children as much as possible from vicious associations, to give them habits of order and cleanliness and to answer their enquiries respecting themselves and the things by which they are immediately surrounded; these accompanied by attention to their small personal wants, and taking care their place of meeting in be properly ventilated at all times will give room for an expansion of ideas that will be of service to them; but our great object must be to force on public attention to the Truth of our great principles.[137]

Specifically, Chartist Sunday schools probably did not number more then a dozen. The Keighley and Bury schools mentioned above may have been started by Chartists. Stockport had a Chartist school in 1841, and O'Neill's Christian Chartist church in Birmingham had a Sunday school attached, as did the Hunslet group.[138] Bradford Chartists began a Sunday school in 1839, and a non-sectarian school, though not necessarily meeting on Sundays, was founded in Bridgeton in 1841.[139] There was in April 1838 a report of a radical school meeting three nights per week in Elland, but no mention is made of Sunday classes.[140] Chartist meetings were often held in schoolrooms, but there is no reason to suppose these were Sunday school rooms or even rooms belonging to the Chartist organization. The Ouseburn Chartists, for example, rented their meeting place from a local schoolteacher.[141] Finally, there was, of course, the famous adult Sunday school associated with Thomas Cooper in Leicester.[142] But most of the schools of which traces remain were founded when

[137] Holyoake Papers, Letter book p. 33, Bishopgate Institute, London, letter dated 15 July 1841. Holyoake was only asking for an official textbook with which he might improve instruction

[138] For O'Neill, the most famous 'Christian' Chartist, see H. U. Faulkner *Chartism and the Churches* (New York, 1916) Ch. 2; for Stockport see *Northern Star* (21 August 1841); for Hunslet see J. F. C. Harrison *Learning* ... op. cit. p. 104

[139] For Bradford see *Northern Star* (26 October 1839; for Bridgeton ibid. (20 February 1841)

[140] Ibid. (14 April 1838) 4

[141] Ibid. (12 June 1841)

[142] See Brian Simon *Studies in the History of Education* (1960) 249–50

the political power of Chartism was already on the wane.[143] Although the 'knowledge Chartists' formed an important part of the movement, their practical educational efforts were minimal and apprently did not include Sunday schools.[144] Neither Gammage or Hovell makes any mention of them. If indeed then there were so few political Sunday schools in this period, the question arises why this should be so.

The reason is that working people did not see ordinary Sunday schools as alien, and therefore no real market existed for rivals. Conversely, those rivals which did exist offered very little that ordinary schools did not. Certainly some of the radical schools of the Peterloo period catered for those who had been expelled from traditional schools for wearing white hats and green ribbons, the sign of the Orator Hunt and the color of the Levellers. But the numbers expelled were small, and many managers soon realized that expulsion only aided the hated radicals.[145] For most of the seventy years covered by this study, the majority of ordinary Sunday schools were very much a part of the working-class community and seldom, if ever, excluded members for political reasons.

Alternative and regular Sunday schools were for most purposes indistinguishable. Rowland Detrosier, the Lancashire socialist and 'infidel', Rev. William Hill, the editor of the *Northern Star*, Isaac Ironside, one of the most prominant South Yorkshire Owenites and later the undisputed leader of Sheffield Chartism, as well as many other working-class radicals managed common denominational schools. There were other institutional ties. The Taunton Radical Association was formed in the Newmarket Sunday school, the Methodist New Connexion offered the Chartists its rooms in Bradshaw, and the Tabernacle Chapel Sunday School in the Potteries performed 'the Factory Lad' at its anniversary.[146]

Alternative schools, on the other hand, offered little that could not be obtained elsewhere. Rev. Joseph Harrison, whose school in Stockport pioneered the movement, can best be described as a radical Christian. His Union for the Promotion of Happiness was opposed to the 'wicked pretenders to wisdom and virtue, who are nursed and cherished by a sordid Aristocracy and corrupt system of government'. It considered itself 'Christian in the truest and fullest sense of the word' and saw its educational function as forming 'such good and moral principles as may lead

[143] Ibid. p. 251

[144] R. A. Jones 'Knowledge Chartism' (unpublished MA thesis Birmingham Univ., 1938)

[145] Kinsey 'Some Aspects ...' p. 23

[146] *Northern Star* (10 March 1838) 5; (24 April 1841) 2; (6 March 1841) 2

the will to the practice of the great Laws of God, as revealed in the Book of Nature and the Gospels, that man may live in harmony with his fellows and with all citizens.'[147] Though the same language would not have been used in ordinary schools, the sentiments were undoubtedly those of any number of Dissenting schools. Harrison himself formed a close link with the Particular Baptists and allowed them the use of his schoolroom for their meetings.[148]

P. T. Candelet, conductor of the Manchester Radical Sunday School, replied in the *Manchester Observer* to critics of his school. It offered, he said, 'no other instruction but such as has a tendency to promote religion, morality, and virtue ... '; no books were used but the Bible, testament and spelling books supplied by the Sunday School Society in London, while the hymn book consisted of a compilation from Watts, Wesley, Mrs Barbauld, etc.; finally, he promised a report and a list of committee members within a year.[149] Even if this was exaggerated and if political texts were used for writing copy, there was little to distinguish this from many other schools.

Co-operative Sunday schools, too, bore a remarkable resemblance to more conventional institutions. Of course, education was all important in the Owenite scheme for the regeneration of mankind, and Sunday schools were certainly intended to play their part in this process. As the teachers at the Salford Co-operative School put it when arguing for a more extensive lecture series on socialist principles:

> We are of the opinion that an entire change must take place in the constitution of society before it can be materially improved; and that arrangements must be made for creating a superior physical, moral, and intelligent race of human beings than any which ever yet existed before we can expect to see any great advances towards a state of permanant happiness. A knowledge of these arrangements and of the principles on which they are founded is given in the writings of the Co-operative authors ... [150]

But while Owenite theory replaced biblical exegesis in the superintendents' or teachers' addresses to students, the cultural values and activities of the schools were not at variance with those of ordinary institutions. The 'attentive, quiet, and orderly' manners of

[147] 'Declaration of the Objects and Principles of the Union Formed at Stockport, 1818, for the Promotion of Human Happiness' enclosed in Lloyd/Sidmouth (17 February 1819) HO 42/184

[148] Phyllis Giles 'The Economic and Social Development of Stockport, 1815–36' (unpublished MA thesis, Manchester Univ., 1950) 143

[149] Vol. 3 (23 January 1820) 825

[150] *Lancashire and Yorkshire Co-operator* No. 8, new ser. (1832) 11

scholars were praised; Sunday schools would provide an alternative 'place of resort for rational amusements' to the pubs or gin parlours in which older students were wont to spend their idle hours drinking, smoking or in some other fashion 'degrading themselves to the level, nay, below that of brutes, in besotted ignorance'.[151] Teachers, it was hoped, would lead students to 'prefer industry and knowledge to indolence and ignorance', would inspire them with 'sentiments of gratitude and mutual affection', and would 'furnish them with just and enlarged views concerning their duty and interest'.[152] A description of an Owenite school's annual treat is also telling.

At the height of the Reform Bill agitation, on Whit Sunday 1832, students from the First Salford Co-operative Society Sunday School took an outing which would have been indistinguishable from that of any other local school. They marched in procession to the river, carrying banners with slogans like 'Ignorance is the cause of vice and misery', 'Love ye one another', 'Peace on earth and good-will to all men'. A packet boat awaited them for the trip to Dunham Park, the seat of the Earl of Stamford and Warrington, and the band struck up 'Rule Britannia' as the vessel was loosed from its moorings. Once on the estate, the children sang hymns, were 'plentifully supplied with currant bread, milk, ginger beer, etc.', and generally 'enjoyed themselves in rustic sports'. On returning home, they once again marched through the town and were once again provided with cakes and milk. Only the substitution of a lecture on Owenite principles for one on the necessity of salvation and the occasional banner proclaiming 'Voluntary equality and mutual Co-operation' betrayed the fact that a socialist school rather than a Methodist one had just returned from its annual treat.[153]

Very little is known about the educational philosophy of Chartist schools. The Stockport Chartist Sunday School announced its opening with the innocuous proposal 'to train children up in the way they should go', a favorite school motto. The *Northern Star* did not push any particular educational line. The general impression is that some Chartists, once the excitement of 1842 had passed, founded Sunday schools as an expression of community solidarity. It was another thing to do, like tea meetings, or dances, or plays. In this way their educational efforts were like those of many a working-class community which maintained a Sunday school with no particular pedagogical bias.

More detailed work might reveal more information on alter-

[151] Ibid. No. 12 (4 February 1832) 1; No. 10 (7 January 1832) 8
[152] Ibid. No. 5 (6 August 1831) 2
[153] Ibid. No. 6, new ser. (1832) 6–8

native Sunday schools. But the recondite nature of the information that is available for the 1810s, 1830s, and 1840s and the abundance of material in the *Northern Star* about ordinary schools supports the hypothesis of this chapter that the latter schools were a part of and not an imposition on the working-class community.

vi. CONCLUSIONS

Sunday schools provided educational, social and recreational services not readily available elsewhere to the working classes. In part, parents sent their children to Sunday school because of these services. But schools developed an ethos and a spirit of their own which transcended any specific benefit they might offer. Old scholars remained on as teachers, letters of thanks from old scholars were common, and even former students who opposed school managers on political issues were effusive in their praise of the school itself. But most importantly for the discussion in Chapter Seven, the culture of the Sunday school, though not explicitly political in its aims, was in its content almost indistinguishable from much of the 'radical' culture of the Owenites or Chartists.[154] Sunday schools were the bastion of the respectable working class from which the leadership of popular politics was drawn.

[154] For description of the cultural life of Owenite Sunday schools, see Eileen Yeo 'Robert Owen and Popular Culture' pp. 65–84 in Sidney Pollard and John Salt, eds. *Robert Owen : Prophet of the Poor* (1971)

7. Sunday Schools and Social Control

i. INTRODUCTION

Modern historians who investigate the social role of Sunday schools agree on two propositions. First, that the schools were agencies of the upper and middle classes which were imposed on the 'lower orders' or the working classes. Second, that they were an important agency in suppressing, with a minimum of coercion, traditional lower-class patterns of behavior which were replaced with conduct more suited to an industrial society. Both points appear in numerous guises and with varying degrees of specificity.

The working classes, argues J. F. C. Harrison, 'had no alternative but to accept the instruction offered in middle-class day and Sunday schools'. The breakdown of the old popular culture and its supersession by formal literary instruction based on the three Rs was the conscious aim of middle-class educationalists who provided these schools.[1] Based on the theories of Weber and his successors, historians have sought and found in evangelical religion the source of all those personal traits and values suited to an industrial society.[2] One scholar discusses Sunday schools in the company of 'various other schemes which were used to discipline the lower orders'.[3] Another cites both charity and Sunday schools as 'the principal channels through which the upper and middle classes sought to impose their social ideas upon the working class' while the latter schools, he argues, were 'even more explicitly geared to manning the growing industries than the former'.[4] E. P. Thompson singles

[1] J. F. C. Harrison *Learning* ... (1961) 40
[2] See for example Reinhard Bendix *Work and Authority in Industry* (New York, 1956) 65–8
[3] Maurice Quinlan *Victorian Prelude* (New York, 1941) 44 and generally 44–50
[4] M. W. Flinn 'Social Theory and the Industrial Revolution' in Tom Burns and S. B. Saul, eds. *Social Change and Economic Change* (1967) 14 and 17

out the Sunday school as one of the institutions created by the middle class in order to wean the working classes from their pre-industrial rhythms of work and play and to inculcate in them the 'time thrift' necessary in an industrial society. The military rules of behavior, the insistence on regularity and punctuality of atten-dance, and undisguised indoctrination are adduced to support the the views of some contemporaries that Sunday schools constituted 'a spectacle of order and regularity' which, as a Gloucester manu-facturer put it, 'made children more tractable and obedient, less quarrelsome and revengeful'. 'Once within the school gates', Thompson argues, 'the child entered the new universe of disciplined time' leaving behind pre-industrial sloth for modern industry.[5]

His *Making of the English Working Class* develops and extends these themes. Here too it is argued that: 'The pressures towards discipline and order extended from the factory, on one hand, the Sunday school, on the other, into every aspect of life: leisure, personal relationships, speech, manner.'[6] Methodism between 1790 and 1830 acted at the same time as the ideology of the oppressed and the oppressor. Of the three reasons given for this curious state of affairs—direct indoctrination, the Methodist community sense, and the psychic consequences of counter-revolution—he argues that 'the first reason—indoctrination—cannot be overstated'. Furthermore, the Evangelical Sunday school is identified as the main agency of this indoctrination.[7] According to Thompson, these schools acted upon Wesley's doctrines of the aboriginal sinfulness of the child; they practised a kind of religious terrorism on the young, convincing them of their spiritual unworthiness and offering hard work, adherence to duty and submission to the wishes of their betters as a kind of exculpatory act. Far worse than being merely agencies of moral rescue, Sunday schools weakened the wills and corrupted the souls of their inmates, making them the victims of an objectively hostile ideology.[8]

Thompson's view of the Sunday school must be considered in the context of his general thesis. 'And class', he argues, 'happens when some men, as a result of common experiences (inherited or shared), feel and articulate the identity of their interests as between

[5] E. P. Thompson 'Time, Work Discipline and Industrial Capitalism' *Past and Present* no. 38 (1967) 84

[6] Thompson *Making* ... p. 401

[7] Ibid. p. 375

[8] Thompson *Making* ... pp. 50, 361, and particularly pp. 375–83; a similar interpretation of the social role of religion in general and of Sunday schools in particular is given in Harold Silver *The Concept of Popular Education* (1965) 36–40 and Sydney Pollard *The Genesis of Modern Management* (1965, Penguin ed. 1968) 228–31, 243

themselves, and as against other men whose interests are different
from (and usually opposed to) theirs.'[9] Between 1780 and 1832
a working class in this sense came into being; in these decades
'most English working people came to feel an identity of interests
as between themselves, and as against their rulers and employers'.[10]
If this model is true, the bourgeois values and precepts of the
Sunday school, indeed the institution itself, ought to have become
increasingly repugnant to the working classes during the industrial
revolution.. Furthermore, the richly varied radical working-class
culture which Thompson describes presumably ought to have
been significantly different from the culture of the Sunday school.

But neither of these things happened. Indeed, the interpretation
of Sunday schools developed most fully in the *Making of the English
Working Class* is insufficiently subtle to encompass the facts. It is
difficult to maintain in any literal sense that Sunday schools constituted an imposition by the middle upon the working class. Many
of those active in founding Sunday schools in both the eighteenth
and nineteenth century were from the working class. The teachers
were almost all from the same social strata as those they taught;
after 1810 some sixty per cent of all teachers had once been students
themselves. Even in those schools where the managers were manufacturers or shopkeepers, teachers played an important part in
deciding the internal policies of the school. While early Sunday
schools in both towns and villages were often financed by the
dominant social class, the change in the early nineteenth century
away from subscriptions to annual sermons as a primary source
of funds meant that the community at large played a more significant part in underwriting the schools.

Fund-raising sermons were a popular and important element of
working-class community life, reported alike in the *Manchester
Guardian* and the *Northern Star*. Indeed, Sunday schools were accepted, patronized, and occasionally idealized precisely because they
grew out of the working class as a means of fulfilling the real and
perceived needs of the community. Any analysis of Sunday schools
as an agency of social control or as an institution through which
certain norms and values were transmitted must take these facts
into account. Therefore, a model which regards Sunday schools
primarily as a weapon in an alleged bourgeois assault on working-
class culture simply will not do. The schools were effective in large
measure because they worked from within and because they were
not merely organs of middle-class propaganda.

[9] Thompson *Making* ... p. 9
[10] Ibid. p. 11

ii. Sunday Schools and the Aims of the Middle Class

In order to put the question of indoctrination in context, it is important to note that Sunday schools represented the first step in the increased specialization of educational activities during the late eighteenth and nineteenth centuries. Children were taken from, or sent by, their parents each Sunday to a school whose function was to do what the parent, or perhaps the isolated clergyman, could not do. But the emergence of children, even temporarily, from the educational nexus of family relationships had enormous political and social ramifications which were not lost on contemporaries.

Sunday schools were advocated by the eighteenth-century Evangelicals and some of their successors as a means of removing children from the corrupt influence of the parent to a morally and politically more salutary atmosphere. 'The children of the poor, by being drawn out of their obscurity into notice and protection are humanized and civilized,' argued a friend of Hannah More.[11] Teachers must begin their work by 'unlearning the children much of what they have been taught' because 'being from the lowest order of people they have not been taught to associate happiness with virtue'.[12] Mrs Trimmer told potential subscribers to her school that the immoralities of the poor, which 'keep their employers in a constant state of suspicion and uneasiness', would be a thing of the past now that the 'education of poor children is no longer entirely left to their ignorant and corrupt parents'. Only good could result from the fact that 'it has in many places become a public business'.[13] Most bluntly put, Sunday school managers could 'at all times exercise authority under a conciliating title, and, while they patronize the children, can insensibly control the conduct of the parents'.[14]

There is little doubt, moreover, that some Sunday schools intended to play their part in restraining political radicalism among the working class. Those founded by the London based, Evangelical dominated, Sunday School Society or by committees of notables in the provinces were a fundamentally conservative response to what was perceived to be a moral and political crisis. Education generally, and the Sunday school in particular, was welcomed as a means of bringing religion to the lower orders which would, it was thought, elevate them above the mire of sin and deprivation into which they

[11] George Horne DD *Sunday Schools Recommended—A Sermon* (Oxford, 1786) 11
[12] Rev. Thomas Stevenson *The Difficulties and Encouragements* . . . op. cit. (1814) 20
[13] Trimmer *Oeconomy* . . . pp. 26–8
[14] [Rev. Richard Raikes] *Considerations on the Alliance between Christianity and Commerce Applied to the Present State of this Country* (1806) 56

had fallen, and thereby assure the harmony and continuity of an hierarchic society of orders. Only as much learning as was necessary to achieve this end was to be offered in Sunday school, and indeed the public was invited to contribute to the project under the assurance that their funds would be used to ensure social stability.[15]

Sermon after sermon, appeal after appeal, emphasized the value of the new institution in restraining the lower orders and maintaining the relationship between the classes which appeared so threatened by the revolutions in France. Mrs Trimmer vouched for the political safety of her schools by including in her guide for genteel patrons a list of 'virtues' which the children were to learn. Among them were civility and gratitude.

> If you are civil you will behave with respect to ladies and gentlemen. You will say, Sir, or Madam, when you speak to them; you will rise from your feet when they come into a room where you are sitting; you will make a curtsey to them when you meet them ... If you have gratitude in your mind you will think yourself much obliged to those who subscribe to the school; and you will take care to improve in every respect, that their money and advice may not be thrown away upon you.[16]

A Baptist preacher noted that: 'Christian knowledge has a tendency to establish the peace of society by teaching each individual to fill up that place which Providence has assigned him', and furthermore that 'a well-instructed Chistian peasantry will constitute the support and happiness of the nation.'[17] The horrors of the French Revolution could only be prevented in England, argued an anonymous member of the SPCK, if the poorer classes were preserved from the doctrine, preached among them by evil and designing men, that all men were created equal. Sunday schools, he said, were of particular importance because they impress on the poor 'while still young and tender the duty of behaving lowly and reverently to all their betters ... and to fear God and honour the King'.[18]

Most public declarations of educational policy in the late eighteenth century espoused the conservative doctrines of a Sarah Trimmer, a Hannah More, or a Jonas Hanway. Whether or not Sunday schools in fact inculcated meekness and submission, it

[15] See Chapter 5, pp. 125–7; Silver *Popular Education* ... gives the most comprehensive review of Evangelical attitudes toward education

[16] Sarah Trimmer *The Oeconomy of Charity* vol. 1 (2 vol. 1801 edn.) 321–2

[17] J. Liddon *General Religious Instruction* ... (1792) 13 and 16

[18] *Introductory Address to the Public on the Importance of Sunday Schools at the Present Time* (Canterbury, 1800) 23

remains true that many of their early supporters wanted them to teach 'a superstitious veneration for the church of England, and to bow to every man in a handsome coat'.[19]

There is also evidence that Sunday schools were occasionally used as centers for middle-class propaganda during the nineteenth century. One witness before Sadler's Committee, for example, claimed that during the spinners' turn-out some two or three years earlier manufacturers had come to the Sunday schools of Manchester to tell children that it was a sin to withstand their employers, that they ought to be subject to them, and that they would be well advised to go back to work. Other instances might be cited, according to this informant.[20] A dresser in Robinson's mill, Stockport, told another committee that the schools of Stockport were controlled by manufacturers, were subservient to their interests, and served as an outlet for tracts and lectures pleading the factory owners' case. His denunciations were taken seriously enough to prompt rebuttals from the incumbent of St Thomas and the overlooker in the mill where the witness, Joseph Sadler, had been employed.[21] Radicals and Chartists on occasion made similar assertions and not without some justification. Indeed some factory owners did require their hands to attend a Sunday school, though not necessarily one provided by the employer.

Finally, the politically charged, overtly conservative children's literature of the 1780s and 1790s continued to be distributed by Sunday schools well into the nineteenth century. All of the evidence so far presented seems to constitute an overwhelming indictment of the Sunday school as an agency of class repression. But there is also considerable, and in the end convincing, evidence on the other side.

The decline of the educative family and the removal of the child from the home into the school is in itself a politically neutral occurrence.[22] The Sunday school was, as has been shown, tightly integrated into the working-class community. When children left the home and entered the very different atmosphere of the school they came into contact with the most literate of their class and imbibed the values of artisan respectability taught there. Though the potential for intergenerational change was great, it was not of a kind generally repugnant to working-class parents.

[19] William Godwin *An Enquiry Concerning Political Justice* vol. 2 (1798 ed.) 299

[20] *Report from the Select Committee on the Bill to regulate the Labour of Children in the Mills & Factories of the United Kingdom*; together with Minutes of Evidence 1831–32 (706) xv. pp. 327 ff.

[21] *First Report of the Factory Commissioners* 1833 (450) xx, D 2 114

[22] See F. Musgrove 'The Decline of the Educative Family' *Universities Quarterly* vol. 14 (1959–60) 377–404

It must also be remembered that the most restrictive definitions of Sunday school education were made as pre-emptive counter-arguments in debate with still more reactionary views. The character modelled on the Author in Hannah More's story of the founding of a Sunday school only advanced the view that her proposed school would be limited to teaching the poor to read the Bible, a book which could only lead to the increased obedience and industry of servants, when the farmer being solicited for funds objected that teaching the poor to read was the surest road to national disaster.[23] The Rev. Johnson Grant's caution to Sunday school scholars to regard all printed work with caution and his conviction that education could only lead to religion and this to loyalty seem less offensive when read beside a ultra-reactionary critique of his words. Sunday schools, noted one such article, had turned out fanatical teachers who led disputations, encouraged scepticism, infidelity and the anti-Christ. 'Those taught to read, to write, to reason', this review concludes, 'we see now grasping with eager curiosity every pernicious treatise within reach.'[24] Evidence of their activities and other publications suggest in fact that when the Sheffield Sunday School Union advertised itself as creating a society with 'each in his station under the final influence of religion' or the Stockport Sunday School devoted most of its 1819 report to recounting its battles against those who would attack Britain's 'matchless Constitution', both institutions were defending themselves against real or imagined threats from the Right rather than expressing the views which activated them during calmer times.[25]

Moreover, by the 1820s a new and more progressive conception of Sunday school education had come into being. The doctrine of self-help and advancement through merit replaced those older views of working-class education as an exercise in the creation of deference. Already in 1794 the Baptist Daniel Turner was pointing out that some of 'the richest jewels of society' had been found among the poor whose advancement should be encouraged through education; the Rev. T. Wood recommended Sunday schools to his fellow Wesleyans by recalling the poverty-to-greatness tradition in English history, and suggesting that the schools would 'excite

[23] 'The Sunday School' in Hannah More *Works* vol. 4 (new ed. 1818) 376–9
[24] Johnson Grant *The Abuses and Advantages of Sunday Schools: a Sermon preached at Ormskirk, Nov. 3, 1799...* (1800) and *Anti Jacobin Review* vol. 7 (1800) 214–17
[25] 'Report of the Sheffield Sunday School Union' quoted in John Salt, 'Early Sheffield Sunday Schools and their Educational Importance' *Trans. of the Hunter Archaeological Society*, vol. 9, part 3 (1967) 183; *Report of the Stockport Sunday School* (1819) 5–13 and particularly 12

in some of the children strong desires after further attainments'.[26]
The advancement of science and learning that would result from
mass education became a common theme. Cardinal Wolsey and
Shakespeare were favorite subjects for Sunday school stories
because of their rise from poverty to greatness, and stories of lesser
men—Sunday scholars who learned the three Rs well enough to
become prosperous merchants—abound.[27] There were, of course,
still sermons and tracts which wished for the restoration of the old
order with its patriarchal benevolence of rich to poor and which
valued Sunday schools because of their role in maintaining the
social order.[28] But by the late 1840s even the Church of England's
Sunday school magazine could praise teaching in its schools as a
step in the process of self-culture and self-improvement; and a
widely read children's magazine of evangelical Dissent could
include in each of its issues a story of 'Pursuit of Knowledge under
Difficulties'.[29] Indeed by the mid-Victorian era the early nineteenth-century Sunday school was almost a symbol of working-class
advancement through self-help. Tens of thousands of men had
achieved prominence based on their Sunday school education,
declared A. J. Mundella. 'From the kinds of qualifications which
will be required in the leading men of another generation or two',
according to a sabbatarian tract, 'it is not too hazardous to say,
that many of the children of our Sunday-schools will become the
rulers or the parents of the rulers of the destinies of the world'.[30]
Local school histories proudly proclaimed the success of their
alumni; Bradwell Methodist Chapel, for example, produced
Ralph Benjamin Somerset, fellow of Trinity College, Cambridge,
Thomas Morton, a quartermaster in India, and the owner of a
large works in Stocksbridge who in turn employed three other
ex-Sunday school men in important positions.[31]

But quite apart from its ideological bent, the coercive and
propagandistic powers of the Sunday school were severely limited.

[26] Turner *Hints* ... (1794) second sermon; Rev. T. Wood *Thoughts on Sunday
Schools: Importance of Knowledge to the Lower Classes of Society* (1815) 8

[27] See for example *SS Teachers' Magazine* (1839) 135

[28] See for example 'Sermon for Sunday Schools on Prov. xxii, 6' reprinted in
Christian Remembrancer vol. 14 (1832) 623–8; the Wesleyans could always be counted
on for right wing views; see for example the quotation from 'Report of the Wesleyan
Methodist Sunday Schools of Lincoln' in Rex Russell *Sunday Schools in Lindsey*
(Lincoln, 1965) 17; or another report in Scruton *Sketches of Old Bradford* p. 103

[29] *C. of E. SS Quarterly Magazine* (1848–49) 274; *The Teachers' Offering or Sunday
School Monthly Visitor* (1850)

[30] *Prize Essays* (1849) 26–27

[31] Seth Evans *Methodism in Bradwell* 89; or for example, Anon. *Founded upon
a rock: A Chronicle of Wesleyan Methodism in Berry Brow* (1897) 17

Since they met on only one day a week they could not, like the public schools of the aristocracy or the less great boarding schools of the bourgeoisie, organize all aspects of their students' lives. As one commentator noted sadly, 'For one day, partially spent in the company of the pious, the children are exposed, during six, to all the moral contagion and impurity of their own dwellings and neighborhoods.'[32] Furthermore, competition for students between rival religious bodies made coercion impossible in the long run. It must be admitted, however, that there is some evidence of Anglican use of compulsion in the 1780s and 1790s which in many ways resembled the Church's efforts to control Methodism through-out the eighteenth century. In those decades, the Anglican clergy, for fear of losing what hold it had on the populace, sometimes used more than superior teaching to prize children from Dissenting schools. It was alleged that they threatened on occasion to withhold relief and exclude families from parish charities; on occasion they even carried out their threats. There was a widely publicized case in Oxfordshire of over twenty families being excluded from the Christmas feast because they refused to send their children to the Anglican school.[33] A fierce controversy in Warwickshire developed into a full scale pamphleteering war in the best eighteenth-century tradition when a Presbyterian minister and his allies accused the Anglican rector and his curate of first bribing and later threatening with loss of employment and eviction certain families who would not send their children to the Church Sunday school. On the other hand the Dissenters made cash payments to their scholars, which might be regarded as bribes but which they justified on the grounds that the pittance involved was merely compensation for the social services lost by failure to attend the parish institution.[34] As late as 1811 Anglican authorities sought to harrass a Dissenting Sunday school in Portsmouth by bringing a prosecution under the Conventicle Act.[35] But, with only a handful of exceptions the market

[32] A. H. Davis *Religious Instruction* ... p. 11

[33] *Evangelical Magazine* vol. 30 (1822) 71

[34] For the Dissenting case of this wide-ranging controversy see Rev. William Field *A Letter addressed to the inhabitants of Warwick in answer to the charges against the dissenters* (Birmingham, 1791) and *A second letter in reply to remarks ... of the Rev. the Vicar and the Curate of St. Nicholas upon the first letter* (Birmingham, 1791); Rev. Benjamin Carpenter *A Letter to the Rev. R. Foley, rector of Old Swinford in answer to charges brought against the dissenters in Stourbridge ... To which is added an account of the proceedings at Lye-waste by J. Scott* (1795); see particularly the section by Scott, pp. 39 ff.; for the Anglican case see Rev. Robert Miller and Rev. Hugh Laugherne *Remarks upon a letter to the printer of the Birmingham Gazette ... and also upon a letter ... to the inhabitants of Warwick ... by W. Field* (Warwick, 1798)

[35] *Evangelical Magazine* vol. 19 (1811) 356–8. For full account see the trial report re-printed from the *Times* (7 August 1811) in *Philanthropist* No. 4 (1811) 388–91

in Sunday school education was relatively free after the turn of the century.

As noted earlier, factory owners occasionally enforced Sunday school attendance. One employee of the Strutt's mill even had his quarterly gift money stopped for not doing so.[36] But the extreme rarity of such instances, the absence of complaints about them from the working people, and the efforts schools made to attract children suggest that by and large attendance was a matter of choice and not of compulsion. There may have been a few cases in which parents were not actually compelled to send their children to a school on the mill grounds but would lose respect if they did not do so. But again the great majority of schools were not attached to a mill or workplace and moral pressure would have been far more difficult to exercise in the pluralist religious environment which characterized even small communities. Because of this pluralism, raw coercive power played little part in the world of Sunday schools. It is, of course, possible that those who managed Sunday schools exercised a measure of control over children and their parents by excluding, or threatening to exclude, radicals and malcontents from the services and the society of the school. But this kind of control is rare indeed; by and large the Sunday school did not interfere with the political lives of scholars or teachers.

The Stockport Sunday School provides a good case in point. The town in which it was situated lay at the center of radical activity during both the Peterloo and Chartist period and was decidedly industrial. More than any other school in England this one was the creature of the manufacturing interests. Modern historians use its annual reports again and again as evidence for the repressive nature of Sunday schools.[37] Although its teachers came almost entirely from the working classes and although in their quarterly meeting they exercised some measure of control over the school's internal affairs, the relations of the school with the community were in the hands of a board of managers composed entirely of industrialists.[38] They were by no means all Tories; in fact, most probably supported the 1832 Reform Act, repeal of the corn laws, and other Whig-radical measures. Nevertheless they were opposed to Chartism, trade-union activity, and any other form of independent working-class radicalism. If the Sunday schools of England exercised a powerful control over working-class behavior through their powers of exclusion, the Stockport School,

[36] Fitton and Wadsworth Strutts ... pp. 256–7
[37] See note 8 p. 188
[38] Names were secured from the *Annual Reports* and occupations determined from commercial directories. All board members are traceable for 1800, 1820, and 1840

therefore, ought to exhibit this facet of social manipulation to the fullest. It does not. In the history of the school from 1792 to 1850 there was only one case of expulsion as a result of internal subversion, namely, an attempt by working-class teachers to assume some of the powers of the middle-class committee. In 1797, Joseph Mayer, the son of one of the school's founders and himself the leading light in the school for half a century, wrote to one Joseph Drake, a teacher, asking him to resign. 'Though the motives which activate you no doubt spring from a consciousness of rendering an essential service, yet conceiving [your] conduct inimical and subversive to the good of the school ... ' he, Drake, would have to be dismissed if he did not resign. The unfortunate Drake's sin cannot be reconstructed, but his enforced retirement became the focus of a move by teachers to bid for increased power. Two weeks after Mayer's letter, on 13 April 1797, a petition was presented to the committee signed by thirteen teachers and by a secretary, Joseph Kinder, on behalf of himself and five proxies (i.e. by nineteen out of about one hundred) teachers. The petition was directed at 'Rules that appear to us subversive of equity and good order', but more specifically against the 'undue authority the committee and visitors have exerted on various occasions, not merely in the schools, but in the expulsion of teachers'. The most important of the constructive parts of the petition called for election of the committee by a majority of teachers and visitors (a division head), for the election of visitors by a majority of committee and teachers, and for the formation of a special tribunal, to hear complaints against teachers, four of whose members were to be selected by the accused.[39]

The response to this petition is telling. A *joint* meeting was called of the committee, the visitors and those eighty-odd teachers who had not signed the document being discussed; Joseph Mayer made a speech against the petition, only one phrase of which, in the form of a motion, is recorded: 'That it be now resolved whether the rules or present plan of government be permanent, or whether they shall be revolutionary.' The vote was not in doubt and the petitioners were informed of their rejection. But they were not immediately dismissed. Ten of the thirteen signatories wrote a note in the minute book stating that they were willing to continue their best efforts until the next quarterly meeting at which time they would propose amendments to the school's constitution.[40] So ends the affair in the committee minute books. But, from a

[39] Stockport Sunday School *Minute Book* (October 1796–March 1800) entries for 31 March 1797, 17 April 1797

[40] Stockport Sunday School *Minute Book* 23 and 30 April 1797

teachers' register dated 1800 and another record of teachers from
an earlier date, the fate of the troublemakers can be learned. None
were present in 1800; seven were listed as dismissed in June 1797
in the record book, one resigned, and Drake had already been dismissed.[41] We do not know what happened to the others. This high-
handed purge might be interpreted as proof of middle-class tyranny
over the school. On the other hand, it must be remembered that the
action was taken with the approval of eighty per cent of the teaching
staff. It occurred just as the right-wing attack on Sunday schools,
at the local and national level, was coming into full swing. Moreover, it was the last time in the history of the school in which anyone
was dismissed for insubordination. For the next fifty-six years the
working-class teachers met each quarter with the committee of
manufacturers with no further confrontations. SCARED ?

There were, however, several dismissals for political reasons
during the years around Peterloo. May 1818 saw a turnout of
between 800 and 1,100 jenny spinners in Stockport, led, incidentally,
by Thomas Worseley, an 1813 alumnus of the Sunday school.[42]
In July rumors reached the committee that one of its teachers,
Mr Jonathan Weston, had held office as secretary to this combination of spinners. A special investigative committee was set up
and reported that the rumor was indeed true and that, to make
matters worse, Weston had also acted as collector at a sermon
given in Ancoats, Manchester, by the Rev. Joseph Harrison who
had only months before founded a rival, radical Sunday school in
Stockport. Weston was called before the committee, apprised
that his transgression was not only sinful but illegal, asked whether
he was sorry for what he had done, and finally suspended for two
months.[43] A year after this episode another teacher, William
Griffith, who had been at the school eight years, was dismissed
because he argued with a visitor over the expulsion of a student,
one James Hopwood, who had worn the radical green—the color
of the Levellers—in his hat.[44] The only major purge of the Stockport
Sunday School also occurred during the late 1810s. One Sunday
in October 1818 twenty-six members of the first class, that of young
men in training to become teachers, refused the order of their

[41] MS. Minute Book of Teachers containing names of all teachers from 1793 to
1818 with dates of their leaving and entering the school and MS. Register S 3/1,
Stockport Reference Library
[42] See Giles 'Economic and Social Development ...' p. 136 and Worseley's
testimony in *First Report of Factory Commissioners* ... 1833 (450) D 2, p. 114
[43] Stockport SS *Minute Book* op. cit. 25 July and 2 August 1818
[44] William Griffith/Joseph Mayer, 22 December 1819 and Mayer/Griffith,
16 January 1820, Stockport Reference Library MS. 5/3

teacher to attend divine worship. These students were ceremoniously expelled in what can only be described as a publicity exercise. An address was presented to the magistrates setting out the reason for the dismissal of the twenty-six; broadsheets were printed giving the school's justification and advertisements were taken out in the London *Courier*, the Manchester *Chronicle*, *Volunteer*, and *Exchange Herald*, the Macclesfield *Courier*, and the Chester *Chronicle*, for the same purpose. Under normal circumstances the offending students' behavior would have been forgiven, provided that they apologized and appeared sufficiently contrite but, the managers' announcement proclaimed,

> in the present case it was un-pardonable, being the result of a premeditated plan contrived by those persons now suffering in jail the punishment of their crimes, and encouraged by some inconsiderate and mistaken parents of these youths ... both parents and children know that we do not allow any to remain in our school, who shew the slightest disobedience either to their teachers, masters, or governors.[45]

Two young ladies were quietly dismissed as teachers shortly after this public announcement because they had 'eaten of the forbidden fruit of the reformers'.[46] Except for the cases discussed there were no further instances in which the managers took action against a student or teacher for political reasons.

In the history of the school, which had enrolled over 50,000 children between 1793 and 1850, four teachers and twenty-eight students were persecuted for their beliefs. Each met his fate between mid-1818 and January 1820, a time when the committee was under enormous pressure from those who wanted to use the political crisis to make a frontal attack on Sunday school education. Rumors had reached the managers that certain members of Parliament were coming to regard Sunday schools as subversive and were planning to move to close the whole lot of them. Several letters arrived at the school from preachers outside Stockport, in effect accusing all Dissenters in the town of being Reformers.[47] The year and a half around Peterloo must therefore be considered a special case when the managers felt that the very existence of the school was threatened from the right. It is significant that there was no

[45] Stockport Sunday School *Minute Book* op. cit. (31 July 1819) printed separately as a broadsheet (12 August 1818)

[46] Joseph Mayer's *Diary*, MS. uncat. Stockport Reference Library, entry for 22 August 1819

[47] James Butterworth MP (Pres. of the Sunday School Union)/Stockport SS (June 1819); N. K. Pugsley/Stockport SS Committee MS. 5/3 (n.d. but *c.* 1818); letter to J. A. James, Birmingham in *Minute Books* (4 August 1819)

mention in the school's minute books of expulsions during the turnouts of 1810–11, the period of acute crisis about 1830, nor during the period 1838–43 when a rival Chartist Sunday school sought to attract its students. When in 1848 some of the young teachers were ' "standing up for their rights" on real chartist princi-ples', the managers did nothing more than write a letter to one of the school's elder statesmen asking him to 'slip over, and explain our "constitution" to them [so that] their importunance might perhaps be reduced to its proper level and station'. Apparently, no further action was taken.[48]

The managers certainly distributed tracts whose message, insofar as it was political, advocated quiescence and maintenance of the *status quo*; they quite probably delivered the occasional lecture to the same effect; they used a crown and sceptre resting on a Bible as an illustration at the beginning of many of their annual reports. But by and large politics were not central to the life of the school. Except during the years 1818–20 the managers were content to leave the worldly convictions of students and teachers outside their sphere of interest. In a town which was at the center of radical politics for most of the first half of the century the working classes seemed oblivious to the politics of those who financed the schools. So far as the middle-class board of managers was concerned, they were content to let sleeping dogs lie and to get on with the recreational, religious and educational work of the Sunday school.

There are occasional references in local histories to expulsions from other Sunday schools; but these are rare. The *Northern Star*, which regularly published accounts of the victimization of Chartists, and continued until 1841 to report annual sermons and feasts of ordinary Sunday schools, is silent on expulsions from Sunday schools. When Chartist schools came into being, they did so with almost no political fanfare. One cannot prove that Sunday schools were not used as a means for the political manipulation of the working classes, but if so, this was certainly not accomplished through purging dissidents from their ranks.

The remaining coercive method Sunday schools could use involved the regulation of the child's or the parent's political behavior through control of funds deposited in various Sunday school societies. The only virtue that an opponent of clothing societies could discern in their continued existence was that they served as a check on children's behavior through their power of

---

[48] 5 September 1848, Heaton Mersey Branch, Stockport Ref. Library MS B/T/2/13

dismissal and consequent loss of contributions and bonuses.[49] The Tutellstairs Chapel Sunday School Friendly Society refused to pay sickness benefits if the illness was brought on by immoral activities which might be taken to include gathering with disreputable political friends.[50] In Burslem, where the sick and benefit society was governed by a committee chosen by popular vote of the membership, expulsion from the Sunday school for bad behavior meant forfeiture of all one's contributions.[51] Though examples could be multiplied, all this is relatively unimportant. Sunday schools operated in a highly competitive and relatively free market place; they exercised what political influence they had through moral persuasion rather than through force.

iii. THE INCULCATION OF VALUES: LECTURES, SERMONS AND PATRIOTIC EXERCISES

If the coercive powers of the Sunday school were limited, so also was the time spent on direct propaganda, and the means available. It is true that Sunday schools might have exercised indirect influence on the political attitudes of children through efforts to form their habits of work and play, both of which are discussed below. The more direct methods, however, were limited to three. Through sermons and lectures, through participation in patriotic festivals and most importantly through the literature they distributed, Sunday schools could work on the minds of students to inculcate values which sustained the *status quo*. Sermons and lectures, however, had severe limitations in this regard. Only about twenty per cent of each day was available for direct propaganda by a school's managers; the remainder of the time was spent in the classroom engaged in religious or educational exercises having no direct political importance. Furthermore, although the subjects of the fifteen- or twenty-minute long exhortations given by the superintendent or his representative have not been recorded it seems unlikely that the only time of the day available exclusively for religious instruction would have been devoted to the more mundane concerns of this world.[52] If the scriptural texts of anniversary sermons are any indication preachers never chose to discuss highly charged social or political issues. 'Feed my lambs', 'Suffer the

[49] *SS Teachers' Magazine* (1846) 163

[50] Ibid. (1841) 812–14

[51] John Young *After One Hundred Years* ... op. cit. (1903) 30–1

[52] See Table 13, p. 106. Hymns, prayer, and taking the roll must have taken a good part of the fifteen to twenty minutes available at the opening of each session

little children to come unto me ... ', 'As ye sow so shall ye also reap', and 'My people perish for lack of knowledge' were the favorite themes for Sunday school sermons. But whatever the subject matter, a short opening exercise or the occasional sermon, even over a period of four to ten years, probably did not have a major impact on the restructuring of working-class life and mores or the maintenance of social stability.

The patriotic exercises organized on occasion by Sunday schools were less a cause of loyalty to Queen and country than a reflection of widespread working-class adherence to the main outlines of the existing political order. The *Northern Star* noted with bewilderment the eagerness with which working-class children and their parents participated in Victoria's coronation celebrations, despite the restricted franchise, in much the same way as socialists at the end of the century were shocked by the Mafeking victory celebration.[53] The 840 students of the Wortley Sion Interdenominational Sunday School, it reported, paraded around town, the girls dressed in white led by a banner reading 'Queen and Constitution'; the boys were preceded by a sign with 'Knowledge and Instruction are the stability of the Throne'.[54] Ironically, throughout the 1840s the *Northern Star* itself published advertisements for pictures of the Queen. The York Church of England Sunday School committee spent £10 on arrangements for the coronation of George iv, treating each child with a 3d. cake after the procession, giving teachers and children in the first class a special medal, and presenting everyone in the school with a copy of 'God Save the King' which they were all taught to sing. Over a thousand of the school's children took part in the coronation procession of Victoria, and their special treat the next year was arranged to coincide with her wedding day.[55] In the Uttoxeter Sunday School children sang a little ditty expressive of their loyalty at the cornerstone-laying ceremony for their new building:

> Victoria! Victoria!
> We hail thy gentle rule
> Victoria the patroness
> Of every Sunday school.[56]

And when the Queen visited Hull in 1854 to knight the mayor, 10,500 Sunday school scholars and 1,200 teachers were at the

---

[53] See *Northern Star* (7 July 1838) 5 for example
[54] Ibid. p. 4.
[55] J. Howard *Historical Sketch ... York SS* op. cit. pp. 39–40, 53
[56] *SS Teachers' Magazine* (1841) 216

station to greet her, each child wearing a commemorative ribbon.[57] Indeed most of the great Sunday school annual processions were graced with banners expressing the scholars' loyalty scattered amongst signs with more religious messages. The royal palace at Hampton Court and the Park at Richmond were meccas for London Sunday school outings, and in the North and Midlands, the country houses of the gentry served as substitutes. Viewed as instruments of bourgeois control the annual encounters with the aristocracy and occasional participation in patriotic exercises were not very important. They were often not organized by the bourgeoisie and in any case were too ephemeral and infrequent to have a major impact. However, they were an important reflection of the relationship of the working class to society and of the subtle ways that class tied itself to the social order.

iv. The Inculcation of Values: Literature, Politics, and Virtue

A far more significant vehicle of propaganda was the vast body of literature with which the working-class child was bombarded. It can be divided into three categories: tracts and reward books given to scholars in school; magazines and periodicals published by denominational or church organizations, by private individuals, or by Sunday school associations; and finally the textbooks which formed the main body of reading material for the boys and girls during school hours. The literature in the first category is so enormous in scope and number of titles that a proper analysis would be a research project in its own right.[58] They range from the most blatantly propagandist and counter-revolutionary tracts to fanciful accounts of heaven and hell to 'books ... such as relate to Natural History, to Biography, to Travels and Voyages, to the History of England, and even to metaphysics', all of which, one reactionary noted, 'are scarcely publications *fit* for the lowest order of Society'.[59] On the one extreme were the tracts of Hannah More and the anonymous writers of the Religious Tract Society, which constituted part of an 'upper-class offensive' against the working-class reader.[60] Hannah More and her colleagues took up their pens

[57] James Sibree *Fifty Years of Recollections of Hull* (Hull, 1884) 40–1

[58] See Chapter 4, pp. 113–19 for a discussion of the scope and volume of publishing for Sunday school audiences

[59] R. Lloyd MA *A Letter to a Member of Parliament (in these days of infidelity and sedition) showing the serious and dangerous defects of British and Foreign Schools* (1819)

[60] See R. K. Webb *The British Working Class Reader 1790–1848* (1955) especially Chapter 2

to combat 'pernicious publications by tracts of an opposing tendency'.[61] Her *Cheap Repository Tracts* are populated by men like Tom Hod the mason who only learns he is unhappy and discontented after reading seditious literature; his friend Jack Anvil the blacksmith shows him the error of his ways and points out that the good gentlemen who manage things will improve the lot of the poor if they are undisturbed by the Levellers toward whom Tom had been sympathetic.[62] The Newcastle collier is Jack Anvil's more industrial counterpart; Patient Joe is his name.

> In trouble he bow'd him to God's holy will
> How contented was Joseph when matters went ill!
> When rich and when poor he alike understood
> That all things together were working for good.
>
> When taxes ran high, and provisions were dear,
> Still Joseph declared he had nothing to fear;
> It was but a trial he well understood,
> From HIM who made all work together for good.[63]

The limits of social mobility in this world are represented by More's Betty Brown who 'by industry and piety, rose in the world till at length she came to keep that handsome sausage shop near the corner', or by Joseph Green who became Squire Brown's head gardener and the superintendent of a Sunday school through possessing traits similar to Betty's. Joseph's rise was perhaps more in tune with the times; he used the skills learned in Sunday school to study botany books thereby advancing him in his profession.[64] The RTS, the SPCK, and indeed the Sunday School Union continued to sell stories of Hannah More, Sarah Trimmer and their followers until the 1840s.[65] New works continued to be written in the old style. One 'advice to the young' tract, which incidentally reprinted the *Newcastle Collier* from the *Cheap Repository Tracts*, suggested that those who are 'clever and promising and who have honest and industrious parents' might rise so far as to become servants to the rich.[66] Another laid out quite clearly the duties of the poor, viz. industry, sobriety and purity, veracity and honesty, subjection,

[61] H. More *Works* ... vol. 1, 341

[62] Ibid. 'Village Politics, by Will Chip, a Country Carpenter' vol. 1, 345–68

[63] Ibid. 'The Newcastle Collier; or Patient Joe' vol. 1, 329–33

[64] H. More *Works* ... vol. 5, 372–96; Betty married the Hackney coachman of the ballad by that name, vol. 1, 325–9; and [anon.] *The History of Joseph Green, a Sunday Scholar* (RTS n.d. but *c.* 1820)

[65] Goldstrom 'Changing Social Context ...' p. 40

[66] [Anon.] *Advice to Sunday Scholars in Rural and Mining Districts with a View to their Future Prosperity and Happiness* (Newcastle-under-Lyme, 1836) 23. Pamphlet is in Salt Library, Stafford

and contentment, but pointed out that in compensation they had been favored by God with peculiar promises and spiritual privileges.[67] A third gives credence to the view of working-class philanthropy outlined in Chapter Two although intended for quite another purpose. Richard Pearson, 'the humble reformer' and carpenter, is outraged by the lack of church attendance and prevalence of sabbath-breaking in his parish. He convinces his neighbor Harper to observe the sabbath. Both then decide to raise a subscription to buy books for a Sunday school; Harper is asked to become a teacher and at first demurs modestly, saying that he would be called preacher or schoolmaster and be made the laughing stock for aspiring beyond his station. Never mind, Pearson assured him, and Harper becomes a teacher well aware of the caution that one in his station must exercise so as not to be thought uppity,[68] *John the Plowman and Mary the Milkmaid*, the *Strawberry Gatherers*, *Colin Cameron or the Herd Boy* are all in the same vein.

The impact of this material was probably minimal. It was not used in week to week teaching and was not even the major form of reward literature. It was seldom anthologized in Sunday school collections and was never condemned in the working-class press or in the autobiographies of trade-union or radical readers which recounted school experiences. Like the mass of literature directed against the working-class reader, there is good reason to think that it missed its mark.[69]

Some tracts and reward books, while not immediately political, dealt with the virtues of hard work, honesty, thrift and perseverance; these will be considered within a subsequent section. Many had nothing to do with morality or counter-revolution. No. 59 in the Union's list, the *Spanish Armada*, was in its second printing of 12,000 copies in 1810 and related to the contemporary world only in feeding anti-papist popular prejudice. *The Powder Plot* was in its third edition of 14,000 copies at the same time; *The History of Lord Cobham* was issued in an edition of 15,000 in 1807.[70] Books of instruction in the Sunday School Union list included works on history and science 'especially adapted to children who had not had the advantage of a learned education'. Of historians 'the most impartial

[67] [Anon.] *The Duties and Encouragements of the Poor* RTS tract no. 22 (n.d. but *c.* 1830) Isa 41:17, Psalms 37:3, James 2:5, Matt. 31:3, Luke 16:22, Mark 12:15 and Phil. 4:12 are quoted for the edification of the poor

[68] 'The Humble Reformer' Sunday School Union tract no. 35 (*c.* 1808)

[69] See Webb *Working Class* . . . p. 81 and Chapters 2 and 3 *passim*

[70] These tracts are in the Angus Library of Regents Park College, Oxford. They are later editions of tracts which appear in *Sunday School Tracts, nos. 1–62* published for the Sunday School Union by W. Kent, London, 1805–11; these are available in the Hull University Library

and dispassionate' authors were selected, and in science, those 'which are acquainted with the latest discoveries'.[71] The military, religious and martyrological aspects of the reformation, the kings and queens of England, and the growth of English liberties, all implicitly at least establishmentarian, were favorite subjects in the former category. Natural history, particularly botany, was the most popular form of the latter. In among the more religious titles of a provincial publisher were a goodly number on this subject and a few on the theme of the honest poor boy succeeding to riches and fame against the heaviest of odds. For example, the *Cabinet of Curiosities* (in two parts) contains articles on the steam coach, on the diving bell and other recent advances in deep-sea diving, on attachments in animals and on the features of African oxen. *Curious Fish* is about the flying, spotted toad, sea-cock and lump fish, with attractive woodcuts of each. There are others which deal with *Foreign Fruits*, *Flax and Corn*, the *Industry of Beavers*, and an assortment of natural curiosities. Fifty-eight per cent of the twenty-eight pages in the firm's elementary reading textbook was taken up with illustrated alphabet and word lists, but after three pages of prayers the remainder is devoted to stories about cows, horses, eagles and ships.[72]

The most frequent subject of Sunday school tracts and reward books was, as might be expected, religion. Here again, however, the range was enormous. From Bunyan's *Pilgrim's Progress*, Foxe's *Book of Martyrs*, the sermons of Rev. John Newton or Milton's *Paradise Lost* to uninteresting little pieces on the deaths of pious scholars or the damnation of the wicked. Although eschatological religion might have considerable political impact, the ostensible subject matter of most of the pamphlet literature was peculiarly irrelevant to this world. True, infidels like Tom Paine, sabbath breakers, liars, thieves, and the like went to hell, while the virtuous Sunday school child went to heaven, perhaps converting his or her parents in the process. But nothing was said in all this vast literature about radicals, malcontents, trade unionists, Chartists, or similar disreputable sorts nor about the kinds of theft or dishonesty—stealing materials, coal, or time from one's employer—which were of particular concern in an industrial society.

The periodical literature associated with Sunday schools was by and large more worldly, though no more political. Some magazines—

[71]'Books for Young People: Instructive, Moral and Entertaining' in the *Sunday School Union Catalogue* (1824)

[72]These were published by Richardson and Son of Derby between 1820 and 1830. They, and the spelling book—*The First Step to Learning . . .* —are bound as 'Chapbooks' in the Bodleian 2703, g.5

C. Pray, sir, what is the power by which steam gives motion to such engines?

M. Expansion; the steam expands.

C. But pray what is expanding?

M. It is enlarging, extending, or spreading out. You know that heat turns water into steam. And one inch of water will, it is said, make one thousand inches of steam. So you will see at once that a quantity of water that will fill a vessel one inch in size, will, when turned into steam, fill a vessel one thousand inches in size.

C. Then would the steam burst a vessel, if the vessel were not large enough to hold or contain it?

M. Yes, if it had no vent, or unless the vessel was made sufficiently strong. Let a gun barrel be part filled with water; and let both ends be firmly stopp'd up; and then let the gun barrel be heated, so as to turn the water inside it, into steam, and the steam will burst the gun barrel, unless the barrel be exceedingly strong.

C. Why when the water was turned or converted into steam, the gun barrel would be too small a vessel to hold or contain it.

M. Yes, and that is the reason why the barrel would burst or be split to pieces. But suppose you had a pipe fastened into the side of the barrel, near the breech or big end of it and suppose there were a cock like a wate

cock, in such pipe, and the other end of such pipe reached into a large boiler; and suppose the boiler to be covered over, and so firmly made up that no steam could possibly get out of it, except by that pipe into the gun barrel, how then?

C. Why the steam would rush into the gun barrel with great violence.

M. It certainly would; but if you turned the cock, it would stop the steam from coming into your gun barrel at all. And suppose you were to put a bullet into the gun barrel; and then turn the cock, and let in a rush of steam, what would follow?

C. Why the steam would drive the bullet out like a shot; just as if sent out with a charge of gunpowder.

M. Very right. And do you know that there are steam guns, which will shoot with as much force as those that use gunpowder. And if a piece of old metal shaped like a bottle-cork were put into the gun barrel, it would be driven out with more force than a bullet.

C. That seems clear.

M. Well, suppose another pipe, a short one, was fixed in the gun barrel, near the big end of it; and this pipe open to the outward air, how then?

C. Why then it would not shoot out at all, for the steam would rush out at the short pipe.

M. Very true; but if there were a cock in

5. *This extract from an account of how railways work from the Primitive Methodist Children's Magazine (Vol. 16 (1840) No. 3) is typical of the 'useful' knowledge genre of Sunday school literature. Note the detail with which the operations of a steam engine are explained.*

Mrs Sherwood's *Child's Magazine* and *Sunday Scholar's Companion*, William Carus-Wilson's *The Children's Friend* or *The Child's Companion*—offered a steady diet of particularly gruesome deathbed scenes and unusually vacuous moral tales. Most of their competitors, however, did not follow their pattern. *The Primitive Methodist Children's Magazine*, for example, combined Bible stories and tales of pious children with quite elaborate six and eight page discussions on how paper is manufactured or with serialized accounts of the development and operation of the steam engine.[73] The juvenile section of the *Baptist Magazine* included articles on astronomy, guides to natural history collections, and of course essays on the kings and queens of England.[74] One of the oldest and, because of its association with the Sunday School Union, the most popular journals was the *Youth's Magazine or Evangelical Miscellany*. In the 1810s it consisted largely of purely religious material, very little of which was evident by the 1830s. In 1837, for example, the largest number of pages given to any single subject was devoted to geology, while a five-part section under the title 'Why am I here' was in fact on the evidence of God in the morphology of various plants and forms of marine life. Biblical history, descriptions of missionary lands, and various amusing anecdotes filled out the volume. Some magazines like the *Teacher's Offering or Sunday School Monthly Visitor* began publication with a fare consisting mostly of moral tales, but, presumably in response to consumer pressure, issued a second volume leavened with a long series on the life of Luther, on eastern methods of keeping time, on how gravity worked, on how the roundness of the earth impressed itself on men, etc. Further volumes had articles on American Indians, on leaves and roots of plants, on snails and on other natural history topics along with series on biblical history and geography and accounts of foreign lands being opened for Christ.[75]

Overt commentary on social issues was rare and oddly ambivalent. The *Sunday School Teacher's Juvenile Magazine*, for example, announced in its first issue that it intended to combat 'the designing men, who under a semblance of patriotism seek their own aggrandizement ... create confusion, bloodshed, and devastation'. But it also intended to 'plead for the cause of the poor, hard-wrought and

[73] Vol. 3, no. 10 (October 1827); vol. 16, no. 3 (1840)

[74] The article on Richard I and the two parts of a King John feature in the 1819 vol. constituted nos. 11–13 of a series going back to Edward the Confessor. Each issue also had a 'nature cabinet' section which offered articles and tidbits of natural history

[75] *Teachers' Offering; or Sunday School Monthly Visitor*, see vols for 1841–2 and 1844–45

much neglected factory child'.[76] The Sunday school periodical press was by and large such that it appealed to the 'respectable' working class as well as to middle-class patrons who subsidized publication costs. When the *Sunday Scholar*, a fairly mainstream children's periodical, appeared in 1840, it was hailed by the organ of the Manchester and Salford Sunday School Union as:

> a new candidate for popular favor. It is a magazine containing sixteen pages, with cuts, for one half penny. We know the parties conducting it, and have the utmost confidence in their anxiety to benefit little children. We welcome it, and trust that it will prepare thousands of younger scholars for our own periodicals.[77]

The Chartist *Northern Star* reviewer was equally enthusiastic:

> [It] is calculated to do considerable service in giving a right direction to the minds of those for whose especial benefit it is intended. The work is for the most part of a practical tendency and is free from that sectarian bias by which similar publications are frequently disfigured.[78]

The vision of the world given by the Sunday school press was that of the educated artisan, of Mrs Gaskell's Job Legh or of a nineteenth-century Adam Bede. The virtues it lauded were, as will be shown more fully later, those of the increasingly 'respectable' working class.

Sunday school periodical literature was at its most political when it came to England's world position. It was not a great leap from missionary stories about Cingalese superstition, Chinese mourning practices, or Indian funeral rites to statements of the inferiority of other races. By the 1850s gory descriptions of Hindoo cruelty, accounts of brave missionaries who struggled to combat barbaric practices, and requests that children pray for the soldiers who put down the Indian mutiny had become items for a popular Sunday school anthology.[79] On the other hand, one must not exaggerate the racism of Sunday school literature. The *Youth's Magazine*, for example, printed an article entitled 'On Bigotry' which pleaded for racial as well as religious tolerance.[80] Another periodical argued that 'children if left to themselves will naturally unite. Their animosities and prejudices are not theirs but their fathers' ... '[81]

[76] Ed. by James Wood of Barnsby, no. 1 (June 1840)
[77] *SS Teachers' Magazine* (1841) January review section
[78] 30 January 1841, p. 3
[79] See C. Kendall *The New Sunday School Reciter* (1859) 93, 128–34
[80] *Youth Magazine* (1837) 379–83
[81] *Sunday School Magazine* (1841) 24

H

The problem with evaluating the significance of all the literature discussed so far is that the historian can not be certain if, and to what degree, it was read by the children to whom it was directed. On the other hand the massive proliferation of titles and the large printings suggest that they did indeed reach a wide and eager market. With textbooks this problem does not arise; they were the main fare of the Sunday school day and an analysis of their content will provide an insight into the minimum social message Sunday schools sought to convey. The preparation of several new spelling books in the 1780s and 1790s suggests that Sunday schools did not find the specialized teaching literature of charity schools suitable for their needs. The earliest of these new texts was prepared by Thomas Burgess, future Bishop of St David's and Salisbury, for use in the Sunday schools patronized by Shute-Barrington. It appears to have been extensively used, since it reached its twelfth edition by 1809. The division of the text is shown in Table 19.

Table 19:[82] *Content of* Salisbury Reader (12*th*, 1809 *edition*) *giving the percentage of total pages in various categories*

Category	No. of pages	Percentage of total pages
Tables of words or letters	15	16
Lessons using vocabulary words	22	23
Stories	13	14
Biblical extracts and questions	29	30
Natural theology proofs	10	10
Miscellaneous	7	7
Total	96	100

There is little to be said about the word tables; following on a rather attractive picture alphabet, each table consists of thirty-six words divided into syllables along with a guide to their pronunciation. The lessons are composed of short sentences which make use of vocabulary words; the themes are most often the attributes of God and the wonder of creation, the evils of sabbath breaking, with a few sentences on the sins of stealing, lying, cruelty to animals, disrupting class, and not paying attention to one's lessons. As for the stories, one concerns a boy who attempts to steal a chicken from a barn yard while the farmer is in church and is frightened away by a dog. As he runs from the dog he begins to imagine all the dogs of the neighborhood barking at him and consequently runs deeper and deeper into the forest where he becomes lost, is

[82] [Thomas Burgess] *The Salisbury Spelling Book with Historical and Moral Extracts from the New Testament* (1786, 12th ed. 1809) from the Leicester University Library

found by a gipsy, and is finally sold into slavery. In one sense, of course, this somewhat gruesome story is highly political. As Cobbett remarked, it is unjust that a hungry man should be punished for stealing food. Furthermore the context of this and other stories about the wickedness of theft are predicated on a society with strict private-property rights. On the other hand this and other stories are strangely unspecific in the kinds of theft they condemn. Actions which at one time had been sanctioned by custom but which during the industrial revolution came increasingly to be defined as crimes— taking scrap metal from engineering works, picking up a bit of coal at a mine, confiscating the occasional bit of silver or even poaching—are nowhere explicitly prohibited. There is almost an unworldliness about many Sunday school moral tales. Furthermore the values urged by this story were so widely accepted among the working classes by the late eighteenth century that it becomes implausible to describe them as in some way imposed by the bourgeoisie. While the definition of theft was in dispute between masters and men, 'thou shalt not steal' as a general maxim was not a class doctrine in this period

The second long story in the *Salisbury Reader* is about a boy who goes from animal to animal trying to get them to play with him during church hours, only to be refused by each. Only by interpreting the interest of the author in sabbath observance as a part of a program of social control does this often charming tale assume any significance beyond itself.[83] The Bible extracts are even less worldly, dealing mostly with the life of Christ—annunciation, nativity, death, resurrection, and Pentecost. Forgiveness is the major theme of the others.[84] Intellectually the most interesting section concerns the natural theology proofs. It is difficult to argue that the writer was terribly serious about wishing to limit the intellectual development of the poor when he describes the purpose of these exercises as:

> to fix in the minds of Children a plain, palpable impression of an active principle within them, prior to, and distinct from any mechanical act of the body. In the instances alleged [on *intending* to read a book] the intention obviously precedes the intended act.

[83] See pp. 135 ff. Some forms of sabbatarianism during the late eighteenth century might indeed be viewed as an attempt by the upper classes to prevent the poor from congregating on their own during their one free day of the week. Although the true basis of nineteenth-century sabbatarianism remains obscure, this class based interpretation becomes increasingly difficult to sustain

[84] Extracts from Acts 2:11–14; 3:12–18; 5:1–2; 10:7–9; 13:16–31; Luke 1:26–35; 15:11–24; 18:9–14; 24:44–53; Matthew 5:33–37, 43–45; 6:14–15; 18:23–25; 21:28–31

The action of the mind is prior to, and therefore distinct from, the action of the body. The impelling power is distinct from the impelled substance; the mind that moves, from the body that is moved.[85]

Burgess's text is thus overwhelmingly rationalist and religious; while the occasional phrase suggesting humility can be discovered, the impact of the work as a whole is far too spiritual for it to have immediate political import.

William Paley, the distinguished theologian, also wrote a reader for Sunday schools which in most respects is like Burgess's. The division of its content is shown in Table 20.

Table 20 :[86] *Content of* Reading Made Completely Easy *(1790[c. 1840 edition])*
giving the percentage of total pages in various categories

Category	No. of pages	Percentage of total
Alphabet and word lists	16	26
Woodcuts of the apostles	4	7
Creed, Lord's prayer, catechism etc.	13	21
Lessons	28	46
Total:	61	100

The lessons are almost entirely devotional; two stanzas of no. 19 are the only passages with any social relevance, and here children are cautioned to 'fear thou the Lord and the King, and meddle not with them that are given to change'. The query, three lines down the page, 'Can a man take Fire in his Bosom, and his Clothes not be burnt?' may have political overtones but there is some doubt that they would be perceived by a ten-year-old beginning reader.[87] In the catechism section the child is instructed to reply to the question 'What is my duty toward ... ?' by saying 'to love honour and succour my father and mother; to honour and obey the King and all that are put in authority under him; to submit myself to my Governors, Teachers, Spiritual Pastors and Masters; to order myself lowly and reverently to all my Betters'. But taken all together the politically relevant sections of this work total less than one page out of over sixty.

In 1805 the Sunday School Union entered the publishing field

[85] *Salisbury Reader* ... p. 104
[86] William Paley DD *Reading Made Completely Easy; or a Necessary Introduction to Reading the Bible* (1790). The 1850 edition borrowed from the Leeds University Library was used for this analysis
[87] Ibid. p. 36

with its four-part spelling book. This enormously popular text—
5,000,000 bound copies between 1820 and 1850—followed the
same pattern as earlier works, though it was far more extensive
and advanced in the material it presented.[88] Part 4 consisted
entirely of a twenty-four-page dictionary notable only for the high
proportion of biblical words that found their way in amongst more
prosaic nouns and verbs. Part 1 is made up of simple lessons, some
devotional, others consisting of sentences advocating honesty,
early rising, work and similar virtues, all of which were, as the
next two sections show, advocated with equal vehemence by working-class educational writers. Part 2 consists of Bible stories from
the creation to the Pentecost, while part 3 reprints extracts from
the Bible—little children blessed by Jesus, sight given to a blind
man by Christ, etc.

It would be misleading to suggest that all Sunday school texts
were entirely devoid of political overtones. Sprinkled in amongst
pious phrases like 'blessed is he that considereth the poor and needy'
and excerpts from the sermons of Newton or Doodridge, one 'reader'
includes a section entitled 'On Duty of Servants to their Masters'
which elaborates on the meaning of 1 Peter 2:18, Colossians 3:22–5
and most commonly Titus 2:9–14.[89] Another book, whose primary
content is of the 'To God will I pray and he will hear my cry; call
on God and he will help thee' variety, also contains the occasional sentence like: 'Mary was not born a lady, and she knew
she must work hard for a living. But she was always cheerful and
happy; she did not wish to be rich, but she wished very much to
be good.'[90] In both of these texts, however, religious and ordinary
devotional material formed the bulk of their contents.

While the readers used in ordinary day schools became pro-
gressively less religious and more immediately concerned with
worldly matters, those used by Sunday schools exhibited the opposite tendency.[91] In the period 1830–60 ordinary reading books
devoted between one-tenth and one-third of their space to religious
matter. The Sunday School Union on the other hand published
a text, which sold about 250,000 copies per year between 1830–50,
composed entirely of scriptural extracts.[92] Most were chosen to
illustrate aspects of the Christian scheme of salvation; in fact,

[88] See p. 114; parts 1–3 were borrowed from the Glasgow University Library;
part 4 from Leeds University Library
[89] The Sunday School Spelling Book in 5 parts (1823) Part 1, class 2
[90] Mrs Thaner The Sunday School Primer; or Child's First Book (1823) pt. 2, lesson 5
[91] See Goldstrom op. cit. p. 141
[92] Sunday School Union Reading-Book Part 1 (n.d. but c. 1830); copy borrowed
from the Nottingham University Library. See particularly pp. 13–15, 20

of the twenty-four pages and twenty-nine sections, only three
sections, less than two pages, are devoted to topics with immediate
social or political relevance. One-third of a page is given over to
the usual passages regarding the obligations of servants to their
masters, about another two-thirds of a page on the virtue of contentment and the sin of covetousness. On the other hand the two-thirds
of a page-long section on 'Justice and Injustice' contains all those
verses so often adapted to radical purposes: 'He that oppresseth
the poor reproaches his maker'; 'For the Lord will plead their
cause, and spoil the soul of those that spoiled them'; 'The wages
of him that is hired shall not abide with thee all night', etc. Taken
as a whole this most widely used of Sunday school readers contributed far more to the religious and thus political culture of the
working class than to their indoctrination.

Finally, whichever elementary textbooks Sunday schools used to
teach beginners, students were weaned from 'readers' as early as
was pedagogically feasible. The percentage of total enrolment
reading in the Bible or the New Testament was taken as an indication of the efficiency or success of a school. And in both Dissenting
and Anglican Sunday schools at least sixty per cent were in this
advanced category of students.[93]

The literature discussed so far constituted the great bulk of the
reading material associated with English Sunday schools during
the period 1780–1850. It was first of all religious. Secondly, it
formed part of the working-class culture of self-improvement with
its concern for history, the natural sciences, and 'useful' knowledge.
Thirdly, it dwelt on a morality advocating honesty and kindness
while condemning sabbath breaking, disrespect to parents, lying and
similar offences. Direct political propaganda as evidenced in the
tracts of Hannah More or in some of the productions of the SPCK
was rare. The religious content of working-class political life and
the aspiration toward respectability, of which self-improvement
was a part, may indeed have limited the revolutionary potential
in English society during the period being considered. But it was
through such channels, and not through coercion or propaganda,
that Sunday schools played a political role. They did, however,
promote certain values often associated with industrial society.

v. The Inculcation of Values: Literature and Work
    Discipline

On paper, the ideal Sunday school child was certain to grow up

---

[93] Baines *Condition* ... Table 3. There is no reason to suppose that the proportion
was lower elsewhere than in the industrial areas surveyed

into the ideal capitalist man or woman. The perfect scholar was
imbued with the puritan ethic:

> ... Of temper sweet and mild
> No angry passions e're were seen
> In this engaging child.
>
> She very soon could knit and sew
> And help her mother too
> For Hannah would not waste her time
> As idle children do.
>
> Each sabbath morn she rose betimes
> And dressed her clean and neat
> Nor ever utter'd naughty words,
> Or loitered in the street.
>
> She knew that God would never love
> Girls that are bold and rude
> And therefore little Hannah prayed
> That he would make her good.[94]

He, or she, went around reciting ditties like:

> In books, or work, or healthful play
> Let my first years be passed
> That I may give for every day
> Some good account at last.[95]

In short he or she was hard working, clean, conscious of the value of
time, obedient, and (although not stated in these rhymes) thrifty
as well. Indeed it has been argued that Sunday schools were middle-
class agencies designed to inculcate just these virtues, that they
were part of an assault on the pre-industrial personality. In support
of this view, it could be pointed out, for example, that Sunday
schools, particularly in industrial cities, were often founded and
financially supported by the manufacturing class; that when asked
their views some factory owners remarked that the discipline and
instruction of the Sunday school caused the children so educated
to be 'more orderly and subordinate than others', 'more tractable,
better behaved', 'improved in their general conduct and habits
of cleanliness' and taken as a whole, more moral and manageable.[96]

---

[94] *The Sunday School Scholar's Gift, or a present for a good child* (Wellington, 1814).

[95] *Teachers' Offering* vol. 4 (1844) 270; it is prefaced by 'Be industrious. It is a discredit to be idle; children's time is valuable; always be doing something; let every young child take for his motto ...'

[96] *Reports from each of the four Factory Inspectors on the effects on the Educational Provisions of the Factories Act; together with joint reports 1839* (42) xlii, pp. 11, 29 and 7

The aesthetic vision of the Sunday school and the factory during the nineteenth century were also remarkably similar. Ure talks of the 'sublime spectacle of witnessing crowds of factory children arranged in Sunday school' or of '1,500 boys, and as many girls, regularly seated upon benches, the one set on the right side, the other on the left'.[97] Seventeen thousand children attending the Halifax Sunday School Jubilee were described in the official report as 'an invading and well disciplined army—well clad and cheerful'.[98] For some, the spectacle of tens of thousands of spindles turning through the motion of the same drive shaft was not dissimilar to thousands of children following the orders of one individual. But from the facts that the virtues favored in Sunday schools were those characteristic of the entrepreneurial bourgeoisie, that this class on occasion praised and supported Sunday schools, and that on some occasions certain observers saw a similarity between the schools and new forms of industrial organization it does not follow that Sunday schools were agents of the middle classes for imposing suitable character traits on children of their employees.

Two questions remain. To what extent can the puritan ethic in this period be seen as a form of bourgeois ideology? Secondly, in what ways, and how successfully, did Sunday schools propagate or instil this ethic? Both these questions must be answered in the context of the facts presented in Chapter Two. Sunday schools were by no means a simple outgrowth of the factory system or even of industrialism. In 1818, Wiltshire, Dorset, Buckinghamshire and Bedfordshire ranked fourth, fifth, sixth and seventh respectively among counties in percentage of their population enrolled in Sunday school. Bedfordshire stood first in 1851, with almost a fifth of the population enrolled, while Huntingdonshire, Rutland, Cornwall and Buckinghamshire were all in the top one-quarter of counties based on *per capita* enrolment. Sunday schools began at a time when the factory system had scarcely gained a foothold and grew to contain millions of children before the factory became the dominant organization of production. They were as much a rural as an urban phenomenon, as much part of an agrarian as of an industrial economy. Furthermore, as has been noted already in this chapter, Sunday school teachers were predominantly working class, funds often came from the working-class community, and indeed the lower orders responded as eagerly to the philanthropic surge of the late eighteenth century as did other strata of society. The great majority of Sunday schools were then neither the direct product of industrialism nor of the middle class.

[97] Andrew Ure *The Philosophy of Manufactures* (1835) 408 and 411
[98] *SS Teachers' Magazine* (1841) 665

Nevertheless they undoubtedly taught the work ethic that is so often associated with the bourgeoisie. Although texts were primarily religious, diligence, cleanliness, punctuality, thrift and obedience were all pressed on students. 'Go to the ant, thou sluggard, think of her ways and be wise,' the children were advised.[99] Follow explicitly the instructions of one's masters even if an alternative method of performing the task seems easier, because: 'they are much better judges how to have their business done. It is your duty to do as they direct; without murmuring or disputing. You should obey them willingly, readily and cheerfully.'[100] There was a rather touching genre of thrift fables in which the child who spent his or her pennies was unable to help the poor while the one who saved his mite could perform an act of charity. There were poems, ditties and anecdotes regarding the 'puritan virtues' in all the tract magazine and textbook literature, but for reasons having to do more with the organization of teaching than with their intrinsic importance, those associated with time received the most thorough treatment. Punctuality was the cardinal virtue of the Sunday school teacher; ill health would result from sleeping past sun-up; as for lateness,

> A little less indulgence in the bed
> A little less contrivance in the head
> A little more devotion in the mind
> Will quite prevent your being so behind.[101]

'Do not lie long in bed, but rise up soon in the morn; pray to God, wash your face, next comb your hair, and then make haste to your book or to your work,' advises a widely read textbook.[102] Jesus was held up to the children as being especially punctual because of his remark at the beginning of the Last Supper, 'And when the HOUR was come, he sat down and the twelve apostles with him' (Luke 22:13, 14).[103]

It would be a mistake, however, to conflate these precepts or ideals into a distinct bourgeois ideology. Indeed, the puritan ethic found some of its most vehement supporters among the leaders of a nascent working class. Cobbett thought that the right to live was associated with the obligation to work.[104] Holyoake, the

[99] *Salisbury Speller* op. cit. p. 29
[100] Peter Waldo *Admonitions to Sunday Scholars* (1835) 47
[101] *Sunday School Magazine* (1841) 72
[102] Sunday School Union *Spelling Book* op. cit. pt. 1, 10
[103] *SS Teachers' Magazine* (1840) 686
[104] William Cobbett *Advice to Young Men* (1829; facsimile edition 1906) 10

Chartist, printed in his reading book a poem on work which would have done well in the harshest of political economy primers:

> I love the banging of the hammer
> The whirring of the plane.
> The crushing of the busy saw
> The creaking of the crane ...
> The puffing of the engine,
> And the fans' continuous boom ...
> The sounds of busy labour,
> —I love, I love them all.[105]

In his 'sentimental alphabet' he claims to hate 'T' because it tires, 'U' because it is unsteady, and 'W' because it wastes.[106] The *Northern Star* published little anecdotes on the 'miseries of indolence', while the spokesmen of another strand of Chartism, Thomas Cooper, was an almost too perfect example of inner-directed man.[107] 'Resolve-application-energy-perseverance: these are the secrets of advancement in knowledge,' he advised his young readers. Having no time should not count as an excuse for not learning, he continued: 'Make it from sleep ... your health might suffer no material injury by occasionally cutting off an hour or two of slumber.'[108] It is scarcely suprising that working-class leaders should have adopted so readily the ethic traditionally associated with the entrepreneurial middle class; the personality traits of the successful business man are, after all, not very different from those of the successful political leader, journalist, or trade-union militant. It was as important for the *Northern Star* as for *The Times* or *Guardian* that its copy be handed in on time, that its distributors pick up their bundles regularly, and that payments be reliable.[109] A congruence between the fundamental values of the middle and 'respectable' working classes is thus natural and not difficult to understand.

---

[105] G. J. Holyoake *Practical Grammar with Graduated Exercises* (1st ed. 1846—quoted here is 8th ed. 1870) 'The Reading Book', from a poem by Francis Gage called 'The Sounds of Industry'

[106] G. J. Holyoake *Practical Grammar* ... op. cit. 'The Word Book' p. 8

[107] *Northern Star* (24 February 1838) 7, 'A want of occupation is not rest/A mind quite vacant is a mind distressed', etc.

[108] Thomas Cooper *Eight Letters to Young Men of the Working Classes* (1850) letter 2, p. 1

[109] Most issues of the *Northern Star* for example carried a 'notes from the editor' section which *inter alia* contained pleas to contributors asking that they hand in their copy on time, to distributors complaining about tardy or altogether neglected pick-ups, etc.

vi. The Inculcation of Values: School Organization and Work Discipline

In real life, however, practice is more important than preaching; and the decisive role of the Sunday school in the development of personality had less to do with what was taught than with how things were taught, with the structural and operational organization of the institution. The structure of authority, the discipline of time and place, to a lesser extent the organization of teaching the rules governing appearance, and the system of rewards and punishments all arose out of the school *qua* school. Though they may have had, and in some cases did have, almost obsessional ideological justification as well, this was largely window-dressing on a reality determined by the nature of the institution.[110] A consideration of these features will allow us to understand how they acted to encourage inner drives and outward behavior appropriate to an industrial society.

In the same way that the authority relationships in the family appear as a small-scale version of these relationships in an organic society, the nature of power in the Sunday school was based on reason rather than on deference; on a rule book rather than long-standing tradition. In contrast with the far smaller charity schools, many of these schools issued rule books or sheets setting out in writing the privileges and obligations of various categories of personnel. Some were quite short, the size of a broadsheet, and were read out to the assembled students and teachers once each month in order to remind everyone of the nature of the social system in which they were participating. Other sets of rules were extraordinarily extensive, going on for over fifty pages and defining in the minutest detail the power relationships that governed the school. Perhaps the Napoleonic Wars inspired the military language in which they were couched: superintendents are colonels, inspectors are majors, teachers are captains, monitors are sergeants, and the best students in each class are the corporals.[111] The set of rules from which this is drawn resembles nothing so much as Ambrose Crowley's regulations for the operation and management

[110] The model in this section is derived, in part, from Talcott Parsons 'The School as a Social System: Some of its functions in American Society' originally published in the *Harvard Educational Review* vol. 24 (Fall 1959) 297–318 and reprinted in A. H. Halsey *et al.*, eds. *Education, Economy, and Society; A Reader in the Sociology of Education* (New York, 1961) 435–55. Parsons' insights are elaborated in Robert Dreeben *On What is Learned in School* (Reading, Mass., 1968) which provides most of the theoretical framework employed here

[111] *Rules and Regulations of the Sunday School held in the Wesleyan Methodist Chapel, Spring Gardens, Doncaster* (Doncaster, 1815) 41

of his iron works. In the Sunday school as in the liberal state or the
large firm, obedience is given to a person not because of who he or
she is but because of the position they fill within a system of law.
Furthermore, both the teaching and the structure of the Sunday
school emphasized that it was rational to act according to these
laws. In secular affairs this rationality might imply that one ought
not to engage in trade-union activity because it was against the
immutable laws of political economy to do so; alternatively, of
course, it might encourage working-class trade-union or political
activism on different but equally rational grounds.

The importance of an authority structure is thus not one of
content but of form. Within the rule-governed world of the Sunday
school the day was divided according to the clock; place, motion,
and relationships to other students or teachers were prescribed
by the system. To begin with, the opening of school was rigidly
defined in all rule books. 'At the *exact time* of commencing the
school', according to a typical example of the genre, 'the superintendent rings a bell, *which* is expected to produce entire silence in
the school, whenever rung.'[112] In some schools children were
asked to memorize key phrases like 'I am to be in School every
Sunday morning at nine o'clock and in the afternoon at a quarter
past one,' or 'I am to be in school at quarter before nine o'clock in
the morning, and half past one in the afternoon.'[113] Both Anglican
and Dissenting schools divided class time into previously determined blocks: there were so many minutes for calling the roll,
another few minutes for prayers, three minutes for distributing
books, forty minutes for reading, twenty for spelling, etc. A schedule
rather than the requirements of the task itself dictated what portion
of the day was to be spent on it. In large schools or in cases where
movement of students was required a bell punctuated class time
and signalled a change of place or subject. Once in the place assigned
to him or her, the scholar was not to move out of it except with
explicit permission. His contact with fellow students was severely
circumscribed by the rules of the school. The second of the 'Rules
and Orders for Children in the Schoolroom' from an Anglican guide
dictated that 'No child shall remove out of place without leave of
the master or mistress; nor play, nor talk, nor whisper, upon any
account.'[114] Most rule books prescribed that scholars not leave
their places at all, if possible, and, if absolutely necessary, then at
least not during the first half hour or hour. That 'not a word be

---

[112] *A Brief Abstract of the Plan of Instruction used in the Sunderland and Bishopwearmouth Sunday Schools* (Sunderland, 1814) 4
[113] *Rawcliffe Sunday School Rules* (Rawcliffe, 1829); *Rules ... Doncaster* p. 11
[114] Horne *SS Recommended ...* (1786) appendix, p. 32

spoken, but to teachers: no looking off books, or learning lessons aloud', or that 'teachers shall not allow the children to talk with each other, or suffer them to be heard getting lessons', or some similar sentence was always included in the school rules. In Stockport only one scholar out of forty could leave his place and then only when in possession of a wooden token or by the 1820s of a written notice. The Doncaster rule book, with unconscious poignancy, labelled its pass LIBERTY.

Smaller schools did not require elaborate procedures for removing scholars from one place to another during the course of the day. But in the industrial towns of the North and Midlands, in London and some of the larger southern towns, where up to 4,500 children might gather under one roof, more care was required. The Stockport scheme is not atypical:

> ... at the sound of the organ, the doors to be opened and the 1, 53, 54, 56 and 2, 27, 28, 29, 30 and 60th classes to retire to their respective rooms, before any other late scholars be admitted. When the 1st and 2nd classes, etc. have retired and the late scholars (duly marked) come in, the first division of the third, and the first division of the fifteenth classes will move off, into the attic, to read; the first division of each class to follow after in a continued line; then the second division of the third and the fifteenth classes to move off in the same order, to their respective writing desks. Let all the movements within the school be performed steadily and deliberately; the greatest attention be paid to order and silence.[115]

Punctuality among both students and teachers was amongst the first, most severe, and apparently most intractable problems facing those who operated schools as it was for those who managed factories or workshops. There was scarcely a week when the Stockport minute books were not filled with exasperated notices like 'not one fifth of the classes start on time', '9.30, not $\frac{1}{2}$ of the rooms with teachers', 'shameful lassitude' or 'unforgivable laziness'.[116] Those schools which paid their teachers, and indeed some which did not, tried to impose fines for tardiness or non-attendance: 6d. for five minutes, 1s. for the next half hour, and 2s. for the entire day in the Anglican schools of Manchester; in Bristol one minute late by the nearest church clock meant a 1s. fine for the superintendent, fifteen minutes tardiness cost teachers 3d.; in Prescott fifteen minutes tardiness resulted in a mere 2d. fine and a whole day's absence

[115] *Regulations to be Observed in the Large Room of the Stockport Sunday School* (Stockport, 1840)

[116] Stockport SS *Committee Minute Books* (January and February 1799)

made the teacher liable for a nominal 3*d*.[117] But as unpaid teachers replaced paid schoolmasters, a system of assessments for failing to perform one's duties became less workable. In fact fines seem to have disappeared almost entirely by the 1820s. The almost obsessive preoccupation in Sunday school magazines and guide books with time discipline was then a result of having to replace coercion with moral persuasion in trying to ensure the regular opening of each week's activities: 'PUNCTUALITY. This is the golden word. Let it be yours. Be at the school and seated in your proper place at least five minutes before the time. No other plan will do.'[118] 'PUNCTUAL ATTENDANCE' is the most important trait of good teacher; lateness leads to unruly students and is therefore 'a radical evil', etc.[119]

When it came to ensuring prompt and regular attendance by children, fines were out of the question. Sunday schools could resort only to repeated pleas in various tracts and magazines: 'Children, be punctual, be punctual, everything is gained by punctuality.'[120] Alternatively, they could resort to direct action. The Nottingham Methodist Sunday School followed a widely publicized method of locking the door of the school ten minutes after opening time, reading the roll and removing the cards of the absentees, then opening the door to admit those waiting after having noted on the absentees' cards that these scholars were late, and finally sending visitors around with the remaining cards to the homes of absent scholars exhorting them to come to school.[121] Though it was claimed that with this method only twenty out of four hundred scholars were late, the fact that it excluded students from the opening service and that it took a great deal of manpower to operate caused it to be rejected by most schools. The third method was to offer rewards for punctual and regular attendance; one ticket might be given for four consecutive Sundays of being on time, a book for a whole quarter of regular attendance, some article of clothing for a year of perfect attendance.

The emphasis placed by Sunday schools on a rule-governed order, a rigid discipline of time and place, was undoubtedly buttressed by ideological supports. For those concerned with combating 'the vicious doctrine which teaches the lowest member

[117] *Rules of the Manchester Church of England Sunday Schools* (Manchester, 1815) ... *of the Bristol Methodist Sunday Schools* (Bristol, 1817) ... *Prescott Sunday School* (Prescott, 1812)

[118] *SS Teachers' Magazine* (1843) 249

[119] Ibid. (1833) col. 234

[120] *Sunday School Magazine* (1841) 249

[121] *Evangelical Magazine* vol. 6 (1798) 56; *Essay on the Formation and Management of Sunday Schools* (1813) 8

of society to regard himself as on the level of the most dignified', not only the principles taught, 'but the manner by which they are communicated' were relevant.[122] On a more practical level, a teacher's trade magazine began an article on Sunday school discipline with 'Order is heaven's first law' and ended with 'Let all things be done decently and in ORDER'.[123] As one guide put it, the precise method of conducting a school might vary, but 'let it never be forgotten, that what is done must be done upon a system'.[124] In short, the medium was very much the message.

Many teachers must have believed that 'the ill usage of every minute is a record against us in heaven', or that there was something beautiful and pleasing about rows of children quietly and precisely doing their lessons. But the ideology was grounded in reality; it was justification for a system more than its cause. If several hundred people are to engage in an activity like teaching or learning in one place and time, it is clear that the beginning and end of the exercise must be synchronized. In the confines of the Sunday school—8 square feet per student was a generous allotment—free movement would have led to chaos. As for restrictions on talking to one's fellow students, these might be viewed as an attempt to instil a sense of independence and a drive for personal achievement. But in a single room containing dozens of teachers each with their ten or twelve students working on different lessons, it could also quite plausibly be interpreted as a means of preventing pandemonium. The discipline of time and space as well as the structure of authority in the Sunday school, much as it may resemble the regime of the factory, did not evolve as a handmaiden to new forms of organization. Rather, the school and the factory as organizations were susceptible to the same problems and arrived at similar solutions. That two contemporaneous institutions faced with the same problem evolved similar remedies does not indicate that one was subservient to the other.

The ubiquitous rule requiring students to appear at school cleanly washed and neatly dressed is similarly open to a dual interpretation. On the one hand, it set school apart from the child's other experiences and emphasized the fact that different behavior was required there than in the street, workplace or home. Furthermore, both the health and the air of the school undoubtedly benefited from a certain minimum standard of cleanliness. On the other hand it sprang from that peculiar English confusion between cleanliness and godliness: a clean face, combed hair, and neat

[122] Rev. Richard Raikes *Considerations* ... (1806) op. cit. p. 57
[123] *SS Teachers' Magazine* (1833) col. 193–203; see also (1832) col. 334–35
[124] *Hints on the Establishment and Regulation of Sunday Schools* (1836) 10

clothes in Sunday school were taken by the managers and by many
of the parents as a sign of stability, order and normality in the rest
of a child's life. Special preparation for Sunday school also implied
an acknowledgement of the specialness of the sabbath and constituted, in effect, a ritual act of observance. But as Chapter Six has
shown, none of these characteristics is unique to the bourgeoisie.
In this period they differentiate the rough from the respectable,
a division which does not correspond to that between a working and
a middle class.

Methods of teaching and the manner in which students were
rewarded or punished clearly owe more to ideology than to structural necessity. Some semblance of a system might be required,
but it would presumably have been possible to encourage children
to help one another in performing an exercise and so to re-inforce
a feeling of communal striving and communal achievement.
But it appears that this was never done in Sunday schools. Some of
the stricter regimes were clearly designed to inculcate a sense of
individual competition and of achievement while making failure as
conspicuous and painful as possible. For example, in one system a
spelling lesson might proceed as follows: 'the teacher shall pronounce
the word—Industry; the first scholar says 'Industry-diligence',
the second scholar 'I-n', the third 'd-u-s', the fourth 't-r-y,
diligence'.[125] Then the teacher pronounces the word again and
another scholar pronounces and spells it syllable by syllable. If
one scholar makes an error, the next one down the line tries to
perform the task and the one who finally succeeds takes the place
of the others, passing in front of those who, by failing, go to a lower
position. The top scholar moves into a higher class at the end of
the day. A similar system of public rewards, though without the
stigma of failure, lies at the core of the so called collective system,
recommended by the Sunday School Union and the Anglican
Sunday School Institute. Certain reward systems were veritable
replicas of the market place, bringing scriptural knowledge within
the shadow of the cash nexus. The Bristol Methodist Sunday School
Society, with several schools under its jurisdiction, published a kind
of tariff: 8d. for memorizing the catechism no. 1, 1s. 3d. for no.2 and
1s. 2d. for the somewhat shorter no. 3; the gospel of St Mark, if
recited with sufficient precision, earned 2s., St John a half crown,
St Matthew, St Luke, the Acts and Proverbs were worth 3s. and
all the Psalms brought 5s. to the scholar blessed with a prodigious

[125] This particular illustration is taken from *Rules of the Stockport Wesleyan Methodist
Sunday School* (1837) appendix. But, some version of this system is found in a number
of rule books and is based on the monitorial methods of Bell and Lancaster

memory.[126] Few schools were quite so wedded to business practice. But even in more moderate systems virtue earned a wage just as it was meant to do in the world at large. The influential *Evangelical Magazine* recommended paying one ticket for each Sunday's good behavior and redeeming these tickets for 3d. cash at the end of the quarter; in other schools certificates for various kinds of virtue were worth different amounts.[127]

It would be misleading to argue that Sunday schools had a uniform system of teaching or of rewards and punishments. The author of a teacher's manual running to over 350 pages gave up in despair trying to describe the range of rewards and censures, claiming that another book of equal length would be required to do the job.[128] One basic generalization, however, can be made. This is that there was great reluctance in Sunday schools to exercise severe discipline and that stress was always more on rewards than on punishments. The result was that the apparent rigidity of the rules in theory was greatly softened by the unwillingness to enforce them in practice by a system of penalties. Whether the reasons for this laxity were pedagogical theory, theological scruples or a fear of losing pupils does not affect the result. Almost from the beginning of Sunday schools, corporal punishment was condemned as inappropriate for the sabbath; similarly any form of punishment arising out of anger or impatience on the part of the teacher was condemned. That hated figure, the wicked and quick tempered day school-master of working-class autobiographies occurs with extreme rarity in remembrances of Sunday school. The pioneer days when Raikes could burn the fingers of a student on a stove, the managers of a midland school hoist a student up in a basket, or force a child to hold a Bible at arm's length for hours on end were looked back on, after the turn of the century, as regrettable instances of a benighted era. Punishments which induced a sense of shame in scholars were more common. Students might be forced to wear a sign saying 'LATE' or 'SWORE' or 'UNRULY'; they might be made to sit on a form in the center of the room; or they could be threatened with public expulsion during which they would be subjected to a stern lecture and then escorted to the door by a cadre of their former schoolmates.[129] But this too was frowned upon in

[126] *Rules of the Bristol Methodist Sunday School Society* (Bristol, 1831)

[127] *Evangelical Magazine* (1798) 17

[128] R. N. Collins *The Teachers' Companion designed to exhibit the principles of Sunday School Instruction and discipline* (1840) 196. He then proceeds to discuss the question for the next 58 pages

[129] Harris, ed. *Robert Raikes* ... (1887), *Centenary Volume of the Bank Str. Sunday School, Manchester* (1907); Collins *Teacher's Companion* ... p. 271; Pratt *Black Country* ... op. cit. p. 172

more enlightened circles, both Anglican and Dissenting. If virtue had to be rewarded at all—and there was some controversy about this—then these rewards should consist of books and tracts or of tickets which could be exchanged for such reading material; punishment should consist of confiscation of rewards or of with-holding them altogether. As this view of punishment became more widely accepted, however, it forced managers to give little gifts to all students so that there would be some thing that could be taken away in case of improper behavior. Although there is no way of knowing precisely how various schools operated their reward systems, the inspection of a large number of anniversary accounts leaves the impression that most children on the annual or quarterly feast day were likely to receive something or other. So, as an analogue of the world at large, this aspect of the Sunday school was probably not very effective.

Several other factors softened the impact of the teaching regime and overall discipline in creating suitable work habits. First, while the Sunday school as a whole was a large complex organization, each class was far smaller than that of the modern school. Ten students per teacher was an average, with many groups as small as five or six.[130] A child's experience of the school was therefore less of the large and ordered world of the school at large and more of the less regulated and more family-like atmosphere of the small class. Furthermore, although teachers were expected to follow a definite regime of instruction, ensuring that each student learned systematically and was accordingly tested on what he or she was meant to learn a number of factors made the teacher more like a parent than an impartial mentor. The most basic of these was the ambiguity of goals in the Sunday school; secular learning which could be tested, and even objective biblical knowledge, were only one part of the task. Conversion, a sense of seriousness, and love of God were far more important, at least in the eyes of those who wrote about schools. Teachers were therefore encouraged to develop a highly personal relationship with the children in their class, to get to know their homes, and most importantly to let love and kindness guide their dealings with their classes.[131] This of course conflicted with the far more impersonal role assigned to the instructor in his or her role as purveyor of knowledge alone. For example students who read poorly were nevertheless encouraged so that they would not come to dislike Bible reading; teachers were praised who, though deficient in learning, were highly religious; and the specific

[130]See Chapter 4, pp. 108–10

[131]See Chapter 1, pp. 17–18; 'treat them [students] like your family' advises the *Evangelical Review* (1812) 174

relationship a child had toward his parents, arising from the Evangelical ideal of the home, was taken as a model at least as often as the universalistic model of the pupil-teacher relationship in a modern school.

All these features of the school worked against the inculcation of suitable work discipline. They mitigated the rational, orderly, impersonal aspect of the Sunday school and indeed account for the widespread acceptance of the independent schools by communities which at the same time rejected those of the National and the British and Foreign Societies. On the other hand, the Sunday school was far more a part of the industrial world of large-scale enterprise than of the artisan-workshop era. If there was a certain mechanistic quality about their discipline and an aggressive commitment to the puritan virtues, it was not because of the school's specific relationship with factory owners or other managers of large-scale enterprise. It was because both the school and the factory were part of the same stage of historical development in which it was, and is, more difficult to maintain humanistic values.[132]

vii. The Inculcation of Values: Sunday Schools and the Use of Leisure

The role of Sunday schools in transforming working-class leisure was far more profound and pervasive than their part in political propaganda and repression. Their very being was dependent on the existence of leisure; they constituted an alternative way of spending Sunday and had to compete with other activities for the time of children who worked during the week. The child who spent his or her day in Sunday school was therefore taken out of the street or field, away from football, dice, hoop-spinning, or simply noisily playing about. The schools also sounded the alarm against leisure activities which, though not directly injurious to the cause of sabbath education, offended the aesthetic sensibilities, the ideas of what constituted civilized behavior, or simply the practical economic or political judgments of those who managed or taught in them. In place of the proscribed amusements, the Sunday school offered the 'rational pastimes', the outings, walks, railroad excursions, the teas and meetings which formed the core of respectable working-class leisure until the growth of large-scale public entertainment in the late nineteenth and early twentieth century. Neither in its negative nor its positive modes can the Sunday school

[132] This paragraph is based partly on the formulation of the relationship between schools and society in Ivan Illich *Deschooling Society* (1972)

be regarded simply as an agent of the bourgeoisie molding a recalcitrant working class into conformity with alien values. A certain puritanism, a passive if not an active rejection of the 'picaresque hedonism' of the lower orders in the eighteenth century, was too much a part of radical working-class culture in the nineteenth century for so unambiguous a class interpretation to be valid. Nevertheless, the ascendency of bourgeois sensibilities—the decline of bear-, bull-, and badger-baiting, the end of old style pugilism, the growth of the temperance movement, the decline of public violence, and not least the establishment of the Evangelical sabbath—were all part of the cultural underpinnings of the new industrial society which Sunday Schools helped to establish.

A certain amount of their hostility to leisure activities was not directed so much at the activities themselves as at their competition with school attendance. School directors were heirs to men like the Rev. William Grimshaw, the Evangelical perpetual curate of Haworth in the 1750s and 60s, who began by suppressing Sunday football and, when the children took to spending the sabbath on the moors playing various games, was said to have dressed up as an old woman in order to sneak up on them, take their names, and order them to appear before him.[133] When a report was brought in to Adam Rushton's Sunday school near Macclesfield during the late 1830s that certain students belonging to the school were playing football in an adjacent field during class hours, an expedition was organized, the ball captured, and the offending youths brought back into the school.[134] The children at the Haslingden Sunday School during the early nineteenth century were described in 1898 as 'semi-barbarous youths who were collected from the moors and vales' about town and who, 'previous to attending the school spent sabbath days in wrestling, fighting, bull-baiting, cock-fighting, and football playing'.[135] Most of these were objectionable in themselves, but football was included in the list primarily because it competed with the school.

Of course, practical, sabbatarian and moral motives easily became intertwined. Newcastle-upon-Tyne Sunday schools fought a long battle against Sunday races first because they happened on Sunday, second because racing and the gambling that went with it were sinful, and third because they cut into attendance by fifty per cent.[136] An element of self-interest also motivated the Stockport Sunday School managers in their efforts. A sabbath

[133] L. E. Elliot-Binns *The Evangelical Movement in the English Church* (1928) 27
[134] Rushton *My Life* ... p. 46
[135] John Stott *Notices* ... p. 110
[136] *SS Teachers' Magazine* (1833) col. 255

patrol was set up in 1807 to scour the fields around Stockport for children who might be playing there and to bring them to school for more suitable sabbath recreation. Two years later a complaint was lodged with the magistrates to close a fruit shop where scholars gathered, and a discussion some months afterward sought for ways to deal with the street corner society that was growing up around a sweetmeats shop. In 1817 the school's committee wrote to constables asking them to take some action against 'boys playing football and c. [etc.] on the outskirts of town'.[137]

But by the mid-1820s, in Stockport and elsewhere, excepting parts of London, the problem of other activities competing directly with Sunday schools had largely disappeared. It was no longer mentioned in minute books, nor was it discussed in the trade press of the Sunday school movement. The sheer numbers in Sunday school by 1832 suggest that while adults might still have lounged about on Sundays it had become customary in all strata of the working class to send the children to school on their day off from work. Sabbath patrol and the efforts of the magistracy cannot alone explain the success of Sunday schools in suppressing less desirable amusements. In fact, the drive to remake working-class leisure patterns had much deeper roots.

The social and political context of leisure changed rapidly after 1750 and with it came efforts to provide new alternative recreation. Conservative Evangelicals embraced the Sunday school as an instrument for gaining control over the free time of children, and through them that of their parents. The loss of control had resulted in dire consequences on two levels. First, it was widely believed that only sin and profligacy could come from working-class leisure. It was this way of thinking which prompted a farmer in one of Jonas Hanway's Sunday school lessons to tell children that 'you will be delivered from many evils you are otherwise exposed to' as he gave them specially designed tools that made it possible for them to begin work at an earlier age than hitherto possible.[138] The habits of idleness which uninstructed youth were thought to acquire would, as one sermon to the Sunday School Society put it, fill the land with villains, render property insecure, crowd our jails with felons, and bring poverty, distress and ruin upon families'.[139] Profligacy among the poor, another clergyman argued, was the result of a want of education and 'the abuse, through life, of the leisure afforded them by the institution of the

[137] Stockport SS *Minute Books* (29 March 1807); (19 March 1809); (3 March 1814); (10 February 1817)
[138] J. Hanway *Comprehensive View* p. 197
[139] W. Jesse *The Importance of Education* (1785) 6

Lord's day'.[140] But no grand theories were necessary to spur efforts to control working-class leisure.

Even if the crime rate *per capita* declined in the late eighteenth century, rapidly increasing population and the growth of productivity probably caused an increase in the absolute number of crimes committed. The theft and violence decried by contemporary observers had some 'basis in reality.'[141] Furthermore both modern studies on the weekly cycle of crime and contemporary descriptions of leisure activities suggest that much mischief might indeed have been done on the sabbath or other holidays. While working life became ever more tightly controlled, leisure, and particularly the free time of the young, became increasingly free at the end of the eighteenth century. The declining importance of apprenticeship and the reluctance or inability of masters to enforce the strict moral regulations of the indenture certificate undoubtedly contributed to petty crime and the nuisance potential of the young. No longer did masters insist that those under their control not ' ... play at cards, dice, tables, or other unlawful games ... not haunt taverns or play houses ... not commit fornication'.[142] One Birmingham magistrate blamed the increased crime of the 1820s on the abeyance of precisely these regulations.[143] Furthermore, the Church's traditional role in controlling Sunday activities was severely curtailed, in practice if not in theory, by the late eighteenth century and probably much earlier. It could not compel attendance nor could it enforce the canon which proscribed loitering near the church during services and gave the churchwardens power to remove idle persons. And even if the importance of these factors is exaggerated, it must not be forgotten that there were simply more people, and especially more young people, alive during the industrial revolution than ever before. Had there been no change in patterns of crime or mischief, there would still have been an increased number of such instances.[144]

Less than thirty years ago fifty per cent of all juvenile offences in England were committed during the leisure time provided by

[140] Rev. D. Turner *Hints* ... (1794) 44

[141] See J. J. Tobias *Crime and Industrial Society in the Nineteenth Century* (London 1967) Chapters 1–3, and J. M. Beattie 'The Pattern of Crime in England, 1660–1800 *Past and Present* No. 62 (February 1974) 47–95

[142] The proscribed activities are listed in more or less this form on most apprenticeship indentures. The wording here is taken from a candle maker's certificate from 1756 in the author's possession

[143] Sir John Eardley in *SC on Criminal Commitments and Convictions* (2nd Report) 1828 vi 545 , pp. 419 ff., esp. 445–6

[144] See Leon Radzinowicz *A History of English Criminal Law and its Administration from 1750* vol. 1 (1948) 399–427

Saturday and Sunday holidays.[145] In the eighteenth century it was widely believed that sabbath leisure led to crime and that the Sunday school, by filling those leisure hours, caused a commensurate reduction in illegal activities. One of the most publicized fruits of the Painswick, Glos., schools was that farmers and their servants could go to church without fear for their property and without posting a guard. While in former days 'even the most vigilant was plundered', property in the Sunday school era was safe.[146] The farmers in Hannah More's fictionalization of her Sunday school enterprises in Mendip were finally won for the cause when they were made aware of the increased safety of their orchards on Sundays.[147] In contributing to Sunday schools, wrote another early supporter, one was not only helping to save souls but also preventing sabbath day 'pilfering, stealing and depredation'.[148] While prior to the existence of Sunday schools the working classes were surly and insolent to their betters on the sabbath, after an education they were far more civil.

Undoubtedly, some of those who founded and worked for Sunday schools sought to control working-class leisure in order to control crime in general, and most particularly that crime committed in violation of the sabbath. But others, the great majority of the working men and women who taught in the schools, did so because they believed that leisure on the sabbath and at other free times should be well spent, either in preparing for the next life or in improving oneself for a happier and more prosperous earthly existence. For them the remaking of patterns of leisure was part of the culture of self-help, self-improvement, and, above all, respectability.

Sunday schools waged their battle for the control of children's leisure in three ways. First, through education as itself a morally regenerative enterprise; second, through the support of temperance and other reform campaigns; and third, through the provision of counter-recreation. Like religion, education was thought to have a transforming effect on all it touched. The recreations of the educated man, the man who could use his mind, would not be those of the ignorant; education changed man the beast to man the angel, or so it was thought. Rational amusement, made possible by literacy, was therefore touted from the pulpit and in the bourgeois and the working-class press. The Methodist bookseller, James Lackington, was one of the first to point out that Sunday schools

[145] Cyril Burt *The Young Delinquent* (1944) 159
[146] *Gentleman's Magazine* (1787) pt. 1, pp. 73–4
[147] H. More, *Works* . . . vol. 4, 361–90
[148] *The Good Effects of Sunday Schools* . . . introduction

would not only improve the ability of adults to contribute to science and, through the increase in book clubs, drive out ignorance and superstition, but would cause reading to take the place of idle hours mis-spent in a pub. This was all to the good, he added, since these developments could only increase the sale of books and the profits of booksellers.[149] The *Gentleman's Magazine* supported Lackington, and its correspondents generally defended the existence of a widespread working-class reading public when it came to be attacked some years later.[150] The Rev. Robert Hall, the famous Baptist preacher, argued that knowledge 'by multiplying the mental resources [has] a tendency to exalt the character, and, in some measure, to correct and subdue the taste for gross sensuality'. The poor man, Hall predicted, would find entertainment at home by reading and thus not be tempted to 'repair to the public house for that purpose'.[151] In fact, except for those early evangelical sermons which emphasized the role of Sunday schools in keeping the working class in its place, most pronouncements on Sunday education stressed its role in furthering the march of intellect.

The sentiments of the bourgeois pulpit that 'the educated would spend their leisure time in scientific pursuits rather than in low and vicious indolent occupations' was echoed in the working-class press.[152] Drink and the drinking place provided the focus of much working-class recreation, both in the town and the countryside, during the nineteenth century; and it was this form of recreation which came under the heaviest attack by Sunday schools. 'Extreme wickedness pervades this town at large,' proclaimed one early Sunday schools sermon, 'ale houses are crowded with the slaves of riot and drunkenness, whilst clammering and wantonness, strifes and envying mark the conduct, and disgrace the character of various orders of society.[153] 'The drunkenness, the debauchery, riot and confusion', noted a London sermon, would only be suppressed by religious instruction and, since this was lacking amongst the upper and middle classes who were consequently given to sin and depredation, it was particularly important that the gospel be spread to the poor. Sobriety, according to a Wesleyan spokesman, was one of the aims of Sunday schools; 'health of body, by means of temperance and action' was one of its

[149]James Lackington *Memoirs of the First Forty-Five Years of the Life of James Lackington . . . in a Series of Letters to a Friend* (1791) 386–91, esp. 389
[150]*Gentleman's Magazine* vol. 62, pt. 1 (1792) 208; vol. 71, pt. 1, (1801) 491–2; vol. 71, pt. 2, pp. 691, 1087–88
[151]Rev. Robert Hall *The Advantages of Knowledge to the Lower Classes* (1810) 4–5
[152]Rev. T. Allin *The Diffusion of Knowledge . . .* (1825) 16
[153]*Wigan Sunday School Society, Plan* (1785) vi

'principles and designs'.[154] The drunkard in Sunday school literature invariably came to a bad end, unless he was saved from the
abyss through the virtuous example of his or her child. His life,
it was usually pointed out, was a precarious one. In a typical story
two men are discussing a boast by one of them that he had thirty
or forty more years of life left to him, as evidenced by the fact that
he could drink three bottles of porter each day. Ah, says the other,
you may not live thirty hours; and, as expected, the next day the
porter drinker climbs a ladder while intoxicated, falls off, and dies.

But, while excess drinking was universally condemned, neither
Anglican nor Dissenting Sunday schools took a consistent stand on
the question of organized opposition to drink. In the late eighteenth
and early nineteenth centuries Sunday school teachers in
Manchester and the surrounding towns still went to the alehouse
during breaks in their schedule. Ale was the common beverage at
Sunday school meetings in much of the north until the 1840s.[155]
Much to the disgust of the *Northern Star*'s correspondent, children
were served beer and buns at a Sunday school celebration as late
as 1841; Macclesfield Church scholars were rewarded with drinks
of wine in 1848, and earlier in the century children in Bristol drank
their toasts in strong English ale.[156] All this, of course, did not go
unnoticed by temperance organizations. The *London Teetotaller*
claimed that in the Launceston Wesleyan Sunday School, forty-four
out of seventy-four students who could be traced were drunkards.[157]
Not so, replied a spokesman for the school; so outlandish an accu-
sation could only be made out of malice by two teachers who were
angry that students who had not signed an abstinence pledge
were allowed to remain enrolled. A split in the teetotal ranks
between long- and short-term pledge factions, and pro- and anti-
music factions, further complicated the issue.[158] The *London
Temperance Intelligencer* claimed that in a school near the Metropolis
91 out of 100 boys were known drunkards and someone else asserted
that 38 out of 65 children at another London school could be
similarly classified.[159]

Despite such accusations, individual Sunday schools and regional
Sunday school associations played a key part in the fight against

[154]Rev. T. Wood *Thoughts on Sunday Schools: Importance of Knowledge to the Lower
Classes of Society* (1815) 13–14
[155]J. Ward *Rise and Progress . . .* p. 85
[156]*Northern Star* (8 September 1838) 4; *Church of England Sunday School Magazine*
(1848–49) 284–5; *SS Repository* vol. 2 (1814) 31
[157]*SS Teachers' Magazine* (1846) 351
[158]Ibid. p. 447
[159]Ibid. p. 535; *Sunday School Magazine* (1839–40) 359

drink. 'Some of the most conspicuous of the famous and heroic band of Preston temperance advocates of the first period, were trained and fitted for their work in his Sunday school,' according to Joseph Livesey's biographer.[160] Teetotal Sunday schools were started in Bristol in 1834, Warrington in 1836, and Hayle in 1845: That vast youth temperance organization, the Band of Hope, was founded in 1847 by Sunday school workers.[161] 'Every little boy and girl should belong to a temperance society for this is the way both to do good and to get good,' suggested the widely circulated organ of the Manchester and Salford Sunday School Union.[162] The same magazine reported on a railroad outing by a thousand children during race week in Carlisle, when they were 'regaled in teetotal style with two large plum cakes and abundance of rich new milk'.[163] Birmingham Church of England Sunday school teachers went so far as to found a new sick society so that they would not have to belong to one which met in a pub.[164] Though not on so organized a basis, Sunday schools put their weight behind the suppression of all those activities traditionally associated with drink—animal sports like bear- and bull-baiting, badger and cock fights, prize fighting, gambling, and card playing—which, along with drinking itself, were the principal pub recreations. They also opposed cruelty to animals and indeed any manifestations of the baser human passions.

The Rev. Thomas Allin's sermon on the morally elevating aspects of knowledge, for example, digressed to praise Martin's bill for the curbing of cruelty to animals; the spirit of the bill was that of the Sunday school, he said. The *Teacher's Offering* featured stories on this theme. A lady who wept at sentimental novels but allowed her servant to bleed a turkey to death by slitting a small vessel under its tongue was condemned for cruelty and hypocrisy; the evil of blood sports was pointed out in a story of boys in New Hampshire who killed a bear only to discover that he had been their pet while still a cub. A good man, it was pointed out, followed the biblical maxim of being merciful to his animals; those who rob nests, beat dogs and such are rendered most like Satan, moral charity began with kindness to animals, etc.[165]

[160] J. Pearce, ed. *Life and Teachings* ... p. xxxvii
[161] P. T. Winskill *The Temperance Movement and its Workers* vol. 1 (1891) 118–19 and vol. 2, 191–200; *SS Teachers' Magazine* (1845) 341. See also p. 250 below
[162] *Sunday School Magazine* (1846) 124
[163] Ibid. p. 232
[164] *C. of E. SS Quarterly Magazine* (1848–49) 392
[165] Allin *The Diffusion* ... p. 32; *Teacher's Offering* (1841) 250; (1844) 117–22; (1850) 296; *SS Teachers' Magazine* (1848) 351–3; *The Salisbury Spelling Book* p. 28

The aesthetic revulsion against these activities and violent sports generally felt by the evangelical founders of Sunday schools is apparent in outbursts like that of the poet Cowper against a local Olney variety of hockey. Even Roman boys were not so delighted by the 'filthy aspersions' manifested in this game of 'dashing each other with mud, and the windows also'. 'It will be well if the Sunday school may civilize them to a taste for more refined amusements,' he concluded.[166] But even without such well-articulated objections there was clearly a widespread opposition among Sunday school workers against the drunkenness and brutality of traditional fairs, wakes or races and the violence of popular recreation generally. This was matched by a systematic attempt, through the development of counter-recreations, to replace the old with more acceptable new leisure time activities.

Raikes's famous attraction at Painswick was in fact a move to supplant a traditional church ale with all its 'drunkenness and every species of clamour, riot and disorder' by entertainment exhibiting to the vulgar 'the superior enjoyment to be derived from quietness, good order, and the exercise of that benevolence which Christianity peculiarly recommends'.[167] From Raikes's day onward Sunday schools were active in the provision of even more elaborate kinds of alternative attractions. On a relatively modest scale the Wesleyan Sunday school children in Bilston received a bun and some tea on the day of the yearly Newton wake in October; on 26 and 27 September in Uttoxeter when 'almost every sinful amusement [was] introduced for the purpose of alluring unguarded youth into the paths of folly and sin', the Sunday school teachers invited scholars 'to meet them ... and to regale them with plum cake [etc.] when also addresses suitable to the occasion [were] given and each child [was] presented with a book and tract'.[168] The 'annual folly fair' on Easter Monday in Blackburn was counteracted by a day of sports in the country, while in Newcastle the June races were met by a procession with brass bands followed by the inevitable treat and speeches from such 'respectable' working men as the temperance reformer Thomas Whittaker.[169] Some counter-attractions were even more explicitly designed to be of an 'improving' nature. On the third day of the races the children of the West Warwick Sunday schools were presented with

166 *The Letters of William Cowper* ed. J. G. Frazer vol. 2 (1912) 367

167 F. A. Hyett *Glimpses of the History of Painswick* (Gloucester, 1928) 50–1; *Gentleman's Magazine* vol. 57, pt. 1 (1787) 73–4

168 J. Freeman *Bilston Wesleyan Methodism* (Bilston, 1924) 125–6; *SS Teachers' Magazine* (1843) 24

169 *Sunday School Magazine* (1841) 145; *SS Teachers' Magazine* (1848) 333–4

a show, which included 'among the good things .... panoramic views, objets d'art and science, a galvanic battery [etc.]'[170] Anglican school children in Burton spent the evening of 5 January 1847, 'in a most happy manner, being highly entertained by the exhibition of the magic lantern'.[171]

Gradually, counter-attractions became larger and more elaborate. Offshoots of the famous Manchester Whit Walks, which began in 1802 to keep children from the Kersal Green races (scourge of all morality in all south Lancashire), included expeditions of more than thirty boats to Dunban park and treats for several days running.[172] In 1844 the Wigan Sunday School Union reported that 'in order to withdraw so large a number of young persons from the demoralizing fascination of the racecourse', they had organized an outing by rail to Bootle, near Liverpool, for some 4,000 children and teachers from the Wesleyan, Dissenting and Roman Catholic schools. Of 2,000 additional Anglican school children, 1,000 had gone by boat to the mineral springs at Whittle and 1,000 by rail to Fleetwood.[173]

Perhaps the richest of outings was offered by the Church schools of Macclesfield 'for the purpose of counteracting and destroying the evil effects produced on the youthful mind by frequenting the fair which is held about the festival of St Barnabas'. In 1843, 800 children and teachers went by special excursion train to Trentham Park, Staffordshire, home of the Duke of Sutherland. While some of the teachers were shown around the gardens, others led discussion groups among the girls; the boys amused themselves with 'the more noble game of cricket, while some solitary stragglers, it would seem, were admiring nature's scenery'. At various times during the day the children received pies and 'good fresh whole milk', and when they finally returned to Macclesfield, they received a bun and glass of British wine before being dismissed. Another Anglican school in Macclesfield and one in Hursfield made similar outings.[174] In most parts of England in the mid-nineteenth century the Sunday school anniversary or outing had, for the children at least, supplanted the traditional yearly feast. In Buckingham, Bedford and Oxford, the Sunday school tea drew the young away from the drunken Whitsuntide celebrations of the friendly societies; in mid-Cornwall Sunday school dances replaced those of the

---

[170] *Sunday School Magazine* (1846) 232

[171] *Staffordshire Advertiser* (9 January 1847) I owe this reference to David Philips

[172] *Sunday Schools 100 Years Ago* Bretherton Collection, Methodist Archive (Sarah/Ann, 3 June 1836)

[173] *SS Union Magazine* (1849) 222–3

[174] *C. of E. SS Quarterly Magazine* (1848–49) 284–5

traditional June Fair.[175] In all of the places already mentioned outings, treats and train rides supplanted visits to the races or fairs, or, at the very least, limited the attendance of children there.

Sunday schools were thus undoubtedly advocates of refinement and respectability. It is more difficult, however, to determine if they were therefore on the side of the middle classes against the working classes, or the side of counter-revolution against revolution. There were compelling tactical as well as ideological reasons that kept organized working-class politics out of the politics of moral reform. But the vices condemned by the Sunday school were almost as often condemned in the working-class press and in the writings of important spokesmen. A certain puritanism pervaded many of these writings, which suggests that the division in society between the decadent, pleasure-seeking and idle classes on the one hand and the upright, serious and hard-working classes on the other was as important in the minds of their authors as the imputed antagonism between a middle and a working class.[176]

In an article entitled 'A New Mode of Supporting the Revenue against the Sobriety of the Reformers', the editor of the *Black Dwarf* reported in 1819 that card playing had recently been permitted in Westminster public houses with full knowledge of the magistrates. This, it argued, encouraged drunkenness and gambling, while at the same time discouraging the reading of newspapers and discussion. The new freedom was therefore part of an anti-reform conspiracy. 'Paganism has again become the fashion of the day, as Bacchus and his votaries are called in to support the tottering system.'[177] In one satire Wooler hinted that as reformers turned to water, the liquor tax would be transferred to that beverage, while in another he suggested that the loyalists would turn to the bottle as radicals abhor excisable liquor.[178] Cooper twenty years later told his audience: 'Let the titled, who fatten on your toil, and yawn for idle ease and pleasure ... play at filthy cards, or gaming of any description.'[179] 'No entertainment is so cheap as reading,

---

[175] See Alan Howkins *Whitsun in 19-century Oxfordshire* Ruskin History Workshop pamphlet No. 8 (Oxford, 1973); Random checks in Buckinghamshire and Bedfordshire newspapers for Whitweek in the late 1830s and 1840s confirm Howkins' finding. For example see *Buckinghamshire Herald* (13 June 1840) or *Buckinghamshire Chronicle*, (24 June 1848). M. A. Courtenay 'Cornish Feasts and "Feasten Customs" ' in *Folklore Journal* vol. 4 (1886) 235

[176] See Brian Harrison *Drink ...* p. 33 and his 'Religion and Recreation in Nineteenth Century England' *Past and Present* no. 38 (1967) 105–25, esp. 121–2, for a similar hypothesis with respect to moral-reform movements

[177] Vol. 3 (1819) col. 852

[178] *Black Dwarf* vol. iv (1820) 139–142

[179] T. Cooper *Letters* op. cit. 'Knowledge is Power' p. 8

nor any pleasure so lasting,' pointed out another Chartist publication which in the same volume noted the enormous costs of the liquor trade and the fact that 'ninetenths of all those engaged in the accursed traffic ... are the deadly enemies to both your civil and religious liberties.'[180] The *Northern Star* described a bull and terrier fight as 'one of those disgraceful exhibitions'; prize fights were variously referred to as 'a brutal and unmanly exhibition [between] ... two fools', 'a disgraceful scene', and 'another of our wealthy and aristocratical displays of brutality and man-debasing exhibitions'.[181] For many Chartists as for those who worked in and supported Sunday schools the purpose of education was, as a speaker at the great radical meeting in Macclesfield, 6 October 1838 noted, to 'accustom the individual to seek his pleasure from things which afford it of the highest and most enduring description'.[182]

Of course, Sunday schools cannot be adduced to explain the general decline of fairs and wakes. Their demise was part of the slow death, already well under way in the eighteenth century, of the traditional order. Some festivals, like the London fairs, were suppressed by the magistracy; others, like the Cotswold games, were prohibited by acts of Parliament, a victim of overlarge crowds and new sensibilities. Religion generally and Sunday schools in particular were only one of the forces making for the new attitudes which rejected old pastimes.[183] Nevertheless, for three reasons the schools were instrumental in the process of reforming working-class leisure. They were part of a larger, systemic transformation of pre-industrial to industrial society. They offered a relatively refined form of leisure activity which many working-class men and women already embraced, at least for their children if not for themselves. And finally, their efforts by and large grew out of the community they sought to influence rather than being imposed on it from the outside.

But by helping to form cultural linkages between classes Sunday schools contributed to the stability of Victorian society and the success of a capitalist economy. There is no more telling comment on the politics of recreation than a report in the *Norwich News*

[180] Chartist Circular (26 June 1841) 388; (17 October 1840) 227; (3 October 1840) 219 ff.

[181] *Northern Star* (24 March 1838) 5; (21 April 1838) 5; (16 June 1838) 5; (6 February 1841) 5; and also (23 June 1838) 5

[182] *Northern Star* 'Report of the Great Radical Meeting in Macclesfield' (7 October 1838) 7

[183] See further, Robert W. Malcolmson *Popular Recreations in English Society, 1700–1850* (1973)

of 1846. Five thousand working-class children and three thousand spectators were taken by rail for a day at the sea:

> We are glad, too, to perceive in this and similar instances, evidence of the growing tendency in religion to associate itself with the innocent amusements and social enjoyment of the poor, and thus to promote a genial intercourse between all classes ... more has been done by modern evangelical religion to raise the scale of social recreation; and by breaking down the rigid barriers of caste, to bring high and low into happy harmony, than by all the well meant but quixotic antics of Young England ... Sunday school outings are better adapted to regenerate society, than the revival of the maypole and the antiquated rubbish of the Book of Sports.[184]

viii. CONCLUSIONS:

The repressive, middle-class dominated Sunday school of Hannah More or William Fox was a rarity by the early nineteenth century. Within two decades of their founding Sunday schools had become one strand of a uniquely working-class cultural constellation. In their literature and teaching they stressed moral and ethical as against overt social or political values. Honesty, orderliness, punctuality, hard work and refinement of manners and morals may all have been congruent with the industrial system and thus in the interest of the bourgeoisie but they were not therefore middle-class values. The great divisions in early nineteenth century society were not between the middle and the working classes but between the idle and the non-idle classes, between the rough and the respectable, between the religious and the non-religious. All of these divisions ran across class lines. The puritan ethic was therefore not the monopoly of the owners of capital; it was the ideology of those who worked as against those who did not. Sunday schools were effective in the transmission of certain values precisely because these values were those of the working-class men and women who taught in and supported the schools.

Furthermore, the life of the Sunday school mirrored an aspect of working-class life which has received short shrift from historians. In it the comparative strength of cohesive over disintegrative forces in society were reflected. The five years between 1838 and 1843 saw not only the publication of the People's Charter, the

[184] *SS Teachers' Magazine* (1846) 483–4

Newport risings and the Plug Riots but also a parade in Bolton of 12,000 working-class children celebrating the Queen's coronation.[185] In 1841 as Chartist agitation was growing, 1500 children in Blackburn marched out of the town on Easter Monday for a day of pleasure. 'Masters and servants, parents and children were united in the most innocent sports' under the sponsorship of the Sunday school.[186] The 'Age of the Chartists' witnessed scenes like that of the banker Joseph Gurney standing on the platform in Norwich waving to 5,000 Sunday school scholars as their train left the station. The children responded by singing 'The Fine Old English Gentleman' to the music of the band. [187]

[185] Rothwell *Memorials* ... p. 163
[186] *Sunday School Magazine* (1841) 146
[187] *SS Teachers' Magazine* (1846) 394–6

8. Conclusion

This book has argued that the Sunday school was largely the creation of the working-class community and as such deserves a place in its history; that it was the product of the infinite inventiveness and ingenuity of men and women who, under the most adverse conditions, created a culture of discipline, self-respect and improvement within which to wage the battle for social justice and political equality; and that the prism of the Sunday school reveals qualities and textures in working-class life absent from a vantage gained exclusively through the history of political struggle. The conclusions to previous chapters provide an outline of the argument which therefore need not be repeated here. Nevertheless, the overarching questions of the role played by education and religion in determining the relationship of the English working class to bourgeois society and to the new industrial order remain to be posed if not resolved. The Janus-like, profoundly ambiguous quality of both religion and education in the context of nineteenth-century England makes an unequivocal assessment of their social function at the same time tempting and impossible.

It is clear that a bourgeois world view triumphed in the nineteenth century largely through consent, not through force. The middle classes established a moral hegemony in England; their concept of reality 'diffused throughout society in all its institutional and private manifestations, informing with its spirit all taste, morality, customs, religious and political principles, and all social relations, particularly in their intellectual and moral connotation.'[1] and swept away both its working-class and its aristocratic competitors.

Literacy and the hunger for books, which Sunday schools helped

[1] G. A. Williams 'The Concept of "Egemonia" in the Thought of Antonio Gramsci: Some Notes on Interpretation' *Journal of the History of Ideas* vol. 21, 4 (Oct.—Dec. 1960) 587. Hegemony, it should be noted, is taken to be predominance gained by consent rather than force by one class over another

to produce, were a component of the psychological revolution which accompanied and made possible the industrial revolution. The printed word, it has been argued, opened the reader to a new range of goals, but more importantly to a new range of exploitation: 'The inner-directed man, open to 'reason' via print, often develops a character structure which drives him to work longer hours and to live on lower budgets of leisure and laxity than would have been deemed possible before. He can be driven because he is ready to drive himself.'[2] Literacy itself was an agency through which the working classes were driven or were taught to drive themselves to create wealth for their masters and to accept their values. Furthermore, the creation of a mass reading public made possible the manipulation of thoughts and opinions on a scale hitherto impossible. That long and, in a European context, unique experiment in which the upper orders invested considerable time and money in the education of the lower classes appeared finally to have borne fruit on the eve of the industrial revolution.

There is little doubt that literacy alters the personality structure of those who possess it in ways congruent with the requirements of industrial society; and furthermore, that during the late eighteenth and nineteenth centuries the printed word was frequently used as an agency of covert and on occasion of perfectly open indoctrination. But on balance the early enemies of Sunday schools who feared that the new institutions would create a generation of readers of seditious and corrupting books and newspapers were nearer the truth than those supporters who extolled the schools' counter-revolutionary virtues. Working-class radicalism was predicated on literacy. From the LCS to the Chartists the new politics were distinguished from mob action—that most common of earlier expressions of discontent—by its degree of organization, its articulateness, and its reliance on an educated audience to consume its pamphlets, broadsheets, and newspapers. As Chapter Six argued the world of learning, self-improvement and respectability symbolized by the Sunday school was intimately tied by personnel and spirit to the world of parliamentary reform, trade unionism, and the struggle for the Charter. Henry Solly's fictionalized biography of a Chartist opens with a group planning a meeting at the Sunday school.[3] And even the farm labourers arrested in the Kent Risings of 1838 had almost all been to Sunday school and were regular readers of religious books.[4] Men, like the minister of Bel-

[2] David Riesman *The Lonely Crowd* (New Haven, 1952) 91

[3] Henry Solly *James Woodford, Carpenter and Chartist* (1881)

[4] F. Liardet 'State of the Peasantry in the County of Kent' in Central Society of Education *Reports* vol. 3 (1839) 128

grave Chapel, Leeds, may have felt that Sunday schools constituted the formidable and impregnable pass through which working-class radicalism would not go, but, in fact, the centers of Sunday school activity were precisely those towns and cities most hospitable to radical and revolutionary politics in the period 1780–1850.[5] In short, for whatever reason it was offered, working-class education in the nineteenth century vindicated at any rate the less lurid fears of its reactionary opponents.

The counter-revolutionary effects of religion have been recited so often that they scarcely need be repeated. Its direct effects, it is argued, were to convince the poor that their station in life had been divinely ordained and therefore not open to change, and that in any case not this world but the next ought to be the concern of pious men. Indirectly, religion absorbed the psychological energies born of frustrated revolution; it contained the political fervor of the poor by providing it with a readily available alternative focus. Finally, the ideology of working-class politics, grounded as it was in scripture and in the tradition of Dissent, was inappropriate to the development of a revolutionary consciousness. Although capable of expressing a hatred of injustice and inequality, it was not up to articulating a more fundamental critique of society and, worse still, blocked a language which had just this capability. If one accepts Marx's notion that religion is 'the fantastic realization of the human being inasmuch as the human being possesses no true reality', and that the 'struggle against religion is therefore indirectly a struggle against the world whose spiritual aroma is religion', then the lack of such struggle implies an acceptance of the world as it is.[6] Religion, on this model, is by its very nature counter-revolutionary.

But, it is perfectly clear that the political role of religion varies over time and between cultures.[7] If, during the industrial revolution, the working classes became increasingly reluctant to attend worship on Sunday, participate in church life, or join a chapel congregation—all as yet unproven propositions—they did not therefore become estranged from all forms of religious expression. Charles Booth noted that in the 1890s London working men were great on all forms of discussion and that while any subject would suffice, '. . . religious subjects are the most popular; and after the organized debate is over, little groups of men remain, crowding

[5] Rev. Richard W. Hamilton *The Institutions of Popular Education* (Leeds, 2nd ed. 1846) 52

[6] From the *Critique of Hegel's Philosophy of Right* in T. B. Bottomore and M. Rubel, eds. *Selected Writings on Sociology and Social Philosophy* (1956) 26

[7] Guenter Lewy *Religion and Revolution* (Oxford, 1974)

in, all heads pushed forward and ears strained ... Neither intelligence nor interest is lacking; but neither intelligence nor interest leads to public worship.'[8] Sunday schools provided a new and unprecedentedly wide sphere of lay activity within both Anglicanism and Non-conformity. They formed part of a distinct religious subculture on the periphery of Church or chapel based religion but organizationally and in style of operation apart from it. Furthermore, working-class parents chose to send their children— over 2,000,000 in 1851—to schools whose curriculum was based on scripture. Their motives were doubtless complex but they certainly included a desire to impart at least some measure of religious upbringing. A firm grounding in scripture was the accepted norm and formed the basis for much of the imagery of the radical press and the rhetoric of broadsheets and meetings. ·.

Working-class politics was largely the creation of people steeped in religion and the Bible. Eschatology need not lead to quietism; it could and did inspire a vision of a better, even radically different, earthly reality. Thomas Spence, whose followers made up the left wing radical politics in the 1810s denounced religion as a delusion but at the same time wrote and thought in the metaphors of the Bible. The judgment of the dead and the glory of the New Jerusalem in Revelations (Chapter 21) were interpreted as applying solely 'to the nations, great and small, leagured with anti-Christ ... and to the restoration of the New Jerusalem state of happiness on earth; and not in heaven'. The biblical Rechabites were cited because of their opposition to private property and the fall of Judas attributed to the wickedness of a market in land.[9] As an opponent of Sunday schools and advocate of secular education put it in a report on the Kentish peasant risings, 'The narratives and lessons contained in the sacred writings may be turned, as they often have been, not merely into sources of error, but into authorities for wrong.'[10] The late disturbances, he added, were undoubtedly of a religious nature. While Jabez Bunting was inveighing against revolutionaries and radicals, the great Chartist meeting at Peep Green on Whit Monday 1839 opened with one of Wesley's hymns:

> Peace doubting heart! my God's I am;
> Who formed me man forbids my fear

[8] Charles Booth *Life and Labour of the People in London: Third Series, Religious Influences, Vol.* 1 (1902) 87–8

[9] T. M. Parssinen 'Thomas Spence and the Origins of English Land Nationalization' *Journal of the History of Ideas* vol. 34, no. 1, 139

[10] Liardet, Central Society of Education *Reports* vol. 3 (1839) 129

> The Lord has called me by my name,
> The Lord protects me, for ever near. [11]

The condemned Luddites marched to the scaffold singing:

> Behold the Saviour of mankind
> Nailed to the shameful tree!
> How vast the love that him inclined
> To bleed and die for me.[12]

The working-class reader of the *Black Dwarf* understood what Wooler was trying to say when he compared the attitude of the Anglican priesthood to that of Caiaphas and the high priests against Jesus, and the Tory and the Whig parties to the Sadducees and Pharisees.[13] That a radical poster beginning with 'Abolish Church Rates' could also include '"No prohibitionary bread laws" Gen. 1:29' and '"No prohibitionary meat laws" Gen. 9:3' is further testimony to the depth of biblical culture among the working class.[14] If it is true that 'For every socialist created by *Das Kapital*, a thousand have been created by the Bible', then, far from being an agency of repression, Sunday schools were a spring which nourished the embryonic labor movement.[15] Protestant Christianity is intrinsically neither revolutionary nor oppressive; but in nineteenth-century England it provided the language of radicalism.

The period 1780–1850 witnessed the birth of a working-class culture that was deeply rooted in that ethic of education, religion and respectability which was embodied in the Sunday school. English working-class politics lacked a revolutionary ideology, a rhetoric of 1789 less because of religious education than because England did not experience a '1789'. And this latter fact is due to the stability of English society and the cohesion of its ruling class and not to the failure of ideology taken as an independent variable. The religious, educational and social institutions of the working class must be seen as significant cultural achievements in their own right and not merely as spurs or restraints in the development of revolutionary politics. Sunday schools were largely a creation of the community they served and 'helped to keep the soul alive in a population living under conditions that degrade the mind'.[16]

---

[11] Frank Peel *The Rising of the Luddites* (3rd ed. 1895; Cass reprint, 1963) 263

[12] Ibid. p. 318

[13] *Black Dwarf* vol. 3 (1819) 235; vol. 11 (1823) 590–4

[14] Poster 'Some Principles of Dudley Radicalism' reprinted in G. Barnsby, *Dudley* . . . p. 15

[15] Keith Hutchinson *Labour in Politics* (1925) 9

[16] J. L. and Barbara Hammond *The Town Labourer* 1760–1832 (1917) 248

Epilogue

The history of Sunday schools did not end in 1850. On the contrary enrolments grew until well into the twentieth century; an entourage of auxiliary organizations and a plethora of new publications came into being between the middle of the century and World War I. Statistics of growth belied fears of men like Bishop Wilberforce who in 1868 thought that the increased availability of day schooling and the erosion of religion among the working classes would spell disaster for Sunday schools.[1]

Table 21:[2] *Sunday school enrolments, density and religious affiliation distinguishing between Anglican and others for Great Britain 1851–1961*

Year	No. of Students	Percentage of population in England, Scotland and Wales enrolled in Sunday Schools	Percentage of students in C. of E. Schools
1851	2,614,274	13	36
1881	5,762,038	19	39
1901	5,952,431	16	39
1906	6,178,827	16	39
1911	6,129,496	15	40
1916	5,572,194	13	39
1921	5,256,052	12	38
1931	4,823,666	11	37
1941	3,565,786	8	40
1951	3,047,794	6	37
1961	2,547,026	5	41

[1] Samuel Wilberforce 'Our Sunday Schools and How to Use Them' in *Good Works* (1868) 260–63

[2] In order to insure compatibility of various statistical sources from 1851 to 1961, it was necessary to consider all of Great Britain rather than just England. However, the most significant indicator of Sunday school popularity, the enrolment density, is for 1851 and 1881 roughly the same whether we consider England alone, England

As Table 21 shows, Sunday school enrolment continued to grow until the eve of World War I; it then began to decline and by 1950 had sunk to where it had stood a century earlier. The proportion of the population attending Sunday school, however, reached its peak earlier, probably during the 1880s. It declined to the 1850 level before the Great War and by 1930 was roughly the same as it had been in 1833. The reasons for the growth and decline of Sunday schools in the second half of the nineteenth and in the early twentieth centuries, like those for the stagnation of the growth rate of Dissent or for cycles in religious practice generally, remain obscure. They are probably not linked directly to the fate of organized religion or to the rejection by parents of a scriptural education. There was still widespread support for 'the notion of Sunday school attendence' and indeed even in 1957, 76 per cent of those over the age of thirty had at some time attended Sunday school.[3] Furthermore, while in the first half of the nineteenth century the growth of enrolment was matched by the explosive growth of Non-conformity and by the less easily quantifiable revivification of Anglicanism on the parish level, the two phenomena were less clearly related after 1850. Dissent in any case achieved its greatest proportional hold on the population in the 1840s while the proportion of the population in Non-conformist and indeed in all Sunday schools increased dramatically for at least four more decades.[4] The likeliest explanation for the steady decline in enrolment *per capita* is that the period of attendance by the twentieth century had become increasingly short. Rather than remain in Sunday school to engage in sports, youth group activities, or some other form of recreation, young

and Wales, or England, Wales, and Scotland. That is, in 1851 all three densities are within .5 per cent of 13 per cent; for 1881 all are within .9 per cent of 19.3 per cent. For enrolments in England and Wales in 1851 see *Census: Education* ... 1852–3 [1692] XC. p. clxix; for Scotland in 1851 see *Report and Tables on Religious Worship and Education in Scotland* 1854 [1764] LIX, 545. For 1881 enrolments see Fountain J. Hartley *The Sunday School Army; its Position and Progress* (1884) 6–7. Enrolments for 1901 to 1961 were taken from Robert Currie and Alan Gilbert 'Religion' in A. H. Halsey, ed. *Trends in British Society Since 1900* (London 1972). Population for non-census years were arrived at by linear interpolation. Since some denominations did not report Sunday school enrolments for each of the years under study, estimates of enrolments were made by multiplying the denomination's membership in the year or years in question by the membership to Sunday school enrolment ratio for that denomination during the nearest year for which data on Sunday schools are available. So for example, since the Congregational Church of England and Wales did not report enrolments in 1926, church membership for that year was multiplied by 1.36, number of Sunday school scholars per church member in 1921, to arrive at an estimate of enrolment

[3] David Martin *A Sociology of English Religion* (New York, 1967) 42
[4] See A. Gilbert 'Growth of Dissent ...' pp. 38–47

people joined the Boy Scouts or Girl Guides, participated in school directed games, went to the movies or to professional sports matches. As each pupil's stay in Sunday school grew shorter, the proportion of the population on school rolls declined. By 1960, however, the very idea of religious education may finally have been in decline; as against 76 per cent of those over thirty only 61 per cent of those under that age in 1957 had ever attended a Sunday school.[5] Furthermore, those forces which weakened the moral and political force of organized Non-conformity in the late nineteenth century undoubtedly affected Sunday school activities as well. Clearly, an understanding of these complex phenomena requires a level of analysis too profound for this short epilogue. I want simply to suggest that the development of Sunday schools in the period after 1850 must be seen against a broad background of secular change and not simply as a response to religious factors taken as independent variables.

An elderly observer in 1890 would have found the Sunday schools of that year similar to those of his youth in at least one respect. They were still largely the province of the working classes. 'There is a notion getting current in these days of respectability,' argued one commentator in 1856, that Sunday schools are only for the poor; but on the contrary, 'they are for all classes of the community.' Be that as it may, in 1862 the World Sunday School Convention was reminded of the necessity of extending Sunday school education to children of the upper classes and the Anglican Sunday School Institute in the same year stated that Sunday schools at their best would accept all 'infant objects' and not just those of the poor. But in the 1890s a broad social base was still in the realm of the ideal; family religion remained the norm among the higher ranks of society and Sunday schools continued to be essentially working-class institutions.[6]

In many respects, however, the Sunday school of the late nineteenth century was different from that of the period examined in this book. Sir Charles Reed may have spoken too hastily when he told the Congregational Union in 1860 that 'we have done with the drudgery of secular teaching'. Young and not so young men still flocked to the Sunday writing organized by men like W. H. White, the radical Birmingham councillor. They came to these schools, suggested White, so that they could learn to write letters

[5] Martin *Sociology* ... p. 42

[6] Charles Messent *The Autobiography of a Sunday School Teacher* (1856) 212; Groser *A Hundred Years' Work* ... pp. 64–5; *Church of England Sunday School Quarterly Magazine* (July, 1862) 279

and so get better jobs; religion, as he put it, 'got thrown in'.[7] But, except for night classes and special sessions of various sorts for adults regular secular education vanished from the Sunday school by the 1870s.

A plethora of alternative activities took its place. The ideal Sunday school of the 1870s would have contained scholars from three to eighty; it would have contrary to reality 'know[n] no caste, but br[ought] rich and poor into close fellowship'. In addition to religious education it would have sponsored a Christian Endeavour Society, a Band of Hope, a branch of the International Bible Reading Association, recreational evening classes and lantern lectures, gym, cricket, swimming and cycling clubs, class teas, picnics, etc. It would have been affiliated with a Union or Institute which would provide libraries, training schools, and improvement societies for teachers.[8]

In fact, many of these ideals were realized. While both rich and poor did not flock into the schools, older and younger students were in far greater prominence than they had been before. In 1850 it was estimated that about 20 per cent of the students were either infants or over fifteen; by 1890 the Union reported that 21 per cent of its students were in the senior and 22 per cent in the infant division.[9] In the last fifteen years, noted William Groser in 1909, the primary department of the Union grew 34 per cent, the senior 37 per cent and the intermediates only 5 per cent.[10] And there is no reason to suppose that Anglican figures are different. Furthermore, many new auxilliary organizations found roots in the Sunday school. In 1883, for example, the Boys Brigade, a scout-like, militaristic organization for Sunday school scholars between twelve and seventeen was founded for 'the advancement of Christ's kingdom among Boys, and the promotion of habits of reverence, discipline, and self-respect, and all that tends toward a true Christian manliness'. By 1888 the Brigade had 230 companies, 800 officers and 11,000 boys in Great Britain. Ambulance instruction was given in some battalions, company Bible classes were conducted in a military manner and, in general, the Brigade fostered the traits of working-class jingoism. Presumably the Sunday School Union's new magazine *Boys of Our Empire* was designed to further encourage imperial

[7] Charles E. B. Reed *Memoir of Sir Charles Reed* (1883) 42; W. H. White *The Development of the Sunday School System in the Direction of Adult Education* (1886) 6–9

[8] *My Ideal Sunday School: Prize Essays Collected by the Sunday School Union* (1894), see the essay by Alfred Whitby, a Baptist from Bridgewater; for a comparable Anglican text see Rev. R. Adam MA, rector of St. Stephens, Hulme, *Handbook for Sunday Schools* (Manchester, 1871)

[9] SS Union *Annual Report* (Jan. 1891)

[10] William H. Groser *Some Present Day Hinderance to Sunday School Progress* (1909) 7

thinking among the lower orders while at the same time replacing the 'trash serials' so readily available to the young.[11]

Temperance made great inroads into the Sunday school in the later nineteenth century. Although the Band of Hope began in 1839, individual schools, the Union and the Institute were slow to affiliate with the temperance cause. In 1862 the World Sunday School Convention meeting in London received without comment a memorial from the representatives of the Total Abstinence Society.[12] Even in 1893 a representative of the Church of England Temperance Society could still complain that Anglican schools were not as enthusiastic about the Band of Hope as they might be because teachers failed to understand the benefits that would result from affiliation and in any case, were often not as sympathetic to the total abstinence cause as might be hoped.[13] Nevertheless, in 1874 the Union did pass a resolution declaring that a Band of Hope should wherever possible be incorporated into the Sunday school association; and by 1890 some 70 per cent of the Union's scholars, almost a million in number, were indeed members. There were another million members belonging to Anglican or Methodist Sunday Schools, so that total membership by 1890 stood at around 2,000,000.[14] The temperance cause and the Sunday school, were, by the end of the century, firmly allied.

Both the Union and the Institute expanded their activities dramatically during the second half of the nineteenth century. The libraries, teacher training programs, outings, tea meetings, and such grew in size and number. As secular instruction disappeared from Sunday schools, religious instruction became more systematic. Both the Union and Institute as well as newer denominational ones like the Primitive Methodist Sunday School Union founded in 1874 published hundreds of graded lesson plans, courses of study on biblical geography and history, readings for every day of the week or every Sunday, and books on teaching technique. The care which in the decades before had been lavished on guides for the use of alphabet books was now bestowed on works like *The Blackboard in the Sunday School* or *The Chart System of Teaching Sunday School Lessons.* Magazines associated with Sunday Schools multiplied with the Church, the Baptists, Presbyterians, Wesleyan and Primitive Methodists, and the Union adding publications for

---

[11] William A. Smith *The Story of the Boys' Brigade* (Glasgow, 1888) esp. p. 2–4; Groser *Hundred Years' Work* ... pp. 141–2

[12] Groser ibid. p. 64

[13] H. F. Clarke *The Sunday School in Relation to the Band of Hope* (Church of England Temperance Publication Dept. 1893)

[14] Groser *Hundred Years'* ... p. 85; Winskill *Temperance Movement* ... vol. ii, p. 199

students and teachers to those already mentioned in Chapter Four. Some of these were devoted to purely devotional or practical 'how to do it' sorts of subjects. Others like the *Church of England Monthly Magazine for Teachers* reflected the heightened concern of Englishmen for their empire by publishing series upon series of articles on Eastern education, oriental manners, the Arabs and similar subjects. Magazines addressed themselves to the conflicts between science and the Bible and in general to the problems of organized religion in a secular age.[15] The Union expanded its activities into widely divergent areas from Hebrew and Greek classes for teachers to what amounted to a welfare system for the Sunday school community. Between 1886 and 1903, 19,000 children were taken to their Country Homes; the new Home by the Sea built in 1899 received 1200 children during the 1902 and 1903 season. A children's convalescent home begun in 1894 accomodated 250 patients each year and a Home of Rest for Lady Teachers built in the country in 1895 welcomes about 400 urban teachers annually.[16]

There is of course much more that could be told regarding Sunday schools after 1850. This epilogue merely suggests that while a part of the story ends at the middle of the nineteenth century, another strand continues and grows up to the First World War. Indeed a rosy glow seemed to surround the Sunday school in the second half of the century; it was a symbol of English voluntarism, of the ability to muddle through successfully, of the virtues of self-help and of the hopes for upward social mobility. It shared in that sense of goodness which suffused Gladstonian liberalism. The final decline of Sunday schools after the First World War might stand as symbol for the bankruptcy of old ideals and the advent of new ones that replace them.

[15] See for example, *C of E Monthly Magazine for Teachers* vol. 3 (1859) or *C of E SS Quarterly Magazine* (July, 1863) 221

[16] Groser *Hundred Years'* ... pp. 167–9

Appendix 1. Tables 22–4

Table 22: *Examples of working-class founders of sunday schools, 1780–1812* [1]

Date	Name	Place	Occupation or circumstances
*c.*1780	John Moore	nr. Leicester	framework knitter
	Benjamin Underwood	Cotswolds	farm worker
	James Hey	Bolton	bobbin winder
	John Lancaster	Manchester	shoemaker
	Benjamin Barber	Bradwell, Derbyshire	'a poor man'
	William King	Dursley, Glos.	woollen card maker
	William Hallam	Nottingham	framework knitter
*c.*1784	Mr Harris	Taunton	gardener
	John Pounds	Portsmouth	shoemaker
	James Hamilton	Rochdale	tin plate worker
	John & William Tierney	Sheepscomb, Glos.	weavers in a mill

[1] For Moore and Hallam see J. Blackner *The History of Nottingham* (Nottingham, 1815) 127–8; for Hey and King see note p. 24; for Lancaster see *Manchester Guardian* 10 Nov. 1879; for Barber see Seth Evans *Bradwell: Ancient and Modern* (Chesterfield, 1912) 85; for Benjamin Underwood see C. Northcott *For Britain's Children* (1935) 11; for Harris see Joshua Toulmin, DD *The History of Taunton* (Taunton new ed. 1822) 594; for John Pounds see W. H. Watson *The First Fifty Years of the Sunday School Union* (Southport, 1873) 50; for Hamilton see John Ashworth *Strange Tales from Humble Life* (4th series, Manchester 1870) 251; for the Tierneys see F. A. Hyett *Glimpses of the History of Painswick, Glouchester* (Gloucester, 1928) 82; for the man in Blackburn see Rev. John Ward *The Rise and Progress of Wesleyan Methodism in Blackburn* (Blackburn, 1871) 34; for Baldwin see C. Deane Little *Our Old School* (Wigan, 1933) 17; for James Bent see Rev. Allan Spencer *The History of Methodism in Daveyhulme* (Manchester, 1898) 40; for Riding see *125th Anniversary History of the Ardwick, Manchester, Sunday School* (1911) 2; for Noble see Thomas Whitehead *History of the Dales Congregational Churches* (Keighley, 1930) 166; for Lough see

Date	Name	Place	Occupation or circumstances
1785	John Baldwin	Wigan	pewter worker
	James Bent	Daveyhulme, Cheshire	weaver
1786	anon.	Blackburn	three poor men
	John Riding	Ardwick	handloom weaver
1787	Thomas Noble	Newton in Rowlands, Yorks.	blacksmith
	Simon Lough	nr. Newcastle-on-Tyne	labourer
c.1790	Patience Steward	Mendip, Som.	farm servant
	Thomas Cranfield	London	tailor
	Thomas Broadbent et al.	Stalybridge	'a poor, illiterate man with some friends'
	William Emerson	Braithwaite, Yorks. WR.	'humble but zealous'
1791	John Lupton	York	linen weaver
	Thomas Wilkes	Wolverhampton	'illiterate who learned to write to help with starting the school'
1794	James Jones	Bicester	labourer
1798	William Ranyard, John Scott, Joseph Cannon & Peter Pratt	Kingston, Surrey Trowbridge	tallow chandler, shoemaker, ferrier & haberdasher owner of a pickings shop
1799	anon.		
pre-1800	Mrs Brookes	Bilston	wife of a tailor
	James Weston	Walworth etc., Kent	cooper
	Mr Tory	Southhold Yorks. WR.	bombardier

W. Walters *Newcastle Union* ... pp. 88–90; for Steward see More *Mendip Annals* op. cit. p. 28; for Cranfield see his obtuary in *Sunday School Teachers' Magazine and Journal of Education*, new ser. vol. 10 (1839) 10–13; for Broadbent see ibid. new ser. vol. 16 (1845) 365–7; for Emerson see Anthony Steele *History of Methodism in Barnard Castle in the Dales Circuit* (1857) 209; for Lupton see John Lyth *Glimpses of Early Methodism in York* (York, 1885) 171; for Wilkes see Alfred C. Pratt *Black Country Methodism* (1891) 27–8; for Jones see John Dunkin *The History and Antiquities of Bicester* (Bicester, 1816) 114; for Ranyard *et al.* see McLellan 'Educational Activities ...' p. 69; for Trowbridge see *Sunday School Teachers' Magazine* new ser. vol. 18 (1847) 143; for Tory see J. Norton Dicksons *Kirkgate Chapel, Bradford, and its Associations with Methodism* (Bradford, 1903) 62; for the colliers and forge workers see Society for Bettering the Condition of the Poor *Reports* vol. 4, 169–72 and 20; for Davalier and Amos see J. Sturdy *Our Local SS* pp. 18–19; for Littlewood see H. W. Baker *The Story of Methodism in Caton* (Lancaster, 1936) 46; for William Smith see John S. Broad *History of the Origins and Progress of Sunday Schools in Bristol* (Bristol, 1816) 15; for Weston see *The Union Magazine* vol. 2 (1845) 1–5; *Sunday School Teachers' Magazine* new ser. vol. 10 (1839) 42; for Rogers see Eliott *Shropshire Congregationalism* ... p. 50; for Hunter see Walters ibid. p. 232

Date	Name	Place	Occupation or circumstances
	16 anon. men	Gateshead, Yorks.	colliers
	10 anon. men	Kirkstall, Yorks.	forge workers
	Peter Cavalier	Whitby	cabinet maker
1800	James Amos	Whitby	baker
1804	Thomas Littlewood	Vale of Lune, Lancs.	workman
	William Smith	Bristol	servant in linen warehouse
c.1805	anon.	Stowey, Somerset	'a small group of humble people out of harmony with the new clergyman of the parish'
1809	Martha Rogers	Craigforda, Salop	wood ranger's daughter
1812	George Hunter	High Felling, Durham	pit man

Table 23:[2] *The Sunday school periodical press*

a. Magazines for Students

Date	Title
1. 1805	*Youth's Magazine and Evangelical Miscellany*
2. 1815	*Sunday School Child's Repository*
3. 1817	*The Youth's Instructor and Guardian*
4. 1820	*Penny Magazine for Children*
5. 1820	*Friendly Visitor*
6. 1821	*Sunday Scholar's Magazine*; or *Monthly Reward Book*
7. 1821	*The Child's Magazine*

[2]Part a: Egoff *Children's Periodicals* pp. 28–31, is far from a complete list. She gives numbers 1, 5–6, 15, 17, 24, 35–36, 40–42. Numbers 16, 28, 30–31, 34, and 36 are misdated in her list. For number 2 and number 22, see Groser *One Hundred Years*, . . . pp. 140–41; for number 3, see copy in John Rylands Library, Manchester, Hobart Collection. For number 4, see Watson *History*, op. cit. p. 37; for 8 and 12, 14 and 16, see *Eclectic Review* new ser. vol. 21 (1824) 476; for numbers 7, 9–11, and 19 see Rice *The Sunday School Movement* . . . ; number 13, see *Primitive Methodist Magazine* vol. 5 (1824) 94–5; number 18, see *Union Catalogue of Periodicals* number 20, see *Baptist Magazine* vol. 19 (1827) 22; for numbers 25–26, see *The Revivalist* vol. 7 (1838) 70, 420, and for 26 also *SS Teachers' Magazine* vol. 14 (1843) col. 887–90; for number 21 and 23, see St. John *Catalogue of the Osborn Collection* . . . ; for number 27, see *Methodist New Connexion Magazine* vol. 43 (1840) 71. British Museum has entire set; for number 28, see advertisement in January 1841 issue of *Sunday School Magazine* vol. 3, 3rd series; for number 29, see *Sunday School Magazine* (April 1841) advertisement; for numbers 30–31, see *Union Catalogue*. Egoff misdates these; for numbers 32–33, see copies in the Bodleian; for number 39, see P. *Winskill The Temperance Movement and its Workers* vol. 3 (1891–2) 2

Part b: see *Union Catalogue* for all except 6–9 which are given in *SS Teachers' Magazine* new ser. vol. 14 (1843) col. 887–90

Date	Title
8. 1823	*Teacher's Offering; or Sunday School Monthly Visitor*
9. 1824	*The Scholars' Magazine and Juvenile Miscellany* (ed. by T. Albat, Harley: Staffordshire)
10. 1824	*Wesleyan Sunday-School Magazine*
11. 1824	*The School Miscellany*
12. 1824 (?)	*Tract Magazine for Children*
13. 1824	*Primitive Methodist Children's Magazine*
14. 1824	*Gospel Tract Magazine*
15. 1824	*Child's Companion; or, Sunday-Scholar's Reward*
16. 1824	*Children's Friend*
17. 1824	*Child's Magazine and Sunday-Scholar's Companion*
18. 1825	*Sunday Scholar's Magazine and Juvenile Miscellany*
19. 1825	*The Religious Instructor or Church of England Sunday School Magazine*
20. 1827	*Baptist Children's Magazine*
21. 1827	*The Infant Scholar's Magazine*
22. 1831	*Child's Own Book*
23. 1832	*Child's Own Magazine*
24. 1833	*Christian Child's Faithful Friend*
25. 1837	*Sunday Scholar's Annual and Parent's Offering*
26. 1838	*Sunday Scholar's Remembrancer*
27. 1839	*The Missionary Repository for Youth and Sunday Scholar's Book of Missions*
28. 1841	*The Sunday Scholar*
29. 1841	*The Child's Own Book* (annual)
30. 1841	*Child's Bethel Flag*
31. 1842	*Church Missionary Juvenile Instructor*
32. 1842	*Independent Magazine*
33. 1844	*Teacher's Visitor*
34. 1844	*Wesleyan Juvenile Offering*
35. 1844	*Juvenile Rechabite Magazine*
36. 1844	*Juvenile Missionary Magazine*
37. 1845	*The Sunday School Visitor and Magazine for Families*
38. 1846	*Early Days: or, the Wesleyan Scholar's Guide*
39. 1847	*Sunday School Temperance Magazine*
40. 1847	*Church of England Sunday Scholar's Magazine*
41. 1848	*Bible Class Magazine*
42. 1848	*Sunday School Penny Magazine*

b. Magazines for Teachers

Date	Title
1. 1813	*Sunday School Repository; or, Teachers' Magazine* (became *Teachers' Magazine and Journal of Education* in 1831)
2. 1818	*The London Christian Instructor*
3. 1829	*Home Missionary Register and Teacher's Magazine*
4. 1839 (?)	*The Sunday School Magazine and Journal of Christian Instruction*; (3rd series begins 1839 but no earlier volume is traceable)
5. 1843	*Teacher's Penny Magazine*

Date	Title
6. 1843 (?)	*Coventry Sunday School Union Magazine*
7. 1843 (?)	*Church of England Sunday School Union Magazine*
8. 1843 (?)	*British and American Teacher's Magazine*
9. 1843 (?)	*Lesson System Magazine for Sunday School Teachers*
10. 1843	*Teacher's Manual* (Anglican)
11. 1844	*Sunday School Union Magazine*
12. 1848	*Church of England Sunday School Quarterly Magazine*

Table 24 :[3] *Publishing account of the Sunday School Union*

Year	Spelling book, pts. 1–4 (x1000)	Other Reading Texts (x1000)	Math. and Grammar	Total Texts sold (x1000)	Total whole-sale value of stock sold (£)
1821	—	—	—	—	1,300
1822	—	—	—	—	1,568
1823	—	—	—	—	1,744
1824	305	48	2,750	380	2,964
1825	242	64	2,000	308	4,330
1826	198	19	3,000	220	4,808
1827	192	31	2,500	248	—
1828	230	45	3,150	278	6,043
1829	188	82	4,500	238	5,024
1830	172	130	—	302	—
1831	203	140	2,000	345	—
1832	132	125	—	257	7,719
1833	153	118	5,000	276	7,030
1834	160	219	5,000	384	7,442
1835	199	335	—	534	7,621
1836	226	264	12,000	502	7,897
1837	89	126	10,000	225	9,074
1838	270	194	—	464	—
1839	196	319	5,000	520	8,914
1840	156	178	15,000	349	—
1841	221	224	7,000	452	9,140
1842	126	222	15,000	363	9,554

[3] Calculated from the *Minutes of the Committee of the Sunday School Union at the Depot* vols. 1–4, uncatalogued MS kept in the offices of the National Council for Christian Education, Redhill Surrey; for value of sales 1821 to 1826 see the letter of resignation from John A. Brown, secretary of the depot in *Minute Books*, vol. 1, 20 Oct. 1826. Dashes indicated that no information was available. To calculate the total wholesale value of stock from 1821 to 1850 I estimated values for years during which no information was available by using the value of sales from the closest earlier year for which there was evidence. Since sales figures grew consistently this practice underestimates the total value of stock sold

Year	Spelling book, pts. 1–4 (x1000)	Other Reading Texts (x1000)	Math. and Grammar	Total Texts sold (x1000)	Total whole-sale value of stock sold (£)
1843	174	185	13,000	372	8,827
1844	114	201	5,000	320	—
1845	192	267	19,000	398	—
1846	126	308	10,000	444	9,719
1847	116	235	7,000	358	8,782
1848	129	320	10,000	459	8,750
1849	138	256	10,000	409	—
1850	140	188	12,000	349	—
Total	4,787	4,843	106,900	9,809	206,248

Appendix 2. The Relationship between the Availability of Day Schooling and the Success of Sunday Schools in Various Localities

Chapters Four and Six suggested that, in part at least, Sunday schools served as a supplement to weekday education and, furthermore, that they were thought of as such by parents when they chose a Sunday school for their children. Indeed it is this feature of the Sunday school which led nineteenth-century commentators as well as modern historians to relate the development of these 'part-time' schools to the curtailing of educational opportunities caused by industrialization with its concomitant child labor requirements. A local historian of Scarborough remarked in the early nineteenth century that Sunday schools failed to prosper in his town because there was little industry and small demand for the labor of school age children.[1] John Glyde made the same point with reference to Suffolk but then admitted that no regular relationship existed between the opportunities for weekday instruction and the popularity of Sunday schools.[2]

More recently Michael Sanderson has argued that industrialization in Lancashire brought with it a new demand for child labor, which in turn caused a shift from full-time to part-time instruction.[3] 'If industrial conditions lay behind the move to part time education', he continues, 'one would expect this form to predominate in these [industrial] areas, while non-industrial areas continued with day schooling.' He then compiles an index for Sunday school and weekday school attendance in thirteen towns

[1] Thomas Hinderwell *The History and Antiquities of Scarborough* ... (2nd ed. York, 1811) 253

[2] John Glyde *Suffolk in the Nineteenth Century: Physical. Social, Moral, Religious, and Industrial* (London, Ipswich, 1856) 253

[3] Michael Sanderson 'Social Change and Elementary Education in Industrial Lancashire' in *Northern History* vol. 3 (1968) 131–54, esp. 150–1

and thirteen fylde villages in Lancashire by dividing the greater attendance figure into the lesser, obtaining thereby a fraction less than one. In towns, for 12 out of the 13 cases, Sunday schools predominate with an index ranging from .15 for Bolton to .90 for Accrington. Conversely in the villages day schooling predominates in 12 out of 13 cases with indices ranging from .25 to 1.00.

There are two parts to Dr. Sanderson's argument. First, the amount of weekday schooling available was a significant determinant of the amount of part-time, i.e. Sunday school, education that was available. And second, industrialization curtailed the former and thus influenced the rise of the latter kind of instruction. The second point is not immediately relevant here; in Lancashire the factory system may indeed have increased the demand for child labor, thus reducing educational opportunities and contributing to the rise of Sunday schools. On a national scale, however, the first point is not valid.

A regression of the number attending Sunday school on the number attending day school for the cities and boroughs in England in 1851 yields a completely insignificant $r^2 = .042$.[4] In other words a test of the hypothesis that the number in day school in a locality determines the number in Sunday schools to a significant extent, i.e. that $f(y) = kx$ where y is the number in weekday school and x is the number in Sunday school, reveals that the relationship between the two is almost completely random. The same test at the county level in 1818, 1833 and 1851 reveals regression coefficients of $-.35$, $-.238$, $-.073$.

But even if significant correlations were obtained, the total number in either kind of school cannot be used to make assessments of the substitution of one for the other. There may, for example, be a large number in day school and a large number in Sunday school with very little overlap between the groups. As noted in Chapter Four students might attend the former and then attend the latter as a form of continuing education. For example, using Sanderson's method, Bristol would have a 'Sunday school predominates' index of .69, higher than Ashton-under-Lyne, Bury, Oldham, and Manchester. Yet in Bristol less than one-third of those in any kind of school attended Sunday school exclusively, roughly the same proportion as in rural Rutland. Conversely in Manchester and Bury, with their lower indices, 52.5 per cent and 54.5 per cent respectively of those receiving any form of instruction, relied exclusively on Sunday schools.

To gauge the degree of substitution of Sunday for day schooling

[4] *Number of day schools . . . in each city and borough* op. cit. 1852–53 (514) lxxix. 714, 4–8

one would need to know the preferences of a substantial number of families faced, over time, with the decision of which school to choose for their children. If substitution occurred, then one would expect to find rising costs, direct or indirect, of weekday schooling reflected in decreased attendance at these schools and increased attendance at the far cheaper part-time institution. Unfortunately no such series exists and no more concrete conclusions than those already offered in Chapters Four and Six can be put forward here.

Bibliography

This bibliography contains all works cited in the text of the book and a small number of additional studies which were found useful in the course of research and writing. It is not divided, as is customary, into primary and secondary works because of the nature and range of sources used. Instead the following classification scheme is used:
I. Manuscript sources
II. Printed sources
  a. Parliamentary papers
  b. Unofficial reports
  c. Sunday school manuals, guidebooks, and rules
  d. Sermons, tracts and addresses
  e. Textbooks and fictional material
  f. Biographies, collected biographies, and autobiographies
  g. Local studies, histories, and reports
  h. General works: Pre-1900
  i. General Works: Post-1900
  j. Periodicals: long runs
  k. Perodicals: single issues
  l. Unpublished theses
Unless otherwise noted, the place of publication is London.

I. Manuscript Sources

Chetham's Library, Manchester
    Minutes of the Manchester Sunday School for all Denominations, 1784–1820 MS A6, 3–6
Manchester Central Reference Library
    Directory and notes in Fred Lewis' *Directory of the Towns of Manchester and Salford for 1788 . . . 1842*. 738. L4

Methodist Archive Centre, City Road, London
    Everett, Rev. [James] 'Sunday Schools in Manchester' n.d.,
Bretherton Collection
    Rider, C. 'History of Sunday Schools in Manchester' signed
and dated December 10, 1825 on final page
    Letter Rev. H. Kellett/Rev. Thomas Sayham. February
24, 1820
    Manchester London Road Sunday School; an Account of
Sunday Schools 100 Years Ago, Bretherton Collection
National Christian Education Council, Robert Denham House,
Redhill, Surrey (formerly the Sunday School Union)
    Minutes of the Committee at the Depot,
    Vol. 1 15 November 1822 to 16 April 1829
    Vol. 2 16 April 1829 to 15 November 1837
    Vol. 3 20 January 1837 to 16 February 1844
    Vol. 4 16 February 1844 to 31 December 1850
    Minutes of the Committee of the Union
    Vol. 1 18 July 1810 to 23 February 1814
    Vol. 2 23 February 1814 to 14 May 1817
    Commonplace Book 20 May 1828 to 27 June 1844
National School Society, Great Peter Street, London
    Files for Manchester, Stockport, and Warrington
Nuffield College, Oxford
    'Directory of Labour' a typescript biographical dictionary
prepared by G. D. H. Cole. Copy on open shelves
Public Record Office
    George III. Correspondence H042/174–182
Staffordshire Record Office
    Scrapbook of the Leek Sunday School D 1114/1
    Admissions Register of the West Street Methodist School, Leek
D 1114/2
Stockport Reference Library
    Enrolment Registers 3 vols. 1797–1860
    Minute Books of the Committee 5 vols. 1797–1850
    Teachers Register 1799
    Diaries of Joseph Mayer 8 vols. 1806–51
    Returns Prepared for the Second Factory Commission 1833
    Stockport Sunday School Letters 1818–20

II. PRINTED SOURCES

    a. *Parliamentary papers*

*Select Committee on the State of the Children in Manufacturies of the
United Kingdom* 1816 (397) iii

Second Report from the Select Committee on the State of Education among the lower orders in the Metropolis 1816 (427) iv

Digest of Return to Circulars from Committee, of the state of schools and means of parochial instruction 1819 (224) ix

General Table showing the State of Education in England 1820 (151) xii

Select Committee on Criminal Commitments and Convictions (2nd Report) 1828 (545) vi

Report from the Select Committee on the Bill for Regulation of Factories; together with Minutes of Evidence 1831–2 (706) xv

First Report of the Commissioners oppointed to collect information in the manufacturing districts relative to the Employment of Children in Factories ... : *with Minutes of Evidence and Reports of District Commissioners* 1833 (450) xx

Supplementary Reports from Commissioners appointed to collect information in the manufacturing districts, relative to the Employment of Children in Factories ... *with Minutes of Evidence and Reports of District Commissioners* 1834 (167) xix

Report from the Select Committee on the State of Education, with Minutes of Evidence 1834 (572) ix

Abstract of answers and returns relative to the State of Education in England and Wales 1835 (62) xliii

Report from the Select Committee on the Education of the Poorer Classes in England and Wales, together with Minutes of Evidence. 1837–8 (589) vii

Report from each of the Four Factory Inspectors on the Education Provisions of the Factories Act; together with joint reports 1839 (42) xlii

Report of the Assistant Commissioners on Hand-loom Weavers 1839 (159) xlii.511; *Part II* 1840 (43-I) xxiii.49; *Part III* 1840 (43-II) xxiii.367 *Part IV* [*Midland District*] 1840 [220] xxiv.1; etc

Minutes of the Committee of Council for Education 1840 (254) xl; 1844 (84) xxxviii

Report of the Commissioners on Hand-loom Weavers 1841 [296] x.273

First Report of Commissioners for inquiring into the employment and condition of children in mines and manufactories 1842 [380] xv.1

Reports and evidence of Sub-Commissioners, Appendix to First Report, Part I 1842 [381] xvi.1

Appendix to First Report, Part II 1842 [382] xvii.1

Second Report of the Commissioners inquiring into the employment of children ... [*Trades and Manufactures*] 1843 [430] xiii.307

Appendix to Second Report, Part I, with Reports and Evidence from Sub-Commissioners 1843 [431] xiv.1; *Part II* 1843 [432] xv.1

Report of the Special Assistant Poor Law Commissioners on the Employment of Women and Children in Agriculture 1843 [510] xii

Index to the Second Report and Evidence of the Children's Employment Commission. 1845 [608] xlii.195

Report of the Commissioners appointed to inquire into the condition of the framework knitters 1845 [609] xv.1

Appendix to Report of the Commissioners oppointed to inquire into the condition of the framework knitters: Part I. *Leicestershire* 1845 [618] xv. 151; Part II. *Nottinghamshire and Derbyshire* 1845 [641] xv. 665

Report of Committee on the State of Education in Municipal Boroughs of Manchester and Salford 1852–53 (499) xi

Number of Day Schools and Sunday Schools, and Day Scholars and Sunday Scholars, in each City and Borough, in England and Wales 1852–53 (514) lxxix. 714

Religious Worship [1851] *Census* 1852–53 [690] lxxxix

Education [1851] *Census* 1852–53 [1692] xc

Report and Tables on Religious Worship and Education Scotland [1851] *Census* 1854 [1764] lix

Special Reports on Educational Subjects 1894 (c. 8943) xxiv

b. *Unofficial reports*

Baptist Annual Register edited by J. Rippon (1798)

Central Education Society *Reports* vols. 1–3 (1837–9)

Manchester Sunday Schools belonging to the Established Church *Annual Report* (Manchester, 1818, 1819)

Methodist New Connexion *Minutes of the Annual Conference* (1820–41)

Methodist Conference *Minutes* (1805–43)

National Society *Annual Reports* (1812–16) (1837) (1846)

Society for Bettering the Conditions of the Poor *Of the Education of the Poor … Digest … containing a selection of these articles with reference to education* edited by Sir T. Barnard (1809)

The South Lincolnshire and Isle of Ely Sunday School Union *Second Half Yearly Report* (1816)

Liverpool Baptist Association *Circular* (1832)

London City Mission *Report* (1846)

Stockport Sunday School *Annual Reports* (1793–1860)

The Sunday School Teachers' Re-Union (Leeds, 1848)

The Third Cooperative Congress *Proceedings 23 April 1832* edited by William Carpenter (1832)

Wesleyan Education Committee *Report* (1843)

c. *Sunday school manuals, guidebooks and rules*

Brief Abstract of the Plan of Instruction used in the Sunderland and Bishopwearmouth Sunday Schools (Sunderland, 1814)

Rules of the Bristol Methodist Sunday School (Bristol, 1817)

Rules for the Management and Internal Government of the Burslem Sunday School, instituted 1787 (Burslem, 1821)

Rules of the Methodist Sunday School, St. John Street, Chester, instituted 1782 (Chester, 1782)

Rules of the Doncaster Sunday School (Doncaster, 1815)

'Rules of the Enford Sunday School' in *Orthodox Churchman's Magazine* vol. 5, 25–7 (1803)

The Plan of a Society Instituted A.D. 1798 ... for the Establishment and Support of Sunday Schools in London and its Vicinity (1811)

Plan of a Society Established in London for the Support and Encouragement of Sunday Schools (1787) (1788) (1789) (1797) (1812)

Rules of the Society for the Establishment and Support of Sunday Schools in London (1802)

Rules and Orders for the Government of Sunday Schools in Manchester (Manchester, 1786)

Rules of the Prescott Sunday School (Prescott, 1812)

Rules of the Rawcliffe Sunday School (Rawcliffe, 1829)

Rules of the Southwark Sunday School Society (1797)

Regulations to be Observed in the Large Room of the Stockport Sunday School (Stockport, 1849)

Rules of a Sunday School Society established at St. Paul's Chapel, Wigan, for instructing poor children (Wigan, 1807)

Adam, H. *Handbook for Sunday Schools* (Manchester, 1871)

Anon. *Essay on the Formation of Sunday Schools* 3rd edition (1813)

Anon. *Hints on the Establishment and Regulation of Sunday Schools* (1836)

Anon. *Sunday School Reform* 3rd 1000 (n.d., *c.* 1870)

Anon. *Sunday School Teachers' Handbook* (1848)

Anon. 'Treatise on Sunday Schools' in four parts in *Primitive Methodist Magazine* vol. 5 (1824)

Clarke, H. F. *The Sunday School's Relation to the Band of Hope* (1893)

Collins, R. N. *The Teacher's Companion: designed to exhibit the Principles of Sunday School Instruction and Discipline* (1842)

Cooper, J. A. *The Senior Class; a Prize Essay* (*c.* 1847–50)

Davids, Louisa *The Sunday School* (1847)

Davis, A. H. *Religious Education* (1826)

Garrett, Rev. Charles *The Relationship of Sunday Schools to the Band of Hope* (1883)

Groser, William H. *Some Present Day Hinderances to Sunday School Progress* (1909)

Inglis, James *The Sabbath School and Bible Teaching* (*c.* 1847–50)

James, Rev. J. A. *The Sunday School Teacher's Guide* (Boston, 1819)

Lockwood, Rev. J. Traviss *Sunday Schools: How to revive and utilize them* (Oxford, 1868)

Mags, Rev. J. B. *The ABC of Christian Endeavour from a British Standpoint*

Miller, David *The Organization of Our Sabbath Schools* (Edinburgh, 1880)

Prize Essays collected by the Sunday School Union (*c*. 1894)

Rafles, Thomas *The Sunday School Teachers' Monitor* (Liverpool, 1816)

Reed, Charles *Infant Class in the Sunday School; a prize essay* (*c*. 1848–50)

Sargeant, F. J. *Sunday School Teaching practically considered* (*c*. 1847–50)

Sunday School Reform (*c*. 1870)

Trimmer, Sarah *The Oeconomy of Charity* (1787)

Watson, W. A. 'The Senior Class' reprinted in *Teachers' Magazine* vol. 12 new series (1841)

Watts, Isaac *The Improvement of the Mind* (1820)

Wigram, J. C. *Practical Hints on the Formation and Management of Sunday Schools* (1833)

Wilberforce, Samuel *Our Sunday Schools and How to Use Them* (1868)

William, Brooke *Plans of the Sunday-Schools and School of Industry, established in the City of Bath* (Bath, 1786)

Wilson, Rev. B. W. *Plain Hints for Sunday School Teachers* (n.d. *c*. 1870)

d. *Sermons, tracts and addresses*

'A Minister of the Gospel' *An Important Question Discussed* (Sheffield, 1824)

Address of the Southwark Sunday School Society Instituted 1799 (1803)

Adkin, Rev. Lancaster *The Sabbath: A sermon preached at the Parish Church of St. Stephen's, Norwich, to promote the establishment of Sunday schools* (Norwich, 1785)

Allin, T. *The Diffusion of Knowledge among the Labouring Classes: Promotive of Public Good* (1825)

Anon. *An Address to parents earnestly recommending them to promote the happiness of their children, by a due regard to their virtuous education* (Uxbridge, 1787)

Anon. *Advice to Sunday Scholars in Rural and Mining Districts with a View to their Future Prosperity and Happiness* (Newcastle-under-Lyme, 1836)

Anon. *An Appeal to Members of the Church of England on the Subject of Sunday Schools with especial reference to effects of lay agency* (1823)

Anon. *The Importance of Sunday Schools at the present Crisis . . . By a Member of the Society for promoting Christian Knowledge* (Canterbury, 1800)

Anon. *A Plain and Serious Address to the Parents of Poor Children on the Subject of Schools* SPCK (*c.* 1800?)

Anon. 'Sermon on Sunday schools on Prov. xxii. 6' in *Christian Remembrancer* vol. 14, 623–8 (1832)

Baines, Edward *Letters to the Rt. Hon. John Russell on the State of Education* 7th edition (Leeds, 1847)

Barker, Rev. Joseph *Mercy Triumphant, or Teaching the Children of the Poor to write on the Sabbath Day . . .* 3rd edition (1843)

Bayley, Cornelius *An Address to the Public on Sunday Schools* (Manchester, 1784)

Beilby, Porteus, Bishop of Chester *A Letter to the Clergy of the Diocese of Chester Concerning Sunday Schools* (1786)

———*A Sermon preached in the Cathedral Church of Chester, February 4, 1787, for the benefit of the Charity Schools in that City and with a view of recommending the establishment of a General Sunday school there* (Chester, 1787)

Berington, Rev. Joseph *An Essay on the Depravity of the Nation with a view to the promotion of Sunday Schools etc* (Birmingham, 1788)

Brocas, Thomas *God No Respector of Persons, but Loving to Every Man* (Shrewsbury, 1808)

Bunting, Rev. Jabez *A Great Work described and recommended in a sermon preached May 15, 1805 before members of the Sunday School Union* (1805)

Burges, Rev. George *A discourse on the necessity and duty of enlightening the human race* (1797)

Burgess, Rev. Richard *Letter to the Revd. W. F. Hook, D. D. . . . on his Proposal for a plan for the Education of the People* (1846)

Burn, Rev. Edward *A Reply to the Revd. Dr. Priestley's Appeal to the Public . . . in vindication of the clergy and respectable inhabitants of the town* (Birmingham, 1792)

Burnaby, Rev. Andrew *Two Charges delivered to the clergy of the Archdeaconry of Leicester in the years 1786 and 1787* (1787)

Carpenter, Rev. Benjamin *A Letter to the Rev. R. Foley, M. A., Rector of Old Swinford in answer to the charges brought against the Dissenters in Stourbridge . . . To which is added an account of the proceedings at the Lye-Waste by J. Scott* (1795)

Cobbett, William *Advice to Young Men* (1829)

Collins, Rev. Thomas *A Sermon Preached at Burnley in Lancashire, Nov. 4, 1787, on the Institution of Sunday Schools There* (1788)

Cooper, Samuel, DD *The necessity and duty of the early instruction of children in the Christian religion—a sermon* (1790)

Cooper, Thomas *Eight Letters to Young Men of the Working Classes* (1850)

Courtenay, Henry, Bishop of Bristol *A Sermon Preached ... May 28, 1795, Being the Time of the Yearly Meeting of the Children Educated in the Charity Schools* (1796)

Deacon, Francis and John Gamble *A letter on the importance of Sunday Schools addressed more especially to such of the General Baptist churches as have not established them* (1808)

Detrosier, Rowland *An Address ... on the Necessity of an Extension of Moral and Political Instruction Among the Working Classes* (1831); with a memoir by James Shuttleworth in 1834 edition

Dore, Rev. James *A Sermon preached at Maze Pond, Southwark Sept. 27, 1789 for the Benefit of the Society Established in London, for the Support and Encouragement of Sunday schools in different counties of England* (1789)

Edwards, Rev. John *Letters to the British Nation ... occasioned by ... a pamphlet, entitled 'A Reply to ... Dr. Priestley's Appeal to the Public on the subject of the Riots in Birmingham'* ... (Birmingham, 1791)

Farrar, Rev. A. *The religious instruction of children enforced*; *Sermon to Hull Sunday School Union* (Hull, 1820)

Farrell, Rev. John *The principles of sound policy delineated ... or observations on the necessity of educating the poor* (Wigan, 1785)

Field, Rev. William *A letter addressed to the inhabitants of Warwick in answer to several charges ... against the Dissenters ... by the Rev. Mr. Miller* (Birmingham, 1791)

————*A Second letter ... in reply to Remarks ... by ... the Vicar and the Curate of St. Nicholas* (Birmingham, 1791)

Fifteen Pamphlets on the Blagdon Controversy (Bound together and catalogued under Hannah More in the Bodleian Library) (1801-02)

Foley, Rev. Robert *A Letter to Dr. Priestley, in answer to his late publication, entitled 'An Appeal ...'* (Stourbridge, 1793)

Glasse, Rev. Samuel *The Piety, Wisdom and Policy of promoting Sunday Schools ... 24 Sept., 1786* (1786)

Grant, Rev. Johnson, *The Abuses and Advantages of Sunday Schools*; *a sermon preached at Ormskirk* (1800)

Greenwich Union Society *Reply of the Union Society of Greenwich for promoting Sunday schools and preaching the Gospel: to a pamphlet ... by the Revd. Dr. Wollaston ... A Country Parson's Address ... By a member of the Union Society* (1800)

Grinfield, Rev. E. W. *The Bulwarks of the English Church ... To which are added some observations on the origins and progress of Parochial Libraries* (Bath, 1820)

Hall, Rev. Robert *The advantages of knowledge to the lower classes: a sermon preached at Harvey Lane, Leic. for the benefit of Sunday schools* (1810)

Hanway, Jonas *A Comprehensive View of Sunday Schools* (1786)

————*Letters on the Importance of the Rising Generation of the Labouring part of our fellow subjects* (1767)

Hill, Rev. Rowland *An Apology for Sunday School* (1801)

Horne, Rev. George, DD *Sunday Schools Recommended—a sermon delivered at St. Alphage, Canterbury* (Oxford, 1786)

Horsley, Samuel, Bishop of Rochester *Charge . . .* (1800)

'INVESTIGATOR' *A Vindication of the Measures Lately Adopted by the Trustees of the Wesleyan Methodist Chapel, Burslem, in Reference to the Sunday School Conducted on their Premises* (Burslem, 1836)

[Jackson, Rev. Samuel] *Wesleyan Sunday Schools as they are and as they Ought to Be* (1854)

Jesse, Rev. W. *The Importance of Education* (1785)

Kaye, Sir Richard, Dean of Lincoln *A Charge delivered to the Clergy at the archdeaconry of Nottingham* (1786)

Lancaster, Joseph *An Address to the Friends and Superintendent of 'Sunday Schools'* (1809)

Liddon, Rev. John *The general religious instruction of the poor, the surest means of providing national happiness; A sermon on Sunday Schools* (1792)

Lloyd, R. *A Letter to a Member of Parliament (in these days of infidelity and sedition) showing the serious and dangerous defects of British and Foreign Schools* (1819)

Lucas, Rev. Robert *Three Sermons on the Subject of Sunday Schools: with an Appendix containing rules and c. to which are added a few hints on parochial clubs* (1787)

Martin, Rev. Robert *An address . . . on the Impropriety and Sinfulness of Teaching Children to write on the Lord's Day* (Bury, 1819)

Mayer, J. A. *Candid Animadversions on the Revd. Thomas Whitaker's four letters* (1798)

A Defence of Sunday Schools: attempted in a series of letters addressed to the Revd. M. A. Olerenshaw (1798)

Miller, Robert *The Duty of Parents Considered in a Sermon preached in the Methodist Chapel at Dewsbury Yorkshire, Sunday March 16, 1800* (Wakefield, 1800)

Miller, R. M. *The Religious Instruction of Children and Youth Recommended to Christian Parents* (1820)

Miller, Rev. Robert and Rev. Hugh Langherne *Remarks upon a letter to the Printer of the Birmingham Gazette, dated Oct. 14, 1791 and also upon a letter . . . by W. Field* (Warwick, 1791)

Morris, Rev. John Webster *A discourse delivered at Clipstone . . . in favour of Sunday schools and c., March 11, 1792* (Market Harborough, 1792)

Myddleton, Rev. C. P. *A Sermon in Defence of Sunday Schools* (Manchester, 1798)

Noel, Rev. Baptist W. *The Sanctification of the Sabbath and the Blessings attached to it* (1836)

Olerenshaw, Rev. M. (of Mellor) *A sermon [on Gen. ii, 3] on the sanctification of the Sabbath and on the right use ... of Sunday schools* (Stockport, 1797)

'One of Yourselves' *Is the Union Right?* (1843)

Owen, Rev. T. E. *Methodism Unmasked or the Progress of Puritanism* (n.d. *c.* 1800)

Peters, Rev. William *An exhortation to that greatest of Charities, Rescuing the Infant Poor from Sin, and educating them in the Principles of Virtue and Religion—on Prov. xxii, 6* (1787)

Pitt, William Morton *Plan for the extension and regulation of Sunday Schools* (1785)

Pretyman-Tomline, G. Bishop of Lincoln *A sermon on Matthew ii, 5 delivered May 31, 1804, Being the time of the yearly meeting of the Children educated in Charity Schools ...* (1804)

Priestley, Joseph *An appeal to the public on the subject of riots in Birmingham ...* (1791)

———*A second appeal ... to which is added a letter from W. Russell* (Birmingham, 1792)

Prize Essays on the Temporal Advantage of the Sabbath (1849)

Raikes, Rev. Richard *Considerations on the Alliance between Christianity and Commerce Applied to the Present State of this Country* (1806)

Religious Tract Society *The Duties and Encouragements of the Poor* (n.d. *c.* 1820)

Shute-Barrington, Rev., Bishop of Salisbury *A Letter to the Clergy of the Diocese of Sarum ...* (Salisbury, 1789)

———*Charge to the clergy of the diocese of Sarum* (1797)

Stevenson, Rev. Thomas *The difficulties and encouragements attending the communication of religious instruction to the children of the poor: a sermon delivered: the Methodist Chapel, Halifax Lane, Nottingham, April 11, 1814 before the Nottingham Sunday School Union* (1814)

Toulmin, Rev. Joshua *The Rise, Progress and Effects of Sunday Schools considered in a sermon preached at Taunton Mar. 28, 1789* (1789)

Townsend, Rev. John *Hints on Sunday Schools and Itinerant Preaching in a Letter to the Bishop of Rochester* (1801)

Turner, Rev. Daniel *Hints on religious education; being two sermons in favour of Sunday Schools* (1794)

Turner, Rev. William *Sunday Schools Recommended in a sermon and appendix concerning the formation, conduct and expense of these schools* (Newcastle-upon-Tyne, 1786)

Vipond, W. *The Scriptural Method of Governing and Instructing Children* (Canterbury, 1807)

Waddy, Rev. Samuel *A Sermon on the Importance and Obligation of Early Religious Education* (Manchester, 1838)

Ward, Rev. Valentine *Observations on Sunday Schools; Principally to their connection with the divine worship on the Lord's Day. Instruction in the Art of Writing and the pastoral duties of Christian ministers* 2nd edition (Leeds, 1827)

Watmough, Rev. A. *Observations on Teaching the Art of Writing in Sunday Schools* (1832)

Watson, Rev. R. *Sermon preached at Stockport for the Benefit of the Methodist Sunday School* (1806)

——*Sermon to the Sunday School Union* (1819)

Watson, Richard, Bishop of Llandaff *Charge* ... (1788)

——*Charge* ... (1809)

Whitaker, Rev. Thomas *Four Letters to Mr. J. Mayer of Stockport in his Defence of Sunday Schools* (1798)

Wollaston, Francis *A Country Parson's Address to His Flock, to Caution Them Against ... the Wolf in Sheep's Clothing, or Jacobin teachers of sedition (Chiefly against the Union Society of Greenwich)* (1799)

Wood, Rev. T., *Thoughts on Sunday Schools: Importance of knowledge to the Lower Classes of Society* (1815)

Workman's Testimony to the Sabbath (1851)

e. *Textbooks and fictional material*

Anon. *The Sunday Scholar's Gift, or a present for a good child* (Wellington 1814)

Anon. *Sunday School Gleanings* 2nd edition (1823)

Anon. *The Sunday School Spelling Book in five parts* (1823)

Bickersteth, E[mily] *Plain Sunday Readings for Plough Boys* (1856)

Bronte, Charlotte *Shirley: a tale* (1880)

Burgess, Thomas, Bishop of Salisbury *The Salisbury Spelling Book, for the use of Sunday Schools* 2nd edition (1786); 12th edition (1809)

Chapbooks (n.d. *c.* 1830)

'A Friend of Sunday Schools' *The Sunday School Treat to Richmond Park* (1860)

Gall, James *Key to the one Book for teaching children to read* (Edinburgh, 1832)

Holyoake, G. J. *Practical Grammar with Graduated Exercises* (1846); 8th edition (1870)

Kendall, C. *The New Sunday School Reciter* (1859)

[Maurice, Mary A.] *Glenrock Sunday; or Lessons Illustrative of a Simple Method of Conveying Religious Instruction to Children of the Poor* 2nd edition (1840)

MacCarthy, George *The Rise and Progress of Sunday Schools, A Poem* (Sudbury. 1816)

Messent, Charles *The Autobiography of a Sunday School Teacher* (1856)

Milhouse, Robert *The Sonnets and Songs of Robert Milhouse, with a biographical sketch of the author, edited by John Potter Briscoe, FRHS* (1881)

More, Hannah *The Works of* ... a new edition, 18 vols. (1818)

Paley, Rev. William *The Young Christian instructed in Reading and in the Principles of Religion* (Carlisle, 1790; London, 1855)

A Practical Catechism for the instruction of children especially those of the Sunday School ... with prayers (Warrington, 1787)

Religious Tract Society *The Death of an Infidel: or the last Hours of the Hon. Francis Newport* no. 16 (n.d. *c.* 1820)

———*The History of Joseph Green, A Sunday Scholar* (n.d. *c.* 1820)

———*The Repentance and Happy Death of the Celebrated Earl of Rochester* no. 6 (n.d. *c.* 1820)

———*The Sunday Scholar* (n.d. *c.* 1830)

Richardson, William *Dialogues for Sunday Schools on Interesting Topics* no. 1 (1822)

Solly, Henry *James Woodford: Carpenter and Chartist* vol. 1 (1885)

Stockport Sunday School Memoir Book (1797 ff)

Sunday School Union *Catalogue of the Book Repository (No. 1), Paternoster Street* (1824)

———*Introduction to Reading, Parts 1–3* (1830) with yearly editions

———*Spelling Book, Parts 1–4* (1812) with yearly editions

———*Tracts, nos. 1–62* (1806–11)

Mrs Thaner *The Sunday School Primer; or Child's First Book* (1823)

Trimmer, Sarah *The Sunday School Primer, or Child's First Book* (1823)

Waldo, Peter *Admonitions for Sunday Scholars* (1835)

Watts, Isaac *Divine Songs* (Facsimile reproduction of the first edition of 1715 with an illustrated edition of circa, 1830. Oxford, 1971)

Wesley, Revs. John and Charles *Poetical Works of John and Charles Wesley collected and arranged by G. Osborne, DD.* (1871)

f. *Biographies, collected biographies, and autobiographies*

Anon. *Bennett Street Memorials* 2nd edition (Manchester, 1868)

Anon. *A Brief Memoir of the Late Mrs. John Richards* (Wednesbury, 1854)

Anon. *When I was a Child, by an 'Old Potter'* introduction by Robert Spence Watson (1903)

Arch, Joseph *Story of His Life* (1898)

Ashworth, Rev. John *Life and Labours*, by A. L. Calman. (Manchester, 1875)

————*Strange Tales from Humble Life* 4th series (Manchester, 1870)

Atkinson, Rev. Miles, Vicar of Kippax *Practical Sermons . . . to which is prefixed a short memoir of the life and character of the author* vol. 1 (1812)

Austin, R. *Robert Raikes, the Elder, and the Gloucester Journal* (1915)

Bamford, Samuel *Passages in the Life of a Radical* 2 vols. (1844)

Barker, Joseph *Life* (1880)

————*Memoirs of Several Eminent Christians, lately members of the Methodist New Connexion* (1839)

————*Teachings of experience, or, Lessons I have learned on my way through life* (1869)

Barr, David *Climbing* (1910)

Braidley, Benjamin *Memoir* (1845)

Brierley, Benjamin *Home Memories* (Manchester, 1886)

Bunting, T. P. *Life of Jabez Bunting* (vol. 1 (1859); vol. 2 (1887)

Burney, Fanny *Diary and Letters of Madame* d'Arblay (1842–46)

Burns, Jabez *A Retrospect of forty-five years' Christian ministry* (1875)

Burt, Thomas *Autobiography* (1924)

Cappe, Catharine *Memoirs of the Life of the late Mrs. Catherine Cappe* edited by Mary Cappe (1822)

[Carter, Thomas] *Memoirs of a Working Man* (1845)

Cecil, J. *The Works of the Reverend Cecil, M. A., with a Memoir of His Life, arranged and revised by Josiah Pratt* (1827)

Chalmer, Alexander *The General Biographical Dictionary* vol. 25 (1812)

Clarke, Adam *Adam Clarke Portrayed* edited by James Everett, vol. 2 (1843)

Collier, Mrs. *A Bible-Woman's Story* edited by Eliza Nightingale (1885)

Cooper, Thomas *The Life of Thomas Cooper; written by Himself* (1872)

Dalley, William A. *The Life Story of W. J. Davis, J. P.* (Birmingham, 1914)

Davis, Arthur Paul *Isaac Watts: His Life and Works* (1948)

Eastman, P. M. *Robert Raikes and Northamptonshire Sunday Schools* (1880)

Edwards, George, MP *From Crow-Scaring to Westminster* (1922)

Everett, James *Adam Clarke Portrayed* (1843)

Farningham, Marianne *A Working Woman's Life: an autobiography* (1907)

Fish, Rev. Henry *Memoir of Joseph Pearson of Bath* (Bath, 1849)

Griffin, James *Memories of the Past* (1883)

Harford, John S. *The Life of Thomas Burgess, Bishop of Salisbury* (1840)

Harris, J. Henry, ed. *Robert Raikes: The man and his work* (1899)

Herford, Brooke *Travers Madge*: *a memoir* 3rd edition (1868)

Hillocks, James Inches *Life Story*; *a prize autobiography* (1860)

Hodder, E. *The Life of Samuel Morley* (1887)

Hodgson, Robert *The Life of the Rt. Revd. Beilby Porteus* (1811)

Hutchins, John H. *Jonas Hanway* (1940)

Ivimey, J. *Memoir of William Fox, Esq.* (1831)

Kelly, Edith and Thomas, ed. *A Schoolmaster's Notebook* vol. 8 3rd series (Manchester, 1957)

Kendall, Guy *Robert Raikes*: *A Critical Biography* (1939)

Lackington, James *Memoirs of the Forty-Five Years of the Life ... in a Series of Letters to a Friend* (1791)

Livesey, Joseph *The Life and Teachings of ..., comprising his Autobiography* with an introduction by John Pearce (1886)

Lovett, William *Life and Struggles in Pursuit of Bread, Knowledge, and Freedom* (1876)

McCabe, Joseph *Life and Letters of George Jacob Holyoake* (1908)

MacDonald, Frederic W. *Reminiscences of My Early Ministry* (1912)

Mann, Tom *Memoirs* (1923)

Memorials of the Founders ... of Bennett Street Sunday School, with additions by Benjamin Milner (1882)

Milner, Isaac, ed. *Practical Sermons of the Late Reverend Joseph Milner, M.A. .... to which is prefixed an Account of the Life and Character of the Authur* 2nd. edition (Cambridge. 1801)

More, Hannah *Life and Correspondence* edited by William Roberts (1834)

Nichols, John *Literary Anecdotes of the Eighteenth Century* vol. 5 (1812–15)

Nunn, Rev. William, M.A. *Memoirs of the late ...* ed. by Rev. Robert Pym (1842)

Padgin, George *James Montgomery* Robert Raikes Historical Society Bulletin no. 15 (1965)

Paley, Rev. William *A Life ...* in the *Works of William Paley* edited by Alexander Chalmer, vol. 1 (1821)

Pearson, A. *Life of William Hey* (1822)

Reed, Charles E. B. *Memoir of Sir Charles Reed* (1883)

Rhodes, Elizabeth *Memoir* (1829)

Rushton, Adam *My life, as a farmer's boy, factory lad, teacher and preacher, 1821–1909* (1909)

Saville, John, ed. *Dictionary of Labour Biography* (1972)

Skinner, Rev. John *Journal of a Somerset Rector ... 1772–1839* edited by Howard Coombs and Arthur Bax (1930)

Somerville, Alexander *Autobiography of a Working Man* (1848); edited by J. Carswell (1951)

Soutter, Francis William *Recollections of a Labour Pioneer* (1923)

Swan, Guida, ed. *The Journals of Two Poor Dissenters, 1786–1880* (1970)

Tillett, Ben *Memories and Reflections* (1931)

Timpson, Thomas *Mirror of Sunday School Teachers* (1853)

Torr, Dona *Tom Mann and his Times* vol. 1 (1956)

Turner, J. Arthur, ed. *The Life of a Chimney Boy* (1901)

Watson, James *A Memoir of the fight for a free press in England ... by James Linton* (1880)

Webster, G. *Memoir of Robert Raikes* (Nottingham, 1873)

Whittaker, Thomas *Life's Battles in Temperance Armour* 3rd edition (1888)

Williams, Gwyn *Rowland Detrosier—A Working Class Infidel* (York, 1965)

Wilson, John *Memories of a Labour Leader* (1910)

Winstanley, David *A Schoolmaster's Notebook*, edited by E. and T. Kelly, 1957.

g. *Local studies, histories, and reports*

Abbreviation: *JRSS* = *Journal of the Royal Statistical Society*.

Adkin, Rev. Lancaster *Proceedings for Sunday Schools and a Plan of that in St. Stephen's, Norwich* (Norwich, 1785)

Allin, Rev. Thomas *Four Letters to the Revd. John Maclean, minister in the Wesleyan Methodist Connexion, on his defence of Wesleyan Methodism* (1835)

Anon. *An Account of the Celebration of the Jubilee of the Macclesfield Sunday School, May 6, 1846* (Macclesfield, 1846)

Ashworth, Henry 'Statistics on the present Depression of Trade at Bolton; showing the mode in which it affects the different Classes of a Manufacturing Population' *JRSS* vol. 5, 74–81 (1842)

Austin, Roland, 'The Dursley Sunday School Established 1784' *Transactions of the Congregational Historical Society* pp. 228–33 (April 1929)

Axon, William E. *The Annals of Manchester* (Manchester, 1886)

Bain, W. J. *A Study of a Rock: but not geological ... A paper on the early history of Sunday Schools, especially in Northamptonshire* 2nd edition (1875)

Baines, Edward *The Social, educational, and religious state of the manufacturing districts; with statistical returns of the means of education and religious instruction in the manufacturing districts of Yorkshire, Lancashire, and Cheshire* (1843)

Baker, H. W. *The Story of Methodism in Caton* (Lancaster, 1936)

Bardsley, C. W. *Memorials of St. Anne's Church, Manchester* (Manchester, 1877)

Barnsby, G. *The Dudley Working Class Movement 1832–1860* (Dudley, 1970)

Birmingham Statistical Society 'Report on the State of Education in Birmingham' *JRSS* vol. 3 (1840)

Blackner, John *The History of Nottingham* . . . (Nottingham, 1815)

Bretherton, Francis Fletcher *Early Methodism in and around Chester. 1749–1812, etc.* (Chester, 1903)

Brigden, Thomas Edwin *The Old Leek Sunday School. A Centenary Record, 1797–1897* (Leek, 1897)

Broad, John S. *History of the Origins and Progress of Sunday Schools in Bristol* (Bristol, 1816)

Brockett, Allan *Nonconformity in Exeter, 1650–1875* (Manchester, 1962)

Carter, W. B. *History of the Nottingham Sunday School Union* (Nottingham, 1869)

Chapman, S. D. 'The Evangelical Revival and Education in Nottingham' *Transactions of the Thoroton Society* vol. 66 (1962)

Cobbett, R. S. *Memorials of Twickengam* (1872)

Cossons, Arthur 'The Villagers Remember' *Transactions of the Thoroton Society* vol. 66 (1962)

Courtney, M. A. 'Cornish Feasts and "Feasten Customs" ' *Folklore Journal* vol. 4 (1886)

Dale, Thomas P. *A History of Brunswick Chapel, Bury* (Bury, 1897)

Davis, C. H. *History of the Silver Street Sunday School Society* (1904)

Dickins, J. Morton *Kirkgate Chapel, Bradford, and its Associations with Methodism* (Bradford, 1903)

Dunkin, John *The History and Antiquities of Bicester* (Bicester, 1816)

Dyson, J. B. *History of Wesleyan Methodism in the Congleton Circuit* . . . (1856)

Edgell, Rev. E. W. 'Moral Statistics of the Parishes of St. James, St. George, and St. Anne, Westminster' *JRSS* vol. 1, 478 ff (1838)

Elliot, A. *A Slight Sketch of the Rise of Sunday Schools in Windsor* (Windsor, 1905)

Elliot, Ernest *A History of Congregationalism in Shropshire* (Oswestry, 1898)

Evans, Seth *Bradwell: Ancient and Modern* (Chesterfield, 1912)
———*Methodism in Bradwell* (1907)

Firth, H. I. 'The Earliest English Sunday School' *Transactions of the Congregational Historical Society* (September 1928) 183–90

[Fletcher, John] *Greenhill Methodist Sunday School, Block Lane, Oldham, 1849–1949* (Oldham, 1949)

Freeman, J. *Bilston Wesleyan Methodism* (Bilston, 1924)
———*Black Country Studies and Sketches* (Bilston, 1930)

Fripp, C. B. 'Report on the Condition of the Working Classes in Bristol' *JRSS* vol. 2 (1839)

Glew, E. L. *History of the Borough and Foreign of Walsall* ... (Walsall, 1856)

Glyde, John *The Moral, Social, and Religious Condition of Ipswich* (Ipswich, 1850)

————*Suffolk in the Nineteenth Century* (Ipswich, 1856)

Greg, J. 'On the State of Agricultural Labourers in Northumberland' *JRSS* vol. 1 (1838)

Hadley, George *A New and Complete History of Kingston-Upon-Hull* (Kingston-upon-Hull, 1788)

Haigh, William B. *Leeds Synopsis of Wesleyan Methodism in Yorkshire* (Leeds, 1830)

Hawkes, Joseph *The Rise and Progress of Wesleyan Sunday Schools, Luton* (Luton, 1885)

Hickey, J. E. *History of the Dukinfield Sunday School* (Dukinfield, 1928)

Hinderwell, Thomas *The History and Antiquities of Scarborough and Vicinity* 2nd edition (York, 1811)

Hindmarsh, L. 'On the State of Agriculture and Agricultural Labourers in Northumberland' *JRSS* vol. 1 (1838)

Holden, Joshua *A short History of Todmorton* (1912)

Hole, William *Light, more light! On the Present State of Education amongst the working classes of Leeds* (1863)

Howard, J. *Historical Sketch of the Origin and Work of the York Incorporated (Church of England) Sunday School Committee established 1786* (York, 1887)

Hurt, J. S. *Bringing Literacy to Rural England* (London and Chichester, 1972)

Hyett. F. A. *Glimpses of the History of Painswick* (Gloucester, 1928)

Jessop, Rev. William *An account of Methodism in Rossendale and the neighbourhood, etc.* (Manchester, 1881)

Kirkham, J. *Centenary History of the German Street Sunday School* (Manchester, 1903)

Langford, John A. *A Century of Birmingham Life from 1741–1841* (Birmingham, 1868)

Laycock, J. W. *Methodist Heroes of the Great Haworth Circuit* (Keighley, 1907)

Little, C. Deane *Our Old School. 150 Years of Wigan Methodism* (Wigan, 1933)

Lyth, John *Glimpses of Early Methodism in York and the Surrounding District* (York, 1885)

McClatchey, Diana *Oxfordshire Clergy 1777–1869* (Oxford, 1960)

Manchester Statistical Society *Report on the State of Education in Bury* (1835)

———*Report on the State of Education in Manchester in 1834* (1835)

———*Report on the State of Education in Salford in 1835* (1836)

———*Report on the State of Education in Liverpool in 1835–36* (1836)

———*Report on the State of Education in Bolton* (1837)

———*Report on the State of Education in York, 1836–37* (1837)

———*Report on the State of Education in Pendleton, 1838* (1839)

———*Report on the State of Education in the County of Rutland in the year 1838* (1839)

———*Report on the State of Education in Kingston-upon-Hull* (1840)

Matthews, A. G. *The Congregational Church in Staffordshire* (1924)

Mellor, R. H. *A Short History of the Macclesfield Sunday School, 1796–1946* (1947)

Mellors, Robert *Men of Nottingham and Nottinghamshire ...* (Nottingham, 1924)

Moore, B. *History of Wesleyan Methodism in Burnley and East Lancashire* (Burnley, 1899)

More, Martha *Mendip Annals, or a Narrative of the Charitable Labours of Hannah and Martha More in their Neighbourhood* edited by Arthur Roberts (1858)

Musgrove, John *The Origins of Methodism in Bolton* (1865)

Nicholson, Francis and Ernest Axon *The Older Non-Conformity in Kendal* (Kendal, 1915)

Northcote, Hon. A. F. *Notes on the History of Monks' Eleigh* (Ipswich, 1930)

Noake, John *Notes and Queries for Worcestershire* (1856)

Parkinson, Ann *The Beneficial Effects of Sunday Schools in Dukinfield* (Hackney, 1816)

Parsons, Edward *The Civil, Ecclesiastical, Literary, Commercial and Miscellaneous History of Leeds, Bradford ...* (Leeds, 1834)

Pearce, Robert *Methodism in Portland and a Page of Church History* (1898)

Picton, Sir James *Memorials of Liverpool* vol. 1 (1873)

Pilkington, W. *The Makers of Wesleyan Methodism in Preston* (1890)

Plaisted, Arthur H. *The Manor and Parish Records of Medmenham, Bucks* (1925)

Pratt, Alfred C. *Black Country Methodism* (1891)

Prentice, Archibald *Historical Sketches and Personal Recollections of Manchester* (1851)

Prince, W. H. *The Romance of Early Methodism in and around West Bromwich* (1925)

Reeve, R. *History of Maze Pond Sunday School, 1801–1901* (1901)

'Report on the State of Education among the Working Classes in the Parish of West Bromwich' *JRSS* vol. 2 (1839)

Roberts, Richard *History of Methodism in Almondbury* (1864)

Rose, E. A. 'Cornelius Bayley and the Manchester Methodists' *Proceedings of the Wesley Historical Society* vol. 34, 152–8 (September, 1964)

Rothwell, Stephen *Memorials of the Independent Chapel, Folds Road, Bolton* (Bolton, 1887)

Russell, Rex C. *Sunday Schools: The Miserable Compromise*, vol. 2 of *A History of Schools and Education in Lindsey, Lincolnshire* (Lindsey 1965)

Salt, John 'Early Sheffield Sunday Schools and their Educational Importance' *Transactions of the Hunter Archaeological Society* vol. ix, part 3, 179–84. (1967)

Scruton, William *Pen and Pencil Sketches of Old Bradford* (Bradford, 1889)

Sheldon, W. C. *Early Methodism in Birmingham* (Birmingham, 1903)

Smith, Rev. Benjamin *History of Methodism in Macclesfield* (1875)

Spencer, Rev. Allan *The History of Methodism in Daveyhulme* (Manchester, 1898)

Statistical Society of Bristol 'Statistics of Education in Bristol' *JRSS* vol. 4 (1841)

Statistical Society of London 'Second Report on the State of Education in Westminster' *JRSS* vol. 1 (1838)

———'Report on the State of the Working Classes in the Parishes of St. Margaret and St. John, Westminster' *JRSS* vol. 3 (1840)

———'Fifth Report and Summary of the Education Committee' *JRSS* vol. 6 (1843)

———'Report of the Education Committee on the Borough of Finsbury' *JRSS* vol. 6 (1843)

Steele, Anthony *History of Methodism in Barnard Castle in the Dales Circuit* (1857)

Stott, John *Notices of Methodism in Haslingden* (1898)

Sturdy, J. *Our Local Sunday Schools, 1806–1906* (Whitby, 1906)

Sutton, John F. *The Date Book of Remarkable and Memorial Events Connected with Nottingham . . .* (1852)

Swift, R. C. 'Methodist Sunday Schools in Nottingham' *Proceedings of the Wesley Historical Society* vol. 23, 17–20, 36–40 (1961–2)

Telford, John *Two West End Chapels: Sketches of London Methodism from Wesley's Day* (1886)

Thomis, Malcolm I. *Politics and Society in Nottingham 1785–1835* (Oxford, 1969)

Toulmin, Rev. Joshua *The History of Taunton* New edition (Taunton, 1822)

Walters, W. *The History of the Newcastle-on-Tyne Sunday School Union* (Bristol, 1870)

Ward, John *The Borough of Stoke-on-Trent in the Commencement of the Reign of her Most Gracious Majesty* ... (1843)

Ward, Rev. John *Historical Sketches of the rise and progress of Methodism in Bingley* ... (Bingley, 1863)

———*The Rise and Progress of Wesleyan Methodism in Blackburn* (Blackburn, 1871)

Westerdale, Thomas *Centenary History of the Radnor Street Day, Sunday, and Ragged Schools* (1898)

Whitehead, Thomas *History of the Dales Congregational Churches* (Keighley, 1930)

Wild, W. I. *The History of the Stockport Sunday School* (1891)

h. *General works*: pre-1900

Allen, W. O. B. and Edmund McClure *The History of the Society for Promoting Christian Knowledge, 1698–1898* (1898)

Anon. *The Story of the Religious Tract Society* (1898)

Arnold, Matthew *Culture and Anarchy* Popular edition (1909)

Baines, Edward *History of the Cotton Manufacture in Great Britain* (1835)

Bowles, John *Reflections on the Political and Moral State of Society at the Close of the Eighteenth Century* (1800)

Campbell, Rev. John, *Letters on Wesleyan Methodism in England and the Colonies* (1847)

Carlisle. F. *Endowed Grammar Schools in England and Wales* 2 vols (1818)

Cecil, Rev. Richard *Works* edited by Josiah Pratt (1811)

Cowper, William *Letters* edited by J. G. Frazer, 2 vols (1912)

Dearden's Miscellany vol. 2 (1839)

Dunn, Henry *Popular Education* (1837)

Eden, Sir Thomas *The State of the Poor* vol. 1 (1798)

Evans, David *The Sunday Schools of Wales* (1880)

Farr, William *Vital Statistics* (1885)

Godwin, William *An Enquiry Concerning Political Justice* vol. 2 (1797)

Hamilton, Richard Winter *The Institutions of Popular Education* 2nd edition (1846)

Hartley, Fountain J., FSS *The Sunday School Army: Its Position and Progress* (1884)

Hill, Frederic *National Education: Its Present State and Future Prospects* 2 vols (1836)

Howitt, W. *The Rural Life of England* (1838); 2nd edition, corrected (1840)

Hudson, J. W. *The History of Adult Education* (1851)

Jones, William *The Jubilee Memorial of the Religious Tract Society containing a Record of its Origins, Proceedings and Results, AD 1799–AD 1849* (1850)

Kirby, Charles *The Early Days of Sunday Schools* (1869)

Ludlow, John M. and Lloyd Jones *The Progress of the working Classes, 1832–1867* (1867)

Marx, Karl and F. Engels *Marx and Engels on Britain* (Moscow, 1962)

Marx, Karl *Selected Writings in Sociology and Social Philosophy* edited by T. B. Bottomore and M. Rubel (1956)

Mayer, S. R. T. *Who was the Founder of Sunday Schools?* (1880)

Overton, John Henry *The English Church in the Nineteenth Century, 1800–1833* (1894)

Peel, Frank *The Rising of the Luddites* 3rd edition (1895); Cass reprint (1968)

Polwhele, Rev. R., ed. *The Enthusiasm of Methodists and Papists considered by Bishop Lavington* New edition (1833)

Prentice, Archibald *Historical Sketches and Personal Recollections of Manchester (Intended to Illustrate the Progress of Public Opinion from 1792 to 1832)* (1851)

Romaine, Rev. William, *Letters*, in *Works* (1809)

Senior, Nassau *Letters on the Factory Act* (1857)

Smith, William A. *The Story of the Boys' Brigade* (Glasgow, 1888)

Stock, Eugene *The History of the Church Missionary Society* vol. 1 (1899)

Taylor, Adam *The History of the English General Baptists* vol. 2 (1818)

Traill, H. D. *Social England* vol. V (1896)

Ure, Andrew *The Philosophy of Manufactures* (1835)

Watson, W. H. *The First Fifty Years of the Sunday School Union* (Southport, 1873)

————*The History of the Sunday School Union* (1853)

Wesley, Rev. John *Journals* ... in 8 vols. edited by Nehemiah Crunock (1914)

White, W. H. *The Development of the Sunday School System* (1886)

Winskill, P. *The Temperance Movement and its Workers* 4 vols (1891–2)

[Wright, Thomas] *Some Habits and Customs of the Working Class Journeyman Engineer* (1867)

i. *General works*: post-1900

Altick, Richard *The English Common Reader* (London and Chicago, 1957)

Argyle, Michael *Religious Behaviour* (1958)

Armitage, W. H. G. *Four Hundred Years of English Education* (Cambridge, 1964)

Bayne-Powell, Rosemund *The English Child in the Eighteenth Century* (1939)

Beattie, J. M. 'The Pattern of Crime in England' *Past and Present* no. 62. (Feb. 1974)

Bendix, Reinhard *Work and Authority in Industry* (New York, 1956)

Binns, H. B. *A Century of Education. Being a Centenary History of the British and Foreign School Society* (1908)

Blaug, Mark *An Introduction to the Economics of Education* (1971)

Booth, Charles *Life and Labour of the People in London: Third Series, Religious Influences* vol. I (1902)

Briggs, Asa, ed. *Chartist Studies* (1959)

Broadbent, Arnold *The First 100 Years of the Sunday School Association* (1933)

Brown, Ford K. *Fathers of the Victorians* (Cambridge, 1961)

Burgess, H. J. and P. A. Welby *A Short History of the National Society 1811–1961* (1961)

Burt, Cyril *The Young Delinquent* (1944)

Coventry, Peter *Poor Monkey: the Child in Literature* (1957)

Cranfield, G. A. *The Development of Provincial Newspapers, 1700– 1760* (Oxford, 1962)

Currie, Robert *Methodism Divided* (1968)

———'A Microtheory of Wesleyan Methodist Growth' *Proceedings of the Wesley Historical Society* vol. 26 (October 1967)

Darton, F. J. *Children's Books in England: Five Centuries of Social Life* (Cambridge, 1958)

Deane, P. and W. A. Cole *English Economic Growth 1688–1959* (Cambridge, 1963)

Dobbs, A. E. *Education and Social Movements, 1700–1850* (1909)

Dreeben, Robert *On What is Learned in School* (Reading, Mass., 1968)

Edwards, Maldwyn *After Wesley: A Study of the Social and Political Influence of Methodism in the Middle Period* (1935)

Egoff, Sheila *Children's Periodicals of the Nineteenth Century* (1951)

Elliot-Binns, Leonard *The Early Evangelicals: a religious and social study* (1953)

Everett, Alan 'Nonconformity in Country Parishes' Joan Thirsk, ed. *Land, Church, and People: Essays Presented to Professor H. P. R. Finberg* (Reading, 1970)

Faulkner, H. U. *Chartism and the Churches* (New York, 1916)

Fitton, R. S. and A. P. Wadsworth *The Strutts and the Arkwrights, 1758–1830* (Manchester, 1958)

Flinn, M. W. 'Social Theory and the Industrial Revolution' Tom Burns and S. B. Saul, eds. *Social Change and Economic Change* (1967)

Foster, Charles *Errand of Mercy: The Evangelical United Front, 1790–1837* (Chapel Hill, 1960)

George, Dorothy *London Life in the Eighteenth Century* (1925)

Gray, Benjamin K. *A History of English Philanthropy* (1905)

Groser, William *A Hundred Years' Work for Children* (1903)

Halsey, A. H., Jean Floud, and C. Arnold Anderson *Education, Economy, and Society* (Glencoe, 1961)

Hammond, J. L. and B. *The Town Labourer 1760–1832* 1917)

Harrison, Brian 'The Sunday Trading Riots of 1855' *The Historical Journal* vol. 8 (1965)

———*Drink and the Victorians* (1871)

———Religion and Recreation in Nineteenth Century England' *Past and Present* no. 38 (1967)

Harrison, J. F. C. *Learning and Living, 1790–1960* (1961)

Higson, C. W. J. *Sources for the History of Education* (1967)

Hill, Christopher 'The Uses of Sabbatarianism' *Society and Puritanism in Pre-Revolutionary England* (1964)

Hobsbawm, Eric *Labouring Men* (1968)

Hollis, Patricia *The Pauper Press. A study in working-class radicalism in the 1830s* (1970)

Holt, Raymond. *The Unitarian Contribution to Social Progress in England* (1938)

Howkins, Alun *Whitsun 19th Century Oxfordshire* (Oxford. 1973)

Hutchinson, Keith *Labour in Politics* (1925)

Illich, Ivan *Deschooling Society* (New York, 1972)

Inglis, Brian 'Patterns of Worship in 1851' *Journal of Ecclesiastical History* vol. 11, no. 1 (1960)

———*Churches and the Working Class in Victorian England* (1963)

Johnson, Richard 'Educational Policy and Social Control in Early Victorian England' *Past and Present* no. 49, 96–120 (November, 1970)

Jones, M. G. *The Charity School Movement* (Cambridge, 1938)

Kiernan, V. 'Evangelicalism and the French Revolution' *Past and Present* no. 1 (1952)

Laqueur, Thomas W. 'English and French Education in the Nineteenth Century' *History of Education Quarterly* (Spring, 1973)

———'Literacy and Social Mobility during the Industrial Revolution' *Past and Present* no. 44 August, 1974)

———'Working Class Demand and the Growth of Elementary Education, 1750–1850' forthcoming in Lawrence Stone, ed. *Education and Society* (Baltimore, 1976)

Lewy, Guenter *Religion and Revolution* (Oxford, 1974)

Malcolmson, Robert W. *Popular Recreations in English Society* (Cambridge, 1973)

Marshall, Dorothy *The English Poor in the Eighteenth Century* (1926)

Martin, David *A Sociology of English Religion* (New York, 1967)

Mathews, H. F. *Methodism and the Education of the People, 1791–1851* (1949)

Musgrove, P. W. 'The Decline of the Educative Family' *Universities Quarterly* vol. 14, 377–404 (September, 1959–60)

Namier, Lewis and John Broke *The House of Commons, 1754–1790* (1964)

Neuberg, Victor *The Penny Histories: A Study of Chapbooks for Young Readers over Two Centuries* (1968)

Northcott, William C. *For Britain's Children: The Story of the Sunday School Union 1803–1952* (1952)

Owen, David *English Philanthropy* (Cambridge, Mass., 1964)

Parsons, Talcott 'The School Class as a Social System: Some of its Functions in American Society, A. H. Halsey, Jean Floud, and C. Arnold Anderson *Education, Economy, and Society* 434–55 (Glencoe, 1961)

Parssinen, T. M. 'Thomas Spence and the Origins of English Land Nationalization' *Journal of the History of Ideas* vol. XXXIV, No. 1 (January-March 1973)

Pelling, Henry 'Religion and the Nineteenth Century British Working Class' *Past and Present* no. 27 (1964)

Pollard, Sydney *The Genesis of Modern Management* Penguin edition (1968)

Poynter, John *Society and Pauperism, English Ideas on Poor Relief* (1969)

Quinlan, Maurice *Victorian Prelude* (New York, 1941)

Radzinowicz, Leon *A History of English Criminal Law and its Administration from 1750* vol. 1 (1949)

Reid, F. 'Socialist Sunday Schools in Britain, 1892–1939' *International Review of Social History* vol. 11, part 1 (1966)

Reisman, David *The Lonely Crowd* (New Haven, 1952)

Rice, Edwin W. *The Sunday School Movement, 1780–1917 and the American Sunday-School Union* (Philadelphia, 1917)

Rubinstein, David *School Attendance in London, 1870–1904: A Social History* (Hull, 1969)

Sanderson, Michael 'Social Change and Elementary Education in Industrial Lancashire, 1780–1840' *Northern History* vol. 3 (1968)

Sangster, Paul *Pity my Simplicity: The Evangelical Revival and the Religious Education of Children, 1738–1800* (1963)

Saul, S. B. and Tom Burns, eds. *Social Theory and Economic Change* (1967)

Schofield, R. S. 'Dimensions of Illiteracy' unpublished paper presented to the Cambridge New Economic History Conference (September, 1972)

Siegel, Sidney *Nonparametric Statistics for the Behavioral Sciences* (New York, 1956)

Silver, Harold *The Concept of Popular Education* (1965)

Simon, Brian *Studies in the History of Education, 1780–1870* (1960)

Simon, Joan 'Was there a Charity School Movement' Brian Simon, ed. *Education in Leicestershire* (Leicester, 1968)

Soloway, R. A. *Prelates and People*; *Ecclesiastical Thought in England, 1783–1852* (1969)

Tholfsen, Trygve R. 'The Intellectual Origins of Mid-Victorian Stability' *Political Science Quarterly* vol. 86, no. 1 (March, 1971)

Thompson, E. P. *The Making of the English Working Class* (1963)

———'Time, Work Discipline and Industrial Capitalism' *Past and Present* no. 38 (1967)

Thompson, Kenneth A. *Bureaucracy and Church Reform: the organizational response of the Church of England to social change 1800–1965* (Oxford, 1970)

Townsend, William J. *et al. A New History of Methodism* 2 vols (1909)

Wadsworth, A. P. 'The First Manchester Sunday Schools' *The Bulletin of the John Rylands Library* vol. 33 (March, 1951)

Walsh, John 'The Anglican Evangelicals in the Eighteenth Century' *Aspects de l'Anglicanisme* (Paris, 1974)

Ward, W. R. *Religion and Society in England, 1790–1850* (1972)

Warren, Howard C. *A History of Association Psychology* (New York, 1921)

Warren, W. *The Wesleyan Movement in the Industrial Revolution* (1930)

Wearmouth, Robert Featherstone *Methodism and the Working-Class Movements of England, 1800–1850* (1937)

Webb, R. K. *The British Working Class Reader, 1790–1848: Literacy and Social Tension* (1955)

Wertheimer, Egon *Portrait of the Labour Party* (1929)

Whitaker, W. B. *The Eighteenth Century English Sunday* (1940)

Williams, Gwyn A. 'The Concept of *Egemonia* in the Thought of Antonio Gramsci: Some Notes on Interpretation' *Journal of the History of Ideas* vol. 21, no. 4 (October-December, 1960)

Williams, Raymond *The Long Revolution* (1961)

Wrigley, E. A. *Population and History* (1969)

Yeo, Eileen 'Robert Owen and Popular Culture' Sidney Pollard and John Salt, eds. *Robert Owen: Prophet of the Poor* (1971)

j. *Periodicals*: long runs

Anti-Jacobon Review 1798–1802

Arminian Magazine to 1797, then *Methodist Magazine* to 1821,
then *The Wesleyan Methodist Magazine* 1784–1850
   Baptist Magazine 1810–45
   Black Dwarf 1818–23
   British Critic 1800–1802
   Chartist Circular 28 September 1839–9 July 1842
   Christian Child's Faithful Friend 1833
   Christian Observer 1802–27
   Christian Remembrancer 1819–24
   Church of England Magazine 1836–45
   Church of England's Sunday Scholar's Magazine 1850
   Church of England Sunday School Quarterly Magazine 1848–50
   Child's Magazine and Sunday Scholar's Companion 1824
   Eclectic Review 1805–30
   Evangelical Magazine 1793–1845
   Friendly Visitor edited by William Carus Wilson 1820, 1824–7
   Gentleman's Magazine 1784–1832
   Independent Magazine 1842–4
   Lancashire and Yorkshire Co-operator 1831–2
   The London Christian Instructor to 1824, then *The Congregational
Magazine* 1818–45
   Manchester Observer 1818–20
   The Methodist New Connexion Magazine and Evangelical Repository
1798–1850
   New Moral World 1840–43
   Northern Star 1838–43
   Orthodox Churchmen's Magazine 1801–1808
   The Philanthropist 1811–19
   Primitive Methodist Children's Magazine 1827
   Primitive Methodist Magazine 1819–50
   Protestant Dissenter's Magazine 1794–7
   The Revivalist 1838–40
   The Sunday School Magazine and Journal of Christian Instruction
1839–50
   Sunday School Manual 1843
   Sunday School Repository or Teacher's Magazine to 1831, then *Sunday
School Teachers' Magazine and Journal of Education* 1813–16; 1831–50
   Sunday School Union Magazine 1844–50
   Teacher's Offering; or Sunday School Monthly Visitor 1840–50
   Union Magazine for Sunday Schools 1844–50
   Youth's Magazine 1837; 1848–50

   k. *Periodicals*: single issues

British Magazine vol. 3 (1833)

Buckinghamshire Chronicle 24 June 1848
Buckinghamshire Herald 13 June 1840
Church of England Sunday School Monthly Magazine for Teachers vol. 3 (1859)
Church of England Sunday School Quarterly Magazine vol. XVI (1863)
Cobbett's Annual Register vol. 2 (1802)
European Magazine vol. 14 (November 1788)
Manchester Chronicle 27 November 1819
Manchester Exchange Herald 12 October 1819
Manchester Guardian 10 November 1879
Manchester Mercury 10 August 1784; 1 July 1800
Morning Chronicle 15 November 1849
The Patroit 11 December 1843
Philanthropic Magazine vol. 1, no. 1 (1827)
Sunday Scholar's Magazine; or Monthly Reward Book (1821)
Sunday School Teacher (1830)
The World (June 1787)

1. *Unpublished theses*

Cumberland, A. G. 'Protestant Non-Conformity in the Black Country 1662–1851' MA thesis, Birmingham University, 1951

Ellis, George 'The Evangelicals and the Sunday Question' PHD thesis, Harvard University, 1951

Gilbert, Alan 'The Growth and Decline of Nonconformity in England and Wales ... before 1850' DPHIL Thesis, Oxford University, 1973

Giles, Phyllis 'The Economic and Social Development of Stockport, 1815–36' MA thesis, Manchester University, 1950

Goldstrom, J. M. 'The Changing Social Context of Elementary Education as reflected in school books in use in England, 1800–1870' PHD Thesis, Birmingham University, 1963

Jones, R. A. 'Knowledge Chartism' MA thesis, Birmingham University, 1938

Kinsey, W. W. 'Some Aspects of Lancashire Radicalism, 1816–1821' MA thesis, Manchester University, 1922

McLellan, A. 'Congregationalism and the Education of the People' MA thesis, Birmingham University, n.d.

Stigant, Paul, 'Methodism and the Working Class, 1760–1821. A Study in Social and Political Conflict' MA thesis, Keele University, 1968

Watson, J. E. 'The Educational Activities of the Baptists in England during the XVIIIth and XIXth Centuries with Particular Reference to the Northwest' MA thesis, University of Liverpool, 1947

Index

Pre